An Uncommon History of Common Things

NATIONAL GEOGRAPHIC

WASHINGTON, D.C.

CONTENTS

Foreword 6 • About This Book 10

Foreword

Everything has a story behind it, and some of the commonest things have the most uncommon stories. This book is a wide-ranging compendium of mini-essays on the curious origins of everyday things, both symbolic and concrete, ranging from the thumbs-up gesture to the red-and-white-striped barber pole. Because so many of the things covered here are so familiar, we seldom give them much thought. How often do we wonder why we knock on wood, or how the dollar sign came to be? The more we see actions performed or objects used, the less we tend to ask questions about them. But asking those questions can lead to fascinating and enlightening answers.

This book provides those kinds of answers. It is full of opportunities for the reader to think, How interesting. That's something I didn't know. I didn't know, for example, exactly how pockets within pants evolved from pouches or "purses" full of valuables that used to hang from a belt outside whatever a person was wearing. To better protect the pouch from "cutpurse" thieves (now known as pickpockets), people cut a slit in their outer garments so that the purse could be concealed and still leave its contents easily accessible. From that practice to a man's pants pocket was, over time, just a matter of sewing. Women continued to wear their pouches beneath their full skirts until more fitted styles and safer societies encouraged a return to the practice of carrying a purse outside one's clothing.

Because so many of the things and traditions covered in this book are centuries old, stories of their origins have often become the stuff of legend and lore that has been embellished over time. The entry on "crossing your fingers" is a wonderful little essay on one of the most widely practiced gestures in the Western world. How interesting then to learn how it may have evolved from pagan practices that predate the Christian cross.

The origins of more modern practices make equally interesting reading. The story behind the now familiar peace symbol reminds us that all things, whether symbolic gestures or clever toys, have a beginning. This book's essay on the "ban-the-bomb" symbol is wonderfully specific, telling us the name of the person who designed it and for what particular purpose. Who knew that the symbol was a deliberate superposition of the semaphore alphabet symbols for *N* and *D,* standing for nuclear disarmament?

Another fascinating story has to do with the discovery of Silly Putty, which engineers at first called Nutty Putty. The funny material—which could be formed into a ball that would bounce higher than any other and could also be flattened over the Sunday comics to take up a colorful image of whatever it touched—was the result of a wartime quest for a cheap substitute for rubber. Although Nutty Putty did not find its way into military use, the more innocently named Silly Putty became a great hit with children.

Among my favorite essays in this book is the one on blue jeans. Its story "involves a purpose from India, a fabric from France, and a business idea from California." I learned that 16th-century sailors bought "thick cotton indigo-dyed cloth" in the vicinity of Mumbai (Bombay), near a fort called Dongarii. The material was taken to Italy, where it inspired an industry that exported a similar material out of Genoa. This came to be known as *bleu de Genes,* or "Genoa blue," which was made into pants and came to be called "blue jeans." A related fabric was known as *serge de Nîmes,* after the French port, from which the familiar term "denim" derives.

The entrepreneur who put this all together was Levi Strauss, the manufacturer of what I wore and called "dungarees" as a child in New York, not realizing that in using that name I was evoking the very remote origins of Levi's in the vicinity of a fort in India. My wife, who grew up in a different part of the country than I, has always questioned my use of the word "dungarees" for what she calls "jeans." Now I can read her the entry in this book that shows that my term reflects the more remote historical origins.

These mini-essays are models of concision. Though entire books have been written on the history of devices like the bicycle and the pencil and the zipper, here the stories of these familiar objects—and many more—are summarized in just a few paragraphs. These might whet the appetite for a fuller story, should the reader so desire, but they also serve as a reliable digest of the key ideas, providing the gist of the history, for the essence of each is nicely encapsulated.

In all the artifacts we read about in this book, we can see the creativity and ingenuity of our human ancestors. Everything was created, invented, and developed for a purpose; everything is the result of a kind of everyday engineering. Like modern engineers who are called upon to solve problems that arise in the course of living in a technological society, so the oldest and most enduring things that everyday people devised in times past came about in the course of organizing civilization itself.

These stories equip us to view the world of things in a fresh way. The next time we see people shrug their shoulders, we might remember that we read here the movement may be "one of the most instinctive and universal of human gestures," and when combined with upraised palms may also be among the oldest ways of nonverbally saying, "I don't know." We might also remember that shoulders shrugged in conjunction with raised eyebrows and pursed lips say, "I'll think about it." We don't need a book to tell us these things, of course, but the book does tell us why we do some of the things we do and reminds us of how subtle our means of communication can be.

Every book can be read in many different ways, and all readers have their own favorite ways of progressing through a volume. Though, like every book, this one can be read serially from front cover to back, this is also a book that lends itself to the random sampling method, in which the reader dips in here and there at this time and that, as schedule and circumstance allow. However it is read, this is a book to keep on the bookshelf, ready to refresh our memory about April Fools' Day or split-level houses.

With its wealth of information and a great deal of food for thought, this is a book that will reward the reader with old memories of things of the past and with new knowledge of things of today. And, like any book worth reading, it will change the way we look at the world and the people who inhabit it and how they themselves have changed it.

—*Henry Petroski*

About This Book

AN UNCOMMON HISTORY OF COMMON THINGS TELLS THE STORY OF HOW HUNDREDS OF everyday things came to be what they are. Pencils, buttons, forks, coffee, and napkins are just some of the humble items that we take for granted but depend on greatly. Who first thought of removing the hull from the red coffee "cherry," roasting it, grinding it, and then steeping it into the liquid we consume daily? What garment frustrations or embarrassments led people to discover they could hold their clothes together with a combination of small, flat disks and holes in fabric? Some of these short histories describe necessity as the impetus to invention; other inventions were the result of fortuitous accidents. Some of the descriptions shed light on misconceptions, while others fill in gaps in popular knowledge. Over the course of nine chapters, organized by topic, we explore the earliest known origins and current uses or observances of hundreds of things. We start with Food & Drink, then move on through Seasons & Holidays, Ceremony & Customs, Symbols & Markings, Hearth & Home, Garments & Accessories, Medications & Potions, Toys & Games, and Tools & Innovations. Within each chapter, look for subheads, fast facts, uncommonly known trivia and historical items, and timelines. One characteristic all of these things have in common: our lives would be quite different without them.

CHAPTER INTRODUCTION
Each of the nine chapters starts with a full-spread introduction, which gives the overview of the topic and describes what is included —and not included—in the chapter, using examples from the text. At the top of the page, a quote from a famous personality provides a humorous or popular opinion of the topic.

Within each chapter, the items are divided into sub-topics, each with its own introduction, to explain what you'll encounter there and why it's significant. A color photo of each item is followed by three lines of "fast facts"—interesting tidbits about etymology, alternative uses, best examples, and inventor's name and date of invention, if known. The item histories span earliest known origins through modern usages.

UNCOMMONLY KNOWN, PARALLEL HISTORY

Items of special interest are highlighted in Uncommonly Known blue boxes and Parallel History tan boxes. The Uncommonly Known stories reveal little-known facts about familiar things, such as origin, use, or common misconception. Parallel Histories put entries in historical context, describing related world and local events, competing items, and the impact of their invention, evolution, or usage.

TIMELINE

Each timeline focuses on a specific topic (such as footwear, currency, clocks, etc.) and follows its evolution throughout history, from the earliest known appearance of the item through to its modern form. Dates and spacing on the timelines are approximate, providing a broad overview of the progression of technology, style, materials, or manufacturing processes that contributed to the development of these important objects.

Life itself is the proper binge.
–JULIA CHILD (1912-2004)

Food & Drink

Natural selection and discriminating palates have seen to it that we choose our foods carefully, so it's not surprising that much of what we consume has been part of our diets for a long time. We've sprinkled salt on our food for thousands of years; there are grains that we have eaten for 17,000 years; for millennia we have steeped tea leaves in hot water. Not that humans haven't made great strides in food production and preparation over the ages; the variety of available foods is greater now than ever. In this chapter we take a look at many of our most common foods and beverages, and track them back as far as we can. Some of our foods date back only to the previous century—the first baking mix, Bisquick, was born in 1931. But it might come as a surprise to learn that chewing gum goes back to ancient times, both in Europe and the Americas. Among other revelations: salt has been used in warfare; the spread of margarine caused an interesting backlash by dairy farmers; ninth-century Arabians were expert distillers. You'll also discover what is the most popular dessert in the United States, which grain was generic for "local grain," and what is the world's oldest alcoholic beverage—and that people may have been consuming it as far back as 10,000 years. The fact that some foods have been on the menu for a long time does not seem to make them any more or less popular than recent items. The birth of cheesecake is separated from that of the peanut butter and jelly sandwich by 2,000 years, yet both these delicacies seem poised for a long and happy future. While we have more packaged, easily prepared foods than did our ancestors, we have more choice in what we eat and thus every reason to fill our shopping carts with the market's best offerings, both ancient and modern.

Daily Fare

Modern nutritionists caution that one of the worst things for human diets is too little variety; the more kinds of foods people eat in a day or week, the more likely they are to get all of the necessary nutrients to make their bodies strong and healthy. Societies have instinctively evolved diets that rely on a diverse array of nutritious staples—and, of course, the choice of those foods depends on geography, religion, climate, culture, and many other things. Following are a few of the foods that modern Americans like to eat, even if not every one of them is entirely healthful.

Pancakes

ALSO KNOWN AS: HOTCAKES, CRÊPES, CRESPELLE, GRIDDLE CAKES, FLAPJACKS, JOHNNY-CAKES, PALATSCHINKEN, NALESNIKI , PANNENKOEKEN

The humble pancake truly spans the globe—regional variations can be found in Europe, Asia, Africa, Central America, and North America. Whether they're called pancakes, griddle cakes, flapjacks, johnnycakes, hotcakes, *Pfannkuchen, crêpes, crespelle, Palatschinken, nalesniki, Pannenkoeken,* blini, or dosa (and that's not a complete list), this common and versatile food starts with a batter, usually sweetened, that can be poured onto a griddle or into a pan and cooked through.

We may never know which culture or cook made the first pancakes, but one Christian tradition may provide a clue: "Fat Tuesday" or "Pancake Day" is the day before Ash Wednesday, which starts the liturgical season of Lent. It was the last day people

could use fat or oils in their cooking before the 40-day fast. In other words, pancakes may have developed as a means of quickly using up cooking fats before they spoiled.

The modern pancake is similar to the Roman flatbread *alita dolcia* ("another sweet"), made from flour, milk, eggs, and spices; they were often served with pepper and honey. The first reference to pancakes in English is in a culinary book from the 1430s.

Native Americans of the Narragansett tribe made a soft batter shaped by hands called a *nokehick.* Other cornmeal pancakes were called Indian cakes as early as 1607, while buckwheat pancakes were made by Dutch settlers, and by 1740, colonists were cooking "hoe cakes" in the fire on the flat blade of that tool.

American pancakes are traditionally served with maple syrup and butter, a practice that may have its roots in the recipe for crêpes Suzette (perhaps originally served by one Monsieur Joseph at the Restaurant Marivaux) that Henri Charpentier, a French maître d'hotel, brought to the United

---

UNCOMMONLY KNOWN ...

Waffles Its batter similar to pancakes, the waffle gains distinction through its cooking method. The "wafer," as medieval people called it, was cooked between hinged metal plates often embossed with heraldic symbols. Today, the waffle's indented pattern (source of the term "waffling," both for fabric and for back-and-forth behavior) provides nooks for toppings.

States in the 1930s. Crêpes Suzette are covered with a sauce of caramelized sugar, citrus juice, and liqueur, and their sweet stickiness brought about a vogue for pancakes with similar toppings.

Breakfast Cereal

THE TOP FOUR MANUFACTURERS ACCOUNT FOR MORE THAN 80% OF INDUSTRY REVENUE: KELLOGG, GENERAL MILLS, POST, AND QUAKER

Cold breakfast cereals composed of flakes were invented in the United States (see Parallel History), but breakfasts of different kinds of grains have been consumed for many thousands of years. Not just a millennia or three, either; emmer and einkorn wheat consumption have been dated back 17,000 years. The word *cereal* derives from the name Ceres, for the Roman goddess of the harvest, and refers to grasses with edible grains or seeds.

Most cereal grains need to be soaked or at least softened with liquid before eating, making a "porridge." An example is the rice congee popular in China, or Indian *poha*. Congee is often eaten cold, but many porridges are served hot, particularly in northern climates.

In their unrefined form, cereal grains are extremely nutritious; the grains contain all the nutrients that the plant in its embryonic form needs to grow. Unfortunately, in some Western countries, milled cereal grains, with fewer nutrients, have become popular because they have a longer shelf life—the outer layers of unmilled grains are high in fat and can spoil more quickly.

Kellogg and Health Foods

William "Will" Keith Kellogg did not set out to invent corn flakes. He was soaking wheat bran to make bread dough in the health sanitarium he ran with his brother John Harvey Kellogg when he noticed that the finished dough was breaking into smaller pieces. He baked the pieces and served them. The crispy wheat "flakes" became a huge hit with the patients, who asked to have packets shipped to them at home after they were discharged. Soon Will discovered that corn made a lighter, tastier flake. He founded the world's first ready-to-eat-cereal company, the Battle Creek Toasted Corn Flakes Company, now known, of course, as Kelloggs.

Although there are many different cereal grains, including spelt, teff, quinoa, barley, sorghum, buckwheat, and grain amaranth, most American breakfast cereals (hot and cold) are based on wheat and oats. Oatmeal, Cream of Rice, Cream of Wheat, and Wheatena are usually served with hot or cold milk and sweetened to individual taste. Residents of southern states often eat hot cornmeal known as "grits" for breakfast, served with butter and salt or sugar. Besides being cheap and easy to make, porridges of cereal grains are easy to digest, and thus are often given to people recovering from illness.

Sandwich

NAMED AFTER THE FOURTH EARL OF SANDWICH, JOHN MONTAGU (1718-92), WHOSE TOWN, SANDWICH, LIES IN EAST KENT, IN SOUTHEAST ENGLAND

John Montagu, the fourth Earl of Sandwich, certainly contributed his title's name to the popular snack of two pieces of bread holding some type of filling. In 1762, Montagu, a notoriously avid gambler, realized that the type of food he'd seen in his Middle and Near Eastern travels would allow him to sate his appetite while remaining at cards.

However, the snack itself dates back to the first-century B.C. Jewish sage Hillel the Elder, who placed lamb and bitter herbs between pieces of matzo bread during Passover; the Romans called this concoction *cibus Hilleli,* or "Hillel's snack." Other cultures, including Middle and Near Eastern, made sandwiches long before they caught on in the West, and in Europe it seems the Dutch *belegde broodje* ("filled roll") was popular a century before the Earl of Sandwich ever saw a cribbage board.

It took a while for sandwiches to progress from late-night men's fare to general society snack, but by 1824, oyster loaves appeared in *The Virginia Housewife,* and by the end of the 19th century sandwiches had become so accepted that they appeared in the 1887 *White House Cookbook.* As sandwiches grew in popularity, they also grew in variety: From ham biscuits to deli Reubens, muffulettas to BLTs, loosemeats to cheesesteaks, Americans found many ways to put meals between pieces of bread. From their British forebears Americans also took the concept of "sandwich bread," also known as the Pullman loaf, that was shaped in a convenient rectangle and had a firmly packed crumb so that sandwich eaters would not lose most of their bread in their laps while eating.

Today sandwiches are made for and eaten at every meal. While many sandwiches are made at home (especially those with sweet fillings, like peanut butter and jelly), the market for custom and prepackaged sandwiches has gotten bigger. Sandwiches like Vietnamese *banh mi* and Scandinavian *smorrebrod* are available everywhere in the world, proving that one man's snack has become the world's favorite.

UNCOMMONLY KNOWN ...

Sliced Bread Invented by an Iowan in 1917, the bread-slicing machine got its commercial start in Chillicothe, Missouri, in 1928 but got its commercial breakthrough when it was used to section nutrient-enriched Wonder Bread in 1930. Though the U.S. government attempted to impose a World War II ban on the machines, it lasted only three months.

Canned Goods

NICOLAS APPERT, PARISIAN CONFECTIONER
1810 | AWARD FOR HIS HEAT PROCESSING METHOD
CANNING ELIMINATES MOST MICROORGANISMS

The history of canned goods owes a great deal to two modern conflicts. During the Napoleonic Wars (1792–1815), the famous French general realized that in order to keep his armies fed, he needed a new method of food preservation. Bonaparte decided to offer a prize to the man who could figure it out, and in 1810, Nicolas Appert won with his method of heating and then sealing food.

Also in 1810, Englishman Peter Durand developed his own way of heating food, then sealing it in unbreakable containers made of tin. For many years, in Europe and the United States, commercial canning methods remained the same (home canners, of course, used glass jars and bottles, sterilizing them in a water bath, as they do today): After preparation, foods would be heated to about 250°F, then sealed into containers. It wasn't until Louis Pasteur's experiments later in the 19th century that people began to understand that the heating process killed off bacteria already contained in the food, and the airtight sealing prevented any further bacteria from contaminating the processed edibles.

The canning process's simplicity is probably why no great leaps in its development were made until World War I, when once again large armies needed foodstuffs that would last a long while and be portable over great distances. Not only did commanders agitate for cheap, high-calorie fare—they also tried different regional favorites in attempts to keep their soldiers happy. This resulted in manufacturers' experimenting with many of the dishes we keep in our cupboards today, like canned bean dishes, pastas, and tomato sauces.

Meanwhile, manufacturers were finally making improvements to the tin cans, which, while strong and convenient, were also prone to leaks and often harbored botulism toxin when leaks were unnoticed or ignored. The new, tin-coated steel, double-seamed cans with welded side seams keep food airtight for much longer.

Noodles

FROM GERMAN "NUDEL" (1770-80)
UNLEAVENED DOUGH CUT INTO STRIPS OR SHAPES
SLANG: "USE YOUR NOODLE" (FIGURE IT OUT)

For many years, several cultures vied for the title of noodle inventor; in 2005, China staked its claim to the honor when archaeologists discovered a bowl of perfectly preserved long noodles in the northeastern area of Lajia.

However, just because the Chinese invented noodles doesn't mean they invented pasta—what Americans knew for years as "macaroni." Pasta is not simply noodles in a different shape; it's actually made from a different wheat. While many types of noodles could be made from *Triticum aestivum,* or soft wheat, macaroni can be made only from *Triticum turgidum* var. *durum,* the "durum wheat" with

a high gluten content that makes possible hard, dry pasta with a long, stable shelf life.

The interesting and important thing that that tells us is that it wasn't the ancient Romans or their forebears the Etruscans who invented pasta, because neither of those groups knew of durum wheat. Who did? It seems to have been the Arabs; in a dictionary compiled by the ninth-century Syrian physician and lexicographer Isho bar Ali, *itriyya* is defined as stringlike pasta shapes made of semolina and dried before cooking. A few centuries later, Arab writers found a variety of itriyya they called *triyakh* in Sicily; it's difficult to know if Sicilians had developed the pasta on their own or through contact with another culture.

Of course, Sicilians and their fellow mainland Italians were responsible for forming pasta made of semolina flour into dozens of forms and shapes, designed for different mouth feels and for serving with different kinds of sauces. In the 1880s, the first significant waves of Sicilian immigrants came to the U.S., bringing their cuisine and its *maccheroni* with them (of course, immigrants from other Italian regions brought their pasta shapes, too; however, Sicilians came in large numbers).

Tortillas

FROM SPANISH "TORTA" (CAKE)
THE FOOD ITSELF DATES TO 10,000 B.C.
ASTRONAUTS EAT THEM IN SPACE TO AVOID CRUMBS

Soft or fried, corn tortillas are an unmistakable sign of Mexican cuisine, and that's partly because maize itself is unmistakably part of the Mexican diet. Maize (from the Latin *Zea mays*) was sacred to the Mexica, or

Aztec, people, supplying their main source of starch, as well as some protein and fat.

Though some corn was eaten green, most of it was stored in ventilated cribs and later boiled in limewater to make a softened gruel called *nixtamal*. This could either be soaked for a tender, starchy dish known as *pozole* or, more often, ground into a mealy flour known as *masa* for tortillas. The traditional method of making tortillas involves a stone slab called a *metate* and a stone roller that's used to turn a lump of the nixtamal into masa. Once that's done, a cook will take a golf ball-size lump of masa between her moistened hands and pat it into a round, flat cake that's thrown on to a hot griddle, or *comal,* for 20 to 30 seconds per side.

The finished tortilla ideally is less than one-eighth inch thick and about six to eight inches in diameter. Tortillas aren't just bread; they're also spoons, forks, serving plates, and the building blocks for other Mexican dishes such as tacos, enchiladas, and burritos. Having cornered 32 percent of the sales for the U.S. bread industry, tortillas trail white bread sales by only 2 percent, making them the second most popular bread type in America, with sales surpassing whole wheat bread, bagels, and rolls. Annual growth for the tortilla industry has expanded 9 percent; in 2002, the U.S. tortilla industry had sales reaching $5.2 billion.

TV Dinners

INVENTOR: GERRY THOMAS
1953 | OMAHA, NEBRASKA
HIS IDEA BECAME THE SWANSON TV DINNER

Frozen meals are a relatively recent innovation, although ancient cultures, including the Chinese and Greek, experimented with cellars made of ice or insulated by snow.

PARALLEL HISTORY

Salt Extraction Industry

Before frozen food, the most practical method of preserving meat involved salting it. The main source of salt in the young United States of America was the ocean along its Atlantic coastline. As salt prices rose, extraction via solar evaporation became the preferred method of obtaining salt, and it involved windmills to pump water into wooden vats that could be covered in case of rain. In the early 19th century Captain John Sears of East Dennis, Massachusetts, proposed some improvements that included the eventual running off of brine into "salt rooms" for crystallization. While his ideas were at first known as "Sears' Folly," the captain's salt works eventually grew to be the largest on Cape Cod, and even after salt production ceased to be profitable for food manufacturing, Epsom and magnesium salts were produced near the Bass River at South Yarmouth.

It wasn't until Clarence Birdseye, a Canadian engineer and avid fisherman, applied freezing technology to food so that it could be marketed as a convenience. However, the public didn't embrace frozen foods until World War II metal needs made canned goods scarce.

Once frozen foods caught on, people started looking for new ways to use them. The war was over, the standard of living was high, and a new style of cooking and dining was on the rise. Into this mix came television, drawing families around it and making people unwilling to spend time on cooking when a particular show was due to start.

But it wasn't the TV itself that inspired "TV dinners"; it was a turkey surplus. In 1953, C. A. Swanson and Sons, a frozen foods company based in Omaha, Nebraska, grossly overestimated the demand for frozen turkeys at Thanksgiving and had 520,000 pounds of extra frozen poultry. A traveling salesman for the company, Gerry Thomas, had experimented with aluminum trays that airlines used for heated food and developed a three-compartment design. He presented his design to the Swansons, filled with turkey and trimmings and made to look like a television, complete with "control" knobs. Most food historians agree that the segmented tray, which kept foods tidy and reminded consumers of childhood, made TV dinners such a success.

On the Side

The phrase "on the side" can refer to a way of serving food as well as the dishes that traditionally accompany a main course. In this section, however, we cover mostly spices and condiments, those items "on the side" that add flavor and savor to our favorite foods. From the most basic—salt—to the slightly more complicated—mayonnaise—these delicious extras have stories at least as interesting as other foodstuffs in this chapter. Don't see your favorite sauce or flavoring here? Get in line. We had room for only the most popular ones.

Salt

FROM THE LATIN "SAL"
IDIOMS: "WITH A GRAIN OF SALT" (WITH SKEPTICISM),
"WORTH ONE'S SALT" (DESERVING)

Salt is more than just a foodstuff. Earth's only edible rock has been used as a weapon —armies once "salted the earth" to prevent enemies from being able to regrow crops. Salt is sacred to many cultures, and was once placed on a baby's lips during baptism in reference to Jesus calling his disciples the "salt of the earth" in Matthew's gospel. It's been used as currency— the word *salary* comes from the Latin *salarium*, or "payment in salt." It's even essential to life— humans once got all of their salt from eating meat, but as agrarian societies developed, more salt was needed as a supplement (every human takes in about 1.6 pounds of salt per year). Ironically, while some salt is needed for survival, overconsumption of salt can cause health problems like high blood pressure.

Salt made civilization possible, since humans were able to preserve food with it and travel distances. Since salt can be produced both through evaporation of seawater and in salt mines, both coastal and inland cultures had access to it, and control of large salt mines has often been a method of empire building. Taxes on salt, such as the 18th-century French *gabelle* and the 20th-century Indian tax, have incited social change and revolution.

Today both sea and mined salt from different countries is available, for both eating and cooking uses. The salt many of us use on our tables was revolutionized by a man named Joy Morton, whose Morton Salt Company now supplies most of the salt in the United States. In 1911, Morton pioneered the use of magnesium carbonate (now calcium silicate) in salt to keep it free-flowing even in humid weather. Morton Salt's slogan, When It Rains It Pours, and logo of a little girl with an umbrella have appeared on its blue packages since 1914.

UNCOMMONLY KNOWN . . .
Salt Superstitions Thrown, sprinkled, or dissolved, salt figures in many superstitious practices, like tossing a pinch of salt over one's shoulder after spilling some. These beliefs stem both from salt's historical costliness and its properties as purifier and preservative, making the mineral a symbol of a good and long life.

Pepper

FROM SANSKRIT "PIPPALI" (LONG PEPPER)
COUNTRY OF ORIGIN: INDIA
ONE OF THE EARLIEST KNOWN AND WIDELY USED SPICES

Although there are many different kinds of pepper fruits around the world, when modern Westerners refer to "pepper," they are usually talking about the dried ground "corns" that are the fruit of the Piperaceae family, with *Piper nigrum* (black pepper) the most common. The black pepper plant is a climbing vine native to India's Malabar Coast that can reach 30 feet or more.

Black, white, and green peppercorns all come from the same plant, growing in spiky clusters on the vines, which are planted on small, carefully tended plots. Each clustered spike (about 50 berries in all) must be picked at a different time depending on the type of pepper desired. Pink "peppercorns" are actually a completely different kind of spice, but sometimes marketed as pepper.

Pepper came to world attention through Roman trade, and after it weakened in the third century A.D., Arabs held control of the spice trade for centuries, trading in Venice, Constantinople, and Alexandria. Pepper was very costly, and European nations wanted a new source of the spice. This fueled the great exploration boom of the Renaissance; for example, Vasco da Gama of Portugal reached Kerala in East India in 1498, and for a century, Portugal ruled the spice route, with Lisbon becoming a wealthy town. In 1602, the Dutch (who had won their freedom from Spain in the 16th century) founded the Dutch East India Company and gained trade supremacy, until after 200 years, the British East India Company gained that power.

Margarine

INVENTOR: HIPPOLYTE MÈGE-MOURIÈS
COUNTRY OF ORIGIN: FRANCE
RECEIVED U.S. PATENT IN 1873

Margarine, once and sometimes still known as oleomargarine, seems a most modern substance, so it might be a little surprising to learn that it's been around

PARALLEL HISTORY

The Spice Trade

One of the most important things to consider about the spice routes is that ancient and medieval peoples who were eager for substances like cinnamon and cloves weren't simply on a quest for tastier food—they sometimes needed spices to preserve food properly, to mask bad flavors, and for use as currency. The European demand for spices that grew primarily in Asia and Africa led to the centuries-long search for new shipping routes that would be faster and safer, avoiding the treacherous Cape of Good Hope at the tip of Africa. Eventually, the search for new routes led explorers to the Americas.

European ships transport goods and spices along a trade route waterway.

for more than a century. Emperor Louis Napoleon III offered a prize to formulate a substitute for butter "for the working class and, incidentally for the Navy." Western Europe was running low on fats and oils, and popular demand for soaps (caused by a rising standard of living) was cutting into vegetable fat sources. A Provençal chemist named Hippolyte Mège-Mouriès mixed beef tallow with skimmed milk.

Mège-Mouriès used something that he and others called "margaric acid," from a slight error by a chemist named Michel Chevreul. Chevreul had isolated a fatty acid that formed "pearls" of animal fat, and he named it after the root of the Greek word for "pearl." Margarine caught on quickly in Europe and in the United States beginning with World War II and continuing through the 1950s and 1960s—so quickly that the powerful American dairy industry pushed back against its supply. Margarine was so cheap that dairy farmers tried everything to slow its production, from having it declared a "harmful drug," to taxing its sale, requiring stores that sold it to have a special license, and, finally, forcing it to be sold without the food dyes that made it look appetizing. Some opponents of the spread even wanted it to be colored pink so it would be truly unappealing.

After a while, many companies began selling uncolored margarine accompanied by a little sack of yellow food coloring that users would knead in so that their margarine would be a buttery yellow. In 1950, federal taxes on margarine were abolished. Tub margarines were introduced in the 1960s, which provided soft, easily usable, butter-colored spread.

Today, many people choose margarine over butter as their spread of choice due to health reasons rather than cost. According to the Cleveland Clinic, a single tablespoon of butter contains 33 of the 200 milligrams of cholesterol recommended as the daily maximum, and 7 of the 10 to 15 grams of saturated fat recommended per day. On the other hand, many people prefer to continue eating butter, while simply exercising moderation. Julia Child famously said, "I don't eat so much butter and cream—just enough!"

Peanut Butter

ORIGINAL INVENTORS: INCAS
89 PERCENT OF AMERICANS EAT PEANUT BUTTER
NUMBER ONE PEANUT-GROWING STATE: GEORGIA

You probably learned in school that African-American agricultural chemist George Washington Carver "invented" peanut butter. It's true that Carver, who figured out 300 different uses for the peanut, discovered that when ground into a paste, peanuts were delicious and filling. However, Carver did not believe in patenting his findings. "God gave them to me," he would say about his ideas. "How can I sell them to someone else?"

Thus Carver's best known concoction didn't make him rich, and he would have said that was just fine. Peanut butter has actually been "invented" and then reinvented many times since the crop's early origins in Brazil, around 950 B.C. The ancient Inca pounded peanuts into a paste, and that was one of the specimens early explorers brought back to the West. It became a commercial crop in the United States, first in North Carolina (around 1818) and then later in Virginia, which became famous for its peanuts.

Many other inventors contributed to peanut butter's development as a popular foodstuff,

---

UNCOMMONLY KNOWN . . .
PB&J Peanut butter and jelly existed independently long before World War II, but it took hungry young GIs (and perhaps the newly available sliced loaves of bread) to think of putting the two spreads into one sandwich. Since the 1940s, this salty-sweet combo has captured the taste buds of Americans young and old.

including Dr. John Harvey Kellogg of Kellogg's cereal fame, who marketed a nut-grinding machine in the late 1890s. However, when Joseph L. Rosenfield of Alameda, California, invented a mixing process to smooth out the previously lumpy peanut butter, the nut paste really took off. Rosenfield licensed his process to Pond's in 1928, which began selling Peter Pan peanut butter. A few years later, Rosenfield introduced Skippy, his own brand of peanut butter, sold in crunchy and creamy styles.

Today more than half of all edible peanuts grown in the United States are used to make peanut butter, and the Procter & Gamble plant that makes Jif brand peanut butter produces 250,000 jars every day. In recent decades, higher numbers of people sensitive to peanut allergies have made peanut butter unwelcome in some schools and childcare centers. However, peanut butter remains a staple, with the average American consuming nearly four pounds each year.

Pickles

MIDDLE ENGLISH "PIKLE" (HIGHLY SEASONED SAUCE)
PROBABLY FROM MIDDLE DUTCH "PEKEL" (BRINE)
PICKLING BREAKS DOWN NECROBACTERIA IN FOOD

Crisp green pickled cucumbers are common sandwich sides around the United States, but anything can be pickled—even a side of beef. While pickled vegetables and fruits most often go by the name "pickles," pickling is a process that has

been around for thousands of years in nearly every culture's foodways, from South Asian hot pickles (which are often made from vegetables and citrus fruits) and Korean kimchi (pickled cabbage and other vegetables) to kosher dills.

Pickling, also known as "corning," involves submerging food in a salt solution, or brine. This solution can also be a marinade with a more acidic edge; the important thing is that the process causes anaerobic fermentation, adding B vitamins and breaking down necrobacteria so that food can be preserved for long periods of time.

The preservational properties of pickling meant that early sailors could bring along salt pork and salt beef ("corned beef" is another term for pickled or salt beef). Pickled foods were originally introduced to American cuisine from English and German traditions, in which brined meats and vegetables (onions, cabbage, cucumbers, carrots, beans, hardcooked eggs) played a large role.

As immigrants from Central and Eastern Europe, especially from Jewish backgrounds, settled in New York and other urban areas, their traditional cucumber pickles became a staple in delicatessens. On New York City's Lower East Side, "pickle men" had shops with large wooden barrels of their different wares displayed near the street. There were so many people working in pickling by 1893 that they formed a trade organization called Pickle Packers International.

Today cucumber pickles can be found whole, in spears, in slices, sizes large and small, and flavors sweet or sour. One of the perennial favorites, "Kosher dills," may or may not be prepared in accordance with Jewish dietary laws (kashruth), but their garlicky flavor is now beloved by Americans of all religious and ethnic persuasions.

Mayonnaise

FROM FRENCH "MAHON" (TOWN IN MINORCA)
MADE FROM EGG YOLKS, VINEGAR, OIL, SPICES
ALSO KNOWN AS: MAYO, SALAD CREAM

The term *mayonnaise* has murky beginnings. Some think it's derived from *mahonnaise,* for the Spanish port of Mahon, where the French defeated the British in a 1756 naval battle, and enjoyed the port's *allioli,* an egg-based sauce flavored with lots of garlic. Others say it's from the French verb *manier,* "to mix or blend." Still others say the word derives from the Old French *moyeu,* egg yolk. We could go on, but the most important thing for connoisseurs to know is that the first recorded English use of mayonnaise was in an 1841 cookbook. Ironic, considering that the always slightly anti-Gallic British rechristened this condiment "salad cream" in 1914—even keeping the name after an attempt to return to "mayonnaise" resulted in a public outcry in 1999.

On a large and diverse continent, regional tastes regulate mayonnaise sales. However, given the dozens of delicatessens in New York City, it won't

surprise anyone to know that the first manufactured mayo was born there, in Richard Hellman's Columbus Avenue storefront in 1905. Hellman packaged and sold his wife's homemade recipe, and it became so popular that in 1912 he built a factory to produce it in larger quantities. He called the new product Hellman's Blue Ribbon Mayonnaise.

Ketchup

FROM THE CHINESE "KI-TSIAP" (FISH SAUCE)
MADE FROM TOMATOES, ONIONS, VINEGAR, SUGAR
ALTERNATE SPELLINGS: CATCHUP, CATSUP

Today "ketchup" is synonymous with "tomato," but its origins are completely different. The thick red sauce takes its name from the Chinese *ki-tsiap,* a savory, fermented fish sauce. Dutch and English sailors brought a taste for the salty stuff back home, but in place of its exotic ingredients tried more indigenous items like walnuts, celery, and mushrooms. Mushroom ketchup (with nary a tomato in sight) is still widely available in the United Kingdom.

When ketchup reached the New World, it coincided with the latest food trend: tomatoes. Tomatoes were indigenous to the Americas (possibly originating with the Aztecs in about A.D. 700), but it took European exploration to introduce them to and popularize them in North America.

UNCOMMONLY KNOWN . . .

Mustard By combining "must" (unfermented grape juice) with seeds of the "Sinapis hirta" plant, Romans made "mustum ardens," or "burning must." Thus our third most popular American condiment, mustard, takes its name not from the "mustard plant," as we often think, but from the vinegar that is usually mixed with "mustard powder" to make the sharp-flavored spread.

Beverages

T he fascinating thing about this section is that whether your tipple is hard or soft, each item in it is based on one substance: water. Without this basic liquid, there would be no coffee, tea, or soda pop; no wine, beer, or liquor. Of course, drinking water is the healthiest way to quench thirst, but human beings appreciate variety, and as you'll read, there are reasons for boiling and brewing and steeping and stewing beverages. While water at its purest is a fine drink, in many times and places water fit for drinking is very hard to find.

Bottled Water

VARIATIONS: SPRING WATER, WELL WATER, PURIFIED
WATER, SPARKLING WATER, MINERAL WATER
WORLD WATER DAY: MARCH 22

P eople are currently debating the purpose of bottled water, since bottles (whether glass or plastic) add more materials to the Earth's overfull landfills; in July 2007, San Francisco ceased using city funds to buy bottled water, and many restaurants have decided to stop serving it. Bottled waters were originally specialty drinks prized for their healthful qualities. Many countries had mineral springs where the wealthy could stay and "take the waters." Both for the wealthy who wanted to take some of the waters away with them and for people unable to afford a visit, these spas and resorts began bottling the mineral water and selling it.

The oldest of these brands in the United States is Mountain Valley Spring Water, from Hot Springs, Arkansas, which has been served in the U.S. Senate since 1904. The next U.S. spring water on the market was Poland Spring, from its namesake in Maine. "Saratoga Water" became very fashionable, despite its strong mineral flavor, since so many Manhattanites liked to travel upstate for the town's horse races as well as its spa.

Europeans have always been greater consumers of bottled water than Americans, for reasons that range from different tastes to availability. Even today, Italy, France, and Germany rank first, second, and third in number of different brands of bottled mineral water produced (585, 493, and 214, respectively), with the U.S. producing just 183. That's also because in the U.S., mineral water isn't as desirable as it once was. American bottled water, as often as not, is "spring water" and "purified water," neither of which necessarily has mineral content, although "purified water" can be treated (and must be labeled as such when sold).

UNCOMMONLY KNOWN ...

Ice Cubes The first refrigerator with an ice cube area was released in 1914. Refrigerators with separate freezer compartments and ice cube trays became common in the 1920s and 1930s, and many readers will remember metal ice cube trays with arms that popped up to release the separate cubes. Today automatic ice-makers and flexible silicone ice cube trays are common.

Tea

FROM CHINESE AMOY DIALECT: "T'E"
THE MANDARIN WORD FOR TEA IS "CH'A"
POPULAR TYPES: BLACK, GREEN, HERBAL

Cultivated for thousands of years in India, tea is now drunk all over the world. The apocryphal story about how the Chinese found tea involves Emperor Shen-nong's hygienic belief in boiled water and a few leaves of a plant falling into his cup around the year 2737 B.C. The emperor found the resulting brew refreshing, and soon China had such an obsession with "cha" that a man named Lu Yu, who wrote the definitive *Cha Jing*, is commemorated by a giant statue in Xi'an. Buddhist monks brought tea from China to Japan a century or so later, where the tea ceremony was developed into a simple but highly formalized ritual that still has a place in Japanese culture today.

It took eight centuries more before tea caught on in the West, introduced by Dutch traders. For a while, tea was all the rage at the French court, with one noblewoman writing that a courtier was

UNCOMMONLY KNOWN...
Tea Bags Thomas Sullivan of Poughkeepsie, New York, began sending out samples of his tea inventory in small silk muslin pouches that allowed customers to smell the tea and test its strength quickly in hot water. Before long, those customers were asking for containers of the bagged tea. Today, tea bags are usually made from filter paper.

known to drink 40 cups each morning. However, tea reached England not through French fashion but through King Charles II's marriage to Catherine de Braganza, whose Lisbon upbringing included a passion for tea drinking.

Once in England, tea became both a stimulating beverage and a mealtime, the latter when Queen Victoria's lady-in-waiting Anne, Duchess of Bedford, began having "a sinking feeling in the afternoon," since lunches were quite spare. She would invite friends in for a pot of tea and some snacks, which often included small sandwiches and cakes. Of course, tea also stimulated famous unrest in the American Colonies, whose resistance to British domination included rejection of a tax on tea that resulted in the Boston Tea Party of 1776, when Colonial insurgents (including Samuel Adams, John Hancock, and silversmith Paul Revere) dumped 342 cases of tea from the decks of East India Company ships into Boston Harbor.

Coffee

FROM ITALIAN "CAFFE," TURKISH "KAHVE,"
AND ARABIC "QAHWAH"
"QAHWAT AL-BUNN": "WINE OF THE BEAN" (ARABIC)

The history of coffee is as stimulating as the beverage we derive from its beans. Legend has it that a goatherd named Kaldi of

Ethiopia discovered the plant when his goats became friskier after eating its berries. More likely is the historical fact that Ethiopian hunters and warriors learned to make primitive energy bars out of coffee cherries and animal fat rolled together. At some point, someone realized that steeping the berries in water made an energy drink.

It was the Arabs in Africa who first tried coffee as a hot beverage. Around the 11th century, *kahve kanes,* or coffeehouses, became popular in the Yemeni port of Mocha. One of the reasons coffee remained so strongly identified with the Arabic world for so long was that its cultivators kept it that way. Coffee was not permitted to be exported; all beans were stripped so that they would be infertile. This was partly to control the lucrative market but also partly because coffee was seen by early imbibers to be an almost mystical substance, since it could induce a kind of "high" (which today's Starbucks addicts know well).

Of course, eventually coffee was smuggled out: An Indian Muslim pilgrim named Baba Budan supposedly left the shores of Africa for a pilgrimage to Mecca with coffee beans strapped to his belly. Once coffee arrived in Eurasia (the first coffee shop there was established in Constantinople in 1475), it quickly spread to other lands. Venice, as an important trading center, became the first European city to welcome coffee. Ironically, after gaining popularity across Germany, France, and England, coffee beans had to be smuggled back across the ocean, to Brazil, to gain the greatest foothold. Brazil now produces most of the world's coffee. Coffee is the world's most popular beverage, with more than 400 billion cups consumed each year.

Among cultures where coffee is widely consumed, nicknames are common. In the United States, people call the morning cup everything from "joe" to "java" to "mud."

UNCOMMONLY KNOWN . . .

Espresso The Italian method of forcing hot water under pressure through coffee produces an intense brew known as espresso. "Espresso drinks," which include the latte (made with steamed milk) and the "doppio" (double shot), became popular in the U.S. in the 1980s and are now widely available through chains such as Starbucks, Caribou Coffee, and Seattle's Best.

Wine Decanters

Modern wine enthusiasts might be surprised to learn that old wine hasn't always been preferred over new. The ancient Greeks and Romans, in fact, prized wine for its freshness and preferred to drink it as soon as possible after its first pressing. The oldest method of preserving wine, olive oil, wasn't meant to keep the wine for years, but rather to keep the wine from aging at all. Thus, a history of wine decanters also becomes a history of changing tastes. Greek amphorae of clay were the easiest way to transport the largest amounts of new wine from vineyard to town center. They were also easily replaced if broken or fouled with a bad batch. Wineskins fashioned from soft leather suited nomadic and transitional societies like the Huns, the Goths, and the Vikings; these containers not only didn't break, they were serving pieces, too. A man could drink straight from a full wineskin without need of a goblet or beaker. Goblets became more important as both Eastern and Western societies grew more stable.

1300 B.C.
Bronze wine vessel
The Chinese made elaborate wine containers, such as this one with animal motif. This bronze three-legged vessel dates to the mid-Shang dynasty.

1500 B.C.
Amphora With its long, narrow neck and dual handles, the ancient Greek clay amphora has a name that comes from the words that mean "to carry by two"; they were used for all sorts of comestibles.

Soda Pop

**ALSO KNOWN AS: SODA, SOFT DRINK, POP,
FOUNTAIN DRINK, FIZZY DRINKS, MINERALS, COKE
SODA JERK: PERSON WHO MIXED THE WATER AND SYRUP**

Carbonated drinks are so widely manufactured and so various it's tough to connect them to their all-natural, single-flavor origins: underground springs. Humans first tasted and enjoyed bubbly water from natural sources, but there is no evidence that anyone attempted to flavor naturally carbonated spring water until the 17th century, when Parisians enjoyed spring water flavored with honey and lemon. In 1767, Englishman Joseph Priestley concocted the first man-made carbonated water, and in 1770 Swedish chemist Tobern Bergmann invented a machine that used chalk from sulfuric acid to add bubbles to still water. In 1832, American John Mathews of Charleston, South Carolina, further refined an apparatus to mass-produce carbonated water and began selling his machines for "soda fountains."

When it comes to how early soda water gained flavors, some historians credit Dr. Philip Syng Physick, known as the Father of American Surgery for his many innovations, including the stomach pump. In 1807, Syng Physick evidently added some flavoring to carbonated water to make it easier for a patient to drink. Other physicians followed suit, and some of their additions resulted in flavors that are still popular, including birch beer and sarsaparilla.

400 B.C.
Wineskin Called a "bota bag," these Spanish containers were usually made of goatskin and lined with tree sap to prevent leaks. The Basque version, distinguished by a red cord, was known as a "zahato."

800
Wine Jug Wine jars morphed into jugs (often with corked tops) as early Europeans turned the fruit of their plentiful vineyards into wine and used their plentiful clay for flat-bottomed containers that could easily be transported in carts.

2000
Boxes The "bag in a box" actually mimics both the wineskin and the cask. While oenophiles have long disdained wines in this type of package, the wine box actually has both taste and environmental advantages.

A.D. 100
Chalice At first the goblet was larger than the base, for sharing as per the Last Supper; then the base became larger than the goblet, so priests could elevate the chalice during Mass. Today most chalices have both elements enlarged for modern congregations.

1400
Cruet In medieval times, most people cut their wine with water, and that practice carried over into churches, where the priest mixed wine from the cruet with water to represent the dual nature of Jesus, human and divine.

Until the mid-20th century, most Americans enjoyed soda water, soda "pop," and other concoctions like "floats" with ice cream at soda fountains. In the 1920s, the first Hom-Pak cardboard tote allowed people to carry out freshly bottled soda pop. By this time, ginger ale, root beer, Dr. Pepper, and Coca-Cola were well established; the bottled-pop trend ushered in fruit-flavored sodas like Nehi and 7-Up, as well as the first diet sodas. In the 1960s, two packaging changes again made soft drinks more available: pop-top cans and plastic bottles. In the 1970s, it was the stay-tab can and vending machines. Today, soda pop is available in many different sizes and shapes of containers. The latest trend is glass bottles topped with metal caps, just like 100 years ago.

Beer

FROM OLD ENGLISH "BEOR" AND LATIN "BIBERE"
WORLD'S THIRD MOST POPULAR DRINK
AFTER WATER AND TEA

Brewing might not be the world's oldest profession, but beer has a firm claim on being the world's oldest alcoholic beverage. Some historians believe that the human discovery 10,000 years ago that grain and water made an intoxicating mix was a catalyst behind the move from hunter-gatherer society to agrarian society: Growing more grains would keep the beer supply flowing.

The oldest known recipe for beer can be found on a cuneiform tablet from circa 4000 B.C. The recipe formed part of a poem written in honor of the Sumerian goddess of beer, Ninkasi. There was a good reason for beer's status in all of these societies as well as later ones. In eras and places where potable water was scarce, fermented drinks made from grains and boiled during the brewing process were generally much safer to drink. When the Puritans landed the *Mayflower* at Plymouth Rock because of dwindling supplies, "especially our beere," it wasn't because they were alcoholics, but because they all needed some unspoiled source of liquids.

Beer as we know it is made with hops, a technique begun around the ninth century in northern Europe because the hop plant helps preserve the fermented brew. However, while hopped beer was perfected and became extremely popular in Germany (and it was German immigrants who created brewing dynasties in the U.S., like Anheuser-Busch), early English peasants nearly revolted at a taste they considered revolting. Even today, unhopped beer or ale is more popular in the United Kingdom than anywhere else.

Much modern beer in the U.S., like milk, is pasteurized, but the most significant development in today's American beers was probably Prohibition. With less beer to go around, the available stuff was usually watered down, giving drinkers a taste for weaker brew.

Lighter beers like Miller, Schlitz, and Pabst were popular through much of the 20th century. As American palates grew more educated in the 1980s and 1990s, small companies began producing "microbrews": beers, ales, and lagers made in smaller batches with specialty ingredients. Microbrews closely resemble the kinds of grain beverages consumed in ancient times and in early America.

Wine

FROM THE LATIN VINUM (WINE)
POPULAR TYPES: RED, WHITE, SPARKLING, DESSERT
"VARIETY" IN WINEMAKING IS THE TYPE OF GRAPE USED

Wild grapes have existed for millions of years. Make that tens of millions—the oldest fossilized vine is dated at about 60 million years old. However, wild grapes are small and sour. The first grapes to be made into wine were domesticated, made possible by cultures that had settled and begun to grow annual crops. The oldest wine container finds have been in what are now modern-day Georgia and Iran (where it was called *mei*). University of Pennsylvania researchers now believe the domesticated grape may first have been planted in Georgia, then spread south.

Just one grape, *Vitis vinifera,* is the species responsible for 4,000 varieties around the world, but only a relatively small percentage of those are cultivated into wine. Wine production dates back about 6,500 years in Greece, and both red and white wine were important in ancient Egypt. Wine became a commodity in ancient Rome, where barrels and bottles first were used for its storage. The oldest existing bottle of wine is from a Roman colony near what is now Speyer, Germany. That bottle contains some olive oil, an early method of preserving the fermented grape juice, before corks came into use.

After winemaking spread from the Roman Empire throughout western Europe, wine became a preferred beverage in nearly all of those countries, with regional types like sherry (from the port of Jerez), Riesling (grown along the Rhine), and Tokay (a sweet Hungarian varietal) gaining favor, too.

All of these varietals were placed in jeopardy in 1863 when the North American root louse *Phylloxera vastatrix* was brought to Europe, decimating European rootstocks for decades. After a Texan horticulturist named Thomas Munson realized the way to save European vines was through grafting them to American stock, the great vineyards were saved, albeit forever changed.

Nowadays, wineries have become much more than the place where the grapes are grown and the wine made. Many wineries are tourist destinations with overnight accommodations and tasting menus that pair foods with wines. They may also act as wedding sites and corporate conference venues.

Most winery-area real estate is expensive. Modern farming techniques have helped wineries figure out ways to get more mileage out of their acreage while not weakening the soil. Such techniques as vertical shoot positioning (VSP), in which the growth of the vines is highly controlled, results in a very neat, tight canopy. Rather than allowing vines to sprawl, VSP promotes sustainable growth. It's also healthier for the vines, making them less susceptible to disease and able to get shading from their neighbors and leading to more uniform quality.

PARALLEL HISTORY

Bathtub Gin

The classic "long drink," gin and tonic is also known as G&T or gin and it, depending on the country, social station, and drinking venue. It may also be the only cocktail that was concocted for a medicinal purpose. British troops that were stationed in hot, damp climates during the 19th century were prone to suffering from bouts of malaria, and tonic water made with Peruvian quinine was found to be the best antimalarial substance. However, quinine (extracted from the bark of the cinchona tree) was quite bitter, and some enterprising officers found that if you mixed it with gin, sugar, and some lime juice, the tonic water was quite palatable and refreshing.

Liquor

FROM LATIN "LIQUERE" (TO BE LIQUID)
ALSO KNOWN AS DISTILLED SPIRITS
SOME POPULAR TYPES: VODKA, TEQUILA, GIN, RUM

Ironically, since the Muslim religion forbids drinking alcohol, the distillation process that produces pure spirits was perfected in the Arab world. Beers, wines, and primitive grain liquors had long been invented and drunk around the world before the alembic still allowed primary inventor Geber to heat wine and separate its alcohol vapor from its fruit in the ninth century.

The process that sets distilled liquor apart from wines and beers is the distillation process. Basically, the four elements involved in making liquor are yeast, a carbohydrate, the fermentation process, and the distillation process. The carbohydrate used can be any starch, such as that present in some vegetables or grains, or the simple sugars in most fruits. First, the yeast and carbohydrate must interact in the fermentation process, then the fermented liquid can be distilled. Liquors have a higher concentration than wine or beer because the distillation process increases their ethyl alcohol content.

By the 12th century, many regions and nations had their preferred types of distilled alcohol, sometimes made from grapes (Italian *grappa*, French *eaux-de-vie*), oats (Irish and Scotch whisky), wheat (Dutch *jenever* and English gin), rice (Japanese sake), potatoes (Russian vodka), and rye (Swedish *akvavit*). The word *alcohol* itself is derived from Arabic (*al* is the definite article, and the second half of the word may be from *gawl,* meaning "spirit"), but as several of the names above indicate, "life water" was also a common early name for these intense liquids.

While many societies, including early American, viewed alcohol consumption with matter-of-fact attitudes during the 17th and 18th centuries, in the more industrially minded 19th century, drinking became a sign of sloth and debauchery. This was due not simply to alcohol's abuse but to its sudden availability—the same governments urging citizens to work and produce more were trying to find ways to use up excess grain.

Adherents of the American temperance movement, which sought to abolish the sale of alcohol, succeeded during the 1920s—Prohibition was enacted nationwide and lasted for nearly a decade before being repealed. While attitudes toward alcohol consumption still vary greatly across the country, with factors like religious persuasion, lifestyle, health concerns, and age coming into play, today there are more types of liquor available than ever before. The millennial trend toward "microbreweries" for small-batch beer production has inspired "microdistilleries" that produce small-batch bourbons, whiskeys, and other types of liquor.

Snacks

Your mother was probably quick to tell you not to spoil your dinner, but you have history on your side when it comes to snacking. Even ancient cultures created small dishes or treats to eat while traveling, and nearly every culture has enjoyed small dishes and treats to serve family and friends at certain times of the day. Some of the modern snacks in this section are fairly substantial, like cheese, pizza, and hot dogs, but when you consider them alongside a miner's Cornish pasty or a farmer's hearty sandwich, their relative lightweight status is apparent.

Swiss Cheese

ORIGINATION: SWITZERLAND'S EMMENTALER CHEESE
PALE YELLOW, FIRM CHEESE RIDDLED WITH HOLES
CHEESE WITH NO HOLES IS KNOWN AS "BLIND"

In countless television cartoons, mice are lured out of their baseboard homes with chunks of the hole-spotted dairy product viewers recognize as "Swiss cheese." This mild yet distinctively flavored *fromage* is a favorite in U.S. kitchens, but that's not because Americans have an obsession with Switzerland. First of all, "Swiss cheese" is a slight misnomer. The cheese we know as "Swiss" does have its origin in a cheese from Switzerland called Emmentaler. Emmentaler is produced in the Emme Valley, part of the Swiss canton of Bern. (Switzerland is home to 450 varieties of cheese.)

Although the appellation "Emmenthaler Switzerland" is protected, "Emmental" is not. Many countries produce some type of Emmentaler, and

in the United States when Swiss and Scandinavian immigrants began producing Emmentaler, the cheese became known simply as Swiss cheese.

Swiss cheese gets its holes (technically known as "eyes") from a bacterium called *Propionibacter* that eats lactic acid produced by two other bacteria (*Streptococcus thermophilus* and *Lactobacillus*). Carbon dioxide released from *Proprionibacter* forces bubbles into the cheese, and that makes the eyes. The propionic acid is also responsible for the nutty flavor and "bite" of Swiss cheese. Americans eat a lot of cheese, maybe even too much: In 1975 the per capita consumption of cheese was 14.5 pounds. By 2006, that number was up to 32.5 pounds. There's good reason for that, at least as far as Swiss cheese is concerned: As a snack or appetizer, Swiss cheese is a satisfying combination of taste and texture. It's a firm enough cheese to be eaten in cubes with fingers or toothpicks, sliced on a cracker, with fruit on a cheese plate, or with cold cuts on bread. Because of its mild flavor, many children like Swiss cheese.

The bigger the eyes in Swiss cheese, the more intense the flavor—because more propionic acid has been generated. The large eyes can make slicing the cheese into uniform pieces difficult. It used to be that Swiss cheese eyes needed to be between $^{11}/_{16}$ and $^{13}/_{16}$ inch (about the size of a nickel) to be stamped Grade A. Now cheese with holes as small as $^3/_8$ inch, about half the originally required size, can earn the highest grade.

Baking Mixes

INVENTOR: CARL SMITH
1930 | CONCEIVED IDEA FOR BISQUICK BISCUIT MIX
BASED ON INSPIRATION FROM A TRAIN DINING CAR CHEF

Many cooking purists eschew packaged baking mixes, but they're not only widely popular in the United States, they were born from a professional cook's efficiency. In 1930, General Mills sales executive Carl Smith returned to a train's dining car too late to order dinner from the menu. He was quickly served a plate of fresh, hot biscuits, and when he asked how it was possible to get something homemade in such a short period of time, the chef showed Smith his pre-mixed biscuit batter.

When Smith took the idea back to his corporate headquarters, everyone realized that the challenge was to create something that could be packaged easily (no lard, butter, or other shortening could be included) and that would taste as good as a home cook's product. By 1931, Bisquick biscuit mix was on store shelves, the first commercial prepackaged baking mix. It was soon followed by scores of others, few of which lasted.

Bisquick has endured, of course, and its success inspired new uses and recipes, which then inspired companies to try different kinds of baking mixes, from muffins to cookies to cakes. Almost every mid-20th-century American home pantry contained at least one box of cake mix. In an era that increasingly valued convenience, the fact that these mixes were nearly complete, needing only a few liquid ingredients like eggs, water, or oil, meant that they saved time, and sometimes money, too.

However, the most important reason baking mixes work for many cooks and places is because of one particular ingredient: baking powder. Baking powder, a combination of acid salts that helps baked goods rise, is highly perishable. Since many households don't or can't replenish their canisters of baking powder frequently enough, packaged mixes are even more convenient, as long as they're used in good time.

Cold Cuts

MOST POPULAR DELI MEATS: TURKEY, HAM
ALSO KNOWN AS: LUNCHEON MEATS, SANDWICH MEATS,
COOKED MEATS, SLICED MEATS

Nearly every culture's cuisine includes some form of sausage and/or cured meat. A list of different types would be as long as this entire chapter! Native Americans made "pemmican," a primitive type of sausage consisting of dried buffalo meat and berries, which could be considered the first American cured meat. Naturally, each group that arrived in this country introduced a different sort of meat product that falls under the category of lunch meat, luncheon meat, deli meat, cold meat, sandwich meat, and more.

Dutch and English settlers would have contributed their softer sausages, which often include some sort of cereal grain mixed with ground meat. English "bangers" are one example, and live on today in some mild deli meats that are sliced, like "Devon sausage." Dutch and German settlers also made mixed sausages and loaf meats like "headcheese" that inspired pickle loaf, Lebanon bologna, and olive loaf. German and Italian immigrants brought numerous varieties of cured meats, including cured sausages like Jagdwurst and salami, as well as pastrami and prosciutto.

The term "cold cuts" came about when refrigeration became more widespread in food markets. These easily spoiled meats were kept in a cold case and sliced to order for customers. Today some deli meats are sausages, some roasts that are sliced (like roast turkey or roast beef), and still others are processed meat products, like chicken loaf or liverwurst. In the United States, cold cuts are most often consumed in sandwiches, and sometimes on buffets, but they are rarely eaten for breakfast as they are in Europe. Today, cold cuts are often purchased presliced and prepackaged, and can even be found in sandwich-making "kits" so that a consumer doesn't need to worry about having on hand different ingredients like a roll, condiments, or cheese.

Popcorn

ORIGINATION: UNITED STATES
TERM "POPCORN" DATES TO ABOUT 1810
AMERICANS CONSUME 17 BILLION QUARTS PER YEAR

Popcorn is an indigenous food product that is also cheap, wholesome, low-calorie, and versatile. However, the word *corn* originally did not refer to cobs at roadside stands as it does today; it's Old English for "local grain." The "corn" in the Bible (e.g., Ruth "among the alien corn") probably meant barley. In England it would have been wheat, and in Scotland and Ireland, oats. European settlers in the New World called the common grain found there "corn," although its proper name is "maize" (*Zea mays*).

Maize has grown in the Americas for millennia, and has been popped for at least 2,500 years. The oldest popped whole ears of corn were discovered in New Mexico. Popcorn pops when water and oil trapped between its dense endosperm and hard hull boil up when heated. The pressure forces moisture into the endosperm and the outer hulls crack. Many people, including the early colonists, ate sweetened popcorn, sometimes with milk poured over it, for breakast. The Massachusetts Wampanoags, who introduced popcorn to the first Thanksgiving feast in Plymouth, even made beer from leftover popcorn that they would ferment like any other grain.

Around the 1890s, popcorn became a common snack food, partly because of that era's health-food boom. Most popcorn (70 percent) is bought and consumed at home, and produced in Illinois, Indiana, Iowa, Kansas, Kentucky, Michigan, Missouri, Nebraska, and Ohio. Some of the remaining 30 percent is eaten at cinemas, popcorn having gained popularity with moviegoers in the 1920s. One nostalgic popcorn-making method for modern Americans is Jiffy Pop, a foil-topped pan with a handle; its top becomes an aluminum mushroom cloud when shaken over heat.

PARALLEL HISTORY

Nachos

As befits its belly-filling qualities, the popular snack known as nachos came about out when some people had the munchies. It was 1943 in Coahuila, Mexico, and a group of military wives from the nearby U.S. Army base of Eagle Pass came into the town's Victory Club looking for hors d'oeuvres after the restaurant had closed for the evening. Head chef Ignacio "Nacho" Anaya threw together deep-fried triangles of corn tortilla with cheese and jalapeño peppers and baked them briefly until the cheese melted. Before you could say "Bueno appetito," the cheesy, crispy dish had been devoured. The Modernos Restaurant in Coahuila's Piedras Negras serves the original recipe.

Graham Crackers

REV. DR. SYLVESTER GRAHAM
1829 | AMERICA
ORIGINALLY FROM BRAN AND GERM LAYERS OF WHEAT

Open any diaper bag or mom's tote and you're likely to find some graham crackers. The low-sugar, high-fiber treats are considered ideal kid fodder but rarely tempt anyone over the age of ten. So most adults might be surprised to learn that these wholesome baked goods were created as part of a dietetic regimen to combat "carnal urges"—that's right, good old-fashioned lust.

The Reverend Sylvester Graham (1794-1851) of Bound Brook, New Jersey, after whom the crackers are named, developed the recipe for his mild baked good in 1829.

Graham—who had no formal medical training—promoted a diet of fresh produce, whole grains, and a small amount of protein. Spices, red meat, and most dairy were forbidden; the diet was supposed to reduce impurity. While the diet never caught on (despite being de rigueur at one point for students at Oberlin College by one of Graham's followers), the graham cracker did.

The Rev. Graham made his crackers with coarse-ground, full-fiber graham flour, which is not made from anything called "graham" but instead means a flour that incorporates the full bran and germ layers of winter wheat. Like his diet ideas, that recipe was soon replaced with something more appealing to a wide range of tastes, marketed by Nabisco in the late 19th century. Today many well-known graham-cracker manufacturers omit graham flour from their formulas entirely; the modern versions share more with British whole-meal biscuits than with Graham's original "crackers."

For campers and cooks, that's not such a bad thing. A perennial favorite, "s'mores"—the treat of softened chocolate and toasted marshmallow sandwiched between two graham crackers that is typically cooked over a campfire—was first mentioned in the 1927 *Girl Scout Handbook*. Cooks rely on the tasty, crumbly powder of graham crackers for pie crusts and bar cookies.

Hot Dogs

ALSO KNOWN AS A FRANKFURTERS
"HOT DOG" SLANG FOR ONE WHO SHOWS OFF COMPLEX
MANEUVERS OR TO EXPRESS DELIGHT

Everyone makes jokes about what goes into hot dogs. "You don't want to see the sausage being made" has grown into a catchphrase about avoiding the inner workings of things like politics and business because many people think that the finely ground, highly spiced contents of a sausage casing might be anything from bits of offal to bits that are truly awful, like vermin droppings.

This isn't fair to American's favorite version of sausage. Hot dogs did not originate as a catchall for butcher castoffs. They come to us from Germany, where sausage-making is an elaborate art. Two cities contributed to the "Frankfurter wiener" that we now know as a "hot dog"; in Vienna, or Wien, a Frankfurt-trained butcher concocted the "wiener-frankfurther." At about the same time, the early 1850s, the Frankfurt butcher's guild created a new sausage called a "frankfurter" with a slightly curved shape. Legend has it that the shape came about because one of the butchers had a dachshund, and that's how Americans came to call the cooked sausage a "hot dog."

That might not be true, but it is true that the long, mild "wiener sausage" came to the U.S. with German immigrants. In 1867, Charles Feltman opened the first hot dog stand on New York's Coney Island. While Feltman sold his sausages on rolls, as Germans and Austrians had been eating them for years, credit for the hot dog bun is generally given to St. Louis vendor Antoine Feuchtwanger, who in 1880 asked his brother-in-law to bake long, slender rolls to help keep his patrons' hands from getting burned.

As for the term "hot dog," it may have caught on after a 1902 New York Giants baseball game in which a concessionaire named Harry Mozley Stevens began hawking "dachshund sausages" by crying, "Get 'em while they're hot!"

Pizza

FROM THE ITALIAN "PIZZA" MEANING PIE, TART
PEPPERONI IS THE MOST POPULAR TOPPING
POPULAR VARIETIES: MEAT, CHEESE, VEGETABLE, WHITE

M odern pizza is basically no more than a circle of dough spread with sauce and sprinkled with cheese. It's probably these simple elements that have made pizza a worldwide staple; most cuisines include some kind of flatbread that can be topped with oils, vegetables, and meats. The ancient Greeks made circular dough "plates" that they called *plankuntos*. One of the earliest recorded "ancestors" of pizza is the dough that foot soldiers of Persia's Darius the Great baked on their shields.

The Persian soldiers put cheese and dates on their bread, and over the years olive oil, herbs, honey, pine nuts, goat cheese, and many other foods were tried and enjoyed on flatbreads. Our evidence that pizza was a specialty of Naples, Italy, comes from A.D. 79. The volcanic eruption that buried the Italian city of Pompeii and part of neighboring Neopolis, or Naples, preserved a bakery run by *pizzaioli*, forerunner of today's pizzeria.

For reasons that may never be entirely clear, Neapolitans embraced pizza with gusto, perfecting a chewy crust (Romans prefer theirs crispy) and experimenting with New World tomatoes until the "pizza marinara" was born. Although *marinara* means "of the sea," this pizza had nothing fishy about it—it was simply the favorite snack of sailors and anglers returning to town after weeks offshore.

Naples is also home to the first true modern pizzeria, Antica Pizzeria Port'Alba, which opened in 1830. By the late 19th century, "pizza a la Margherita" had become very popular. This tomato, mozzarella, and basil pie echoed the colors of the newly created Italian flag, and was the favorite of Queen Margherita di Savoia. Thus, when immigrants from the new nation came to the United States, they brought their trendiest pizza with them, and Americans came to regard this simple, tasty combination as the way pizza should taste. By the time Gennaro Lombardi opened the first U.S. pizzeria in 1905 on Manhattan's Spring Street, "pizza pie" had come a long way from its origins as a plate.

Pretzels

SECOND MOST POPULAR SNACK (AFTER POTATO CHIPS)
CAN BE HARD OR SOFT, BITE-SIZE OR LARGE
USUALLY SERVED WITH MUSTARD OR TOPPED WITH SALT

Many people know the story of the early medieval German monk who took a scrap of bread dough, rolled it into a strip, then folded it into the shape of a child's arms folded in prayer. The monks offered these *pretiola* (Latin for "little bribe") to children who memorized Scripture verses and prayers.

These soft treats evolved to have a deliciously hard, dark crust that is created by sprinkling the dough with water while baking, causing a Maillard reaction (nonenzymatic browning), which contemporary bakers usually simulate by dipping finished unbaked pretzels in a sodium bicarbonate solution. The finished pretzels might be sprinkled with salt or sugar, depending on the baker's whim. Eventually, German *brezln* would almost always be served topped with salt crystals, and other shapes became popular, too: Today you can find *brezel broetchen* (pretzel rolls) in round, oval, and log form in German bakeries.

No one knows exactly how Early American colonists knew about pretzels; some historians believe the recipe came over on the *Mayflower*. What is known is that the colonists made pretzels and sold them to the Native Americans. As the popularity of the snack grew, more bakeries made it. That's how the favorite American version, hard pretzels, came to be. During the late 1600s, a baker's apprentice in Pennsylvania fell asleep by the hearth, and the batch of pretzels he was baking was cold, dry, and

hard when he finally retrieved them. Once he'd tried one, he was hooked. His boss must have been, too, or perhaps it was simply the fact that a hard, dry pretzel could be kept and sold for a much longer period of time than a soft, fresh one.

In 1510, a group of Turks attempted to invade the city of Vienna, but they were thwarted when early rising pretzel bakers not only heard something amiss and sounded the alarm for reinforcements, they kept the attackers at bay until help arrived. The Habsburg emperor awarded the guild a special seal in recognition of the bakers' bravery, adorned with a pretzel.

In 1652, Dutch baker Jochem Wessels and his wife, Gertrude, were arrested in Beverwyck, New York (near the modern-day city of Albany), for selling pretzels to the Indians. It was a good business decision for Wessels, because the Indians loved the bready treats so much they would pay any price he asked, but Wessels's peers prosecuted him for using up the best flour for the pretzels and saving leftover product for bread he sold to everyone else: "The heathen were eating flour while the Christians were eating bran."

The first commercial pretzel bakery was established by Julius Sturgis in Lititz, Pennsylvania, a bit later, in 1861. In 1935, the Reading Pretzel Company introduced an automatic pretzel-twisting machine that sped up the process considerably. Perhaps that helped make pretzels the second favorite American snack, behind potato chips and before popcorn.

Today pretzels are eaten in hard and soft, large and small, salty and sweet forms. In the United States, they are often served with mustard but are also popular with other savory dips, and can even be found baked around that very American treat, the hot dog.

Sweets

Research suggests that human beings may develop a taste for sweet substances from their mothers' milk. Regardless, "sweet" is a taste that brings joy to the taste buds. From chocolate to chewing gum, every item discussed in this section is a treat and not necessary for daily nutrition (serious chocoholics will certainly disagree). Although sweet treats are certainly more prevalent since sugar manufacturing grew to its modern proportions, societies throughout the ages have enjoyed some form of sweets, often in the form of honey, or baked into candies or cakes.

Chocolate

MADE FROM ROASTED, GROUND CACAO BEANS
POPULAR TYPES: DARK, MILK, WHITE
COMES IN FORM OF CANDY, SYRUP, POWDER

Considering how many cultures have contributed to chocolate and the many steps in its manufacture, it's small wonder that a substance dating back several millennia has been consumed as a food for only about 150 years. First harvested and used by the ancient Maya, chocolate was initially a beverage, and not a particularly sweet or smooth one. A Spanish missionary said of it in the 16th century: "Loathsome to such as are not acquainted with it, having a scum or froth that is very unpleasant to taste." The bitter blend of ground cacao beans, water, and other local ingredients (including chilies, pimento, and vanilla) was tough to swallow.

No one is completely sure about the derivation of the word *chocolate*. While some dictionaries cite it as Aztec in origin, other experts believe Spanish colonizers coined the word from the Mayan *chocol,* the Mayan *haa* (water), and the Aztec *atl* (water). However, the Mayan verb *chokola'j,* meaning "to drink chocolate together," is another source. Despite its off-putting taste and name, the chocolate drink was intriguing enough to bring back to Europe. While Columbus did discover cacao pods, their appeal was recognized only in 1510 by Hernán Cortés, who brought three chests of pods back. The first commercial shipment of cacao to Europe occurred in 1585 from Veracruz, Mexico, to Seville, Spain.

For the next 250-odd years, chocolate would increase in popularity and availability in Europe. Unfortunately, this also meant that English, French, and Dutch growers relied heavily on slave labor to cultivate crops. One Dutch chocolate manufacturer made a very important discovery in the history of chocolate as food: In 1828, Conrad J. van Houten patented a method for pressing the fat from roasted cacao beans, which meant that the

UNCOMMONLY KNOWN...

Box of Chocolates The first chocolate bar was introduced in 1847 by Joseph Fry & Sons in Bristol, England, and a few years later the public was introduced to enrobed chocolate candies at Prince Albert's Exposition in 1851. Boxed chocolates were sold in both England and America, and first marketed to the masses in 1868, with John Cadbury's packaged creams and bonbons.

cocoa powder and cocoa butter could be separated. Different treatments for the two result in the various delicious confections we now enjoy.

Cookies

ALSO KNOWN AS BISCUITS (U.K.)
IDIOM: "THAT'S THE WAY THE COOKIE CRUMBLES,"
(IT CAN'T BE HELPED), "TOSS [ONE'S] COOKIES" (VOMIT)

Our word for cookies comes directly from the Dutch *koekje,* or "little cake," which is related to the German *kek,* while the British and French *biscuit* seems to derive from the same root as Italian *biscotti,* from the Latin *bis coctum,* or twice-baked. In other words, everyone enjoys cookies—usually small, rounded, flat baked goods based on flour and sugar and some kind of fat.

Everyone got their versions of cookies from seventh-century Persia (modern Iran), where some soldiers once found riverbank "reeds which produce honey without bees." The sugar cane helped ancient Persian bakers begin concocting pastries for which they are still famous, and the small cakes spread to Europe during Spain's Moorish era. Medieval and Renaissance cookbooks in Spain, France,

PARALLEL HISTORY

Chocolate among the Aztecs

You might know that chocolate originated with the Maya and Aztec peoples of Mexico, but you probably don't know that the Aztecs discovered chocolate's endorphin-stimulating properties while trying to make beer. Scientists believe that attempts to ferment cacao pulp led to the discovery that the ground seeds made a more stimulating beverage, which they called *xocolatl.* One of Cortés's men wrote of the foamy brew: "This drink is the healthiest thing, and the greatest sustenance of anything you could drink in the world, because he who drinks a cup of this liquid, no matter how far he walks, can go a whole day without eating anything else."

and England have many recipes for "fine cakes" and "jumbles," including several akin to shortbread, one of the simplest cookies to make (flour, sugar, and butter are the only ingredients).

As with many other foods and beverages, cookies came to the New World via colonization. By 1796, the first recipes for "cookies" were printed in Amelia Simmons's *American Cookery.* Early Americans enjoyed shortbread, gingerbread, and macaroons, all types of cookies that can still be found readily today. The perennially popular brownies may have been made throughout the 19th century, but the first printed recipe for them dates to an 1897 Sears, Roebuck catalog.

As with many foods and beverages, when manufacturing processes and plants grew more sophisticated, homemade cookies lost some glamour to perfectly baked and symmetrical store-bought types, with names like Chips Ahoy!, Oreo, and Lorna Doone. During the late 20th century, older recipes, rustic textures, and unprocessed ingredients influenced large corporations and smaller artisanal bakers alike. Raisin-flecked hermits, cinnamon-scented snickerdoodles, and intentionally lumpy oatmeal cookies can be found at trendy cafés and farmers markets around the nation.

Ice Cream

USUALLY SERVED IN SCOOPS ON CONES
MOST POPULAR FLAVOR IN THE U.S.: VANILLA
ALTERNATIVES: SORBET, GELATO, FROZEN YOGURT

Ice cream's early history is spotty: some ancient civilizations knew about freezing foods, and some of the first iced "creams" (including the snow and syrup enjoyed by

Emperor Nero in the first century A.D.) would resemble sorbets to modern palates. They must still have been delicious, since King Charles I of England in the early 17th century offered his chef a lifetime pension for keeping an "iced cream" recipe secret, for royal palates only.

By the 18th century, recipes for ice cream as we understand it appeared in British and American cookbooks. Several of the Founding Fathers ate ice cream regularly, and Dolley Madison served it at President James Madison's Inaugural Ball in 1809. It was a rare treat, because it had to be prepared in small quantities and served immediately.

Many people helped to develop ice cream into a widely available treat, including African American Augustus Jackson, whose recipes and technique are credited with improving ice cream's overall taste and texture. In 1843, a New England housewife named Nancy Johnson invented and patented the hand-cranked ice cream freezer, which led to later manufacturing progress—by 1851 Jacob Fussell of Baltimore had opened the first commercial ice cream plant.

But it was advances in commercial refrigeration that really paved the way for modern ice cream consumption; when large freezers became available, especially in transport, merchants could start offering lots of different ice creams, all the time. Howard Johnson's 28 Flavors were challenged by Baskin-Robbins's 31 Flavors, with both of those popular chains receiving plenty of competition from the boom in unusually flavored ice creams during the 1980s and 1990s. Today ice cream is available in hard and soft varieties; dozens of flavors, even garlic and basil; full-fat, no-fat, low-fat, French-style, and gelato; in cones, sandwiches, on sticks, and in many other forms. More than 90 percent of U.S. households consume

about 1.5 billion gallons of ice cream every year, making the frozen confection the nation's most popular dessert.

Pie

TERM "PIE" DATES TO ABOUT 1300
MOST POPULAR VARIETIES IN U.S.: APPLE,
PUMPKIN, CHOCOLATE, LEMON MERINGUE

Today a flaky, tender pie crust is a delicacy in its own right, but for hundreds of years, pastry was prized mainly for its strength: A crust had to not only hold its contents together but also serve as a utensil from hand to mouth.

Ancient Egyptians used bread dough to hold a mixture of nuts, honey, and fruits, but pastry as a substance in its own right can be attributed to the ancient Greeks. Their conquerors, the Romans, experimented a great deal with different kinds of fillings for pastry casing, including (but not limited to) eels, mussels, doves, and baby goats. The inventive Romans also made the earliest recorded version of cheesecake, according to Cato.

Since those inventive Romans built many roads and conquered lots of different lands, we know that pies came to quite a few places around the same time. In early medieval England, pies were known as "coffins," in the sense of that word as a container. The use of lard and butter instead of oil made stiffer, more durable pastry possible. Different constructions were used, from deep-sided, open-topped "traps" to broad, flat "tartlets." As cookbooks became readable, printed materials, cooks began to take more care with their ingredients and recipes, since the lady of the house might double-check their work.

Pies, having become an English specialty (Cornish pasties, shepherd's pie, and steak-and-kidney pie are just a few examples), quickly caught on in the 13 Colonies. The phrase "to cut corners" may come from the colonial practice of using round pans (with no corners) for pies, thus allowing more even distribution of scant ingredients to more people. As the new United States of America grew, pies went west with pioneers, who discovered many ways to use preserved fruits and other ingredients encased in dough.

Doughnuts

ORIGIN: DUTCH
POPULAR VARIETIES: GLAZED, FILLED, ICED
ALSO SPELLED DONUT

Fried dough or batter figures in cuisines around the globe, from China's *youtiao* or "oil sticks," to Poland's *paczki,* to Iran's sticky *zooloobiya*. As that quintessentially American cartoon character Homer Simpson might say: "Donuts. Is there anything they can't do?" While fried treats from other lands can be found in the United States, our own indigenous "American donuts" date back to Dutch settlers' *olieboellen* or *olykoeks* (the spelling varies), which were rounded balls of dense dough, sometimes studded with fruit or nuts.

UNCOMMONLY KNOWN ...

American Apple Pie The first record of American apple pie consumption in the 13 Colonies dates back to 1697, a popular dish both because apples were plentiful in the New World and because pies were sturdy fare for pioneer consumption. The verbal identification didn't come about until the 1960s advertising boom made slogans as popular as ... well, apple pie.

The Dutch "cakes" were usually fried in pork fat, and they had a specific problem: If you drop a ball of dough into boiling oil, its outside will turn golden brown long before the center is close to being cooked. An apocryphal tale about how the American version got its name involves cooks who were attempting to help the cakes cook faster by inserting nuts into their centers. No one can confirm the truth of this story, but some versions of it involve a real-life New England woman in the mid-19th century named Elizabeth Gregory, who was well known for her excellent fried cakes. Her son Captain Hanson Gregory either stuck one onto the ship's wheel during a storm or didn't like the nuts and poked them out. Either way, Gregory's cook began taking the center out of his fried cakes with a small circular cutter.

Doughnuts were so popular and ubiquitous in the United States that grateful French citizens cooked and served American-style doughnuts to World War I "doughboys." Since then, the American Red Cross has always had "donut girls" (now guys, too, of course) on hand to provide a baked symbol of comfort and home for soldiers. The first doughnut machine was invented by Russian expatriate Adolph Levitt in the 1920s; by 1934, he was earning about $25 million per year through sales of his machines.

Fruitcake

"FEED" A FRUITCAKE: SOAK IT IN LIQUOR
THE AVERAGE FRUITCAKE WEIGHS TWO POUNDS
THE FRUIT IN FRUITCAKE IS USUALLY CANDIED OR DRIED

Modern Americans have so many fruitcake jokes that there's even an annual Fruitcake Toss in Manitou Springs,

Figgy Pudding

If you've ever heard the carol "We Wish You a Merry Christmas" and wondered what "figgy pudding" is, know at least that it's not fruitcake. "Figgy" or "Christmas" pudding is a concatenation of very old suet-based "puddings," such as mince pies, that were created to preserve meats, and the medieval grain- and fruit-based "frumenty." Over centuries, fruity and spicy ingredients won out, and by the mid-19th century, sweet Christmas puddings had become staples in homes throughout the United Kingdom. Mixed on "Stir Up Sunday," so called because the collect includes a Scripture verse with those words, the pudding includes and is served with copious amounts of liquor like brandy, rum, and stout.

Colorado, where participants are urged to throw the heavy loaves as far as possible during a tongue-in-cheek ceremony. The gag is supposed to be that everybody hates fruitcake. There are certainly some recipes more palatable than others, but the truth is that the forebears of our fruitcake also played a largely ceremonial role.

We know the Romans made a sort of sweetened cake of pomegranate seeds, pine nuts, and raisins mixed into a mash of barley. This concoction was used as a sort of early energy bar by traveling troops, but when it came to northern Europe, it was made lighter with wheat flour and different with hazelnuts and walnuts. The inclusion of nuts was for ceremony rather than taste. At the end of each year's nut harvest, fruitcakes studded with nutmeats would be baked and put away until the following year and eaten in hopes of ensuring a good harvest.

In England, fruitcakes have continued to be extremely popular since Victorian times, and no British wedding or christening is complete without a rich, dark fruitcake covered in marzipan and then finished in fondant icing. "Black cake," famous in Caribbean countries, is a slightly more modern result of the intersection of the Roman fruit "cake" and the European nut harvest.

No one knows for certain when fruitcake began its holiday appearances, but the English tradition of handing out slices of the robust stuff to the poor after carols may have had something to do with it.

During a time of year when fresh fruits were once hard to come by, fruitcake may have been a welcome treat. Light fruitcakes are made with granulated sugar, light corn syrup, almonds, golden raisins, pineapple and apricots, and dark fruitcakes are made from molasses, brown sugar, raisins, prunes, dates, cherries, pecans, and walnuts.

Chewing Gum

FIRST PRODUCED COMMERCIALLY BY: JOHN B. CURTIS
1848 | STATE OF MAINE PURE SPRUCE GUM
WAS THE FIRST GUM MADE IN THE U.S.

The ancient Greeks chewed the resin of the mastic tree; the Maya chewed chicle from the sapodilla, and North American Indians chewed spruce sap (mixed with beeswax, this would become the settlers' first chewing gum). Chewing gum has a long history in the world, and a long history in the United States, too. The first gum produced for commercial sale was State of Maine Pure Spruce Gum, made by John B. Curtis in 1848.

If a Mexican general named Antonio López de Santa Anna, in exile on Staten Island, had not introduced a fellow boarder named Thomas Adams to the Central American chicle, Americans might still be chomping sticky spruce gum. Adams, a photographer, first tried to market the substance for tires, but soon realized it could be flavored to create a longer-lasting chewing gum. Adams New York Chewing Gum went on sale in January 1871, for a penny per stick. Adams's company would eventually merge with six others to become a great conglomerate, and is responsible for the aptly named Chiclets.

Utensils & Containers

I n some parts of this chapter, items listed could conceivably come from many different times simultaneously. But not here; when it comes to how we eat, cook, and store food, technology has changed things consistently from century to century. For hundreds of years, people ate with their hands or with pieces of some kind of bread, then suddenly: knife, spoon, fork (and we didn't miss chopsticks, either). Similarly, long-standing storage methods like casks and jars met their match with the thermos, aluminum foils, and plastic storage containers.

Spoon

FROM OLD ENGLISH "SPON" (CHIP OF WOOD)
SOME TYPES: TEASPOON, TABLESPOON, SOUP SPOON
"BORN WITH SILVER SPOON IN MOUTH" (PRIVILEGED)

S poons are so widely used in our culture that the idiom "born with a silver spoon in his mouth" is a common reference for material advantage. Spoons started out quite humbly, however; the Anglo-Saxon word *spon* referred to a chip of wood that could be used to convey food to the mouth.

The earliest spoons, however, were probably shells, with their curved shape suited to scooping up loose foods like rice, porridge, and stew. Ancient Indians, Egyptians, and Greeks were all known to use spoons of different materials, and many of those had some kind of handle attached, which would have made it easier to take food from a communal vessel. By the Middle Ages in Europe, spoons had become regular household items and were important for cooking as well as for eating.

Around this time, as guilds grew stronger, craftsmen began manufacturing spoons in bronze, pewter, and, yes, silver. Over the centuries, differently shaped spoons were created for different uses, a practice that reached its zenith in Victorian England and the United States. There were soup spoons and spoons for eating ices; berry spoons and sugar spoons; grapefruit, egg, and olive spoons; even spoons for Stilton cheese, beef marrow, and serving absinthe. Nearly all of these were made of sterling silver or silverplate, although a few, like egg and caviar spoons, were made from horn, which would not interfere with the taste of the food.

In many European countries, wooden spoons were commonly used for everything from measuring to meal preparation to eating, and so carving them was done frequently. Wooden spoons might be completely plain, or beautifully carved and polished, and sometimes even quite elaborately chased and decorated. The strongest example is the Welsh "love spoon," today a popular keepsake but once a sign of real romantic devotion.

The most modern form of the spoon, which Americans favor in a large size as a soup spoon or tablespoon and a smaller size as a teaspoon (used for everything from breakfast cereal to ice cream), developed in the latter half of the 18th century. This spoon has a narrower tip and a handle that can be straight or curved at the end.

Fork

FROM THE LATIN "FURCA" (PITCHFORK)
EARLIEST KNOWN: CONSTANTINOPLE, 400 B.C.
SOME TYPES: SALAD FORK, DINNER FORK, DESSERT FORK

The word *fork* comes from the Latin *furca*, or "pitchfork," and it is mentioned in the Hebrew Bible. While forks were made and used in some ancient Egyptian ceremonies, the earliest dinner fork discovered is from Constantinople and dates to about A.D. 400. These early two-tined forks were introduced to Europe in 1005 by Byzantine princess Maria Agyropoulina on her marriage to the future Doge of Venice, Domenico Selvo; she was known to cut her food and then spear it upon "golden forks." However, while people already knew the word for forks, they didn't approve of them. The Roman Catholic Church denounced their use, saying "God in his wisdom has provided man with natural forks—his fingers. Therefore it is an insult to Him to substitute artificial metallic forks for them when eating."

Both because of this religious censure and because their use was seen as somewhat fussy, the fork did not gain favor until several hundred years later (ironically enough, in Italy, the seat of the Catholic faith). Nobles and upper-class people carried their own sets of flatware, a knife and a fork, to dinner parties in a box known as a *cadena*. When Catherine de' Medici married into the French monarchy, forks became common there, and finally, in the 17th century, they became commonplace in England, too. Until that time, the only forks in use were "sucket forks," which enabled the user to spear sticky preserves and fruits and scoop up their sugary syrup with the spoon on the other end.

An Englishman named Thomas Coryate who had traveled in Italy, was one of the first in his country to use the new implement. Italians, adopting the fork to their uses, were the first to add a fourth tine, and the Germans were the first to round the tines slightly, which made it less necessary to switch between fork and spoon.

When metal flatware became easier to manufacture, forks (like spoons) were created for myriad uses: pickle forks, salad forks, cold meat forks, pastry forks. It might have taken a while for the fork to catch on with Europeans, but once they adapted to it, they adapted the utensil itself, as well.

Knife

FROM OLD NORSE "KNIFR" (KNIFE)
INVENTED AT LEAST 2.5 MILLION YEARS AGO
SOME TYPES: BREAD KNIFE, STEAK KNIFE, BUTTER KNIFE

Humans have been making knives for at least two and a half million years, from what we know of Paleolithic tools found in Tanzania. The first knives were probably used for hunting; knives have been made and used as weapons, tools, ceremonial items, and also as eating utensils for longer than any other type of implement.

For thousands of years, people carried their own knives everywhere, including to the table. Knives were used to cut food into individual portions, as well as to spear food from communal pots and trenchers. Of course, since each person had a knife, each person in a dining hall also had a weapon, which often led to violence. In 1669, King Louis XIV of France banned pointed knives on the street and at table, and insisted the cutlers (knife merchants; from the French *coutelier, coutel* meaning "knife") make the ends of knives blunt.

Blunt-tipped knives actually affected American table manners permanently. In the early days of the 13 Colonies, few forks but plenty of knives were imported. These knives, with blunter tips, could not be used to steady food as it was sliced, and the colonists used their spoon to hold food while they cut it, switching the spoon to their right hand when it came time to eat. Even today many Americans put their knife down and switch their fork to their right hand while dining, unlike Europeans, who keep the fork in their left hand throughout a meal.

Table knives are distinct from butter knives, which still have blunt tips but are smaller, used to take a single serving of butter from a master server. Although table knives have blunt ends, their edges are traditionally sharpened and/or serrated for cutting, which is why airports and airlines banned knives completely from food service after the September 11, 2001, attacks.

Chopsticks

TERM DATES TO 1699 (CHINESE PIDGIN ENGLISH)
USED INSTEAD OF A FORK IN MANY ASIAN COUNTRIES
USUALLY MADE OF WOOD OR LACQUERED WOOD

In early Asian society, cooking fuel was sometimes scarce. People discovered that foods cooked more quickly when they were cut into small pieces, and that those pieces were easily speared for eating with one or more of

---

PARALLEL HISTORY

Spork

Getting a straight answer about the origins of the spork is harder than trying to spear a pea on one of its tines. "Spork" is a portmanteau word, combining "spoon" and "fork" just as the spork combines their functions, with its spoonlike bowl extending to three to four tines. Often one tine or side of the bowl includes knifelike serrations. Sporks have been manufactured at least since the 1800s, but the word was not coined until the mid-20th century. Some people believe that the forerunner of "spork" is "runcible spoon," used by Edward Lear in his famous poem "The Owl and the Pussycat." However, "runcible" is a nonsense word.

---

the thin twigs and branches used for the cookfire. That's one possible explanation about how the eating implements known as "chopsticks" evolved in China more than 5,000 years ago.

Another one, with more historical documentation, revolves around the Chinese philosopher Confucius (551-479 B.C.). A dedicated vegetarian who believed that knives were a reminder of killing, he encouraged food preparation, cooking, and serving that did not require knife use at the table. He said, "The honorable and upright man keeps well away from both the slaughterhouse and the kitchen. And he allows no knives on his table."

The slim, usually tapered sticks quickly became the utensils of choice in the "rice bowl" areas of Asia: China, Korea, Japan, Vietnam, and Thailand. They weren't originally called "chopsticks," however; in Chinese Pidgin English, *chop chop* means "quickly." The original word in Mandarin Chinese for the sticks, *zhu,* means "to stop," and after this was found dangerous aboard ships, the word was changed to *kuai,* which means "quick." Today, the ideogram for "chopsticks" in Chinese combines the character for "quick" with the one for "bamboo"— the fast-growing plant that supplies many pairs of chopsticks to the large Chinese population.

Different styles of chopsticks have developed. Chinese chopsticks are the longest and bluntest, and often made of porcelain. Japanese chopsticks, often of lacquered wood, are shorter, and usually have pointed tips to aid in picking apart the bony fish that are a staple of that country's diet.

Korean chopsticks are flatter and tapered and come in stainless steel; Koreans generally use a flat-bottomed spoon for rice and noodle soups, so their chopsticks do not need to be rounded.

Lunch Box

ALSO CALLED: LUNCH PAIL, LUNCH KIT
TIFFIN (INDIA), BENTO (JAPAN)
120 MILLION SOLD BETWEEN 1950 AND 1970

Home-cooked and packed lunches have a long history around the world. Japanese bento boxes have been prepared for nearly 900 years, while India's tiffin-wallahs can still be seen carrying layered tin contraptions holding breads, curry, and salad. In the U.S., metal lunch boxes were the containers of choice for anyone who either could not conveniently return home for a hot midday meal or didn't have someone there preparing one.

In the late 19th century, metal tobacco tins were often frugally recycled as lunch boxes. With their whimsical designs and illustrations, these tins were attractive to youngsters heading off to schoolhouses. Even for children who returned home at noon, a "lunch box" might hold a small snack or bottle of water for the long walk to and from school. This is also when some people began reusing paper sacks from grocery store purchases, which eventually led to companies selling packs of brown paper lunch bags.

Things didn't change much until the advent of television in the late 1940s. Savvy Aladdin Industries produced the first metal lunch box aimed at children, decorated with a decal of Hopalong Cassidy, the lasso-waving star of a new show. Aladdin sold 600,000 of those boxes alone, and soon several other companies had jumped in, and metal lunch boxes were painted with lithographs of cartoon characters, TV stars, and pop idols.

The metal box, combined with a matching thermos bottle, made up the "lunch kit" that millions of American students toted. But the lunch kit changed in 1972, when a group of Florida parents concerned about safety brought about legislation to restrict use of the boxes. While metal lunch boxes were produced until 1987, their sales were affected by the new, pro-safety plastic lunch kits.

Thermos

INVENTOR: SIR JAMES DEWAR
1892 | UNITED STATES
GENERIC NAME: VACUUM FLASK

Before electricity, keeping liquids hot required a flame—something that wasn't always conveniently at hand. However, when Oxford University scientist Sir James Dewar invented a vacuum flask in 1892, we can

---

UNCOMMONLY KNOWN ...

Brown Bags In the early 20th century, when people realized that kraft paper shopping bags were handy totes for midday meals, manufacturers realized that making lunch-size bags might be profitable. The iconic brown paper bag, produced since 1852 by Pennsylvanian Francis Wolle, is still used by countless students and workers today.

be relatively sure that it was heated liquids that concerned people, since the winner of a 1904 contest to name the new flask and its German company submitted "Thermos," after the Greek *therme,* or "hot."

It's not the contents of a Thermos flask that are under a vacuum but the air between the inner glass walls and the outer metal or plastic walls. The insulation is remarkably effective, which is why vacuum-flask design hasn't changed substantially since its 19th-century debut. The rights to the Thermos were sold to three independent companies in 1901, including the Brooklyn-based American Thermos Bottle Company. The flasks were used for expeditions such as British explorer Ernest Shackleton's quest for the South Pole. Improvements in manufacturing and materials—including heat-proof Pyrex glass in 1923—meant vacuum flasks could be used for more than liquids; by the 1950s, they were being used to transport everything from blood plasma to rare tropical fish.

With the 1960s introduction of stainless-steel inner flasks, Thermos bottles became ubiquitous in lunch boxes, picnic coolers, and kitchens (where "coffee butler" thermal carafes were welcomed by caffeine-starved commuters). They became more ubiquitous because stainless steel is relatively cheap and very durable. Although the Western market has embraced vacuum flasks primarily because of their temperature-stabilizing properties, in Asia vacuum-flask cooking has gained popularity: Food heated to cooking temperature is taken off the

---

PARALLEL HISTORY

Freeze-drying

Like using a vacuum flask, freeze-drying is a method of preserving a specific attribute of food under certain conditions. Freeze-drying removes the liquid from food, making it lighter and keeping it edible for longer than would otherwise be possible. Freeze-dried ice cream was developed by NASA on request from astronauts, but the original Neapolitan brick (striped vanilla, chocolate, and strawberry) in its airtight package never took off with the spacebound. It was a huge hit, however, with pint-size would-be astronauts; the crunchy packaged treat is a consistent top seller in the National Air and Space Museum and Kennedy Space Center gift shops.

---

heat and placed in a vacuum flask to finish cooking through. This requires care, as the food must be heated to a temperature that will prevent bacteria from growing, but when done correctly, this method can save a lot of energy, as well as time.

Aluminum Foil

FROM THE LATIN "FOLIUM" (LEAF)
USED TO BE MADE FROM TIN ("TINFOIL")
CONTAINS 92 TO 99 PERCENT ALUMINUM

Aluminum foil, that kitchen ombudsman, is the result of two scientific discoveries. The first one was Charles Martin Hall's method for extracting aluminum from aluminum oxide, developed in 1889, just a few years after he graduated from Ohio's Oberlin College. A Frenchman named Paul-Louis-Toussaint Heroult was developing the same process independently, which is why it is now known as the "Hall-Heroult method," but in the United States we remember Hall particularly because he and financier Alfred E. Hunt founded the Pittsburgh Reduction Company, which became the Aluminum Company of America, or Alcoa—one of the giants of 20th-century industry.

However, extracting aluminum was just the first step. Turning that metal into thin, flexible, impermeable sheets was the next. Enter the firm of J. G. Neher & Sons, which used the Rhine Falls in Schaffhausen, Switzerland, to power an "endless rolling" process. Once consumers had seen how easy and convenient aluminum foil was, they were hooked. We still are. Despite plastic wrap, sandwich bags, reusable plastic containers, and other food storage methods, almost every

American kitchen still contains a reliable roll of aluminum foil.

There's a good reason for that. Aluminum foil blocks light, water, and bacteria, which means it also blocks bad tastes and odors. It can be crumpled and folded to fit almost any container, then uncrumpled and unfolded and washed to be used again. The same malleability that makes aluminum foil so long-lasting also makes it easy to recycle. Aluminum foil is made from an alloy that contains between 92 and 99 percent aluminum. Usually between 0.00017 and 0.0059 inch thick, this foil is produced in many widths and strengths, and has hundreds of applications, including electrical coils, insulation, and transformers.

Before aluminum foil was possible, sheets of tinfoil served some of the same purposes; even today, there are people who call aluminum foil "tinfoil." Even though there are options for storing food, aluminum foil is used in many other food-service applications now, including Tetra Paks for beverages.

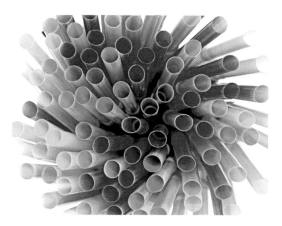

Plasticware

MOST POPULAR HISTORIC BRAND: TUPPERWARE
TUPPERWARE INVENTOR: EARL TUPPER
TUPPERWARE HOME PARTY INVENTOR: BROWNIE WISE

Today there are many different kinds of plastic containers available for food storage, but all of them owe their sales to a man named Earl Tupper, whose idea for molded polyethylene cups and bowls in 1942 launched

---

> **UNCOMMONLY KNOWN . . .**
> **Plastic Wrap** Saran Wrap was discovered when a scientist tried to develop a hard plastic car cover. The resulting pliable film was particularly helpful for covering foods, since it didn't change taste or smell. Saran was based on PVdC, which has a slight toxicity. Newer wraps like Cling and Glad are made from LDPE.

a home-based merchandising empire that still exists. Earl Tupper's formula for his plastics was unusually thick, flexible, and pleasing to the touch. Two things brought his products to the forefront of a postwar society ready for kitchen organization and personal transformation. For the first, Tupper contributed his 1949-patented "burp" seal that allowed users to know that they'd removed all of the spoilage-causing air from their containers.

The second thing, at least equally and possibly more important, was Brownie Wise. Wise was a divorced, single mother who needed a mission. She'd been selling Tupperware as part of her Stanley Home Products parties, and when Tupper looked to her and other Stanley hosts for some new marketing ideas, Wise came up with a home-party plan that has changed little over the past 50-odd years. Although Wise was fired in 1958, her plan launched an empire that provided many a mid-century housewife with extra income—and many even with new careers, especially as the company grew.

Although in recent years Tupperware has reduced its dependence on home parties and increased its direct sales outlets (including a partnership with Target stores), the Tupperware brand remains strong, and many people won't use anything else in their kitchens. Tupperware innovations included modular, stacking containers; expandable bowls; and containers with different kinds of lids, including pour spouts, for different kinds of dry goods and foods.

There are many other types of plastic storage containers now available, but each of them owes something in its design to Earl Tupper's original range. Innovations have been made: Containers are now more resistant to stains, usually odor free, and can be placed in the dishwasher. However, many new plastic containers are also meant to be disposable, which is unfortunate for the environment.

If all the year were playing holidays,
To sport would be as tedious as to work.
—WILLIAM SHAKESPEARE (1564-1616)

Seasons & Holidays

ince the beginning of recorded history, and undoubtedly long before, people have marked Earth's journey around the sun with seasonal festivals and holidays, none more poignant than the ancient winter solstice celebrations, which embraced the return of light to a cold and dark world. Held on the shortest day of the year, these celebrations were offerings to the gods, who had always returned the Earth to light. And so the celebrants were hopeful that the miracle would happen once again, that the days would gradually begin to lengthen and that crops would grow. Of the thousands of holidays celebrated worldwide, we have chosen a couple dozen of those most familiar to readers in the Western world. Divided into the four seasons, these holidays honor saints, parents, war dead, days of independence, and events in religious history. Each one gives us something to celebrate, even the lowly Groundhog Day, with its promise of spring. The original meaning of *holiday*, a word coined sometime before the 12th century, was "holy day," from the Old English *haligdaeg*. These commemorative days were almost all days of religious observance, some involving feasts and festivals. But, interestingly, many early religious holidays were actually transformations of even older pagan holidays. So winter solstice celebrations were accommodated by the Christian and Jewish religions and melded into Christmas and Hanukkah. Likewise, the Roman fertility festival Lupercalia was too much fun to completely disappear, so Christianity named it for a saint and turned it into Saint Valentine's Day. In teasing out the often convoluted history of these holidays, you will also discover a number of entertaining facts and stories—the date of the first Times Square ball drop and the birthplace of St. Patrick (not Ireland), to name but two.

Spring

Spring is a time of liveliness and renewal, evident in the revelry of Mardi Gras, the hope of Easter, and the silliness of April Fools' Day. However, it is also a time when the promise of new life reminds us of lives lost and when we honor the departed during holidays like Passover and through observances like Memorial Day. There's even time for national pride in the form of joyous celebrations like Cinco de Mayo and St. Patrick's Day. Regardless of which holidays they choose to celebrate, all Americans are subject to "springing ahead" during daylight saving time.

"St. Patrick's Day in the Morning."

Saint Patrick's Day

OBSERVED ON: MARCH 17
"ERIN GO BRAGH": IRISH FOR "IRELAND FOREVER"
CELEBRATORY FOODS: CORNED BEEF, CABBAGE, BEER

The traditional death day of Patrick (circa 389-461), the patron saint of Ireland, March 17 is known for spirited parades, beer drinking, and the wearing of anything green. St. Patrick's Day is a religious holiday in Ireland, while in the United States it's an occasion for parties and celebrations of Irish heritage.

Although many legends concerning St. Patrick have proliferated since his death, he was a real person who in about 450 left a credible account of his life called *Confessio*. Born into a wealthy family in Britain, he was kidnapped by pirates at age 16 and sold into slavery in Ireland. After six years, he escaped back to Britain, and then to France after Britain. Eventually, he dreamed he received a letter, "The Voice of the Irish," imploring him to come back to Ireland as a missionary. After a period of study to make up for his lack of education, he followed his dream and began preaching all over Ireland, bringing Christianity to the island nation. He remained there for the duration of his life, baptizing many thousands of people and consecrating some 350 priests.

Patrick's rustic, affable manner and boundless energy won over many an audience. Local Druid priests arrested him numerous times, but he never gave up. Before the fifth century was out, March 17 became an annual day of commemoration. One legend concerning Patrick has him driving all the snakes of Ireland into the sea (to this day there are no snakes in Ireland). In another bit of lore, he explained the trinity of Father, Son, and Holy Ghost by holding up a shamrock, a three-leaf clover. The Irish today often put a shamrock in their lapels on March 17.

UNCOMMONLY KNOWN...
St. Patrick's Day Parade The first St. Patrick's Day celebration in the U.S. occurred in Boston in 1737. Now more than 100 cities hold parades, the largest of which runs up Fifth Avenue in New York. The first such parade took place in 1762, when Irish soldiers marched to show pride in their roots.

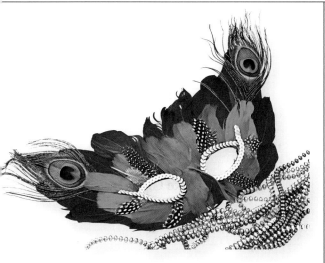

Mardi Gras

OBSERVED ON: TUESDAY BEFORE ASH WEDNESDAY
COLORS: PURPLE, GREEN, AND GOLD
ALSO KNOWN AS SHROVE TUESDAY

Though not technically in spring, Mardi Gras is inextricably linked to Lent. Mardi Gras is French for "Fat Tuesday," and specifically the day before Ash Wednesday, when the Christian season of Lent begins. In European Roman Catholic countries, this Tuesday was the time to use up all cooking fats before the fasting of the 40 Lenten weekdays leading up to Easter.

While Mardi Gras most recently came to the United States from France, its origins go back thousands of years to Roman festivals, which gave the practice its other name, Carnival. The Latin *carne levare* means "farewell to flesh," and these early spring rites usually honored Bacchus, the god of wine and debauchery. When the Roman Catholic Church began modifying various native celebrations to coincide with holy days on the church calendar, Bacchanalia was a natural fit for the weeks preceding Easter.

While "farewell to flesh" might have meant something different to Bacchanalia celebrants (these festivals were probably fertility rites), the church chose to distinguish its ritual by making fasting and abstinence from meat-eating mandatory. This

may have been inspired by Christ's 40 days in the wilderness before his baptism.

For many years, Venice held the most famous Carnevale, but in modern times four celebrations are best known: those in Rio de Janeiro, Brazil; Nice, France; Cologne, Germany; and New Orleans, Louisiana. Mardi Gras came to the U.S. early in the nation's history. In 1699, French explorer d'Iberville explored the Mississippi River from the Gulf of Mexico. He and his crew set up camp on the river's west bank about 60 miles south of present-day New Orleans. Since it was March 3 and a major holiday back home, they christened the site Point du Mardi Gras. While not the only Mardi Gras celebration in the U.S. (others once equally famous include those in Mobile, Alabama, and Biloxi, Mississippi), in the past 50 years New Orleans has become strongly associated with the festival.

Daylight Saving Time

FIRST OBSERVED IN EUROPE ON APRIL 30, 1916
ORGINALLY A WARTIME ENERGY-SAVING MEASURE
OBSERVED BY NEARLY 70 COUNTRIES

Springing forward and falling back have become American rituals—we set our clocks forward one hour in the spring to add a glorious hour of light to our afternoons. Then in fall we get an extra hour of sleep when we set the clock back. Forgetting means arriving late (in spring) or early (in fall) to Sunday-morning appointments.

The idea is credited to Benjamin Franklin, who didn't actually propose setting clocks forward. His plan, laid out in a witty letter to the *Journal de Paris* in 1784, was to make people get up earlier. In what must be one of the earliest investigations of fuel economy, Franklin described the oil a lantern used, saying it was not the same as the light it gave off. His letter turns to the related subject of candle usage, and he concludes that rising a few hours earlier could save Parisians more than 64 million pounds of candles a year. Ever in love of economizing, he suggests putting a tax on every shuttered window that kept out sunlight (and prevented people from rising), and ringing every church bell at sunrise. "And if that is not enough, have cannon fired in every street to awaken the sluggards effectually and make them open their eyes to see their true interests."

In 1907 an Englishman named William Willett proposed setting the clocks forward 80 minutes in spring and summer, but Parliament rejected the idea. Germany and Austria became the first to observe a time change as a wartime energy-saving measure on April 30, 1916. British summer time and a number of other European time-change legislations quickly followed. The United States adopted daylight saving for less than a year in 1918 and 1919, then resurrected it for four years during World War II. In 1967 Congress passed the Uniform Time Act, bringing back daylight saving time. Since then various adjustments have been made to its dates.

UNCOMMONLY KNOWN...

Spring Break Spring used to be the longest break in the school year for children living on farms. Summer vacation is a relatively recent tradition. Before the mid-19th century, children went to school during less busy times on the farm—typically December to March and mid-May to August. In contrast, in urban areas, an 11-month school year was popular among immigrant parents who worked in mills, factories, and shops.

April Fools' Day

ALSO KNOWN AS: SIZDAH BEDAR (IRAN), POISSONS D'AVRIL (FRANCE), HILARIA (ANCIENT ROME), TAILY DAY (SCOTLAND), HULI FESTIVAL (INDIA)

Why do we feel the need to play practical jokes on our friends and family on the first day of April? Or, looked at another way, why on this one day do we excuse people who have a laugh at our expense?

Theories on the origin of April Fools' Day abound, but the most likely takes it back to 16th-century France. The French accepted the reformed Gregorian calendar in the late 1500s, setting their New Year's Day back from March 25 to January 1. The old anniversary continued to be celebrated with a week of festivities, topped off by a final day of merriment on April 1. Pranks were played on those who had a hard time remembering that the date for New Year's had shifted. The gullible were sent on fool's errands, invited to nonexistent parties, and given ridiculous presents. Such people were called *poissons d'Avril* (April fish), because like the newly hatched fish, they were easily caught. The custom did not jump the English Channel until the 18th century; it was known in England as All Fools' Day ("all" perhaps a corruption of *auld*, or old).

Other theories push April fooling back much earlier. Noah reputedly sent a dove out after the great flood, but it was a fool's errand—the bird could find no land. A Roman spring festival honored the goddess of agriculture, Ceres, whose daughter was abducted by Pluto, god of the underworld. Ceres went to rescue her—another fool's errand. Attempts to relate the day to Christian tradition make mention of the mock trial of Jesus; pranks were a reminder of the ridicule Christ suffered at the same time of year. Whatever the origin, April Fools' Day remains a rite of spring, a day for humbling and being humbled.

Passover

ONE OF THE MOST SIGNIFICANT JEWISH HOLIDAYS
THE SEDER FOOD INCLUDES: VEGETABLES, MATZO,
BITTER HERBS, FRUIT/NUT PASTE, AND BOILED EGGS

If you've ever heard someone ask, "Why is this night not like all other nights," you've learned something about Passover. The first night of Passover, when the traditional seder meal is held, is considered holy by Jews around the world. Just as Easter is the most significant holiday in the Christian liturgical year, Passover is one of the most significant holidays in the Jewish liturgical year.

Passover, or Pesach, celebrates the flight of the Hebrews from Egypt, told in the second book of the Old Testament, Exodus. However, that's a huge simplification. The complete Passover story encompasses the long history of the Hebrew settlement in Egypt's Land of Goshen (the eastern part of the Nile Delta), their enslavement by a cruel pharaoh, the birth and coming to power of Moses, and the "exodus" (flight) of the Jews from Egypt with Moses as their leader.

In the days before Passover, Jewish homes are traditionally cleared of any trace of *chametz* (leavening), in remembrance of the hard, unleavened bread that their ancestors had as their only food during the long exodus. Matzo is a crackerlike unleavened bread served in place of bread during Passover (although many people, both Jews and non-Jews, now eat it at other times of the year because they enjoy it).

In remembrance of the hardships their ancestors faced in slavery, on the first and second nights of Passover, the Jewish people hold a seder, which means "order" and signifies the order of the events in the Passover story. There are foods for each stage: sweet *charoset*, a compote of apples, honey, and nuts, to recall the early days in Egypt; bitter

PARALLEL HISTORY

Yad Vashem

The holy feast of Passover commemorates Jewish survival thousands of years ago. The Israeli memorial of Yad Vashem honors those who experienced the horrors of the Holocaust just decades ago. The 45-acre complex on the Mount of Remembrance in Jerusalem was established by the Knesset in 1953 and encompasses memorials, museum halls, an International School for Holocaust Studies, and a Central Database of Victims' Names. One of the important tasks of Yad Vashem is to honor the "Righteous Among Nations," non-Jews who risked their "lives, liberty, or positions" to save Jews during the Holocaust.

The Hall of Names in Jerusalem's Yad Vashem features 600 images of victims in a 30-foot cone.

herbs, symbolizing the years of enslavement; and so on. The ritual is described in a book called the Haggadah that is often among a family's most prized possessions.

As the Exodus of the Jews from Egypt took place in the spring, Passover is always celebrated in the spring. It is celebrated for eight days (seven for Reform Jews), and always begins on the 15th day of the Hebrew month of Nisan.

Easter

TRADITIONS: EGG DECORATING, EGG HUNTS, EASTER BUNNY, EASTER BASKETS, BONNETS
FOODS: HARD-BOILED EGGS, HAM, CANDY

E aster is the most significant Christian holy day, celebrating the resurrection of Christ on the third day following his Crucifixion. But although Easter is one of the oldest Christian observances, it is actually a fascinating combination of ideas from three different spiritual traditions: pagan, Hebrew, and Christian.

According to St. Bede, the name "Easter" comes from Eostre, the Anglo-Saxon goddess of spring and fertility, to whom the month of April was dedicated. Eostre's festival was celebrated at the vernal equinox, the 24-hour period when day and night

---

UNCOMMONLY KNOWN . . .

Easter Bunny Supposedly Eostre, the Teutonic goddess, saved a bird whose wings had frozen by turning it into a rabbit; the rabbit could still lay eggs, and thus the Easter Bunny was born. That may or may not be true, but rabbits are universal symbols of fertility, and in the 19th century, German immigrants brought their tales of "Osterhas," or the Easter Bunny, and his nests of eggs to the United States.

---

are equal. When the early English church looked for a way to incorporate native traditions into its new calendar, it chose "Easter" as the name for this holiday. This word origin is also reflected in the German *Oster.*

However, the other Christian countries have names for the holiday that relate back to its Hebraic roots. The French *Paques,* the Italian *Pasqua,* and the Spanish *Pascua* all relate to *pascha,* or the Hebrew celebration of Passover. Passover commemorates Israel's deliverance from 300 years of bondage in Egypt, and the meal known as the Last Supper that Christ shares with his apostles was more than likely a Passover meal.

By A.D. 100, Easter was an established feast, although not yet movable. The Western and Eastern churches could not agree on when it should be celebrated, with the Eastern churches arguing in favor of a weekday (based on Passover observance), and Western churches taking the position that such a major holy day should always fall on a Sunday.

The problem could not be solved, so Emperor Constantine put it to the Council of Nicaea in 325. While the Council did handle other concerns as well, it ruled that Easter should fall on a Sunday. Not just any Sunday, but specifically the one that follows the post-vernal-equinox full moon. Today, Easter is a "movable feast" that is held on the first day of the full moon after March 21; this means that it can occur on any Sunday between March 22 and April 25.

Over the years, Easter has regained some of its pre-religious symbolism and paraphernalia. Eggs, chicks, rabbits, ducks, and candy all contribute to a sweet celebration of spring's promise.

Cinco de Mayo

POPULAR CELEBRATION IN BOTH
U.S. AND MEXICO
BUT NATIONAL HOLIDAY IN NEITHER

Mexicans and Mexican Americans celebrate the fifth of May with parades, speeches, and fiestas. Contrary to popular opinion, Cinco de Mayo is not Mexican Independence Day. That honor belongs to September 15, when in 1810 Mexico declared independence from Spain. Actual independence was achieved when the final Spanish soldiers left Mexican soil 11 years later. Even more anticlimactically, Mexican independence is now observed on September 16.

Cinco de Mayo harks back to a heroic battle against the French in 1862. Early that year, French troops sent by Emperor Napoleon III landed in the Mexican port of Veracruz. Napoleon wanted to conquer the country and set up Maximilian, Archduke of Austria, as its ruler. A French army of more than 6,500 well-equipped soldiers set out from Veracruz for Mexico City. In the town of Puebla, a ragtag Mexican contingent made up of 4,500 men met them on May 5. The two cavalries clashed first; the French underestimated the ability of the Mexican horsemen and were slaughtered and chased for miles. Meanwhile, the infantries fought in a muddy field, the French confused by herds of stampeding cattle let loose by machete-wielding Indians. French casualties were high, and the day belonged to Mexico.

The battle of May 5 slowed but could not stop the French invasion. With help from Mexican collaborators, the French seized control of the country and by 1864 had established Maximilian as emperor. By 1867 the United States, just recovering from a civil war, pressured France to withdraw from Mexico; Napoleon gave way and called his troops home. (Maximilian stubbornly refused to give up his throne; that year he was assassinated.)

Cinco de Mayo continues as a spirited celebration not only of Mexican heritage but of Mexican-American cooperation.

Mother's Day

SECOND SUNDAY IN MAY
PRES. WOODROW WILSON SIGNED INTO LAW 1914
CELEBRATED IN MORE THAN 100 COUNTRIES

Though the British had long honored mothers during Lent on what they called Mothering Sunday, the idea of setting aside a day in recognition of motherhood did not catch on anywhere else until the 20th century. Reformer Julia Ward Howe first broached the idea in 1870. For the next few decades others tried to stir up interest in regular Mother's Day observances. But credit for making the day stick as a national celebration belongs to a West Virginia schoolteacher named Anna Jarvis.

Born in Grafton, West Virginia, in 1864, Jarvis had a close, loving relationship with her mother. Despite her filial affections and attentions, Jarvis felt guilty she had not done more for her. She set to work campaigning for a national Mother's Day. To push for legislation she sent out letters to congressmen, governors, mayors, newspaper editors, and business leaders across the land. Her hometown church in Grafton celebrated Mother's Day on May 10, 1908, the anniversary of Jarvis's mother's death. Jarvis handed out carnations—her mother's favorite. Finally, Congress approved the proposed bill, and in 1914 President Wilson proclaimed the second Sunday in May to be Mother's Day.

In a sad footnote, Jarvis died childless and impoverished in 1948 in a sanatorium. But the tradition started by a woman who devoted her life to her mother and her mother's memory has spread to many countries. The U.S. leads the way in Mother's Day spending—on cards, flowers, and dinners out.

Today more than 100 countries celebrate versions of Mother's Day. In India, Japan, Finland, Pakistan, and many more, mothers are honored, usually with a special cake, a big meal, and flowers.

Memorial Day

ORIGINALLY CALLED: DECORATION DAY
TRADITIONS: PARADES, BARBECUES, PLACING FLAGS ON THE GRAVES OF VETERANS

Since 1971, Memorial Day has been a federal holiday, observed on the last Monday in May. Parades, speeches, ceremonies and prayers honor those who have died serving the United States in a war. The observance began, though, as a tribute specifically to the fallen of the Civil War (1861-65). Some 25 towns, many in the South where the majority of Civil War soldiers

Ritual Body Markings

Humans are social beings, and social beings in community like to look similar. Long before we could use designer handbags and logo shirts to identify each other, we used the human body as a canvas for painting, piercing, stretching, and etching. Body markings can signify religious affiliation (circumcision) or marital status (bindi), class consciousness (bound feet) or wealth (ear and neck stretching). While some types of body markings draw groups together (ritual scarification) and provide communal identity, other types (modern extreme piercing) are deliberate challenges to received cultural ideals of beauty and normalcy. Some types of markings unify members of one tribe or group against those of another (war paint, gang and organized-crime tattoos). Even the most innocuous body markings are sometimes difficult for outsiders to understand and can thus be frightening or off-putting. Although many modern, Westernized people no longer practice certain body rites, they've replaced them with others: Makeup and piercings are nothing if not the descendants of face painting and neck stretching.

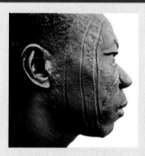

1400 B.C.
Ritual scarification
Scarification or cicatrization alters skin texture through cuts and controlled healing, leaving visible raised keloids that indicate a permanent change in a person's status, e.g., adulthood, nobility, or professional class.

2600 B.C.
Ear stretching
Stretching earlobes, lips, necks, and other body parts signified wealth and status in some cultures. While it looks strange, it's actually a forerunner of today's obsession with plastic surgery.

died, have claimed title to the first Memorial Day celebration—among them Richmond, Virginia; Macon and Columbus, Mississippi; Boalsburg, Pennsylvania; and Carbondale, Illinois.

In 1868 Illinois-born U.S. congressman Maj. Gen. John A. Logan declared May 30 a day for "decorating the graves of comrades who died in defense of their country during the late rebellion . . . and whose bodies now lie in almost every city, village and hamlet churchyard in the land." Most likely he chose the day because flowers would be in bloom. His proclamation was for that year only, but communities around the country continued to hold Memorial Day ceremonies on May 30. Logan, whose congressional career included serving in the House of Representatives as well as two terms in the Senate, was interested only in recognizing the Union dead. Yet within a few years, animosity had waned and flowers bedecked those from both sides of the Mason-Dixon Line.

Not until after World War I was the day's purpose broadened to include the dead of all American wars. In 1966, President Lyndon Johnson declared Waterloo, New York, as the birthplace of Memorial Day. Waterloo's May 5, 1866, ceremony may not have been the first, but it was a formal, community-wide event with businesses closing and flags flying at half-mast, and it was not a one-time celebration.

Today Memorial Day is celebrated at Arlington National Cemetery, as it was in 1868, with about 5,000 people attending. Small American flags are placed on each of the 290,000 graves.

Informally, Memorial Day kick-starts summer for many Americans, who plan outdoor activities around the three-day weekend. However, the festivities usually also include parades and ceremonies of remembrance.

UNCOMMONLY KNOWN . . .

Father's Day Perhaps as it should, Father's Day takes second place. Fewer greeting cards are sent, and the day came on the coattails of Mother's Day. During a Mother's Day sermon in 1909, Sonora Dodd of Spokane, Washington, whose father had raised six children after his wife died, hatched the idea. Spokane celebrated the first Father's Day the next year, but it was not until 1972 that the day—the third Sunday in June—was proclaimed by law.

1000 B.C.
Henna tattoos Some tattoos are intended to be permanent, but henna tattoos for women in Middle Eastern and South Asian societies are elaborate designs created by female relatives for a onetime celebration, usually marriage.

A.D. 1000
Bindi A Hindu married woman's bindi mark, placed on the forehead between her eyes, symbolizes her married status, her spiritual "third eye," and her strength (the color red/vermilion is called "sindoor" and represents Shakti).

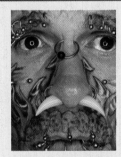

1980
Modern piercings Practiced since ancient times, in the past few decades in the West unusual "neotribal" piercing has seen renewed popularity, especially among some younger people.

1000 B.C.
Circumcision The Hebraic custom of removing an infant boy's foreskin is the only body modification permitted by Jewish law, which forbids tattoos, piercings, deliberate scarring, and other body markings.

1600
Bound feet The old process of foot binding was excruciatingly painful and permanently maimed a noblewoman's feet (called "lotus flowers") so they could not support her.

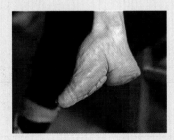

Summer

Summertime's official holidays are few and far between, although many people take personal vacations during this season. And in areas where the weather is relatively mild, informal celebrations like picnics, barbecues, and boat trips abound. In the United States, Independence Day on the Fourth of July means a long weekend and a lot of fireworks, the true beginning to the lazy, hazy weeks known as "the dog days of summer." Many families plan travel during the summer, or children go to recreational camps since American schools are traditionally closed during the summer months.

Fourth of July

INDEPENDENCE HOLIDAY FIRST CELEBRATED
IN PHILADELPHIA ON JULY 8, 1776
U.S. POPULATION IN JULY 1776: 2.5 MILLION

One weekday in an American city, a group of men agreed on a version of a document. This might sound like a rare but welcome occurrence in your own office, except that the day was July 4, 1776, the group was the Founding Fathers, and the document was the Declaration of Independence.

Over the past 200-odd years, some people came to believe that July 4 was the day that the Declaration was ratified by the Continental Congress. That's not true; it was actually ratified on August 2, 1776. However, July 4 was the day that the colonies' Second Continental Congress special committee for drafting a document that would formally sever ties with Great Britain settled on a draft of the Declaration of Independence. The committee included Benjamin Franklin, John Adams, Roger Sherman, Robert R. Livingston, and Thomas Jefferson, who was considered the most eloquent writer and who drafted the document.

Even though it wasn't made official for several weeks, on July 8, 1776, readings of the new Declaration were held in Philadelphia's Independence

PARALLEL HISTORY

Invention of Fireworks

Now a staple of American Fourth of July celebrations, fireworks were discovered in China at least 1,000 years ago. Some believe that their discovery was an accident by a cook who mixed charcoal, sulfur, and saltpeter. When compressed into a bamboo tube, the mixture exploded. No one has explained, however, why a cook might have tamped this volatile compound into a tube. The Chinese themselves credit fireworks to a monk named Li Tian and honor him each April 18. We do know that the Chinese used fireworks and firecrackers, calling them "yanhua" or "smoke flowers." They were thought to frighten off evil spirits. Genoese explorer Marco Polo and Christian Crusaders brought gunpowder back to Europe, where many nations discovered a passion for fireworks.

Square. By the following year, July 4 had become the unofficial day of celebration. Congress was adjourned, bonfires were lit, and bells were rung. By 1791, it had become known as Independence Day. As time went on, other towns and cities held their own festivities, and these became even more common at the end of the War of 1812 with Great Britain.

Despite decades of celebrations, Congress didn't officially establish Independence Day as a holiday until 1870 (in 1941 it was declared a legal holiday, with full pay for federal employees). Today the Fourth of July is observed nationwide with fireworks displays, military salutes, concerts, barbecues, and parades.

Dog Days

NAME FOR: LONG, HOT DAYS OF SUMMER
ALSO REFERS TO: SLUGGISH SUMMER STOCK MARKET,
SLOW SUMMER MONTHS OF CONGRESS

When the summer heat sets in for a long, sultry spell, we've entered the dog days. Traditionally running from July 3 to August 11, the dog days have long been associated with uncomfortable heat, searing sun, steaming pavement, sudden thunderstorms, lethargy, disease, and, at one time, mad dogs. But we have to look elsewhere for the origin of the term.

Ancient Romans noticed that the really hot days came along with the rising of Sirius, the Dog Star, in the Canis Major constellation. Since it's the brightest star in the heavens, they reasoned that it somehow contributed to the sun's heat. Being 8.7 light-years away from Earth and 50 trillion miles

UNCOMMONLY KNOWN . . .

Summer Vacation Depending on the region of the country, summer break for many 20th-century American children historically meant full-time farmwork. Farming kids didn't look forward to long beach vacations; they were part of the labor force for planting and harvesting. Before standardized school years, breaks weren't always during the summer; they varied greatly by the planting and harvesting cycles in different regions, the time period, and the school districts.

distant, Sirius has no effect whatsoever on our temperature. Still, the phrase "dog days" stuck, and the fact that there were more crazed dogs in late summer helped. Pliny (A.D. 23-79) noted in his *Natural History* that there was an increase in attacks by rabid dogs in July and August. His recommended preventive was to feed the dogs chicken droppings.

Near madness himself, the title character in Shakespeare's *Hamlet* (circa 1601) warns, "The cat will mew and dog will have his day." A 1729 British publication, *The Husbandman's Practice*, suggested men should "abstain all this time from woman" and "take heed of feeding violently." It also cautioned, "The Heat of the Sun is so violent that Men's bodies at Midnight sweat as at Midday: and if they be hurt, they be more sick than at any other time, yea very near Dead."

Because the stars gradually shift their positions relative to the sun, Sirius today rises several weeks later than in Roman times. Another 10,000 years and the Dog Star will rise in the middle of winter.

Of course, in recent times we tend to think of sleeping dogs during the "dog days," because the hottest days are when most people simply want to rest and stay cool; real dogs tend to be quite smart in the heat about seeking shade and sleep. Another alternative (although not historically accurate) meaning refers to the stock market. Since bad stocks are often known as "dogs," and summer is a slow time on Wall Street, some people refer to "dog days" in the financial sense, too. Some calendars, like that in the Anglican Book of Common Prayer, list the "Dog Daies" as running from July 6 to August 17, which may be why the feast of St. Roch, the patron saint of dogs, falls on August 16.

Fall

Fall signals harvest and bounty, as well as encroaching darkness and preparation for the winter, so it's not surprising that the major events of this season encompass themes of thankfulness and work. While Labor Day technically comes during summer (fall begins on the autumnal equinox on September 22 or 23), its acknowledgment of toil signals a new season. Ramadan, the holiest month of the Muslim year, comes during the autumn, and so does Halloween, based on the ancient observance of Samhain. However, the holiday that most symbolizes fall for all U.S. citizens is Thanksgiving.

Labor Day

FIRST LABOR DAY PARADE: SEPTEMBER 5, 1882,
IN NEW YORK CITY
CELEBRATED WITH: PARADES, PICNICS, CONCERTS

When the industrial revolution took hold in the United States, growth outpaced the ability of the government to properly regulate working conditions. Overlong shifts, overcrowded facilities, and underage employees were all too common in factories, stores, and other institutions. Many employees feared losing their jobs if they complained. Today's safer, more humane conditions are the result of drastic reforms.

Labor Day always falls on the first Monday in September, but it wasn't always observed. In 1882, the Central Labor Union in New York proposed a day to honor workers. While some records show that Peter McGuire, co-founder of the American Federation of Labor, first suggested the holiday, others show that machinist Matthew Maguire called for a Labor Day while serving as secretary of the Central Labor Union. What we know for sure is that the Central Labor Union celebrated the first "Labor Day" on September 5, 1882, in New York City, and 10,000 workers marched from city hall to Union Square in New York City for the first ever Labor Day parade. This unpaid day off was in honor of all workers and their issues, especially those that were never vocalized to employers. Support grew from the municipal to the state and federal levels, and in 1894 Congress passed an act making Labor Day a national holiday.

In its early years, Labor Day and "Labor Sunday" were serious affairs with speeches, parades to showcase workers, and programs for educating the public about the contributions working men and women make to our society. However, as unions became more organized and people generally more aware of labor issues, the holiday came to function as the end of summer in much the same way that Memorial Day functions as its beginning.

UNCOMMONLY KNOWN...
Harvest Moon The full moon occurring closest to the autumnal equinox (September 22 or 23 in the Northern Hemisphere) is called the harvest moon. Farmers used the early evening light to finish gathering the harvest, and celebrations were widespread. In Asia, mid-autumn Moon Festivals date back 3,000 years.

Ramadan

OBSERVED ON: NINTH MONTH IN ISLAMIC CALENDAR
DERIVED FROM ARABIC WORD MEANING
"INTENSE HEAT" OR "SCORCHING DRYNESS"

The Muslim observation of the month of Ramadan has many parallels with other major world religious observances. For example, like the Christian practice of Lent, Ramadan is a time of inward reflection and material denial. Like the Jewish holiday of Hanukkah, the end of Ramadan (a celebration known as Eid al-Fitr) is a time of joy, gift-giving, and family feasting.

But while it shares characteristics with other religious rites, Ramadan also has its origins in a specifically Muslim event. It is believed that the ninth month of the year (by the lunar Islamic calendar) was that in which the Prophet Muhammad received the first of the Koran's revelations. The exact date, referred to as Laylat al-Qadr, is known only to God and Muhammad, who refused to reveal it so that people would not be tempted to restrict their prayers to one day.

The name of the holy month comes from the Arabic ar-ramad ("scorching heat" or "dryness"). As the fundamental aspect of Ramadan is fasting, it is believed the name may signify the burning desire for drinking water and food. Daily fasting takes place for all healthy adults (the elderly, ill, pregnant or nursing, and children under 12 are exempt) from sunrise to sunset each day until the new moon.

Sunrise is defined as "when the white thread becomes distinct from the black thread." During daylight the devout are forbidden to eat, drink, or smoke.

At sunset, long congregational prayers containing passages from the Koran are traditionally said, because another injunction to the faithful during Ramadan is to read the entire Koran. After sunset, families gather to shop for, cook, and eat the Iftar meal to break their daylong fast. The evening and night hours are often a time of great festivity as people gather.

Halloween

CELEBRATED WITH: COSTUMES, PUMPKINS, CANDY,
TRICK-OR-TREATING, HAUNTED HOUSES
SECOND TO CHRISTMAS IN SPENDING IN U.S.

Nowadays it's a night for costume parties with a ghoulish theme, bobbing for apples, and children going door to door asking for candy, but Halloween has been celebrated in some form for more than 2,000 years.

What has become a night of revelry and fun was for the Celts of Ireland a serious sacred ritual called Samhain, honoring Saman, lord of death. They believed that on Allhallows Eve (October 31), fairies were abroad and mortals were in closest contact with the spirit world—and the spirits were not necessarily benevolent. People attired themselves as demons and goblins, wearing animal skins and heads, and made a noisy procession out to a huge bonfire of sacred oak built by Druid priests. Both the parade and the fire were intended to drive away the spirits of the recent dead who were trying to reinhabit living bodies. After a harvest feast, sacrifices (animal and sometimes human) were made, and fortunes were told from the remains. Then each family carried home a torch from the fire to relight their extinguished hearth fires. Though the Romans conquered the Celts in the first century and banned human sacrifice, Halloween remained alive.

And Christianity had to adapt too—in A.D. 601, Pope Gregory I issued an edict concerning the native beliefs and customs of the peoples he hoped to convert; he wanted missionaries to try to use native beliefs rather than obliterate them. In the ninth century, the Church replaced the supernaturally focused Samhain with a Christian feast, All Saints' Day, on November 1 and, a few centuries later, All Souls' Day (November 2), to honor the dead. While it was meant to diminish the importance of the Celtic deities, this new holy day instead wound up encouraging another celebration: Allhallows Eve, or "Hallowe'en," the evening before All Saints' Day. In this country, the influx of Irish and Scottish in the 1800s revived the pagan spirit festival as a night of amusement and pranks.

Thanksgiving

FIRST CELEBRATED: 1621 IN PLYMOUTH, MA
POSSIBLE MENU: WILD TURKEY, GOOSE, VENISON,
COD, CORN, PUMPKINS, CHESTNUTS

Thanksgiving is the most commonly observed secular holiday on the American calendar. Most Americans, regardless of background or religious affiliation, celebrate this day of gratitude with friends and family.

The first Thanksgiving actually did take place in 1621 at Plimoth (near the modern-day town of Plymouth) in the Massachusetts Colony. The colonists and Wampanoag Indians shared an autumn harvest feast that has become a symbol of cooperation and interaction between English colonists and Native Americans. However, it is important to note that Native American groups had been holding harvest festivals and celebrations of thanks for centuries before this.

While today's Thanksgiving foods are traditionally in the vein of turkey, gravy, mashed potatoes, and cranberry sauce, historians know of only two items that were certainly on the menu at the first feast: venison and wild fowl. There might have been cornmeal, plums, lobster, and leeks, but there definitely wasn't any pumpkin pie, corn on the cob, or anything with milk or eggs.

The first "Thanksgiving Proclamation" was on June 20, 1676, by the governing council of Charlestown, Massachussetts. They called for June 29 to be a day of thanksgiving, but of course, this didn't last forever. While President George Washington called for a national day of thanksgiving in 1789, it was opposed by many people who didn't believe the pilgrims' hardships were worthy of national remembrance; Thomas Jefferson in particular thought the idea entirely wrong.

The modern Thanksgiving came about from the efforts of a magazine editor named Sarah Josepha Hale, whose 40-year campaign of letters and editorials persuaded President Abraham Lincoln in 1863 to sign a bill proclaiming the last Thursday in November a national Thanksgiving holiday. Each President following him proclaimed it so as well, but Thanksgiving did not become a legal holiday until 1941, when Congress sanctioned it as the fourth Thursday in November.

While today's Thanksgiving meal includes many foods the first celebrators wouldn't recognize, its purpose (giving thanks) has been less sullied by commercial concerns than some other major holidays, such as Christmas and Easter.

Winter

Depending on location, winter can manifest itself as a slight dip in temperature or knee-deep snow that lasts until late spring. In the Southern Hemisphere, Christmas may be celebrated poolside, but its origin is tied to the Northern Hemisphere's cold winter solstice. In countries that have large Christian populations, Christmas became so popularly celebrated that other cultures heightened their similarly timed celebrations, such as Hanukkah. Toward the end of the season, all mild-weather lovers can hope for an abbreviated winter on Groundhog Day.

Hanukkah

ALSO KNOWN AS:
FESTIVAL OF LIGHTS, FEAST OF DEDICATION,
FEAST OF THE MACCABEES

Hanukkah (or Chanukkah, or Chanuka . . . we could go on) is a celebratory holiday commemorating the Maccabees' dedication of the Second Temple of Jerusalem. When they took back the temple, the Maccabees saw that the temple lamp had only enough oil to burn for one night—yet it burned for eight, until more oil could be found. This miracle is why Jewish people all over the world celebrate the "Festival of Lights."

In fact, *Hanukkah* means "dedication," and the lighting of the *hanukiyah* (as the menorah is called in Israel) is meant to symbolize the dedication that was shown by the Maccabees as they kept the flame lit for eight days and nights. The menorah's branches are deliberately set apart from each other so the flames will remain distinct and not resemble a "pagan" bonfire.

During the 20th century, Western Jews and especially Jewish Americans began to celebrate Hanukkah with Christmas-type trappings, including home decorations, lavish gifts, and parties. As it was intended, Hanukkah is actually a fairly minor holy day compared with Passover or Yom Kippur. Besides the menorah, traditions common to Hanukkah celebrations throughout the centuries include dishes cooked in oil as a reminder of the lamp, like potato latkes and *sufganiyot*, or jelly doughnuts.

The four-sided dreidel may seem like a child's toy, but in the time of Antiochus, it saved Jews from punishment. Jews were not supposed to gather and read the Torah, so they'd keep a dreidel nearby; if Roman soldiers showed up they could stow the holy scrolls and pretend to play a game.

UNCOMMONLY KNOWN . . .
Dreidel The four-sided top known as a dreidel gets its name from the German word "drehen," "to turn." The sides are marked with the Hebrew letters nun, gimel, hei, shun, standing for "Nes gadol haya sham" or "A great miracle happened there," referring to the container of oil that lasted long enough (eight days) to reconsecrate the Second Temple in Jerusalem after its desecration in the second century B.C.

Winter Solstice

FROM LATIN "SOLSTITUM" (SUN STANDS STILL)
COINCIDES WITH: CHRISTMAS, HANNUKKAH,
DONG ZHI (CHINA), MAKAR SANKRANTI (INDIA)

The official beginning of winter, between December 20 and December 23 in the Northern Hemisphere, marks the shortest day and longest night of the year. Called the winter solstice, the day also heralds the gradual return of light and warmth as the days finally stop growing shorter and begin to lengthen. Celebrations of the solstice have been observed since ancient times with a number of cultural and religious traditions.

The Romans celebrated Saturnalia in December. A week of feasting and orgying honored Saturn, god of agriculture, and included observances of the winter solstice. After the solstice they recognized the return of sunlight by paying homage to Mithras, a Persian god of light born on the solstice. The Greeks had a similar winter solstice festival called Brumalia, an homage to Dionysus. With the rise of Christianity, Saturnalia died out, replaced by Christmas. Though the birth of Jesus was probably not in the winter, Christian tradition since around the mid-fourth century (when it appears in a Roman calendar) has placed it near the solstice, on December 25. Like Mithras, Jesus was considered a god who banished the powers of darkness and brought light to the world. The Jewish Feast of Lights Hanukkah

also takes place in December. The eight-day festival dates to around 165 B.C., when the Jews defeated Antiochus, the Greek king of Syria; they rededicated their temple by lighting holy lamps or candles.

The word *solstice* comes from the Latin for "sun stands still." The Earth's axis is tilted some 23 degrees from its plane of rotation. At the exact moment of the winter solstice the Northern Hemisphere stops tilting away from the sun and begins tilting toward it again—thus, to the ancient astronomers, the sun appeared for a few days not to have shifted its track in the sky.

Christmas

MERRY CHRISTMAS, IN OTHER LANGUAGES:
SROZHDESTVOM KRISTOVYM, FELIZ NAVIDAD,
JOYEUX NOËL, BUONE NATALE, GOD JUL

Christmas is perhaps the most visible Christian holiday; not only is it celebrated by people in many different ways, from secular to solemn; it's a seasonal celebration with secular traditions that have reached, via all types of popular media, into every corner of the world.

Midwinter celebrations have been held for thousands of years. The longest, darkest days of winter called for some kind of warmth, light, and fellowship. The Old Norse celebrated Yule, in which feasts were held as long as a large log would burn, up to 12 days (which may be the origin of the "Twelve Days of Christmas" tradition). Meanwhile, in Rome,

Saturnalia (in honor of Saturn, the god of agriculture) was celebrated for a full week around the winter solstice. It was a hedonistic and chaotic holiday, with peasants in charge while nobles served.

Christmas wasn't originally part of the Christian liturgical year; nor is December 25 mentioned in the Bible. In the fourth century A.D., Pope Julius I chose that date as a church holiday, in large part attempting to give a religious cast to the Saturnalia festivities. First called the Feast of the Nativity, the custom spread to Egypt by 432 and to England by the end of the sixth century. By holding Christmas at the same time as traditional winter solstice festivals, church leaders increased the chances that Christmas would be popularly embraced, but gave up the ability to dictate how it was celebrated. By the Middle Ages, Christianity had, for the most part, replaced pagan religion, but on Christmas, after attending church, revelers would celebrate in a most heathenish fashion, with drinking, games, and mischief.

In the United States, Christmas took some time to settle in. The early Puritan settlers did not celebrate, since they had been influenced by the Protestant Oliver Cromwell and his Reformation government in England. It wasn't until the late 19th century that Americans embraced Christmas; Congress declared it a federal holiday in 1870.

The rise in popularity and subsequent commercialization of Christmas had little to do with religious fervor and everything to do with changing cultural attitudes. In both the U.S. and Europe, attitudes toward family and children were growing more sentimental. This was due to several factors, including higher incomes, more free time, and greater availability of manufactured goods—all part of the industrial revolution.

Santa Claus

FROM THE DUTCH "SINTER KLAAS"
ALSO KNOWN AS: ST. NICHOLAS, SAINT NICK, KRIS KRINGLE, CHRISTKIND, FATHER CHRISTMAS

The fictional Santa Claus as he is conceived of today is fairly uncomplicated: a jolly, fat man in a red suit who brings toys to children all over the world from his home at the North Pole via a reindeer-driven sled. He's just a symbol of gift-giving, generosity, and plenty. Right?

Well, partially right. A monk named St. Nicholas was born around A.D. 280 in what is now Turkey to a wealthy family. St. Nicholas was renowned for his generosity, with legends saying that he gave away all of his inheritance and traveled far and wide helping people. He died on December 6, and that day became his feast day after he was canonized. In Holland, St. Nicholas Day is still celebrated, with children putting out their shoes to receive cookies and candy from "St. Nick."

The Dutch nickname for St. Nick was Sinter Klaas, and as Dutch settlers brought their traditions to the New World, "Sinter Klaas" became "Santa Claus." Novelist Washington Irving further popularized Santa Claus in his book *The History of New York*, in which he deemed St. Nicholas "the patron saint of New York." By the mid-19th century, newly created department stores began to advertise Christmas shopping, often using images of St. Nick/Santa Claus. In 1841, a store owner in Philadelphia hired a man dressed as Santa Claus to climb his store's chimney. It was only a matter of time before stores began to attract children, and their parents, with the lure of a peek at a "live" Santa Claus. In 1822, a New York professor, Clement Clarke Moore, wrote a poem for his daughters entitled "An Account of a Visit from St. Nicholas," detailing a Santa Claus with a portly figure and magical abilities. In 1881, political cartoonist Thomas Nast drew on Moore's poem to create a *Harper's Weekly* cartoon of Santa as a round, happy, bearded man wearing a bright red fur-trimmed suit and holding a toy-stuffed sack.

Kwanzaa

FROM SWAHILI "MATUNDA YA KWANZA"
CREATED BY: DR. MAULANA KARENGA
FIRST CELEBRATED: DECEMBER 26, 1966

Kwanzaa means "first fruits," and is taken from the Swahili phrase meaning the same: *matunda ya kwanza*. Kwanzaa is a secular African-American celebration conceived of in 1966 after the Watts riots by Dr. Maulana Karenga. The seven-day festival, observed annually from December 26 to January 1, is meant to celebrate heritage, pride, community, family, and culture.

"First fruits" or harvest celebrations have been held in African cultures as far back as ancient Egypt and Nubia and include attention to five things: ingathering, reverence, commemoration, recommitment, and celebration.

The seven fundamental activities or principles on which Kwanzaa is based are: Umoja (Unity), Kujichagulia (Self-Determination), Ujima (Collective Work and Responsibility), Ujamaa (Cooperative Economics), Nia (Purpose), Kuumba (Creativity), Imani (Faith). Kwanzaa is represented by seven symbols: Mazao (crops), Mkeka (mat), Kinara (candleholder), Mishumaa Saba (seven candles), Muhindi (ears of corn), Zawadi (gifts), and Kikombe Cha Umoja (unity cup). These are represented by candles in a holder; three of the candles are red, three are green, and one is black. The candle colors represent, respectively, "black" people, their struggle (red), and their future (green).

Each ear of corn represents the children, both in the family and its greater community. Although Kwanzaa gifts are considered mostly a children's thing, other family and community kin may also be given items like a book, which stresses education; a symbol of heritage, which stresses continuity; and other items that show how important culture is to the celebratory group.

Another Kwanzza tradition is the filling of and pouring from a "unity cup." The drinks are poured out of respect for the ancestors, and then the cup is drunk from as a ritual symbolizing unity with them and with the gathered people. Another part

---

PARALLEL HISTORY

Jumping the Broom & Other Slave Traditions

The practice of "jumping the broom" as all or part of a wedding ceremony has several antecedents, including Celtic and West African, and several purported meanings, including fertility, entry into a symbolic new home, and sweeping away old lives. We do know that African-American slaves used broom jumping in their weddings, but whether this was a deliberate incorporation of an African tradition or the substitution of it for a proper ceremony isn't clear. Today, couples "jump the broom" placed on the floor in front of them. An honored friend or family member gives the history of the custom. After the guests count to three, the bride and groom hold hands and leap over it together. Legend has it that whoever jumps higher will be in charge.

of the Kwanzaa ritual is placing all symbols of the seven values on a straw mat on a table everyone can see. This is where the lighting of the candles is held, as well, always beginning on December 26, the first day of Kwanzaa.

The candles are lit in a specific order, beginning with the black candle, which is relit each subsequent day. The second day, the red candle to the left is lighted, and so on, from left to right, until the end of Kwanzaa. Like the candles, the left-to-right sequence honors the people, the struggles, and then the future, in that order.

New Year's Eve

CELEBRATED BY MOST WORLD CULTURES
AMONG THE WORLD'S LONGEST-RUNNING FESTIVALS
OBSERVED WITH: FIREWORKS, CHAMPAGNE, REFLECTION

Celebrations to welcome the new year have been around for more than 4,000 years, making New Year's one of the oldest of all festivities in recorded history. For the Phoenicians and Persians, the year began with the autumnal equinox; for the Greeks it began with the winter solstice. Rites and

ceremonies were held for both purgation of the old year and to express joy in life's renewal.

What had most likely been a harvest celebration morphed into a coronation festival for new kings, combined with a sowing ceremony. The most well known of these new year's observances was held annually in Babylon. The 11-day ceremony began with a high priest ritually washing, then singing to Marduk, their chief god. Plays and parades were staged; fertility gods and other statues were carted to a special building. Following the final day of

PARALLEL HISTORY

Times Square Ball Drop

Millions of merrymakers ring in the new year by watching the ball drop atop One Times Square in New York City. The tradition began on the eve of 1908, when a 5-foot, 700-pound wood-and-iron ball lit with 100 25-watt bulbs descended a flagpole at midnight. Since then, the ball has come down every year except for 1942 and 1943, when the city observed a wartime "dim-out." The most recent balls were 6-foot spheres weighing more than 1,000 pounds and decorated with more than 500 Waterford crystal triangles, 700 lights, and 90 computer-controlled rotating pyramid mirrors.

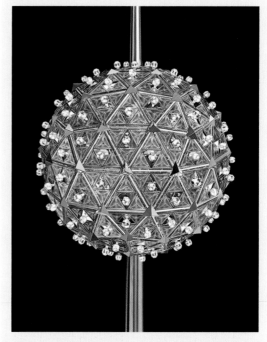

New York City's 2002 New Year's Eve Times Square ball was made by Waterford Crystal.

celebration, the people once more turned their attention to farming.

When Julius Caesar established the Julian calendar in 46 B.C., the year began on January 1, in the middle of winter. New Year's celebrations shifted accordingly. Then Christianity came along and put a damper on pagan celebrations. But not even the church could suppress what had begun to seem almost an innate human need, to mark the Earth making a revolution around the sun. During the Middle Ages the European countries celebrated at various times between mid-December and late March. Not until the 18th century did New Year's settle on January 1 as a universal date. Colonists in the New World celebrated by firing guns or attending church. Iroquois Indians focused on the banishing of evil spirits.

In modern times, New Year's Eve celebrations have grown to include New Year's Day, which is now a federal holiday. All kinds of traditions have sprung up around this symbolic fresh start, from football tournaments (the Rose Bowl) to anthems ("Auld Lang Syne," a Scottish poem by Robert Burns) to foods (hopping John, which includes black-eyed peas for luck). Many Americans consider New Year's Eve a party night, but many others think of it as a time for connection and reflection—it's traditional now to kiss your dearest at midnight.

Another New Year's tradition is making resolutions—personal goals. Since a new year portends new events and new fortune, New Year's resolutions can be singular and simple (be kinder) or multiple and many-stepped (learn Sanskrit, run a marathon, lose ten pounds). Of course, any resolution made is only as good as the maker's determination. Popular methods of keeping resolutions include recording them and enlisting friends as witnesses.

Groundhog Day

PREVIOUSLY KNOWN AS: CANDLEMAS DAY
GROUNDHOG PUNXSUTAWNEY PHIL HAS BEEN
MAKING PREDICTIONS SINCE 1886

The observance of animals emerging from their dens in early spring is a custom most likely going back as long as people have been in the weather-predicting business. Harbingers of spring meant it was time to prepare the ground for planting, so signs in nature were carefully noted from one year to the next.

For hundreds of years, Europeans marked the coming of spring with the emergence of badgers, bears, and other animals from their winter hibernation. German immigrants brought to Pennsylvania a custom similar to our Groundhog Day. If the day the animal comes out is sunny, the animal will see its shadow, grow frightened, and disappear back into its den for six more weeks. The winter will thus be prolonged. On a cloudy day the animal stays out, and spring is just around the corner. Since woodchucks (groundhogs) were plentiful in Pennsylvania, they became the barometer animal. And since they generally emerged in early February, the second of that month was chosen as official Groundhog Day. It was a wonderful instance of confabulating cause and effect. The immigrant farmers probably knew as well as we that though weather determines when the groundhog emerges, the groundhog on one arbitrary day cannot foretell the weather. But traditions die hard.

In warmer climates to the south, groundhogs come out earlier; to the north they come out later. So the farther one is from Pennsylvania, the less reliable February 2 is as a benchmark. And when the groundhogs do come out and test the air, their hunger and sexual drive will determine whether they remain out, not fear of their own shadows. But the Germans were on the right track in trusting the instincts of animals in predicting weather patterns: Modern meteorologists do no better in forecasting the arrival of spring than the lowly groundhog.

Saint Valentine's Day

CELEBRATED WITH: CARDS, FLOWERS CANDY
FIRST MASS-PRODUCED VALENTINES: 1840S
TODAY MORE THAN 1 BILLION VALENTINES EXCHANGED

The day we traditionally give flowers and candy to our sweethearts had its origins in an ancient Roman festival called Lupercalia. Every year on February 15, priests gathered at a cave thought to be the place where Rome's founders Romulus and Remus were nursed by a wolf (*lupus* is Latin for "wolf"). Two youths of noble lineage were then anointed with the blood of a sacrificed goat. They proceeded to go romping through the streets of Rome, lashing at young maidens with goatskin thongs known as *februa* (from the Latin for "to purify" and the root of "February"). The ritual was meant to protect the animals and crops and to ensure the fertility of both animals and owners.

A favorite part of the Lupercalia was the drawing of names for partners likely to become lovers and sweethearts. With the spread of Christianity, pagan traditions mingled with Christian, and by the fifth century A.D. the February festival had acquired the name of a saint. Two third-century martyrs were named Valentine—a bishop who secretly married couples against the emperor's orders, and a man who aided persecuted Christians. (Some scholars believe they were the same person, whose execution occurred during Lupercalia as an entertainment.) Thus, even though the church was not happy about pagan celebrations, a day in recognition of a hero was always welcome. And instead of drawing the names of sweethearts, young men drew the names of saints to emulate. So it was no surprise that Valentine's Day celebrations died off in Italy by the Middle Ages and in France and other countries by the 19th century.

But celebrations continued in Britain, the tradition no doubt bolstered by two literary lions. Chaucer's *Parlement of Foules* (circa 1382) and Shakespeare's *A Midsummer Night's Dream* (circa 1594) both refer to birds pairing off on St. Valentine's Day.

Valentine's Day is big business for stationers, chocolatiers, and florists, who encourage consumers to buy for sweethearts, parents, children, friends, and even colleagues. While some people refuse to so much as send a greeting card, believing that Valentine's Day represents commercial manipulation, others embrace the idea of a day geared toward celebrating romance and friendship and those who are dear.

UNCOMMONLY KNOWN...

Valentine Greetings The first known valentine letter was penned by Charles, duke of Orleans, around 1415 to his wife when he was imprisoned in the Tower of London. In that century the word "valentine" became synonymous with "sweetheart." Gradually it took on the additional meaning of "greeting card." Valentines blossomed in the Victorian era, decorated with hearts, cupids, and lacy borders.

A man without ceremony has need
of great merit in its place.
−BENJAMIN FRANKLIN (1706-90)

Ceremony & Customs

The many customs and ceremonies that give structure to our lives are rituals that we often take for granted, as if they always were and always will be. We meet someone and instinctively extend an arm to shake hands; we get married and go on a honeymoon; someone dies and we have a funeral. But when did people start shaking hands, and why? Where did the custom of the bridal shower come from? Once you start thinking this way, there's no end to the questions you can pose. We trace the histories of more than 30 ceremonies and customs, and find some surprising things. Pink and blue baby colors were once upon a time for the opposite gender they are today. The Pledge of Allegiance did not enter the national repertoire until 1892. The first coffins were made from woven reeds, and the latest, environmentally friendly "ecopods" have a similar construction. Many of the customs are part of daily life—saying "amen" and "gesundheit," for example. Others are special ceremonies we participate in a few times in the course of a life—baby showers, funerals, and so forth. Much of the history, as one might expect, is Judeo-Christian, whereas some customs are only as old as America. Peruse the entries in this chapter and dive in to what pulls you. But don't neglect subjects that may seem overly familiar. Think you know all there is to know about "Here Comes the Bride"? Why don't synagogues play that tune? Are you sure about Viking funeral pyres? If not, read on. As our lives in the 21st century seem ever more complex, our customs and ceremonies take on an increasing importance; they give us comfort and remind us that some things have not changed. They link us to generations past and help guide us through the events, large and small, of our lives.

Courtesies

H umans do certain things to make other humans feel more comfortable and safe. Every courtesy in this section, from shaking hands to opening a door, relates to one of those two things. Reaching out your hand to another person demonstrated that you held no weapon, while keeping your elbows off of the table provided more room for other diners. While we now know that saying "Gesundheit!" after someone sneezes has no immediate effect on the sneezer's health or spirit, we still say it out of custom, and because we like to acknowledge that we're all in this life together.

Shaking Hands

SHAKING HANDS IS A STANDARD BUSINESS GREETING
FIRM GRIP: IMPLIES CONFIDENCE
AVOID: GIVING A LIMP-HANDED HANDSHAKE

L ike so many other rituals, the origins of the handshake are obscure. In ancient Babylonia, a ruler would take the hand of a sacred statue to symbolize the transfer of divine power to human hands. However, the modern purpose of the handshake is quite clear: it's meant to convey open, safe greetings between two people.

Actually, make that "between two men." We do know that handshaking was used several hundred years ago in England to demonstrate that no arms were being carried.

Women rarely carried (or were allowed to carry) weapons, and that's probably why the handshake was not a common greeting for women until recently.

The handshake establishes trust and equality through direct contact. At one time left hands were shaken, because left sleeves often contained concealed weapons, but over time this shifted to right hands, because these were the "sword hands." Early handshakes were really "wristclasps" that at some point evolved into handclasps. While today a handshake conveys respect, it was not always so. George Washington believed handshaking was for common folk and instead preferred to greet people with a bow.

Different cultures around the world now use the handshake as greeting, especially in business situations, but there are variations. The Japanese shake hands frequently, often bowing as well. In some European countries, even if friends know each other well, they shake hands upon meeting. In Kuwait, men never shake hands with women. In some places, like India, a person will grasp your hand in both of theirs as a handshake. Contemporary Americans have a number of new greetings, including the "dap" or fist-bump. However, these trendy gestures will probably not supplant the simple gesture of shaking someone else's hand.

UNCOMMONLY KNOWN . . .

Bow and Curtsy Both the bow and the "curtsy" (a syncope of the word "courtesy") are polite gestures made from one person to another. The bow is a lowering of head or upper body, depending on the formality of the encounter, while a curtsy involves a bob of the head and a bend of the knee.

Saying "Amen"

EXPRESSES AGREEMENT OR APPROVAL
ORIGINALLY FROM THE GREEK AND HEBREW "AMEN"
COMMONLY SAID AT THE CONCLUSION OF A PRAYER

Jews, Christians, and Muslims all use the word *Amen,* but its first use was in ancient Egypt. Amun, the greatest of Egyptian gods, was invoked with the phrase "By Amun!"

In Hebrew usage, some posit that the word came to mean "so be it." Other linguists believe that the Hebraic use of "Amen" derives from *aman,* a primitive root that means "to be firm, confirmed, believe." Regardless of its origin, the word "amen" appears in the Hebrew Scriptures in different grammatical contexts, demonstrating that it was a firmly entrenched linguistic element. In Jewish liturgy, "Amen" is a communal response, an individual charge, and a sacred acronym that signifies "God, trustworthy king."

"Amen" entered the Christian lexicon through the Greek language, and is also found in the Christian Scriptures, expressing a kind of certainty not found in the Hebrew Scriptures or practice. In the early church, "Amen" meant that the people had ratified what the priest had prayed. Perhaps that would account for "Amen Corners" in Christian denominations: sections of a congregation most

---

UNCOMMONLY KNOWN...

Saying Grace Most major religious traditions include a grace or blessing before meals. Whether or not the grace includes a reference or invocation to a divinity, it includes gratitude for the food available. In the United States, it is common for gathered families and groups to say a grace over the Thanksgiving meal in honor both of the current and historical bounty.

---

likely to shout out "Amen!" during a sermon or homily. While most Christian uses of the term follow the Hebrew pronunciation "AH-men," over the years "A-men" has become common among more evangelical groups.

The United States was settled by Christians of the Puritan persuasion, and these churchgoing folk brought a firm belief and practice about responding to prayers, blessings, and exhortations with an even firmer "Amen!" African-American slaves, who created their own means of worship from what they saw in their new home, brought "Amen" into their services and their spirituals.

The word has even entered American politics, with some journalists referring to President Bill Clinton's African-American voting bloc as his "Amen Corner."

Gesundheit

EYES AUTOMATICALLY CLOSE WHEN SNEEZING
A PHOTIC REFLEX CAUSES SOME PEOPLE TO SNEEZE IN
RESPONSE TO SUDDEN, BRIGHT LIGHT

Many Americans automatically say "Gesundheit!" when someone sneezes, without even knowing what the word means, or where it comes from—such is the power of an oft-repeated exclamation like this one.

The word *Gesundheit* is simply German for "healthiness" (*Gesund* = health, *Heit* = state) or "good health." In Yiddish the word is *Gezunterheyt.* Although the common practice of saying "Gesundheit!" began in the early 20th century as thousands of Yiddish-speaking Ashkenazic Jews immigrated to the United States, it had probably already been used for at least a century by Pennsylvania Dutch farmers of German origin. "Gesundheit" can also be used as a drinking salute, but the sneeze response use comes from the proverb *Gesundheit ist besser als Krankheit* ("Healthiness is better than illness").

Other cultures have their own sneeze responses. The ancient Greeks wished each other "long life," while ancient Romans said "Jupiter preserve you," People in Arabic countries say, *Alhamdulillah* ("God be praised"), and Hindus say "Live well!" In Russia, after children are given the traditional response, *Bud zdorov* ("Be healthy"), they are also told *Rosti bolshoi* ("Grow big"). When a child sneezes in China, he or she will hear *Bai sui,* which means "May you live 100 years." Italians say *Felicita,* French say *À vos souhaits* or *Que Dieu vous benisse.* Hispanics have a response for each sneeze that comes in quick succession: *salud* ("health") for the first sneeze, *dinero* ("wealth") for the second, and *amor* ("love") for the third.

Why did people start wishing each other "good health" upon sneezing? It was mainly because in ancient times people thought that the force of a sneeze could propel a person's soul right out of the body. By uttering some kind of incantation or invocation, bystanders believed they could stop evil spirits from taking the sneezer's soul, as well as protect against spirits entering the body. Sneezes were seen as such a powerful phenomenon that

in English there are a number of rhymes relating to them. For example: If you sneeze on Monday, you sneeze for danger / Sneeze on Tuesday, you kiss a stranger / Sneeze on Wednesday, you sneeze for a letter / Sneeze on a Thursday, for something better / Sneeze on a Friday, you sneeze for sorrow / Sneeze on a Saturday, your sweetheart tomorrow / Sneeze on a Sunday, your safety seek / The devil will have you the whole of the week.

PARALLEL HISTORY

The Pope and the Plague

In Rome during the plague of 590, Pope Gregory I ordered unceasing prayer for divine intercession. Part of his command was that anyone sneezing be blessed immediately ("God bless you"), since sneezing was often the first sign that someone was falling ill with the plague. Although the populace did not understand that the sneeze was one source of trasmittal, they may have sensed it was connected to the disease. "God bless you" became a verbal totem invoking divine mercy on the sneezer. The phrase stuck and was still used more than 750 years later when Pope Clement VI dealt with the horrors of a plague, the Black Death of 1348-49, also known as the Great Pestilence.

Pope Clement VI in about 1342, just a few years before the Black Death struck Europe.

Elbows off the Table

MAKES MORE ROOM FOR YOUR DINING COMPANIONS
PREVENTS PUSH/PULL EFFECT ON TABLECLOTH
PROTECTS YOUR ELBOWS FROM GETTING FOOD STAINS

The etiquette reminder to "Keep your elbows off of the table while you eat!" is such a universal experience. For parents trying to teach table etiquette to their children, it may help to know the origins of the custom in order to appreciate, and teach, its importance.

As with many rules of etiquette, "elbows off the table" isn't necessarily about stiff formality or protocol; it's about making sure that other people are comfortable. Elbows get in the way. They can knock another person's arm while it is bringing a fork or spoon to her mouth or tug abruptly at the tablecloth, disrupting dishes and silverware. An elbow can also knock a dish or bowl from the table, or get in the way of a server putting something on the table. In other words, keeping elbows close to one's sides during meal service and while eating serves a practical purpose.

One of the reasons people originally kept their elbows off the table was the crowded dining conditions during medieval times. When there was opportunity at court to dine with the rulers, so many people wanted to say they'd "dined with the king" (or queen or emperor) that they would pack themselves into the space, often sitting shoulder to shoulder on long wooden benches. Under those tight conditions, there was no room for one's arms on the table.

UNCOMMONLY KNOWN . . .
A Hand over the Mouth While Yawning Today we put our hand over our mouth when we yawn so that other people will not have to gaze at our molars or see an obvious sign of fatigue or ennui. However, for hundreds of years, people believed that while yawning, one's soul could slip out, or evil spirits could slip in. Muslims encourage covering the mouth while yawning as a courtesy to others.

Etiquette experts disagree on whether elbows can be on the table when there isn't food around. Is it all right to lean on your elbows while making conversation during cocktails? After a meal? Some say yes, others say use your forearms, and still others say never. The choice can come down to consideration for your and your table companions' personal space and comfort.

Napkin in Lap

KEEPS CRUMBS AND FOOD OFF YOUR LAP
CATCHES CONDENSATION DRIPS FROM GLASS
HANDY FOR WIPING YOUR MOUTH

The humble table napkin has a surprisingly long and varied history. The Spartans used lumps of dough called *apomagdalie,* cut, rolled, and kneaded at table, to wipe their hands. The ancient Romans used lengths of cloth called *mappa* at the edges of eating couches to protect the furnishings.

In the early Middle Ages, people tended to wipe their hands and mouth with the tablecloth, so the French began putting smaller cloths on top of the tablecloth for guests to use (and so that the large tablecloth wouldn't have to be changed so frequently).

By the Renaissance, the standard large napkin for table use was still extremely large, meant for people who ate mostly with knife and fingers. When forks became common during the 17th and 18th centuries, people began to value neatness in dining so greatly that they often didn't use a napkin at all, or if they did, tried to keep it spotless.

Eventually, 30" x 36" became the standard. As dining became more formalized, so did napkin rules. French etiquette guides called it "ungentlemanly to use a napkin for wiping the face or scraping the teeth, and a most vulgar error to wipe one's nose with it," and dictated that diners should not unfold their own napkin until the "person of highest rank" had.

Paper napkins, originating in medieval China, arrived in the West in the early 20th century.

Holding a Door

TRADITIONAL: MEN HOLD DOORS FOR WOMEN
BUSINESS: THE FIRST TO REACH THE DOOR HOLDS IT
HEALTHY PEOPLE HOLD DOORS FOR AGED, DISABLED

Manners can change with the fashions of an era. While people in Victorian times would never have allowed a young woman to be alone in the company of a man for any reason, today women and men

---

Latin American Table Manners

Latin Americans focus on lunch as the big meal of the day, and it's not big simply in quantity but also in time spent and in care taken. After gathering between 1 and 3 p.m. at a well-set table, people in Chile, Venezuela, Brazil, and other South American countries enjoy a meal of several courses. Table manners are taken quite seriously, with proper use of flatware encouraged—even sandwiches and pieces of fresh fruit are eaten with knife and fork. However, the most important element of meals in South and Central America is paying attention to your fellow diners. Properly greeting and addressing everyone, as well as carrying on civilized and polite conversation, is of the utmost importance.

work and live side by side in many different situations. One tradition that has changed a great deal over the past 100 years is the custom of a gentleman helping a woman open the door of a room, building, or a conveyance, be it a carriage, a train car, or an automobile.

This, in large part, arose from practical circumstances. For centuries, women's garments and accoutrements made it difficult for them to maneuver entirely on their own. Helping a woman by opening a carriage or automobile door signaled that a man understood she needed help.

While offering women special treatment with special manners may date back as far as prehistoric times, we know that a particular code of how men of a certain class should conduct themselves had a huge impact. This code was medieval chivalry, and it could be applied to the battlefield, to spiritual warfare, and to courtly love—but in all of those things, the honor of the knight was paramount. When it came to love and women, the knight's duty was to treat all women with carefully constructed protocols, even if he was already attached to a woman in particular. The chivalry of courtly love governed everything from how a woman should be greeted or helped onto a horse (with a sidesaddle, of course), to how doors should be held open to accommodate her dress.

Nowadays, it's considered good etiquette to open the door for anyone who might need assistance, regardless of gender.

Weddings

Everyone wants a unique wedding, but the traditions here have been around for so long that no bride will have any trouble finding that "something old" for her special day. Wedding ceremonies, garments, and symbols come from ancient human motivations and symbols. For example, flowers signify a growing relationship and its potential fruitfulness. A modern bride and groom might choose balloons instead of flowers, but the urge to festoon the wedding venue remains the same. A few traditions, like the chuppah, are unique to specific religions, but their message is also timeless.

Bachelor Party

ALSO KNOWN AS: A "BULL'S PARTY" IN SOUTH AFRICA
THE NUMBER ONE BACHELOR PARTY DESTINATION IN THE
U.S. IS LAS VEGAS, NEVADA

Contemporary American men have raised bachelor party standards to new heights—or brought them to new lows, depending on whether you're invited to the party or you're the bachelor's intended. However, while today's bachelor might be extravagant in throwing a full weekend-getaway bash before his nuptials, he can cite ancient tradition as inspiration for his festivities.

Bachelors have been feted by their friends since ancient Sparta, when a group of men would gather to toast a comrade who was about to be married.

The practice proved popular, no doubt because most cultures believe that marriage means a more responsible, staid, and practical lifestyle. Being married means being answerable to another person. Men decided that one final night of revelry was important for the groom.

Over the centuries the bachelor party has grown from a toast to a full-on party. The modern version might have been born during the Victorian era, when a young man-about-town might have had friends unsuitable to invite to the dinner table in his future married life. A last party with rakes and loose women was supposed to be his way of saying "Thank you, and farewell."

Today's bachelor party is usually planned by a potential groom's brother or best man, and might include drinking, dinner, a bar, cigars, or a visit to a strip club. Even if the party is tame, the hosts might arrange for a limo to ferry guests around, both for the "player" image it provides and for driver safety when everyone is drinking.

What's sauce for the gander is sauce for the goose—the latest trend is bachelorette parties, which are called hen parties or hen's night in the United Kingdom (where the bachelor party is known as stag night). Bachelorette parties aren't as likely to include a stripper or cigars, but they are just as likely to include drinking and games and general rowdiness. In Canada, "stag and doe" events—combined bachelor and bachelorette parties—have become popular.

Bridal Shower

TRADITIONALLY THROWN BY: THE MAID OF HONOR
GUESTS INCLUDE: THE BRIDAL PARTY AND THE BRIDE'S
CLOSE FEMALE FRIENDS, RELATIVES AND IN-LAWS

The background of the bridal shower includes an apocryphal story and a factual history. The time-honored tale is of a Dutch maiden who longed to marry a penniless man. Her father disapproved, and when he told her if she defied him she would have no dowry, the townspeople, who loved the young couple, "showered" them with money and gifts.

No one has any idea if that story contains any truth, but we do know that bridal showers as a group activity were first held in Brussels, Belgium, during the mid-19th century. We also know that some early showers included an upside-down umbrella or parasol filled with gifts, that was then "showered" on the bride-to-be. Before that, in the U.S. as well as Europe, women would often keep "hope chests" filled with items for their eventual married life, such as nightwear, household linens, and quilts. Hope chests were usually filled with handmade, irreplaceable items, although later in American history they might hold china, silver, or family gifts as well.

Hope chests could be kept by young women of any status, but the earliest bridal showers in North America were for the upper class. Entertaining in the home was an opportunity for young debutantes

and their mothers to showcase their family's status, goods, and new connections. The gifts given at showers tended to reflect the idea that the new wife would be a lady of leisure whose main role would be managing the household and its decorative objects, silver, and porcelain. Even as bridal showers became popular among other social classes and gifts became more practical, the tone of these events was focused on a woman's role as homemaker, which meant pots, pans, and dish towels, never desk sets, liquor decanters, or tennis gear. Men were usually excluded from showers, since these events were seen as female territory.

Twentieth-century and modern wedding showers often include silly party games centered on sexual innuendo, and sometimes gifts of lingerie.

Throwing the Bride's Bouquet

SOME BOUQUET TYPES: COLONIAL, ARM, CASCADE
WEDDING GUESTS TRY TO CATCH THE BOUQUET
SYMBOLIZES: GOOD LUCK AND NEXT MARRIED

First there were garlands, then wreaths, then bouquets. Wedding flowers symbolize joy, new life, and love, but for early brides and grooms, they also symbolized safety from evil. That's not all; sage meant wisdom, dill meant lust, and garlic combined with dill? Let's just say that would have been some wedding night.

Generally, attendants at weddings with these aromatic floral arrangements would have carried sheaves of wheat as a sign of plenty. As time went on, more and more blooms were placed in bridal bouquets, and the attendants began to carry flowers as well. The bride's bouquet was larger to showcase her, but it was also meant to provide colors and scents that she might recall later, to give her happy memories. Different floral traditions evolved for brides in different cultures; one that came to the U.S. from England was the practice of having a young female relative known as the "flower girl" scatter rose petals in the bride's path.

The bride's bouquet, like the bride's attire, was considered very lucky. Guests would clamor for bits of the wedding dress, which is one reason the garter toss was instituted. The bouquet, with its promise of fecundity, became something that female guests particularly fought over. It was no doubt a bride who wanted to see her beautiful flower arrangement stay intact who tossed it to a special sister or friend.

The bouquet toss has become a part of many U.S. weddings, especially when there are a number of young, unmarried women in attendance. At the reception, the single women gather in a group so that the bride can "throw" the bouquet to them. Most brides turn their backs to this group and throw the flowers over their shoulders so that they cannot be accused of favoring one woman over another. Many brides have a special, smaller bouquet made up by a florist to "toss" so that they can preserve their carried bouquet as a keepsake.

UNCOMMONLY KNOWN . . .
Throwing Rice Whether guests throw rose petals, birdseed, or confetti, the tradition of throwing something at the newly wedded, like most wedding traditions, relates to fertility and fruitfulness. In ancient times, seeds, nuts, figs, raisins, wheat, and other grains might be tossed to wish the bride and groom a fecund future.

Wedding Veil

CAN BE ADORNED WITH PEARLS, CRYSTALS, LACE
TRADITIONAL JAPANESE WEDDING VEILS
SYMBOLICALLY HIDE "HORNS" OF JEALOUSY AND EGO

Veils on women have a long and controversial history. They've been worn throughout history, originally to provide highborn women anonymity and modesty (in ancient Assyria, prostitutes were forbidden to wear veils). The Hebrew Scriptures contain many references to veiling women with religious significance, as does the Christian New Testament and the Muslim Koran. Veils ensure that the only men to see a woman's face are her own husband and relatives. The only occasion on which a modern Western woman would veil her face is on her wedding day; however, even this tradition is now regarded as old fashioned.

Brides in ancient Rome wore flame-colored wedding veils decorated with pictures of flames to ward off evil spirits who might want to interfere with the wedding proceedings. Some historians believe that women were veiled so that their beauty wouldn't draw the attention of rogues. However, the biblical story of Jacob, whose heavily veiled bride was the homely Leah rather than the beautiful Rachel, demonstrates a different outcome and has grown into the current Jewish practice of *badeken,* in which the groom veils his bride before the ceremony and lifts the veil during the ceremony, to ensure that he knows which woman is involved in the vows.

Of course, while a few brides might have been

veiled to conceal their looks from their future husbands, most brides are veiled as a symbol of purity and chastity. Veils also provide an element of eroticism in a wedding ceremony, since something that is veiled or "off limits" seems quite tantalizing. The idea that a woman is unveiled during a marriage ceremony reminds all present that she will again "unveil" herself to her groom afterward.

Wedding veils could be quite heavy and long, especially during the Victorian and Edwardian eras in the West, when an emphasis on women's sexual innocence combined with well-manufactured textiles resulted in elaborate wedding attire. In the latter half of the 20th century, veils were often very small and simple: netting on a headpiece, or a very short piece of tulle worn as decoration down the back rather than over the face. Bridal veils are now considered less symbolic than aesthetic.

Wedding March: "Here Comes the Bride"

COMPOSED BY FELIX MENDELSSOHN
MENDELSSOHN WAS THE FIRST CONDUCTOR
TO USE A BATON ON A REGULAR BASIS

M any cultures have music specific to weddings, both for the ceremony itself and for the reception. For example, in Egypt there is a wedding rhythm known as the *zaffa*. At Jewish weddings, the bride comes in to a song called the *baruch haba*.

Attendees of many European and U.S. weddings often hear two 19th-century compositions with interesting histories. "Here Comes the Bride," based on the "Bridal Chorus" from Richard Wagner's opera *Lohengrin*, and the "Wedding March," written by Felix Mendelssohn as part of his *A Midsummer Night's Dream*, are both easily identified by most Western listeners.

It is difficult to imagine a connection between either of these joyous bridal marches and violent anti-Semitism. However, Wagner was a vocal opponent of Judaism, and his music was celebrated by the Nazi Party. His attack on the devoutly Lutheran and ethnically Jewish Mendelssohn in an influential essay caused Mendelssohn's "Wedding March" to be played less frequently at German weddings for some decades. Understandably, even today, attendees of Jewish weddings will not hear Wagner's "Here Comes the Bride."

However, Wagner's own composition has bigger problems. In *Lohengrin*, the scene of the "Bridal Chorus" involves a large bed and is quite sexually charged. Conservative Missouri Synod–based Lutheran churches often oppose its use in weddings because of the pagan elements in the opera, while Roman Catholic churches obliquely state that it is a secular and popularized piece of music that does not belong in a sacramental ceremony.

Both pieces of music gained acceptance when they were selected by Victoria, the Princess Royal, for her marriage to the Crown Prince of Prussia on January 25, 1858. Today many brides regard "Here Comes the Bride" as dated. On the other hand, Mendelssohn's "Wedding March" is often played as a recessional at weddings of different faiths. Brides may also instead select a song that has personal associations.

UNCOMMONLY KNOWN ...

Congratulations Versus Best Wishes It is traditional to say "Congratulations" to a groom after a wedding, but "Best wishes" to the bride. The implication is that the groom has made a great "catch," but that it would be impolite to say that the bride had. Like many wedding traditions, this one is rooted in age-old sexism. It is entirely correct to say "Best wishes" to both and avoid the disparity.

Engagement and Wedding Rings

DEBEERS POPULARIZED DIAMONDS
WORN ON THE THIRD FINGER BY ROMANS
SOME BELIEVE DROPPING THE RINGS IS BAD LUCK

These days, engagement rings come first. However, historically, wedding rings take precedence. The history of both involves ideas of women's status, men's behavior, cultural priorities, and religious dogma.

Some historians believe that the first "wedding rings" were lengths of grass tied to a woman's finger in symbolic memory of the cords used to bind her hands and feet after a man had captured her. Rings denoted ownership in ancient Egypt and Rome, too, two places where the use of wedding rings is first recorded. Interestingly enough, Roman wives usually had two rings: a band of gold that they wore in public and a band of iron that they wore at home.

Betrothal and marriage rings were popular in ancient Greece and Europe, as well; the Celts braided hair for rings, and Europeans were fond of the "gimmel," a single ring that could be broken into two or more parts.

The Egyptians and Romans believed that the third finger of the left hand was connected to the *vena amoris* that led directly to the heart, so they wore wedding rings on that finger. In the 12th century, Pope Innocent III decreed that all weddings must take place in a church, and that they must all include a ring for the bride.

Innocent III also declared a longer waiting period between engagement and marriage, and this led directly to a run on engagement rings. While the aristocracy loved using gemstones, it took several hundred years before the first recorded diamond engagement ring, given to Mary of Burgundy by Archduke Maximilan I of Austria in 1477. While diamonds were one of many stones used for engagement rings through the 19th century, a DeBeers Diamond Mines advertising campaign that began in the mid-20th century, A Diamond Is Forever, pushed the diamond forward as the engagement ring stone. Wedding bands now often have diamonds set in them to match these rings, too.

Walking Under a Chuppah

MEANS: "CANOPY" IN HEBREW
SYMBOLIZES: THE COUPLE'S NEW HOME TOGETHER
TRADITIONAL JEWISH MARRIAGES ARE ARRANGED

The bride and groom at a traditional Jewish wedding will take their vows under a chuppah, which at its simplest is a length of cloth (even a prayer shawl, or tallith) stretched between four poles held upright by honored members of the congregation. Symbolically, this structure stands for the groom's house, and the bride's entering it means she accepts him wholeheartedly (and vice versa). The open sides of the canopy mean that the couple will establish a home that's always open to guests and generous in hospitality.

There are several traditions involved with preparing to enter the chuppah and several others with what takes place during the vows. Both bride and groom remove all of their jewelry, so that they may not value each other for material goods; the groom unties all knots in his clothing, so nothing binds them except his vows; both wear white (the bridegroom dons a special tunic called a *kittel*) to demonstrate their purity and freedom from other associations.

Once beneath the chuppah, the bride circles the groom seven times, to demonstrate that just as the Lord built the world in seven days, she is building their new life together starting now. Before exchanging rings, the couple recites their vows before a rabbi and drink from a kiddush cup that symbolizes sanctification .

Then the *ketubah,* or marriage contract, is read aloud. This legally binding document is considered the bride's property, and details the groom's responsibilities toward her; in modern Jewish marriages, the ketubah is often written to include equality for the partners. This document is often elaborately decorated and is framed and hung in the new couple's home.

Following the ketubah, the Seven Blessings *(Sheva Brachot)* are recited over a second kiddush cup, and then the cup is wrapped in a cloth and placed on the floor for the groom to shatter with his foot in recognition of the destruction of the Temple of Jerusalem.

PARALLEL HISTORY

Royal Wedding

As Lady Diana Spencer said "I do" to Charles, Prince of Wales on July 21, 1981, millions around the world were watching the ceremony on TV. It was the first time a royal wedding was broadcast, and what a royal wedding it was. The demure Spencer captured imaginations in Great Britain and beyond during the months of her engagement, and the contrast of her youthful beauty (in billowing satin gown) against the stately pomp made this Westminster Abbey event unforgettable. Even after the marriage ended in 1996, Princess Diana (the title she was officially given on her divorce) remained popular and beloved. When she was killed in an auto accident on August 31, 1997, the whole world mourned.

Honeymoon

TERM DATES TO 1546
QUEEN VICTORIA SPENT HER HONEYMOON
WITH PRINCE ALBERT AT WINDSOR CASTLE

Honeymoons are and always have been about the bride and groom getting away from it all—it's just the reason behind getting away that has changed. In ancient Norse, the *hjunottsmanathr* was a period of time in which the groom took his abducted bride into hiding, ensuring that after a while her family would give up searching for her and the "happy couple" could go and live with his tribe.

Given early wooing techniques, it's understandable that while in hiding the bride and groom each would daily be given a cup of the honey wine known as mead. Thirty days of mead equals "honeymoon." Not quite as romantic as the contemporary practice of taking a long trip to an exotic locale, but definitely purposeful. The more relaxed the new couple became, the more likely they were to conceive, and a pregnancy cemented a union.

After the Renaissance, when both people were a little more sophisticated, postwedding "honeymoon" periods became fashionable as a way to allow the newly married and supposedly chaste bride and groom time to become more intimately acquainted without social obligations. The concept of the honeymoon as a vacation originated in 19th-century Victorian England. Industrial revolution–era advances in transportation made it easier and exciting for newlyweds to board a train or luxury steamer and explore a new locale together. Although the direct translation of the word *honeymoon* in French is *lune de miel*, in France these trips were referred to as *voyages à la façon anglaise* (English-style trips).

As travel methods have multiplied, and especially as air travel has become commonplace, honeymoon trips have multiplied. Fewer modern couples require the kind of reserve and isolation that was once shown to couples on their honeymoon, and so trips may even involve other friends or family, as well as many different kinds of activities, from wine-tasting evenings to sea-kayaking expeditions.

Divorce

FIRST NO-FAULT DIVORCE LAW: 1969, CALIFORNIA
SOME NATIVE AMERCIAN TRIBES' DIVORCE CUSTOM:
LEAVE HUSBAND'S MOCCASINS ON DOORSTEP

The history of divorce, meaning the termination of a marriage prior to the death of either party, is as old as the history of marriage itself. The Mesopotamians had divorces in their society, as did the ancient Greeks. The Greeks required a divorce request to be submitted to a magistrate for approval. In Rome, either the husband or the wife could request a divorce, but dissolved marriages were actually relatively rare. Jewish law includes the right to a *get,* a legally and religiously binding divorce, provisions of which are part of brides' marriage contracts, written into every Hebrew marriage contract, or ketubah.

> **UNCOMMONLY KNOWN . . .**
> **Ketubah and Get** The Jewish marriage contract, the ketubah, is written for the wife's protection and benefit—and that includes divorce, or get. Of course, both the contract and the divorce clause are written for the wife's protection, because in a traditional Jewish marriage, it was assumed that the husband owned everything. Today, ketubahs—and gets—are often written with equality in mind, but they are still just as legally and religiously binding as ever.

This demonstrates an interesting continuity in the divorce timeline: Although many societies and cultures have allowed divorce, most of them have instituted some kind of authority or restrictions over it as well. In other words, dissolving a marriage is seen as a significant matter that requires some oversight.

While many believe that divorce has always been entirely forbidden by the Catholic Church, this is not completely true. Some early Holy Roman Emperors did, in fact, try to make divorce more difficult, but divorce and its twin, annulment, persevered. The resulting church doctrine stated that the sacrament of marriage produced one person from two, and that dissolving that bond was quite serious.

Even as marriage acquired a more civil, legal cast, the grave significance of dissolving the bond remained because divorce was seen as an act working against the public interest. Besides the moral issues involved, divorce was hardest on those with less economic power: the women and children. However, divorce also protected spouses from staying in intolerable situations.

Interestingly enough, the morally rigid Puritans who settled the New World brought with them the more civil and less religious divorce standards of Holland, where they had sought asylum for many years before being granted the right to sail for the Americas. That didn't make divorce common in the United States, but it did make its eventual acceptance interesting: Northern states aligned with the Puritan, Protestant tradition were more likely to allow divorce than southern states aligned with the Anglican, Catholic tradition. For example, South Carolina did not declare divorce legal once and for all until 1949.

Babies

A child's birth is often a moment of great significance for a family, a group, or even a society (think of the French dauphins). From the moment a woman announces her pregnancy, through a safe delivery, she is made much of—then all attention, unsurprisingly, turns to the baby. Although babies are technically just small people, their needs are so distinct and their growth so slow compared with other mammals that adults have developed special literature (fairy tales, nursery rhymes) and signs (pink and blue) related to the period of infancy.

Baby Shower

GUESTS ARE RELATIVES, FRIENDS, AND CO-WORKERS
BABY-THEMED GAMES, FOODS, DECOR, AND GIFTS
USUALLY HELD DURING THE FIRST PREGNANCY

Historians and archaeologists have turned up evidence of celebrations to welcome babies in ancient Egypt and Rome, but it's still unclear whether these were held to celebrate the actual pregnancy (probably after the baby "quickened," or moved, usually during the second trimester), or the birth.

People all over the world at all different times have celebrated the birth of a baby with handmade gifts, both because a new life is cause for joy and because there are specific items a baby needs that a first-time mother probably will not already have: infant-size blankets and hats, diapers, rattles, and feeding utensils. This was especially true in more remote areas, like the American West, where bringing food and necessities to a family with a new baby was seen as a community responsibility.

However, the baby "shower," so called after its bridal equivalent as an event in which a woman would be "showered" with gifts, did not become common until the late 19th century. At that time, it was usually an upper-class tradition held after the baby's birth, to coincide with a christening or baptism. The reason for this was not simply because the family wanted to be sure the baby was healthy, but because most women with enough means went into "confinement" during their last trimester and had not been attending any social events at all.

Baby showers became very popular during the post–World War II baby boom in the United States. The festivities nearly always include cake and silly party games along with presents of baby clothing and gear. Since having the party hosted by a family member might make gifts seem de rigueur, baby showers are usually hosted by a female friend of the expectant mother's. In recent years, showers for

---

UNCOMMONLY KNOWN...

Stork Storks are serious serial monogamists and attentive parents to their storklets, qualities that made them symbols of abundance in ancient times. Storks' fidelity to parenthood, combined with the bird's associations with good fortune, made them a natural choice for Victorian parents looking for a way to explain how babies were made without using any factual language.

couples have become more common as expectant fathers participate more fully in their newborns' births and upbringings.

Passing Out Cigars

USED TO SYMBOLIZE CELEBRATION
FAMOUS CIGAR SMOKERS: WINSTON CHURCHILL,
GEORGE BURNS, GROUCHO MARX

Tobacco is native to the Americas, so passing out cigars at a baby's birth is one tradition that doesn't date back to ancient Rome or medieval Europe. It may derive from the Native American tradition of potlatches in the Pacific Northwest.

The word *potlatch* means "to give away" or "a gift" in Chinook Jargon (a pidgin trade language), and was undertaken by American Northwest Coast Indians, particularly the Kwakiutl. The unique thing about potlatches is that they were both a celebratory occasion and a way to redistribute wealth among tribal members or groups. A family gained status and respect not by the quality or quantity of gifts received, but by the amount of resources given away. This practice might be related to a father's "giving away" cigars, to demonstrate that the new family had abundant resources and the father had status in the community. Most relevant, of course, was the use of tobacco at the ceremony. Tobacco was considered sacred by many Native American tribes. The sharing of it—smoke blown toward the sun in tribute—was a kind of group prayer.

Although the first tobacco plantations were set up in Virginia in 1612, tobacco was smoked only in pipes in the American colonies until Gen. Israel

Putnam brought Havana cigars back to his Connecticut home from Cuba. Before long, cigar factories were set up in the Hartford area, and even today Connecticut continues to make a fair number of high-quality cigar wrapper leaves.

By the mid-1800s the cigar had had become well accepted, and in 1870 it was recorded that one billion cigars were smoked in the U.S. During the Depression in the early 1920s, the total consumption of tobacco fell. Cigar manufacturers promoted their brands with beautifully produced "cigar cards" and boxes, with advertising campaigns encouraging men to pass out cigars for celebrations—like the birth of a baby.

Pink and Blue

THE TERM "PINK" DATES TO 1678
THE TERM "BLUE" DATES TO THE 13TH CENTURY
"BABY BLUE" ONCE SYMBOLIZED GIRLS

Long ago, all babies wore white. While this may have symbolized their purity and innocence, it probably also made for easier laundry days; it's easier to bleach stains out of white garments, and babies do make an awful lot of stains.

When dying and laundry methods got a bit more sophisticated, colors for baby clothes became popular. What were they? Surprisingly, until the 1940s, pink was for boys and blue was for girls. Trendsetters deemed pink a more "decided" color, and therefore most appropriate for boys, while blue was "dainty" and more appropriate for girls.

So how did the opposite become true, since pink is now identified with girls and blue with boys? No one knows for sure. Some historians speculate that the

Nazi use of pink to brand homosexuals led to pink being seen as effeminate. In any case, by the 1950s in America, pink items were for girls and blue items were for boys, and if you weren't sure of a baby's sex, you might buy something in pastel yellow or green.

Of course, this modern choice is supported by modern marketing: There are thousands of items available with this color demarcation by gender, from blankets to sleepers to strollers. But recently researchers discovered that there may in fact be a sex-based color bias that supports feminine pink and masculine blue. British researchers, using a group including people of Chinese ancestry to control for cultural bias, found that women seem to prefer colors on the warm, red end of the spectrum. The scientists believe that women's eyes may be better able to see these colors because they have learned over centuries to spot ripe berries and to identify flushed cheeks as a sign of illness in children.

The latest trend is to dress babies and small children of both sexes in more brightly colored clothing, but blues and greens are still produced more often in boys' styles and reds and purples in girls' styles.

Naming Traditions

NAME: A WORD USED TO REFER TO A PERSON
THE TERM "NAME" DATES TO PRE-12TH CENTURY
"WHAT'S IN A NAME?" –JULIET CAPULET

Globally there are so many different baby-naming traditions that we could devote an entire chapter to them. From the Egyptian *sebooh* ceremony to the

Chinese Red Egg and Ginger celebration, new parents and families regard gathering together and carefully considering an infant's name to be an important way in which to mark a baby's entrance into the world.

The significance attached to names varies throughout cultures. In some societies, such as the Native American Navajo, a name is seen as so powerful that it is never uttered in everyday conversation. Chinese babies are often given "milk names" to ward off evil spirits and misfortune until the child is strong and healthy and given a permanent name. Children in India often have a "family" name used by parents and siblings and a separate, more dignified name for school and outside life.

Protocol for what names can be given varies widely, too. In Spain even today, rules govern which name is given to whom: firstborn daughters are named after the father's mother, firstborn sons are named after the father's father, and so on. French families often use both grandmothers' names for a girl's middle names and both grandfathers' names for a boy's middle names.

Religious tradition also dictates name choices. In Puritan America, names were given to denote virtues: Mercy, Honor, Prudence (interesting that these were usually given to girls). Ashkenazic Jews often name a baby after a deceased relative, bu never a living one. In contrast, Sephardic Jews name babies after their living relatives, but never a deceased one.

The time when a baby receives its name also varies. The Muslim *aqeeqah* takes place seven days after a birth and the Jewish bris and Japanese *osichiya* at eight days, but the Chinese Red Egg and Ginger party is held when the baby is one month old and the Buddhist *namkaran* around three months.

Nursery Rhymes: Little Miss Muffet

A NURSERY IS A ROOM SET ASIDE FOR CHILDREN
THE TERM "NURSERY" DATES TO THE 1300s
MISS MUFFET MAY HAVE SYMBOLIZED MARY STUART

Nursery rhymes are simple: whimsical little stories or nonsense lyrics with rhythm and rhyme. Rhymes, singsong lyrics, and silly sayings have probably been told to children since the inception of spoken language, but the earliest records of nursery rhymes in English date to medieval times. A fuller accounting begins in the 17th century, when people began collecting the rhymes and writing more. During this era, some nursery rhymes, like "Ring around the Rosie" and "Humpty Dumpty," had political symbolism and stories attached to them. The rhymes can be enjoyed by children, but they are also loaded with meaning that adults can understand and appreciate. Given the number of times adults may have had to tell these stories to clamoring children, it is understandable why those rhymes endured.

"Little Miss Muffet," the nursery rhyme that has been linked to the tale of Mary, Queen of Scots, was another tale fraught with political symbolism. By this interpretation, Little Miss Muffet, or Mary Stuart, sits on her tuffet, or throne, and eats her curds and whey before being frightened by a spider, standing for Protestant reformer John Knox, who opposed Queen Mary's Catholicisim.

Most psychologists agree that, regardless of their meaning, nursery rhymes have played, and continue to play, an important role in children's development. Even when the rhymes are about something violent or brutal, they allow children to experience fear and anger in a safe way.

Perhaps that also explains the origin of "La Mère Oie," or "The Goose Mother," depicted as a storytelling angular old woman astride a giant goose. Author Charles Perrault's *Les contes de ma Mère l'Oie,* or *Tales of Mother Goose,* was a collection of stories first published in France in 1697 that included "Beauty and the Beast" and "Cinderella," still well known and beloved today. Despite claims that "Mother Goose" was based on Berthe, the "goose-footed" queen to France's King Richard II, or that she was a 17th-century Boston-area goodwife, experts still maintain that Perrault's "Mother Goose" is the most likely source of the time-honored nursery rhyme teller.

Mother Goose's Melody: or Sonnets from the Cradle was published in England in 1781 and reprinted in the U.S. in 1785.

Patronymics and Matronymics

Once humans began using surnames to differentiate people in related groups, these names took on their own traditions and significance. For example, a family might be known by its trade: "Baker" or "Wheeler." But in some cultures, the last name was formed by taking a father's or mother's name and appending a child's gender to it. In Iceland, a man named Olaf might have a son called Harald; he would be known as Harald Olafsson, and his sister as Sigrid Olafsson. Some families preferred to follow the mother's line; Sigrid Olafsson's children might be called Liv Sigridsdóttir and Leif Sigridsdóttir. In Russia, while surnames nearly always derived from the father's name, they were different for sons and daughters; Ivan's children might be named Mikhail Ivanovich and Anna Ivanovna.

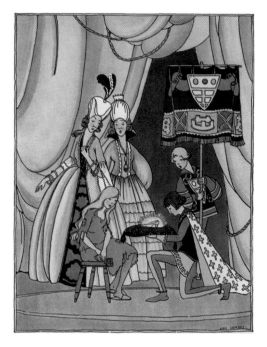

Fairy Tales: Cinderella

THE EARLY CHINESE VERSION HAD A MAGIC FISH
WALT DISNEY'S "CINDERELLA" PREMIERED IN 1950
"CINDERELLA" BALLET BY SERGEY PROKOFIEV (1945)

Some say 340 variations of Cinderella exist; others say 1,500. The point is, the Cinderella story is about hope and dreams: an opressed girl, subjected to harsh treatment from her step-mother and stepsisters. Through her own super-natural powers, she manages to meet, win, and marry the prince of the realm. There are Persian, Egyptian, Armenian, Japanese, Russian, Finnish, and more versions of the classic fairy tale.

The oldest version of the story is from the first century B.C.: The Greek historian Strabo told the story of a Greco-Egyptian slave girl named Rhodopis ("rosy-cheeked") who is forced by fellow servants to wash clothes in a stream while the servants go to the pharaoh's party. An eagle takes Rhodopis's sandal and drops it at the pharaoh's feet. He asks the women to try it on, and when Rhodopis slips her foot into it, he falls in love and marries her.

The ninth-century Chinese tale of "Ye Xian" (Yeh-Shen in the south) is about a girl who befriends a fish. Her stepmother kills the fish friend, but Ye Xian saves its bones, which magically help her prepare and dress for a festival. As she hurries to leave the festival, she loses a golden slipper, which the king ends up with and returns, and then he falls in love with her.

The earliest European tale is "La Gatta Cenerentola," or "The Hearth Cat," which appears in 1634 in the book *Il Pentamerone* written by the Italian fairy-tale collector Giambattista Basile. His tale was the basis of French author Charles Perrault's 1697 "Cendrillon," as well as "Aschenputtel" by the brothers Grimm in the 19th century.

While today most children hearing fairy tales think of the Walt Disney version of Cinderella, golden haired and blue gowned, the truth is that the mistreated waif has a long anthropological history—and use. "Cinderella stories" give people (yes, often women) in straitened circumstances hope that some kind of serendipitous event will change their lives forever and for the better.

Of course, "Cinderella stories" have also inspired women (and men) to debate the fable's moral of patience to the point of passivity. The older ver-sions of Cinderella have given way to a plethora of new versions, including the famous Disney ani-mated movie and novels like Gail Carson Levine's *Ella Enchanted* (now also a movie). There's even a "politically correct" Cinderella, in which Cinder-ella's initially alluring but confining clothes inspire all the women in the kingdom to don comfortable clothes and shoes.

But Cinderella herself isn't the only one who fas-cinates listeners, readers, and viewers. Nearly every character in this classic fairy tale has a certain hold over the popular imagination, from the wicked stepmother to the fairy godmother to the charm-ing prince who takes Cinderella away from her life of drudgery. The longevity of these archetypes is a large part of the story's appeal. Nearly every human being balks at an authority figure, wishes for a mag-ical solution, and hopes for a benefactor who will change our circumstances. In other words, we all want to live happily ever after.

Funerals

Mark Twain said that the only certainties in life were death and taxes, but while some people manage to avoid a year or two of audits, no one avoids the Grim Reaper. It's worth noting that the items and customs in this section are really for the loved ones who are left behind with memories. The fascinating thing about death traditions is that they're probably one of the few things overall that have become less rather than more elaborate over the centuries. But perhaps that's because few people have the means to build and furnish a proper pyramid these days.

Death Traditions

MOST CULTURES RITUALIZE BURIAL
TO DIE: ALSO KNOWN AS CROSS OVER, PASS
AWAY, DEPART, EXPIRE, PASS ON, PERISH

Modern Western death traditions owe something to a number of different cultures. Although it would be too complicated to discuss each one in depth here, there are a few common threads that deserve to be mentioned.

First, upon death, almost every culture has some kind of ritual centering around preparing the corpse for its final journey. In Egypt, as many of us know, the body might undergo the mummification process and then be outfitted with food, pastimes, clothing, comrades, and other items necessary for a trip. Jewish and Muslim protocol calls for nearly immediate burial, while Christian and other religions may take days or weeks for final interment. Though our modern funeral homes and embalming techniques may not resemble earlier methods, they still relate to them, because viewing a corpse is considered to be important for the living friends and family.

Second, the burial or disposal of the body usually involves some kind of ceremony, which can include a service at a place of worship (e.g., a funeral Mass) and a graveside rite, as in the Roman Catholic tradition, or the construction of a special device (such as a burning pyre in India or a ship in Norse countries).

Third, after a body has been buried, interred, or otherwise committed, most cultures include some kind of meal in honor of the deceased. Again, this meal is for the living, and is especially meant to make sure that the grieving people closest to the dead person continue to receive nourishment. The term "funeral baked meats" comes from William Shakespeare's *Hamlet*, referring to the Western custom of providing large portions of food that

UNCOMMONLY KNOWN . . .
Wake Today wakes are usually held in funeral homes the day or evening before a funeral. In some cultures the wake is quite solemn—e.g., the Jewish tradition of sitting shivah—while for the Irish, among others, the wake is a chance to reminisce about the dead person in a loving and lively fashion, complete with stories, songs, and jokes that relate to his or her memory.

can be served for some days following the funeral. Funeral meals can be quite simple affairs (coffee, a buttered roll, and anything chocolate, such as in Belgium) or more elaborate sit-down affairs.

Hearse

VEHICLE USED TO TRANSPORT A BODY TO BURIAL
VENICE'S HEARSES ARE SPECIALIZED GONDOLAS
"HEARSE" ALSO A TRIANGULAR CANDLEHOLDER

Our modern word *hearse,* referring to the vehicle that carries a casket from a funeral home to a cemetery, derives from the Latin *hirspex,* meaning "harrow" or "rake." A harrow was a horse-drawn piece of agricultural equipment that raked up the top layer of soil (unlike the plow, which drew deep furrows).

Of course, many early conveyances for corpses and coffins would have been drawn by horses, but the word (which probably came to us via the French *herce*) came to refer to a framelike structure built around and above the coffin on which mourners could hang epitaphs. This frame resulted in the enclosed fashion we see in modern hearses, but it also echoed another use of the word *harrow:* In Christian tradition, Jesus Christ "harrows" hell, descending to the underworld in order to "rake up" the righteous souls sent there before his death and resurrection. The "herce" eventually became two pieces: Its framework was represented in the vehicle, and its tributary aspect was represented by a candelabra on the bier.

Eventually, the vehicle became a horse-drawn carriage, and the candelabra became a drape of flowers. As automobiles became common, so did motorized hearses. One of the first was used in a 1909 U.S. funeral procession. Hearses evolved to make funerals proceed with what is considered greater solemnity and ease, including features such as curtained windows, motorized lifts for the casket platform, and heavy-duty chassis/suspension.

While many Western hearses are fairly similar, an unusual type can be found in Japan: Some hearse automobiles are outfitted not with a coffin bay but with a miniature, ornate Buddhist temple. In Venice, Italy, some gondolas are outfitted to function as hearses, since there is no other way to transport a coffin through the city's canals.

PARALLEL HISTORY

Viking Funerals

One of the most interesting things about Viking funerals is that most of them did not involve a ship set ablaze and launched on the waters, but instead involved carefully planned ship-shaped burial plots marked off by stones. These tumuli, or burial mounds, can still be seen in Denmark, Sweden, and Norway. The burning of the body, however, usually did take place and was very important in Norse spirituality, because the hotter the flames and the higher the smoke, the nearer the kin believed their beloved came to Valhalla, or heaven. Much of our knowledge of the particulars of a thane's funeral comes from the account of tenth-century traveler and writer Ahmad ibn Fadlan, who detailed the ritualized sacrifice of a thrall (slave) during a chieftain's burial.

The romanticized (and false) notion of a Viking funeral: a blazing boat pushed out to sea.

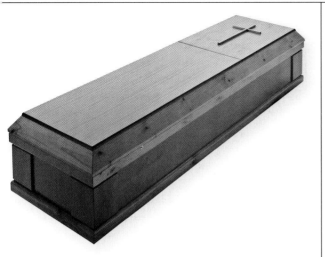

Coffin/Casket

COFFIN: CONTAINER FOR A CORPSE
CASKET: BOX FOR STORING SOMETHING VALUABLE
ALSO USED: URNS, MOLDED CLAY, TURTLE SHELLS

Many modern people use the words *coffin* and *casket* interchangeably, but their meanings are distinct. A coffin is a box that has been constructed for centuries to hold human corpses; it has eight sides and is wider at the shoulder/bust area and narrower toward the feet, an anthropoidal shape. Any box made for a body's burial can be called a coffin. A casket, on the other hand, is actually a box used to store something precious. The term became widely used among 19th-century U.S. funeral homes, in the belief that it had fewer negative connotations.

The earliest coffins may have been woven from reeds or constructed from bark or logs. However, ancient societies and religions did not share the Judeo-Christian imperative of in-ground interment, and many burial containers were meant to stay aboveground, like Roman sarcophagi, which were carved stone containers. Sarcophagi were widely used before the first century B.C. for important persons, including saints, clerics, and monarchs.

While sarcophagi gradually lost popularity due to their expense and the limited crypt and floor space in houses of worship, some families and cultures found that they could have the solemnity of a stone crypt outside by building mausoleums.

Mausoleums take their name from King Mausollos, the Persian satrap of Caria. His burial structure was one of the Seven Wonders of the Ancient World, but today the most famous mausoleum is probably India's Taj Mahal at Agra, which contains the remains of Mumtaz Mahal, the favorite wife of Mogul Emperor Shah Jahan.

Some mausoleums are quite elaborate, containing belowground crypts and fully functional chapels. The pyramids of Egypt are technically mausoleums, too, in that they hold the bodies of the deceased.

However, most families couldn't possibly afford to build a mausoleum of such grand proportions. In modern times, it is common for a church or memorial garden to have an underground "crypt mausoleum" where many interments can be made, not just those of a single family.

The manner of interment, the funeral rites, are strongly tied to culture, religion, and finances. Over the past few hundred years, England's "potter's fields" were where the penniless and destitute were buried in pauper's graves. Plain pine coffins have long been the lowest common denominator, allowing people regardless of circumstance a dignified end. The irony, of course, was that since many could afford a plain wooden box, people found all kinds of ways to make the boxes fancier and more elaborate in order to demonstrate wealth and status or honor the deceased.

Today, from casket materials, to hardware, to luxurious linings, these burial tools can be as customized as any car or house. Most caskets are fairly dignified, but there are quirky ones, too. In Ghana, several artists specialize in painted metal caskets that can be made in the shape of an animal, vehicle, special symbol, or building. An American company sells furniture made out of coffins, including a sofa and a glass-topped coffee table.

As industry developed and the American burial process became more of a business, manufacturers and customers became more and more obsessed with delaying and even stopping the natural decomposition of dead bodies. "Caskets" were made of various metals (ultimately lead) that would not allow vermin and plant growth to penetrate their sides, while special gaskets were created

Burying the Dead

Human beings have buried other humans for thousands and thousands of years. The earliest ritual burial site that historians agree on is in Israel, at Qafzeh. The Skhul Cave remains there date back 130,000 years, and its red clay-touched remains demonstrate the human need for some kind of death acknowledgment. There are many reasons for burial: preventing spread of disease and contamination, showing respect for the dead, providing a last look at a dead loved one for family and friends, honoring religious rituals and cultural practices. In many cultures, clothing, artifacts, equipment, weapons, and even food and drink were buried with a body or bodies in order to assure supplies in the next world. A culture's beliefs about the afterlife have a great deal to do with its burial techniques. A tumulus or burial mound was often used by early, indigenous societies with strong beliefs about the journey required after death. Orthodox Jewish tradition dictates that people be buried as they were born, free of tattoos, piercings, or other bodily modifications. Muslims bury corpses with their head facing the holy city of Mecca. One of the most fascinating things our timeline shows about burial traditions is that many of them coexist or are rediscovered centuries after their first appearance. For example, the Egyptians used sophisticated embalming techniques with highly engineered mausoleums, or pyramids. Viking burials combined cairns with outfitted tombs with pyres. Modern crematoriums combine the idea of a pyre with the closure of a mausoleum. Naturally, attitudes about social rank play into burial practices. From the Egyptian pharaohs to European monarchs to modern billionaires, people in power often seek to mirror their earthly status in their burial places. King Tut had a tomb filled with golden objects, while English royalty prefers to use prime real estate. Beliefs play a strong role in burial of the dead, as do societal needs. In land-strapped Japan, cremation is mandatory. As Westerners have grown more environmentally conscious, they have taken the Japanese attitude into account, as well as considering more eco-friendly options, like biodegradable types of caskets.

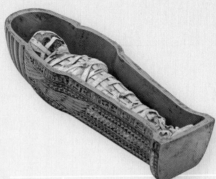

3300 B.C.
Mummy
Ancient Egyptian mummies' levels of mummification differed according to rank and cost. More expensive techniques resulted in a better-looking corpse.

4000 B.C.
Tumulus While today tumuli, or burial mounds, are often seen solitary, many ancient sites had hundreds and even thousands of them clustered in one area.

900
Viking tumulus
Elaborate Viking funerals often involved ritual sacrifice of peasants, given large amounts of strong drink before their "roles." The graves, ship-shaped tumuli, were outlined with stone markers.

that let gases out but no moisture in. Having come to the point where caskets are nearly foolproof, people have realized that they are also environmentally unsound. Allowing bodies to decompose naturally is healthier for the Earth, uses fewer of our limited resources, and is more in tune with modern knowledge about what actually happens to physical bodies after death. In this millennium, a person who opts for interment over cremation might choose to be placed in an "ecopod" made of pressed plant material—and shaped remarkably like an anthropoidal coffin.

350 B.C.
Mausoleum Mausolus, an ancient governor of Caria, was the inspiration for this term. Though in ruins today, his burial structure was so impressive that it was named one of the seven wonders of the ancient world.

A.D. 400
Suttee Through banned on multiple occasions (as recently as 1987), suttee (meaning "good woman" or "chaste wife" in Sanskrit) is the custom of a Hindu widow burning herself, or being burned, on her husband's funeral pyre

1000 B.C.
Urn Funerary or cinerary urns have been used since ancient times as vessels to contain cremains. First made of clay, they can now be found in many different materials.

FIRST CENTURY A.D.
Columbarium The Romans in the first and second centuries, used "columbarium" (which means "dovecote") as a name for a structure containing multiple funerary urns because the stacked urns resembled stacked cages.

1500
Caskets were originally quite plain and simple, but people quickly began to carve, paint, and festoon them according to resources and financial means.

2000
Ecopod Made of biodegradable paper and other fibers, the sleek ecopods can be customized just like caskets, but are designed to be used in "green" cemeteries where decomposition is natural.

All-American

The United States of America is a very young country compared with other nations, yet judging from the number of entries in this section, it has lost no time in cultivating strong, proud national traditions. Today we think of "The Star-Spangled Banner" and the Fourth of July as having very long histories, so it may surprise some readers to learn the amount of time it took for these and other bits of Americana to become official. The most important thing that ties each of these items together is a belief in a government of the people, by the people, and for the people.

Stars & Stripes

THE 13 RED AND WHITE STRIPES REPRESENT
THE 13 ORIGINAL COLONIES
THIS BECAME THE OFFICIAL U.S. FLAG IN ABOUT 1779

Also known as Old Glory, the U.S. flag has been called the Stars and Stripes since 1777 when the miniature British Union Jack in the old flag's upper left corner was replaced with a blue field of 13 white stars (one for each of the Original 13 Colonies). On June 14 of that year, the Marine Committee of the Second Continental Congress passed the resolution stating that "the flag of the United States be made of thirteen stripes, alternate red and white; that the union be thirteen stars, white in a blue field, representing a new Constellation." Why the Marine Committee? Because

flags and "jacks" were primarily used on marine craft for identification, and in an era of naval warfare, this could be crucial to both diplomacy and battle supremacy. The 1777 flag was adopted as the national standard by Congress on June 14 that year. It was updated in 1795 to reflect the addition of Vermont and Kentucy and was the version about which Francis Scott Key wrote.

Folk rumors that Washington designed the flag and Philadelphia's Betsy Ross sewed the prototype are likely untrue. However, it is unclear exactly who designed it. New Jersey's Francis Hopkinson claims to have designed it during his tenure as Chairman of the Continental Navy Board's Middle Department, and even asked for payment: a "Quarter Cask of the Public Wine." However, he was denied because he already was a salaried member of Congress and was not the only person to have submitted a design. We may never know all of the people who did, but we do know that the Stars and Stripes underwent 26 changes as states were admitted to the Union from 1777 to 1960, when Hawaii became the 50th.

UNCOMMONLY KNOWN . . .

Taps Gen. Daniel Butterfield composed the words and music for the bugle call known as "Taps" during the days after the Seven Days' Battle near Harrison's Landing, Virginia, in the American Civil War. Butterfield, dissatisfied with the existing "lights out" call, wrote a simple and informal piece that is now played not just for lights out but for funerals, memorials, and other solemn occasions.

21-Gun Salute

SALUTING BY CANNON BEGAN IN THE 1300s
A 21-GUN SALUTE IS THE HIGHEST NATIONAL HONOR
THREE VOLLEYS ARE FIRED AT FUNERALS

Firing salutes has existed for centuries, and at one time indicated that arms were being rendered harmless by dislodging their ammunition. Similarly, North African tribes would trail their spear points on the ground to demonstrate peaceful intentions.

Ships entering a port would generally discharge seven shots because of that number's auspicious connotations, which included a biblical reference: God rested on the seventh day after creation. This led to 21-gun discharges once ships had a greater supply of powder. While this number varied, in the mid-18th century the British navy's custom of 21-gun salutes was in place, and naturally rubbed off on the new British colonies in America.

Thus, a 21-gun salute grew to be considered a high honor around the world, although the U.S. did not agree on this procedure until August 1875. In 1810, the national salute was defined as being equal to the number of states in the Union, which at that time was 17. The War Department further decreed that the salute be fired by all U.S. military installations at 1 p.m. (later at noon) on Independence Day. Whenever visiting a military installation, the President was to receive the same salute, and in addition to salutes offered to the President and heads of state, the U.S. Navy traditionally held a salute on Washington's Birthday. The 21-gun salute became the standard in a new U.S. Navy regulation issued on May 24, 1842.

The three volleys fired at military funerals come from an old battlefield custom: Two warring sides would cease hostilities to clear away their dead, and the firing of three volleys meant that the dead had been properly cared for and battle could resume.

Presidential Inauguration

NOW TAKES PLACE IN JANUARY FOLLOWING THE
NOVEMBER PRESIDENTIAL ELECTION
FREQUENCY: HELD ONCE EVERY FOUR YEARS

In 1782, at his headquarters in Newburgh, New York, Gen. George Washington refused the offer of a crown and kingship from his officer corps but accepted the office of President. If Washington had been a different man, the United States of America might celebrate coronations. Instead, every four years, a presidential Inauguration follows two and a half months on the heels of a presidential election.

Washington was sworn into office on April 30, 1789. After that, presidential Inaugurations were held every four years on March 4; the date of January 20 wasn't ratified until after the 20th Amendment. In 1937, President Franklin D. Roosevelt was the first to be inaugurated on that day.

On Inauguration Day, both the new President and the Vice President takes the oath of office on the steps of the U.S. Capitol. The Vice President is sworn in first, and precisely at noon, the new President takes his or her oath. Presidents are allowed to swear or affirm, although only President Franklin Pierce ever chose the latter. According to tradition, Washington began the tradition of kissing the Bible after being sworn in, and also added the words "So help me God" to his oath, which some other Presidents have chosen to do.

During years in which January 20 falls on a Sunday, the President-elect takes his oath privately that day, with a public ceremony on the next day. In addition to George Washington, two Presidents, Calvin Coolidge and Lyndon Johnson, have been sworn in away from Washington, D.C.

After the swearing-in ceremony and the Inaugural Address, some Presidents have chosen to walk from the Capitol to the White House, affording spectators a glimpse of the new Chief Executive and his entourage.

UNCOMMONLY KNOWN...

State Funeral State funerals are held for heads of state and people who have attained national significance. In the United States, state funerals are held for Presidents (elect, sitting, and former), as well as anyone deemed of national significance by a sitting President. A sometime component of these solemn but deliberately low-key occasions in the case of a military leader is the procession of the casket by caisson (drawn by six horses of the same color, three of them with mounted riders from the Army's Old Guard) through the nation's capital.

The Pledge of Allegiance

RECITED WHILE STANDING,
WITH RIGHT HAND HELD OVER THE HEART
PHRASE "ONE NATION UNDER GOD" ADDED IN THE 1950S

Before discussing its history, here is the Pledge of Allegiance:

"I pledge allegiance to the flag of the United States of America, and to the republic for which it stands, one nation under God, indivisible, with liberty and justice for all."

According to Title 4, Chapter 1, Section 4, U.S. Code, "It should be recited by standing at attention facing the flag with the right hand over the heart. When not in uniform men should remove any non-religious headdress with their right hand and hold it at the left shoulder, the hand being over the heart. Persons in uniform should remain silent, face the flag, and render the military salute."

Here is the first, original, version of the Pledge of Allegiance:

"I pledge allegiance to my Flag and the Republic for which it stands, one nation, indivisible, with liberty and justice for all."

How did "one nation under God" get in there?

The answer includes more than a bit of controversy, and it will probably surprise many U.S. citizens to realize that the Pledge, as we refer to it informally, has nothing to do with the Declaration of Independence, the Constitution of the United States of America, or even any of the Founding Fathers. This pledge was penned in 1892 by Francis Bellamy, a Christian Socialist, and published in a children's magazine in celebration of the 400th anniversary of Christopher Columbus's discovery of America.

Interestingly, at one time the Pledge of Allegiance was recited partially with right arm extended and pointing toward the flag, but after the outstretched arm became identified with Nazism and fascism after World War II, the entire Pledge was recited with the right hand placed over the heart.

In the 1950s a Roman Catholic organization successfully lobbied to have the words "under God" added to the Pledge of Allegiance. At the time, President Eisenhower thanked the group for this, but if he had lived to hear the ensuing controversies from different secular and religious groups, he might have rethought the decision. Today some people believe that students should recite the Pledge in its entirety, while others believe students should be able to "opt out" of making a pledge they don't agree with; neither side has finished arguing about this.

For example, adherents to the Jehova's Witness religion do not say the pledge because they believe that doing so is a type of worship prohibited by their tenets.

"The Star-Spangled Banner"/ National Anthem

WRITTEN BY FRANCIS SCOTT KEY,
SEPTEMBER 14, 1814, IN BALTIMORE, MARYLAND
FIRST TITLE: "DEFENCE OF FORT M'HENRY"

Today we are accustomed to identifying the words "Oh, say can you see / By the dawn's early light" as the national anthem of the United States of America. However, even though the song's lyrics were penned in 1812, it didn't gain that designation until 1931.

During the War of 1812, a young Washington lawyer named Francis Scott Key accompanied John Skinner to the British fleet in Chesapeake Bay. It was 1814, and they were trying to get their friend Dr. William Beanes released from British custody. Beanes had been captured by the British following the Battle of Bladensburg and the burning of Washington, D.C. Beanes had treated several injured British seamen, and because of this, the British commander agreed to let him go—but only after a planned attack on Fort McHenry, in Baltimore's harbor, had been carried out. He insisted on keeping Key and Skinner in custody overnight while the attack was waged.

The fort was, of course, flying the U.S. flag, and Key watched it until it became too dark, knowing that if the flag came down, the fort would have surrendered.

At dawn, when he saw the flag still flying, Francis Scott Key was inspired to write a poem. All he had was the back of an envelope, and he scribbled down "Defence of Fort M'Henry," which was first circulated as a handbill, and then published on September 20, 1814, in a Baltimore newspaper.

It became popular and was sung to the tune "To Anacreon in Heaven," a popular English song. "The Star-Spangled Banner" was regarded as the national anthem of the United States by the Army and the Navy, but it was not official until 1916, when President Woodrow Wilson issued an executive order. In 1931 an act of Congress confirmed it.

"The Star-Spangled Banner" is notoriously difficult to sing, even for professionals, let alone ordinary citizens. To promote better knowledge of the song, The National Anthem Project was begun in 2005 and celebrates National Anthem Project Day each September 14 on the National Mall in Washington, D.C. The project's supporters claim it will help music education in schools.

Statue of Liberty

SCULPTOR: FRÉDÉRIC-AUGUSTE BARTHOLDI
DEDICATED ON OCTOBER 28, 1886
SITS ON 12-ACRE LIBERTY ISLAND

A joint effort between the U.S. and France, the massive copper Statue of Liberty was commissioned in 1876. Sculptor Frédéric-Auguste Bartholdi was supposed to

---

PARALLEL HISTORY

Ellis Island

Although much of American history lessons focus on the nation's political founding, one of the most powerful forces in the United States of America from its beginnings has been immigration. The indigenous American Indians were joined by European explorers, who were joined by more European settlers, and the chain of immigrants coming to the country's shores has not stopped. However, during the 19th and early 20th centuries, huge waves of immigrants from Ireland, Italy, and eastern Europe poured into New York Harbor, escaping poverty, famine, political oppression, and religious persecution. Most of these people, exhausted and often ill from long ocean passages and unable to speak fluent English, were herded through immigration processing at Ellis Island in New York Harbor, approximately 12 million in all until the center was closed in 1954. Today Ellis Island has become a symbol of opportunity to the Americans whose ancestors greeted it as the first stop en route to a new life.

---

complete it in time to celebrate the centennial of the American Declaration of Independence, but both countries had trouble with financing, and Bartholdi had trouble with engineering.

The first problem was overcome through various fund-raising efforts on both sides of the Atlantic, with the French funding the statue, and the Americans the pedestal. For the second problem, the engineering issue, Bartholdi had to appeal to Alexandre Gustave Eiffel, the designer of the Eiffel Tower. Eiffel lent his skill to the project, designing a supporting framework weighing 120 tons. The statue itself was completed in France in 1884 and transported to New York Harbor in 1885 in 350 individual pieces packed in 214 crates. There it waited for the pedestal to be built. The pedestal was finally finished in April 1886, allowing erection of the finished work. Four months later, on October 28, 1886, the Statue of Liberty was dedicated.

Originally, the Statue of Liberty was set inside the 1812-era Fort Wood on Bedloe's Island. After 1901, the War Department gained responsibility for the fort and its famous "resident," and both became a national monument in 1924. The Statue of Liberty's care was once again transferred, this time to the National Park Service, in 1933, and in

1956, the entire island was renamed Liberty Island. On May 11, 1965, Ellis Island was also transferred to the National Park Service and became part of the Statue of Liberty National Monument. In 1984, at the start of the statue's restoration, the United Nations designated the Statue of Liberty as a World Heritage site.

Unknown Soldier

HOLDS UNKOWN SOLDIERS' REMAINS FROM
WORLD WAR I, WORLD WAR II, KOREAN WAR
SOLDIERS GUARD THE GRAVES 24 HOURS A DAY

After World War I, in which so many countries lost so many service members, many nations began honoring their war dead by dedicating a tomb to an "unknown." In an era before forensic science made it possible to identify corpses through DNA or other types of evidence, it was common for some bodies to remain unidentifiable, and this type of monument acknowledged that everyone's contribution was honored—not simply those who could be properly named.

On March 4, 1921, the U.S. Congress approved the burial of an unidentified American soldier from World War I in the plaza of the new Memorial Amphitheater in Arlington National Cemetery. The tomb's design was selected in a competition won by architect Lorimer Rich. The flat-faced white marble sarcophagus, carved from stone quarried in Marble, Colorado, includes neoclassical figures representing Peace, Victory, and

> **UNCOMMONLY KNOWN ...**
>
> **GI Joe** The GI Joe action-figure doll has delighted many little boys since its first appearance in the 1960s. The doll is based on the American GI, or "general infantry-man," an Army designation that was slangily known as a grunt. GIs were commonly the soldiers who had the hardest and most dangerous duty, and after the Allied victory of World War II, famously known as the soldiers who helped secure that victory.

Valor, as well as six wreaths representing the major battles of World War I: Ardennes, Belleau Wood, Chateau Thierry, Meuse-Argonne, Oisiu-Eiseu, and Somme. The western panel, which faces the cemetery, is inscribed with the words: "Here Rests in Honored Glory, An American Soldier Known But to God."

The sarcophagus was placed above the grave of the Unknown Soldier of World War I. West of the World War I Unknown are the crypts of unknowns from World War II (north) and Korea (south). Sparkling white marble slabs lie on the plaza to mark these graves. Between the two lies a crypt that once contained an unknown from Vietnam. His remains were identified in 1998 as 1st Lt. Michael Blassie and removed.

The Tomb of the Unknowns, also known as the Tomb of the Unknown Soldier, has no official name, but it does have an official guard. Members of the U.S. Army's Old Guard, a special company within the Third Infantry Regiment, watch over the monument 24 hours a day, every day of the year, and have done so since 1937, even during blizzards and hurricanes. The guard is changed in an elaborate and careful ceremony once a day and is considered by the soldiers who are part of it to be the highest honor they are given in the military.

While on his silent duty, an Old Guard sentinel crosses a 63-foot rubber-surfaced walkway in exactly 21 steps. Facing the Tomb for 21 seconds, he turns again, pauses a further 21 seconds, then retraces his steps. The sentinel always bears his weapon away from the Tomb, but if a person should attempt to intrude on the Tomb's restricted area, the sentinel will halt, bring his rifle to port arms, and break silence.

Girl Scouts and Boy Scouts

LORD BADEN-POWELL (BOY SCOUTS) | 1908
JULIETTE GORDON LOW (GIRL SCOUTS) | MARCH 12, 1912
SCOUT MOTTO: "BE PREPARED"

The Boy Scout organization was founded in 1908 by Lord Robert Baden-Powell of England and quickly grew into a worldwide phenomenon. By 1910, 21 countries including the United States had Boy Scouts organizations of their own.

The burgeoning movement soon recognized the need for more leaders and training, as well as for groups for younger boys. However, one of the most significant new parts of the Scouts family was the creation of a similar organization for girls. Lord Baden-Powell and his sister Agnes Baden-Powell began the Girl Guides in 1910.

Two years later, in 1912, Lord Baden-Powell took a cruise to the West Indies and met a high-spirited and adventurous woman named Olave. Despite the 32-year age difference, they soon married. Lady Olave Baden-Powell dedicated herself to the development of the scouting movement as Chief Guide of the Girl Guides in the U.K. Meanwhile, in the U.S., girls could only watch their brothers enviously.

That all changed as the result of the fiery determination of an American woman named Juliette Gordon Low. An exceptionally talented, educated, and well-traveled woman, she was living in England with her British husband, William, when the couple separated. He died shortly thereafter, and Gordon Low began looking for a meaningful endeavor to which she could devote her energy. When she met Baden-Powell, she was inspired to take his scouting idea back home to the girls of Savannah, Georgia. She made a now historic call to a cousin to tell her, "I've got something for the girls of Savannah, and all of America, and all the world, and we're going to start it tonight!"

Gordon Low held the first Girl Scout meeting in America on March 12, 1912. Girl Scouting retained its historic ties to Girl Guides through the World Association of Girl Guides and Girl Scouts. There are now four world centers where Guides and Scouts travel to participate in international exchange and education programs.

While Gordon Low was and is considered the undisputed founder of Girl Scouts in the U.S., Boy Scouts in the U.S. had several early champions, at least two of whom battled for control over the young organization. Ernest Thompson Seton, who had founded a 1901 boys' outfit called the Woodcraft Indians, merged his group with the Boy Scouts in 1910 and became the Boy Scouts of America's first Chief Scout (1910-15). His wrangles with

PARALLEL HISTORY

Lord Baden-Powell and the Scouts

We wouldn't have today's Scouts movement without British imperialism. Although Great Britain committed many sins in the name of colonialism, its stiff-upper-lip upper class did develop quite a talent for traveling around the globe and making do with whatever they had at their disposal while "abroad." One of the model examples of can-do fortitude was Robert Stephenson Smyth Baden-Powell, the first Baron of Gilwell, a lieutenant general in the British Army who served for 34 years. Lord Baden-Powell (as he was known) wrote several military reconnaissance books that became popular with boys, and used his experience to write 1908's "Scouting for Boys." Its success led to Baden-Powell's trying out his ideas about training youths at a camp—and the Scouts were born.

1911-elected Chief Scout Executive James West resulted in the ousting of Seton in 1915. However, Seton's contribution to the early Boy Scouts has not been forgotten. In 1930, the first Cub packs were allowed to register with the Boy Scouts, providing the opportunity for younger boys to join.

State Fair

ORIGINALLY FOR SELLING LIVESTOCK,
NOW INCLUDES SHOWS, GAMES, COMPETITIONS
FIRST STATE FAIR: NEW YORK, 1841

The Latin *feria*, which is still used to mean "fair" in some Romance languages, also means "holy day." Whenever there were large groups of people gathered together, there was usually some kind of worship involved.

The early church realized this and began sponsoring fairs on feast days that provided revenue to the church. Church fairs grew into town fairs, and these grew into regional fair, too. Countries all over the world have regional fairs, but the American state fair is singular because of the number of states in the U.S., as well as the folksy focus of most state fair celebrations.

The precursor of all U.S. state fairs is the 1765 Windsor, Nova Scotia, agricultural exhibition, still in operation today. Over the border, state fairs owe their start to a New England farmer and woolen mill owner named Elkanah Watson. In 1807, Watson, who was looking to attract more business, brought

---

UNCOMMONLY KNOWN . . .

4-H At state and county fairs all over the country, 4-H youth, ages 9 to 19, compete for prizes in categories ranging from livestock to crop growing to sewing and baking. The symbol of the U.S. Department of Agriculture's 4-H program for youth—created in the early 1900s—is a four-leaf clover with an "H" on each leaf. They stand for Head, Heart, Hands, and Health and were meant to remind its members of the important qualities necessary for farm life. The organization now includes nonfarming children as well, encouraging development of leadership and good citizenship in "learn by doing" programs.

---

some of his merino sheep to stand beneath an elm in the public square of Pittsfield, Massachusetts. He clanged an old ship's bell with a piece of iron, hoping to encourage the locals to raise the same kind of sheep. A few years later, Watson held a "Berkshire Cattle Show" and received entries including 386 sheep, 109 oxen, 9 cows, 7 folds, 3 heifers, 2 calves, and 1 boar.

Watson's open-air technique led to others' trying his approach, and soon town and county "fairs" that mostly dealt with selling and trading and evaluating livestock were opening around the country. Today there are rodeos and livestock shows and auctions separate from state fairs, but livestock exhibitions still play an important role in most state fairs.

New York State opened the first state fair in Syracuse in 1841. Michigan followed suit in 1849, and the briefest perusal of history pages for individual state fairs will show that they just kept opening through the late 19th century and on into the early 20th. Some states (Washington, Texas, Oklahoma, Michigan, for instance) are either so large or have such diverse agricultural and farming communities that they have two or three state fairs.

A typical state fair will receive several hundred thousand visitors, although very large fairs, like the State Fair of Texas, receive up to three million. They come to see technology (usually, but not limited to, agricultural equipment), livestock displays, live entertainment, cooking and handicraft contests, fairway games, carnival rides, and food vendors. Displays from 4-H clubs are always popular, as are counting the number of food items sold on a stick.

Symbols & Markings

We open this chapter optimistically, with the thumbs-up. The gesture, from fourth century B.C. Rome, said yes to life in a very literal way back then. Many symbols and signs have, since antiquity, and even prehistory, been a way for people to show a positive outlook, despite the dangers, real and imagined, that confronted them. Think of the peace sign, crossing the fingers, knocking on wood—these and other symbols and practices express the human capacity for hope. Likewise, when we applaud, salute, or give red roses, we, like those before us, are giving the thumbs-up sign in a tangible way. We approve, and so we say yes, well done despite the obstacles. Then there are symbols that express our concerns about the dangers confronting us. The skull and crossbones, the broken mirror, the evil eye—how these symbols came about makes for a fascinating jaunt through man's perception of himself in his world. The skull and crossbones, for example, arose during the Black Death of the 14th century; it was intended to remind people both of their spiritual duty and their need to enjoy life. Divided into five sections, this chapter takes a look at gestures, signs, superstitions, tributes, and body markings. Some of these are viewed today as simply for fun, or self-expression. Their purposes long ago were often deadly serious. Tattoos, for instance, were meant to ward off evil, bring fertility, or designate slaves; crossing fingers was a pledge between two people, more binding than a contract because it invoked magical powers. Whether you read the entries in order or skip about, you will certainly pick up any number of great cocktail party tidbits and factoids, and you will begin to make your own connections between our times and the past.

Gestures

Body language, particularly that involving the hands, has in the course of human history evolved into a rich vocabulary, expressing in ways both subtle and blatant things that verbal language cannot. Anyone who has ever tried to get along in a country where the tongue is not one's own knows how useful gestures can be. Sign language may in fact be older than verbal language—it is no coincidence that apes have been taught hundreds of communication gestures. In this section we examine a few of the more well-known gestures, varying in age from the prehistoric shoulder shrug to the high five.

Thumbs-up

INDICATES: APPROVAL OR "GOOD WORK!"
THUMBS DOWN IN ANCIENT ROME MAY HAVE MEANT
"SWORDS DOWN," THUS SPARING THE LIFE OF THE LOSER

You like what your friend is wearing; your office mate is going to ask for a raise; you want to wish your son good luck in the 50-yard freestyle. You raise your thumb. If you really want to show enthusiasm, you raise two. The thumbs-up gesture is prevalent in American culture, usually meaning something as vaguely benign as "hello" or "have a good day."

The gesture most likely dates back to Etruscan gladiatorial contests from the fourth century B.C.

Spectators shouted and extended their thumbs down when they wanted the defeated warrior to be executed. The Latin phrase meaning "thumbs turned down" refers to this ancient blood sport and its tragic end. If, on the other hand, the gladiator fought well and bravely, the spectators might raise their thumbs, indicating they wished the winner to spare his life.

But why use the thumb instead of another digit? Historians from the time of Julius Caesar explained that infants learn to open their hands, extending their thumbs out, while the infirm lose mobility in their digits, especially their thumbs.

Another theory has it that the outward-extended thumb stood for life, while the thumbs down signaled death. That idea seems to have originated from a painting by 19th-century French artist Jean-Léon Gérôme. An alternative supposition is that it

PARALLEL HISTORY

White Flag of Surrender

As a symbol for truce, cease-fire, or surrender, the white flag goes back at least to the Roman Empire, when historian Cornelius Tacitus referred to such a device in A.D. 109. The Chinese of the Han dynasty were using white flags around the same time. In American history, perhaps the most famous white flag was ordered raised by Lord Cornwallis after the long siege at Yorktown, Virginia; a drummer boy tapped out a request for parley. The patriots were ecstatic, for they knew the symbol meant the British Army was surrendering. The Geneva Convention now recognizes the use of a white flag.

actually means "thumbs turned," not thumbs down. The turned thumb (in what way is unclear) meant the gladiator should die; a "thumb in front," signaled he should live.

High Five

GESTURE OF CAMARADERIE, CONGRATULATIONS
MORE ELABORATE HAND-SLAPPING ROUTINES CAN
SIGNIFY MEMBERSHIP IN A SOCIAL GROUP OR TEAM

An office: Two men in suits approach each other, raise their right palms, slap hands, then continue on their separate ways. Decorum is maintained. The scenario owes its origins to the original high five, the wildly exuberant palm-to-palm slap by athletes after a touchdown, an important basket, or just about any big score.

More than one person is credited with the first high five. The Louisville Cardinals basketball team, winners of the 1980 NCAA championship, had two players, Derek Smith and Darrell Griffith, who at least made the gesture a part of popular culture. The latter, also known as Dr. Dunk or Dr. Dunkenstein, was, at six feet four, one of the outstanding dunkers of all time. An earlier episode has Glenn Burke of the Los Angeles Dodgers running out to high-five Dusty Baker in 1977 after a Baker home run.

The gesture appears to have grown out of a hand-slapping greeting in black urban hip culture. The

recipient offers an open palm and says "gimme five" (meaning five digits) or "gimme some skin." Numerous variations of the high five have come about. The low five is a back-to-back palm-slapping gesture, arms extended downward. People across a room or open space can mime a high five to each other, the gesture sometimes referred to as an "air five." A simple congratulation or expression of enthusiasm is often rendered by touching palms or fists. And athletes sometimes celebrate with a ritual leap and midair chest-to-chest bump, a maneuver that requires balletic timing and the teammates' highly intuitive sense of each other's intentions.

Crossing Your Fingers

GESTURE OF GOOD LUCK OR SUPERSTITION
TYPICALLY DONE IN PRIVATE OR BEHIND THE BACK
ALSO SPOKEN: "I'LL CROSS MY FINGERS FOR YOU"

Who hasn't at some point crossed her fingers for good luck? At sports events, before tests and job interviews, even for someone's health, the crossing of fingers is probably, after praying, the most widely used superstitious gesture in the Western world. It's so easy to do, and it can't hurt. Even a simple "I'll keep my fingers crossed for you" will suffice, whether you actually do it or not.

The practice comes from western Europe, during the days of paganism. Long before Christianity, the cross was a powerful symbol, signifying perfect unity; it was thought that good spirits resided at the intersection of the cross. Early Europeans believed that a wish made in the presence of a cross was secured at that intersection until the wish came true. The original crossing of fingers was a gesture made by not one, but two people—they formed the cross by placing their index fingers together at right angles. In this way, the wish for luck was a kind of incantatory spell between them, where one would wish for some advantageous outcome for the other person.

Over time people realized they could get similar benefits by crossing their own fingers, one index finger over the other at the second knuckle. A further modification resulted in what we use today—the middle finger crossing over the index finger to form a St. Andrew's cross. For something really important people cross the fingers of both hands. Crossed fingers have been used in history not only for luck but to avoid bad luck, or to stop what one says from coming true. At some point, the gesture became appropriated by children as a way of blamelessly telling a lie. Hiding the crossed fingers behind one's back was a way of protecting the fibber from the evil consequences of fibbing. Young people today sometimes hook fingers in order to express agreement or nonverbally seal a deal—the practice comes from the earliest finger crossing.

UNCOMMONLY KNOWN ...

V for Victory Winston Churchill is credited with popularizing this two-finger sign of courage during World War II. He may have gotten it from a Belgian radio announcer who frequently played the opening notes of Beethoven's Fifth Symphony, which mimics the Morse code for the letter V. President George H. W. Bush flashed the V one morning while jogging and told reporters it was "Julius Caesar ordering five beers."

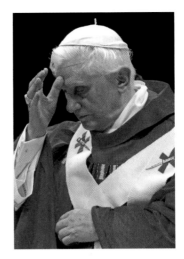

Crossing Your Heart

RELIGIOUS-TURNED-CASUAL GESTURE
SIGN OF THE CROSS: BLESSINGS, LUCK, PROTECTION
"CROSS MY HEART": SWEAR TO TELL THE TRUTH

A child says, "Cross my heart and hope to die." She might even add, "stick a needle in my eye." She has just told a story that's hard to swallow; the cross-my-heart oath underscores her sincerity by expressing her willingness to undergo pain or even death if she is not telling the truth.

The expression stems from a Christian ritual known as the sign of the cross. Dating from at least the 13th century, the ritual involves bringing the thumb, forefinger, and middle finger together—symbolizing the holy trinity. Adherents then touch their forehead, sternum, one shoulder, and the other shoulder, indicating the four points of the cross, or crucifix. Western Christians now go from left shoulder to right, while Eastern Christians go from right shoulder to left. As each point is touched, the worshipper may say, "In the name of the Father, and of the Son, and of the Holy Ghost, Amen," or the equivalent incantation in Latin.

The sign of the cross is now made most commonly by Catholics and Orthodox Christians. It is performed when entering a church, before a prayer, when venerating icons, before taking Communion, and at other times to profess Christian faith or to invoke divine blessing or protection—for example, upon exposure to blasphemy. Some people cross their heart for luck at simple tasks.

So when a child makes an X over her chest and says, "Cross my heart," she is making a sacred vow in imitation of Christian ritual.

The practice of placing the hand or a hat over the heart during the Pledge of Allegiance and the national anthem was adopted into the Flag Code signed by President Franklin D. Roosevelt in 1942.

Shrugging the Shoulders

GESTURE INHERITED FROM OUR MAMMALIAN ANCESTORS, WHO LIFTED THE SHOULDERS AND LOWERED THE HEAD IN A SIGN OF SUBMISSION

One of the most instinctive and universal of human gestures—shrugging the shoulders while raising the palms—may also be one of the oldest. We use the shrug in a number of different situations. It generally says, "I don't know." But add raised eyebrows and pushed-out lips and the gesture can mean, "I'll think about it" or "Why don't you think about it?" In other contexts a simple shrug means "Whatever" or "I don't really care."

Gestures have always been a part of human communication, and though they have been analyzed scientifically since the early 1900s, they are still imprecisely understood. A recent article links the palms-up shoulder shrug with similar gesturing among chimpanzees that means, broadly, "Give

me something." It could be food or help. The stance seems generally to indicate helplessness and often goes along with an apology or alibi: So I got lost and I'm late (shoulder shrug, raised palms)—I'm sorry. Gimme a break.

Anthropologist David Givens calls this a "gestural by-product" passed down through vertebrates for hundreds of millions of years. Ancient reptiles pushed their spines lower to the ground to indicate submission. Similarly, when primates raise their shoulders, they effectively lower their heads into a protective, unthreatening position. By contrast, primates display dominance by straightening the spine, which lifts the head and thrusts the chest out; the palms rotate downward.

By the Renaissance, authors on manners were critical of overusing gestures. A 1540 book cautioned English readers not to shrug "as we see in many Italians." Yet the shoulder shrug, with its rich ambiguity of meaning, remains popular with people as divergent as New York cabbies and French politicians.

Hands Joined in Prayer

OTHER WAYS TO PRAY:
ARMS RAISED TO SKY, KNEELING WITH HEAD BOWED, HOLDING HANDS WITH OTHERS, LYING FACEDOWN

Early Hebrew and Christian worshippers typically opened their arms out as if imploring heaven. The hands-held-together posture came about later and not, as often claimed, in imitation of a church steeple. The joining of hands in prayer is not referred to in the Bible, and in fact did not appear in the Christian Church until the ninth century. The gesture seems to be in imitation of the bound hands of prisoners. By joining the hands together as if they were tied or shackled, a worshipper showed his or her humility and submission to God's will.

Actual binding of the hands as a symbol of subjugation and servitude can be traced back to an early Germanic tribe. According to Roman historian Tacitus (circa 56-circa 120), people were allowed into a sacred grove only after being bound "as a sign of dependence and as a public homage to the power of the gods." Greeks and Romans likewise ceremonially bound their hands as a symbolic way of binding the devil.

OK Sign

IN SCUBA DIVING, THE GESTURE
INDICATES "I'M ALL RIGHT!"–NOT TO BE CONFUSED
WITH THUMBS-UP, WHICH INDICATES "ASCEND"

The "OK" sign is a very common gesture, made with thumb and index finger forming a ring and the other three fingers extended upward. It is used in the United States

to signal that "everything is fine." However, the gesture has long been known as the "OK sign," and so a brief explanation of the term "OK" is in order.

It's difficult to discern the origins of the word "Okay." According to various people at various times, it might have entered American English from the Choctaw *okeh* (meaning "It is so"), the West African Wolof *waw-kay* (meaning "I agree"), or a newspaperman's abbreviation of the phrase "oll korrect" (which might have been misspelled deliberately so that copy editors would know to remove it before typesetting).

However, the most researched and well-supported story involves the "oll korrect" anecdote. Historian Allen Walker Read explained in his early 1960s work that in mid-19th-century Boston there was a fad for abbreviations like OFM ("our first men," or leading citizens), and SP ("small potatoes"). Around 1839, OK for "oll korrect" was first used, but it became widespread after Martin van Buren's supporters appropriated OK to show approval of their candidate, who handily came from Old Kinderhook, New York. Opponents used it sarcastically: "Out off Kash, Out of Kredit, and Out of Klothes." As the campaign progressed, the media used even sillier combinations ("Orfully Konfused"), and after this campaign, the term was firmly rooted in popular speech.

Signs

Since prehistoric people first painted cave walls, signs have been used to condense meaning into a few lines or squiggles. While the ancients had a wide palette of symbols associated with magic and religion, many current signs are employed in science, the economy, and other practical fields. The skull and crossbones has a medieval origin; today it is useful on bottle labels. More recently, the peace symbol originated in the late 1950s. Some signs are so pervasive and important—e.g., traffic lights—that we have recruited them into spoken language. We "green-light" a proposal or project we like.

Skull and Crossbones

LOGO FOR GROUPS RANGING FROM ATHLETIC TEAMS TO BANDS TO MARVEL COMICS' "THE PUNISHER"
SKULL AND BONES: SECRET SOCIETY, YALE UNIVERSITY

As a modern symbol, the skull atop a pair of crossed bones warns us against poisons, explosives, and other dangers. The labeling of harmful or deadly substances with a skull and crossbones dates to around the mid-19th century.

The symbol itself seems to go back only as far as the 14th century. According to 19th-century British author Ebenezer Brewer, although the ancient Egyptians displayed a skeleton at banquets as a reminder of death, the skull and crossbones wasn't used as a symbol until much later. During the mid-1300s, the Black Death, or bubonic plague, swept across Europe, wiping out one-fourth of its population. It was not uncommon then to see skeletons lying in streets or in public spaces, awaiting burial. Skulls began to appear in artwork and as decorative motifs. The meaning of the death's-

PARALLEL HISTORY

Parallel History: Jolly Roger

Contrary to popular belief, "Jolly Roger" isn't the name of the skull pictured on the most famous pirate ship flag. It's the name of the kind of flag, which we know since two pirates (Bartholomew Roberts and Francis Sprigg) were using the term "jolly roger" for their flags in 1721 and 1723, and their flags bore neither skull nor crossbones. Variations showed possible foes that a pirate vessel adhered to no country's rules, and might do anything in a fight or to gain plunder. By the time Edward England, John Taylor, Sam Bellamy, and John Martel flew the black flag emblazoned with skull and crossbones, the Jolly Roger had become an icon.

Marginally successful pirate Jack Rackham (aka Calico Jack) flew this Jolly Roger.

head, or memento mori (reminder of death), was twofold. It reminded people of their mortality and thus the need to be prepared should they suddenly go to meet their maker, but it could also—especially when adorning a drinking cup or pub—express the idea that since life is short, one had best make the most of it. In other words, eat, drink, and be merry, for tomorrow we die.

The skull also symbolized man's corruptible nature—the temptations of the flesh compared with loftier concerns of the soul. The symbol was intended as a spur to prayer, repentance, and renunciation of worldly things. It continued to appear in Renaissance and Baroque art as a more general symbol of time, eternity, and wisdom. And just as Hamlet waxes philosophical while holding the skull of the jester Yorick (in the 1601 Shakespeare play), so it was not uncommon for scholars and other professionals to keep a skull on their desk as a philosophical memento mori. The skull, with or without the accompanying bones, was an immediate evocation of our own frailty—all of us will soon become nothing but the bones supporting us—and of Christ's promise of eternal life—his Crucifixion took place at Golgotha, from the Hebrew word for "skull."

Peace Symbol

CREATOR: GERALD HOLTOM
APRIL 4, 1958 | BAN THE BOMB MOVEMENT
MARCH FROM LONDON TO ALDERMASTON

A raised-arm cross, turned upside-down and framed within a circle: The peace symbol would seem to have emerged

spontaneously with hippies in the 1960s. The truth is that it was deliberately designed in 1958 for use in a protest march.

The creator was a London textile designer named Gerald Holtom. The march, supporting the Ban the Bomb movement, was sponsored by a group of citizens called the Direct Action Committee Against Nuclear War. Hundreds traversed the 52-mile passage from London to Aldermaston, a town where nuclear weapons were made. Holtom had been a conscientious objector during World War II, so he eagerly took it upon himself to come up with a symbol the marchers could use in the antinuke protest. His idea was brilliantly simple: Combine the semaphore signals (an alphabet signaling system using two flags) for the letters *N* (nuclear) and *D* (disarmament). The *N* semaphore figure has the arms angled down; the *D* has one arm straight up, the other straight down. The result suggested another meaning to Holtom—a person in despair, his arms stretched downward.

The symbol made its first public appearance on April 4, at the start of the four-day march. Newspaper pictures sent the image around the world. The first appearance in the U.S. was on April 14, 1958, when a photo of the marchers was published in *Life*. One of the marchers, a follower of Martin Luther King, Jr., introduced the symbol to America's civil rights movement. When the Vietnam War broke out in the 1960s, protesters took up the symbol. It quickly became a countercultural icon. Critics of the peace movement claimed it was an anti-Christian emblem, suggesting an inverted broken cross; others decried it as the footprint of a chicken. Yet the versatile peace symbol has endured for half a century and seems unlikely to disappear anytime soon.

Traffic Light

GARRETT MORGAN
NOV. 20, 1923 | U.S. PATENT NO. 1,475,024
PATENT "TRAFFIC SIGNAL"

The early Romans introduced a number of traffic controls—one-way streets, parking laws, road crossings, and possibly traffic circles. The first actual traffic signal was installed on a 22-foot-high pole in London's Parliament Square in 1868. It was a manually operated signal with red and green lanterns; shortly after its installation it exploded, injuring the policeman operator.

After the introduction of the automobile at the turn of the century, traffic in cities began growing rapidly. Cars, horse-drawn wagons, bicycles, and pedestrians all had to figure out how to safely cross intersections at the same time. Accidents were common. After witnessing one such accident,

---

PARALLEL HISTORY

Tinker Case

In 1965 Mary Beth Tinker, an eighth grader in Des Moines, Iowa, decided with her brother and a friend to wear a black armband decorated with a white peace symbol. They were wearing them, they said, not to protest the Vietnam War but to express their sorrow for the war's death toll. School administrators not only banned the symbols, they suspended the students wearing them. The two families filed suit. Though lower courts ruled against them, the U.S. Supreme Court decided in their favor. "It can hardly be argued," said the majority opinion, "that either students or teachers shed their constitutional rights to freedom of expression at the schoolhouse gate."

Garrett Morgan, son of former slaves, invented an automatic electric traffic signal, which, according to his 1923 patent, "may be readily and cheaply manufactured." The device was installed in Morgan's hometown of Cleveland, Ohio, in about 1918. It had red and green lights and a buzzer that sounded before the light changed.

Shortly after this, traffic lights began appearing in Detroit and New York with red, yellow, and green lights. The colors were most likely adopted from railroad signals in use since the 1830s. Red had always meant "stop." But green was for "caution," and clear, or white, for "go." In the early 1900s a train crash occurred when a conductor mistook a broken red lens for a "go" signal. After this, green became "go" and yellow "caution."

Morgan sold his invention to the General Electric Corporation for $40,000. Among his many other inventions was a sewing machine and a gas mask; in 1920 he founded a Cleveland newspaper. After a long and successful career, he died in 1963 at the age of 86.

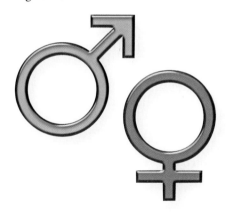

Male & Female Symbols

ORIGIN: MIDDLE AGES, VIA ROME
FEMALE SYMBOL: ASTRONOMICAL SIGN FOR VENUS
MALE SYMBOL: ASTRONOMICAL SIGN FOR MARS

We may know them best as symbols from women's lib or gay culture. Or perhaps we recall biology classes in which male fruit flies were labeled with a circle from which an arrow points obliquely up to the right, females with a circle from which hangs a cross. These gender symbols are used in many fields, but they stem from the Middle Ages by way of Roman mythology.

When astronomers of the Middle Ages (also known as astrologers then) wrote up their predictions and observations, they used symbols to designate the planets. To designate Mars they used what we now call the male symbol; for Venus, they used the female symbol. These logically became associated with male and female, since Mars was the Roman god of war, and Venus the goddess of love.

The reasons for the symbols themselves is less clear. One explanation is that they mimic the genitals. The male symbol is more obviously mimetic. The female symbol is sometimes called the "mirror of Venus," since it looks like a handheld mirror—a beautiful woman likes to admire herself in a mirror, hence the symbol. Some scholars believe that the symbol is a sloppy version of the Greek letter phi for phosphorus (from *phosphoros*, "light bringer" or "morning star," another name for Venus); the error became standard practice. All these explanations point to the possibility that the astrologers merely adopted male and female symbols already in use.

The symbols are still used in modern astronomy for Mars and Venus. They also appear in chemistry and metallurgy to represent iron (male) and copper (female). A warrior's weapons were made of iron; "copper" has the same root as Cyprus, the place where both copper and Venus originated.

Symbols demarcating the sexes are common across cultures. For example, the Chinese yin-yang specifically refers to male/female energy and the Indian *mithuna* signifies male-female duality represented by an entwined couple.

UNCOMMONLY KNOWN ...

Euro History Since 1999 the euro has been the basic monetary unit of the European Union. Its symbol, according to the European Commission, is a glyph representing the Greek letter epsilon, in tribute to the cradle of Western civilization; the letter also begins the word "Europe" and the parallel bars denote the currency's stability. But a former senior art director of the European Economic Community, Arthur Eisenmenger, says he designed the symbol as a logo in 1974 by combining the letters "C" and "E."

Currency

Since primitive times, when an even trade of goods was not possible, currency becomes necessary for transmitting value. As a result, there have been as many symbols for currency as there have been written forms of accounting to record them. At times, even the currency itself was a symbol, such as Native American wampum (used by such tribes as the Algonquian and Ojibwe), which was believed to have spiritual power. Besides wampum's value as currency, it was also used to record history, transmit messages and function as jewelry. Our timeline runs from livestock to plastic and includes shells, silver, paper, wood, and gold, too. Rather than show the written symbols for the different forms of currency, we're showing the currency itself. The materials are significant because they show not only things that are valuable to particular civilizations (cows, precious metals), but also how the importance of a currency's material has waxed and waned depending on the era and the economy of a culture.

1200 B.C.
Cowries The smooth, shiny, variegated shells of the Cypraeidae family of mollusks were long coveted by humans for decorative and financial purposes in Africa, China, and India.

6000 B.C.
Cattle Cows were often a commodity in early agrarian societies; their low maintenance and high food return made them valuable. Their use was so pervasive for so long that our word for "fee" derives from the Old English "feoh," or cattle.

Dollar Sign

FROM THE DUTCH "THALER" (BOHEMIAN COIN)
FIRST CIRCULATED U.S. DOLLAR: 1792
"YOU BET YOUR BOTTOM DOLLAR" (YES, DEFINITELY)

As a shorthand for "money," the dollar sign appears everywhere from pop art to sweepstakes announcements to the eyes of greedy cartoon characters. But "$" is mostly used to indicate that the numbers it precedes are of dollars. The origin of the symbol most likely dates back to 15th-century Spain.

When King Ferdinand II of Aragon pushed the Moors out of Spain in 1492, he marked the occasion by adding to his coat of arms two ornate columns, representing the two pillars of Hercules. Why? In taking the Iberian peninsula, he also claimed the Strait of Gibraltar, whose easternmost headlands (at the neck of the strait) were known in mythology as the pillars of Hercules. The Greek hero was said to have set the pillars there—the rock of Gibraltar in Europe and Jebel Musa in Africa—while performing his 12 labors. Ferdinand's heraldic pillars also had a ribbon draped around them, with the Latin words *Plus ultra* ("further beyond"), because that same year Columbus discovered the New World.

After Spanish explorers began bringing back gold and silver from the New World, newly minted coins were stamped with the heraldic device—twin pillars and an entwined ribbon. The symbol became especially associated with the Spanish peso, or piece of eight (equaling eight reales). The U.S. dollar, first minted as silver in 1794, copied the Spanish peso's weight and value, thus "two bits" refers to a quarter and eight bits to a dollar. Eventually the two lines through the S of the dollar sign became one, though as a plural the two lines are still sometimes used.

A.D. 312
Solidus Roman Emperor Constantine introduced the round gold coins, which weighed 4.5 grams and remained in use for nearly six centuries, their base value maintained by frequent reminting.

1450
Wampum Native American culture used wampum extensively, though not only as a form of currency. Foreign traders helped make wampum a widespread medium for exchange because of their shortage of money.

1792
Postal order Established in Great Britain in 1792, but it wasn't until fees were reduced to make it profitable that the Post Office decided to take it over, in 1838.

806
Paper money Early Chinese copper coins were of such small value that large strings of them were needed for most purchases. A copper shortage in the ninth century forced Emperor Hien Tsung to issue the first paper money, which was treated as temporary.

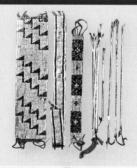

1951
Credit card First "charge plate" issued was Diner's Club. Charge cards required that a balance be paid in full each month, while a credit card provides an interest-bearing line of credit.

Superstitions

Irrational beliefs or practices handed down through successive generations, superstitions started as a result of ignorance or fear about something as innocuous as a person who looked different. Often superstitions were ways to explain bad luck (walking under a ladder) or to reverse the effects of bad luck (knocking on wood). Either way, the superstition took (and still takes) for granted that there are supernatural forces at work in our everyday lives. Though major religions explain the perpetuation of some superstitions (such as the use of four-leaf clovers), others appear to stem from mythology.

Four-Leaf Clover

CLOVER SPECIES: TRIFOLIUM REPENS
CHANCES OF FINDING IN WILD: 1 IN 10,000
ALSO KNOWN AS SHAMROCK

Though botanists came up with seeds for producing them back in the 1950s, there's still a thrill in finding a four-leaf clover in the wild. The fabled little herbs, hiding inconspicuously among patches of normal three-leafers, have long been thought to bestow luck on the finder.

According to Irish legends and Julius Caesar, the druids of the British Isles and Gaul were the ones who first believed in the luck of the four-leaf clover. The druids were an ancient Celtic priesthood who held religious rites in sacred oak groves. The Romans, who conquered Europe starting around 300 B.C., tried to stamp out Druidism; later, Christians accused the Druids of practicing magic and wizardry, and when the Celts became Christianized in the fifth and sixth centuries, the religion came to an end.

The druids' oak grove rituals involved collecting four-leaf clovers and mistletoe (another good-luck charm). A key part of the ritual involved animal, and possibly human, sacrifice; the disposition of the charred remains could foretell the future. It is unclear how the plants were used, but their rarity likely gave them elevated status. In addition, the four-leaf clover is in the shape of a cross, which well before Christianity was a magic symbol, representing, among other things, the cardinal directions. Druids may have believed that having a four-leaf clover gave one the ability to see witches and devils, and thus the power to avoid them.

Illustrating how an exception becomes a rule, the term "cloverleaf," used since the 1930s for a kind of

---

UNCOMMONLY KNOWN . . .

Wishbone Sometime before 400 B.C., the Etruscans, living in what is now Tuscany in Italy, used fowl to divine the future. After these soothsaying birds were killed, their clavicles (collarbones) were dried in the sun. A person who then touched the bone while making a wish would have his wish fulfilled. From this evolved the tradition of two people pulling the bone apart—the one with the larger piece gets his wish.

looping highway interchange, refers to a four-lobed configuration. The plants themselves, by the way, are genetic anomalies found in common-variety white clover; they occur at the rate of 1 in 10,000.

Knocking on Wood

ACTION CAN ALSO BE SPOKEN:
"KNOCK ON WOOD" OR "TOUCH WOOD"
FAMOUS USE: 1966 HIT "KNOCK ON WOOD" (EDDIE FLOYD)

K nocking or touching wood after saying something boastful is a long-standing superstition going back in apparently independent lines to ancient Greece and pre-Columbian North America. Tree veneration was common in many ancient cultures, among them that of woodland Indians, who as far back as 4,000 years ago regarded trees, particularly oaks, as places where sky gods lived after descending in lightning bolts. If a person boasted of future success in battle or of a good harvest, the event was almost certain not to occur. But by knocking on a tree one could appease the god within, and reverse the effect of the boast. The ancient Greeks developed a similar practice nearly 2,000 years later. In other lands, other trees were considered the most sacred—the sycamore in Egypt, the ash in Germany.

Medieval Christian scholars contended that the "knock wood" tradition sprang from early Christians who touched wooden crosses to ask God's forgiveness. They may have done so, but the superstition seems to have been adapted by Christians

from a pagan habit already in place. Knocking on wood has persisted as a way not only of canceling out the ill effects of a boast but also of ensuring that some misfortune, which we have just mentioned or witnessed, does not befall us. The act says, in effect, "There but for the grace of God go I." Today we continue to knock on wood—any kind handy. Unlike saying, "I'll cross my fingers for you," when we say "knock on wood," the words themselves don't suffice—often an inconvenience in a car or other wood-free environment.

Black Cats

CONSIDERED LUCKY IN SOME ENGLISH FOLKLORE
"THE BLACK CAT": 1843 STORY BY EDGAR ALLAN POE
"LE CHAT NOIR": 19TH-CENTURY PARIS CABARET

M any people are familiar with the superstitious belief that a black cat crossing one's path brings bad luck. Probably fewer are aware that cats were once held in such high esteem that such a belief would almost be heresy. As far back as 3000 B.C., when the Egyptians domesticated cats, felines of all colors were honored family pets. Laws protected them from harm, and when one died the family—rich or poor—would mourn the loss and often preserve the cat in a bronze or wood mummy case. Cats continued to be venerated, particularly in the East, until the Middle Ages.

With the rise in urban population during medieval times, the cat population soared. Cats were no longer such rare creatures. At the same time, a hysterical fear of witches swept across Europe. In England alley cats became connected with the lonely crones who often fed them. Many such old women were burned at the stake for witchcraft, and since it seemed logical that evil power had been transferred either from or to a creature that by nature is sly and aloof, their cats were burned too. Black cats were especially associated with black magic and thus feared; many people considered them the nighttime manifestation of witches.

PARALLEL HISTORY

Witch's Familiar

The black cat was but one of a veritable menagerie of witches' companions that, since the Middle Ages, have been known as familiars–a spirit in animal form that guards and serves. Goats, pigs, dogs, rabbits, toads, and mice have all been considered familiars. The witch could, in some traditions, change into the familiar's shape, or the familiar could assume a human-animal form or appear as a demonic being. The familiar helped the witch in return for suckling at the witch's "third teat," a deformity that was a sure sign of a witch during the height of witch hysteria in the late 1500s.

To the superstitious, this horned toad might once have seemed a shape-shifting witch or demon.

If England started the trend, France ran with it. In the early 1600s the French burned thousands of cats every month, attempting to eradicate the species. King Louis XIII stopped the cat-killing campaign in the 1630s. Black cats have endured, their mystique carried through the centuries. Folklore has it that to reverse the bad luck of a black cat crossing your path, you should walk in a circle, then go backward across the spot where it happened and count to 13.

Walking Under a Ladder

IF YOU CAN'T WALK AROUND, TO AVOID BAD LUCK: CROSS YOUR FINGERS, SPIT AFTER PASSING UNDER, DON'T SPEAK UNTIL YOU SEE A DOG

According to folk wisdom, walking under a ladder brings bad luck. Taking the long way around seems an obvious way to protect yourself from falling objects, but the roots of the superstition have nothing to do with any immediate danger.

To the Egyptians of 3000 B.C., wood was scarce and a ladder was a good-luck sign. Some people even carried miniature ladders as amulets. Ladders were often put within the tombs of Egyptian pharaohs so that they could get to heaven. The sun god Osiris was rescued by ladder from the spirit of darkness. Furthermore, triangles were thought to represent a sacred trinity of gods—the tombs of the kings were built as pyramids because of the triangle's significance. Any commoner who walked beneath a triangular arch was guilty of transgressing upon holy ground. Since a ladder leaning against a wall forms a triangle, to break the plane of that space was to tempt the wrath of the gods.

Among Romans, if someone accidentally walked beneath a ladder, he could reverse the bad luck with a *fico* (from the Latin for "fig" or "vulva"). This sign of contempt was made by putting the thumb between the first two fingers and pointing it at the ladder. Christian tradition also reinforced the fear of walking under a ladder. The ladder leaning against the crucifix was not for the ascent of a god but for the killing of one. Thus the ladder became a symbol of evil and death. In 17th-century England, condemned criminals had to walk beneath the gallows' ladder; executioners skirted it.

Evil Eye

ALSO KNOWN TODAY AS: WITHERING GLANCE,
STINK EYE, OR DEATH ROLL
ROLLING THE EYES SHOWS ANNOYANCE OR DISBELIEF

B elief in the evil eye—the idea that a person can harm others with a glance—was common in many ancient traditions.

Early Jews, Christians, and Muslims supported the belief, as did pagan practitioners, particularly in the Mediterranean. The evil eye appeared in Greece as far back as the sixth century B.C., when it adorned drinking vessels. In Greek and Roman legends, the basilisk (or cockatrice) was a dragon that could kill with a glance or a breath. This power, when held by a person, could be either a gift or an affliction. Sorcerers claiming the evil eye could make money by using their talent to bewitch someone's enemy. Yet its deadly use was often considered involuntary. Thus, a person with abnormal eyes—crossed, cloudy, protruding, or any number of other unfortunate conditions—might be said to have the evil eye and could therefore be put to death. In a Slavic folktale, a father fearful of having the evil eye blinds himself in order to avoid harming his own children.

Many folklorists believe the evil eye tradition comes from the reflective properties of the pupil. A person staring into someone's eye could see a tiny image of himself, which in some cultures may have been frightening. The word "pupil," in fact, comes from the Latin *pupilla* ("little doll"). But then everyone would have an evil eye. A more likely scenario would give the evil eye to a person whose eyes were different and thus didn't perfectly reflect the viewer.

Today you can buy talismans to ward off the evil eye—glass balls painted with concentric blue and white circles, or decals with stylized eyes. But for the most part, the remnant of the superstition occurs in such expressions as "withering glance" and "giving the stink eye."

We now know that a person's glance can't cause physical harm, but the powerful anger in an "evil eye" might prove harmfully distressing.

Number 13

TRISKAIDEKAPHOBIA: FEAR OF NUMBER 13
FAMILIAR 13s: AMERICAN COLONIES, BAKER'S DOZEN,
ALEX RODRIGUEZ, DAN MARINO, WILT CHAMBERLAIN

Of all superstitions, fear of the number 13, called triskaidekaphobia, is the one with the most influence still in the modern world. More than 80 percent of high-rises lack a 13th floor; many hospitals have no room number 13; France and Italy rarely have 13 as a house address; airports often skip gate 13 and airplanes don't include a 13th row. Most telling, up to $900 million is lost every Friday the 13th because of people not flying or conducting business on this double-whammy day.

Folklorists trace this numeric nervousness to a pre-Christian Norse myth. Twelve gods were having a dinner party in Valhalla, their heaven. An uninvited 13th guest named Loki arrives. A known mischief-maker, Loki then arranges for Hoder, the god of darkness, to shoot Balder the Beautiful, god of joy, with a mistletoe-tipped arrow. Balder dies and the Earth is shrouded in darkness.

A sense of foreboding and doom has attended the number 13 ever since. The Christian story of the Last Supper fit readily into the Norse framework. Judas is the last disciple to show up, making 13 at table; the next day he betrays Jesus. In ancient Rome, covens were reputedly made of 12 witches; the 13th was the devil.

Numerologists place some of the blame on 13's unfortunate position after 12. A "complete" number, 12 can be divided evenly into halves, thirds, and fourths; it is the number of the disciples of Jesus, signs of the zodiac, months in a year, gods of Olympus, labors of Hercules, tribes of Israel, and people on a jury. Adding one unbalances the completeness of 12. But nobody seems to complain about a baker's dozen, the tradition of giving 13 baked items instead of 12, stemming from a 1266 British law levying stiff fines on bread companies that cheated.

However, another rationale behind the fear of the number 13 that has ancient roots is the Egyptian belief that spiritual ascension came in 12 stages in this life. The 13th stage was the afterlife—and, of course, nothing could be known about it. Anything to do with 13, then, was shrouded in mystery and had to do with death. For the ancient Egyptians, this bestowed a kind of reverence for the number 13, the symbol of the afterlife. However, subsequent cultures simply took the association and made 13 part of their overall fear of death.

Finally, the number 13 has some even more ancient associations than with the Egyptians—those having to do with female power. Thirteen had been revered in prehistoric goddess-worshipping cultures because it corresponded to the number of lunar (menstrual) cycles in a year (13 x 28 = 364 days). The "Earth Mother of Laussel," a 27,000-year-old carving in the Lascaux caves in France, shows a female figure holding a horn with 13 notches. It is thought that fear of the feminine (including the inability to conquer or contain its power) might have been associated with fear of the number 13.

PARALLEL HISTORY

Friday the 13th

According to one survey, fear of bad things happening on Friday the 13th afflicts from 17 to 21 million people in the United States. The phobia combines fear of the number 13 with superstitions about Friday. By biblical tradition, Friday was the day Jesus was crucified. Some biblical scholars also maintain that Eve tempted Adam on a Friday and that Cain slew Abel on a Friday the 13th. But, again, Norse legend may be the true source. Friday was named for Frigga, goddess of the sky. With the onset of Christianity, she was banished and considered a witch; for centuries Scandinavians called Friday "witches' Sabbath."

Tributes

Conquerors of old demanded tribute in the form of food, money, and services. Today we use the word "tribute" to refer to homages paid to worthy individuals. Hence a great performance "demands" tribute in the form of applause; a superior officer is honored with a salute; a diploma is conferred upon a college graduate. The history of these familiar tributes is often long and surprising—from the moon cakes of the Greeks came birthday cakes, and toasting started with actual toast. Just as in the past, we use tributes today to mark special occasions, thus paying tribute to both honoree and tradition.

Applause

FROM THE LATIN "APPLAUDERE" (TO CLAP)
CLAQUE: ORGANIZED BODY OF PERSONS HIRED TO APPLAUD A PERFORMANCE

Put your hands together to welcome the new member. Give a hand to the talented young singer. Let's hear it for this outstanding group of athletes. How do we show our approval? By clapping our hands together. No other body part works so well in making a loud noise, except the vocal cords. We'll get to them later.

Just as apes thump their hands on their chest, so primitive man likely learned that clapping was a handy sound producer. We know that Romans applauded speeches and dramatic performances they liked. Actors sometimes at the end of a play told the audience to "clap your hands" or express appreciation "in the usual manner."

University students, whose hands were occupied with paper and pen, could compliment good lectures by stamping their feet. Orchestra members, hands holding instruments, showed approbation of their conductor in the same way. Young women were taught "ladylike" applause: holding one hand steady while clapping the other against it, thought to be more refined than vigorously moving both hands together.

A different kind of applause developed in British parliamentary institutions. Those who approved of what a speaker was saying would often shout, "Hear him! Hear him!" This was directed to people who might not be paying attention. A shortened form evolved, and today we still use "Hear! Hear!" to voice acclaim to a speech or part of a speech.

Operagoers traditionally shout "Bravo" after a particularly moving aria if the singer is male, "Brava" for a female; for a group with at least one male the cry is "Bravi," and for a group of women it's "Brave" (pronounced brah-vay). American audiences also whistle, but in some countries whistling is equivalent to booing.

UNCOMMONLY KNOWN . . .
To Clap or Not to Clap Applause after movements of symphonies and concertos is considered in poor taste, though this tradition did not arise until the late 1800s. Music critic Alex Ross believes it started with the temperamental German composer Richard Wagner, who demanded silence throughout his (lengthy) operas. In less formal music, clapping is almost de rigueur after every song or solo (in jazz).

Salute

GESTURE OF RESPECT OR OBEDIENCE
OTHER FORMS OF SALUTING: CANNONFIRE, GUNFIRE,
AERIAL FLYOVERS

Everyone is familiar with the crisp military salute as a sign of respect and courtesy. But where did it come from, when is it used, and how is it performed?

The modern salute likely goes back to the late period of the Roman Empire. Assassinations were on the rise, and so a citizen approaching an official was required to raise his hand to show he was unarmed. Later, armored knights would show their faces to each other by flipping open their visors with their right hands. The gesture evolved into removing, or simply touching, one's hat.

In the early 19th century, British military personnel were required to clap a hand to their hat and bow when they passed a superior officer. By the middle of the century, the hand clap was replaced by the hand touching the hat, palm outward. The British navy saluted with the palm down and away from the viewer so as not to present a tar-stained hand to a superior. The United States military salute resembles this practice: The right hand snaps to the forehead, palm down, forearm at a 45-degree angle, eyes on the officer. Soldiers are expected to salute higher-ranking officers, including those of friendly foreign countries, when the officer is within 30 paces and at no less than six paces. Sailors on ships salute an individual only at the first meeting of the day. Salutes are returned by the ranking officer. Prisoners may not salute. Salutes are also made during the national anthem and at ceremonial occasions.

Diploma

FROM GREEK "DIPLOMA" (FOLDED PAPER, DOUBLING)
ORIGINALLY MADE OF SHEEPSKIN
SOME UNIVERSITIES STILL WRITE THEIRS IN LATIN

The graduate of an educational institution comes away with a document proving he or she has fulfilled the requirements for graduation. Such a document is called a diploma. The word *diploma* is from the Latin for "passport" and the Greek for "folded paper," and once referred to any official or state charter. Sometime in the past 400 years the word came to mean a document under seal conferring an honor or privilege, then gradually to mean the document one receives at a high school or college graduation ceremony.

Educational diplomas were once called sheepskins, and sometimes still are. That's because they were actually made from vellum—a very thin, fine-grained lambskin upon which the information was handwritten. The document was then rolled and tied with a ribbon. *Parchment* was another word for sheepskin, but it came to refer to a kind of tough, translucent paper resembling sheepskin. Parchment academic diplomas became the norm, with the ready supply of paper, and starting in the early

20th century they were bound in leather, perhaps to confer a more official, sheepskin appearance. The diploma was at this point sometimes called a testimonial, a term still used in the United Kingdom.

A few colleges still confer either a sheepskin diploma or offer it as an option. Of a recent graduating class at Amherst College, 87 percent chose the traditional sheepskin, while others preferred "a vegetarian option" and had their diplomas printed on archive-quality, cotton-stock paper. Of these, many objected to sheepskin's being the default option.

Diplomas are also conferred upon those earning higher degrees. Such certificates, indicating medical or law degrees, are traditionally framed and hung in offices as proof of the recipient's education.

(living and dead). A 50th-birthday cake was made with wheat flour, olive oil, honey, and grated cheese.

The modern birthday cake, however, may have begun in medieval Germany, where a *Kinderfeste* was held in celebration of the birthday of a young child. Early in the morning, the child was presented with a cake topped by lighted candles. During the day the candles were kept burning (and replaced when necessary); the cake was eaten after dinner. The candles numbered one more than the child's age. What we now call "one to grow on," they called the "light of life." The child would blow out the candles with one breath to ensure that his wish, which had to be kept secret, would come true.

Birthday Cake

MAKE FROM A BOXED MIX OR FROM SCRATCH
POPULAR TYPES OF CAKES: SHEET, CUP, LAYER
FROSTING TYPES: BUTTERCREAM, ICING, GANACHE, GLAZE

The practice of giving a birthday celebrator a cake is a long-standing tradition going far back in Western culture. The ancient Greeks baked round or moon-shaped honey cakes and bread as a tribute to Artemis, a moon goddess. Candles gave the cakes a moon-like glow. Whether the Greeks celebrated birthdays with cakes is unclear. The Romans almost certainly did. Private celebrations were held in honor of friends and family, while public birthdays celebrated cities, temples, and emperors

Toasting

GESTURE OF HONOR OR GOOD FORTUNE
FROM THE ROMAN TRADITION OF
ENJOYING SPICED TOAST WITH WINE

When we raise a glass and say a few words in honor of someone, we are offering a toast. The tradition dates back yet again to the ancient Greeks and Romans. By the sixth century B.C., a common way to get rid of enemies was to poison them; hence, to show that a beverage was safe to consume, a host would drink to a guest's health by taking the first sip.

Credit the Romans with adding the actual toast. As a pledge of friendship, they would drop a piece of spiced toast into the communal cup of wine they raised at a ceremony or other celebratory function. It turns out that the toast not only added a sweet flavor, the charcoal content could help make a vinegary wine more flavorful by reducing its acidity. Though the Romans could not have understood the chemistry, they no doubt appreciated the mellowing effect of the toast.

The clinking of glasses just after a toast developed in 17th-century England, where it was believed that the bell-like noise had the power of banishing the devil. By the next century, the title of toastmaster was created to designate the one who presides over a banquet and its after-dinner speakers. It was also during the 18th century that the tradition of drinking to the health of some celebrated person, not present at the table, came into being. This celebrity, often a beautiful woman, was referred to as the "toast of the town." So ingrained was the custom of toasting that in 1803 an English duke maintained that every glass should be dedicated to someone, and if any dinner guest was untoasted it was a direct insult.

Red Roses

SYMBOL OF: BEAUTY, DELICACY, ROMANTIC LOVE
"MY LOVE'S LIKE A RED, RED ROSE" –ROBERT BURNS
CAN ALSO REPRESENT DECEIT OR DANGER

The tribute of red roses for a loved one has a long and colorful history. One legend maintains that red roses came about when Eve kissed a white rose in the Garden of Eden. Another legend has it that Cupid—the

Roman god of erotic love—bled on white roses. In yet another, Harpocrates, god of silence, happened upon Venus, goddess of love, in the act of lovemaking. Cupid, Venus's son, bribed him into silence by giving him the first rose in the world. The rose thus became a Roman symbol of silence and, since roughly the fifth century B.C., a rose carved into a ceiling indicated a place where diplomats could gather in secret, or sub rosa.

Dionysus the Younger, tyrant of Syracuse (fourth century B.C.), ordered his house filled with roses for the parties he had with young women of the city. The wealthy Romans would lie on beds of roses, wearing garlands and crowns of roses. During a party of Roman Emperor Elagabalus (third century B.C.), several Roman nobles were supposedly suffocated when tons of rose petals were dropped on them. The ancient Romans so loved roses that they imported them in barges from Egypt, and when the growing season was over they filled their fountains with rosewater. Cleopatra (queen of Egypt from 51 to 30 B.C.) reputedly strewed a room with red rose petals so that their perfume would intoxicate Mark Antony.

Greek physician Galen (second century A.D.) is credited with inventing a rose oil perfume known today as attar of roses; Persian women used rosewater as a potion to bring wandering lovers home; an ancient Chinese aphrodisiac called for a mixture of prunes, sugar, olives, and rose petals to be drunk during fourth-month rose festivals; and English colonial women made a love stimulant by marinating rose petals in brandy.

Hair & Body Marking

Welcome to the weird and wonderful world of body markings, where the faddish and modern meet the ancient tribal. Here we learn how the subcultures of the pierced and painted developed from long-standing cultures around the globe. Multiple nose rings? North Africans have had them for centuries. Dreadlocks? Islamic dervishes and Christian ascetics were on to them long before the Rastafarians. The art of the tattoo may be more than 10,000 years old. Indeed, there may not be a way of marking or decorating the body that was not already in vogue somewhere long ago.

Dreadlocks

SYMBOL OF RASTAFARIAN MOVEMENT
BEARER OF BRAIDED AND MATTED "LOCKS" (HAIR)
LIVED IN DREAD, OR FEAR, OF GOD

The term *dreadlocks* entered the English language in the 1950s with the rise of the Rastafarian movement among Jamaica's poor blacks. One precept of the movement was a prohibition on cutting the hair. The long hair was then matted or braided into ropelike strands and coils. The wearer of such locks lived in dread or fear of god (Jah), hence the term dreadlocks developed for the hairstyle. But the hairstyle itself was in vogue for centuries before the word dreadlocks was coined.

The Rastafarian vow of uncut hair may have been taken from the book of Numbers (6:5), the fourth book of the Bible: "All the days of the vow of his separation there shall no razor come upon his head: until the days be fulfilled . . . he shall be holy, and shall let the locks of the hair of his head grow." Author Timothy White, in a biography of Rastafarian singer-songwriter Bob Marley, contends that the directive came from Leviticus 21:5: "They shall not make baldness on their head. . . ."

The tradition of the hair linking the wearer to the divinity and divine powers occurs in early Hindu legend. The god Shiva and his followers are often depicted with long, twisted locks of hair. In one legend Shiva gathered up the Ganges in his hair to keep it from flooding the Earth. Similarly, many ascetic and mystic groups within larger religions have advocated the wearing of long, braided hair, among them the Sufi and dervishes of Islam, the sadhus of Hinduism, Christian Coptic monks, and Jewish Nazarites (including Samson). In Central America before the 16th-century Spanish conquest, Aztec priests wore long, matted locks of hair. And in Australia, mummified Aborigines with long locks have been unearthed.

Tonsure

FROM THE LATIN "TONSURA" (SHEAR, CLIP)
IN MIDDLE AGES, DISTINGUISHED CLERICS FROM LAITY
EXEMPTED PRIESTS FROM SECULAR CRIME

Several religions have performed tonsuring—clipping or shaving part of the hair—as a ritual initiation to a higher, more devoted stage of religious life. The word derives from Latin (see above); Roman barbers were known as tonsors.

The tonsuring ritual probably began among the early Greeks and Semites; hair cuttings were offered to the deity. Such haircuts were possibly an imitation of the shaven heads of slaves, and thus a tonsure was a symbol of servitude to God. Another theory suggests that tonsuring mimicked male baldness and thus gave a young novitiate a badge of respectability.

Early Christian ascetics developed the tonsuring ritual that became standard practice by the seventh century in the Catholic Church. This ritual was performed on men being initiated into the clerical order and thus eligible for priesthood. In the Roman, or St. Peter's, tonsure, the crown of the head was shaved, leaving only a fringe of hair to symbolize the crown of thorns worn by Christ before his Crucifixion. The Greek tonsure (also called Eastern, or St. Paul's, tonsure) was a complete head shaving; this practice gradually evolved into a close-cropped haircut. A third tonsure was known as the Celtic (St. John's)—hair forward of a line across the top of the head from ear to ear was shaved. Tonsuring continued until it was abolished in 1972 by Pope Paul VI.

Buddhists still perform tonsures during monks' novice ordination ceremonies, and again when they become full-fledged monks. Subsequently, monks maintain a clean-shaven face and head. Many boys in Thailand and Burma undergo tonsure and spend a short time in a monastery for religious training. Hindu boys are given a tonsure that leaves a tuft of hair on the crown of the head.

Tattoos

FROM TAHITIAN, TONGAN, AND SAMOAN "TATAU"
ONE OF THE OLDEST FORMS OF SYMBOLISM
CAN SYMBOLIZE RANK, STATUS, MEMBERSHIP

Who dreamed up the idea of injecting pigment under the skin to create pictures of roses and anchors and animals? Whether it started out as an accident, or a prank pulled by some bored tribesmen, it turns out that tattooing is one of the oldest forms of artistic expression. Cave paintings date the practice to at least 8000 B.C., and tattoos occur in nearly every ancient culture around the world. The earliest tattoos known to date appear on the body of the "Iceman," a Bronze Age man discovered in the Tyrolean Alps during the melting of a glacier. The body had been frozen for more than 5,000 years; it bore tattooed stripes on the lower back and right ankle and a tattoo cross behind one knee. The tattoos could have been merely ornamental, or they might have denoted a tribal affiliation or have been applied as protective or healing tokens.

Many ancient Egyptian mummies are marked with tattoos, perhaps the oldest being that of Amunet, a priestess from 4,000 years ago. Her tattoos likely had some religious or spiritual purpose, though it's also possible they had a sexual reference as well—scholars speculate that tattoos on females may have been fertility talismans. The early Greeks and Romans also used tattoos, primarily to mark slaves.

Piercings

FROM THE LATIN "PERTUSUS" (TO THRUST THROUGH)
MOST COMMON PIERCING: EARLOBE
OTHER POPULAR SPOTS: BROW, LIP, NAVEL, NOSE

L ike tattooing, body piercing has a long history among primitive cultures. In Genesis, a servant of Abraham gives a golden earring to Rebekah. In Africa and other places where tattooing did not gain a foothold—

due in no small part to the fact that tattoos did not show up well on dark skin—piercing has been practiced for centuries. Tribes in Mali and Ethiopia pierced their ears and lips with rings to enhance their beauty and during ceremonial rituals. In India, the Middle East, and North Africa, nose rings indicated tribal status and wealth—the more nose rings a young woman wore, the larger her bridal dowry.

The Maya of Central America (A.D. 250-900), among the most elaborate of body art practitioners, not only tattooed their body and face but also pierced their ears, nose, lips, and other body parts, stretching the holes larger with incrementally bigger piercings. In North America, the Mandan, Sioux, and other Native Americans pierced their breast with slivers of bone from which they were suspended by thongs during purification ceremonies called sun dances—the self-inflicted pain was considered an offering to the creator and a symbol of death and rebirth.

Nipple piercing had a brief period of popularity in 1890s London and Paris. The practice has reemerged in recent years, popularized by male rock stars.

Ear piercing became a mainstream practice starting in the 1960s. The practice is so common that it can be done in a matter of minutes and is offered by doctor's offices, dermatologists and jewelry stores. Nowadays, pierced earrings are so common it is difficult to find the clip-on variety.

According to the *New York Times*, belly-button piercing went mainstream in 1993 when model Christy Turlington appeared at a London fashion show with a navel ring. The next day model Naomi Campbell followed suit, showing off a belly button adorned with a gold ring set with a pearl.

Hearth & Home

Since long before the beginning of recorded history—for perhaps tens of thousands of years—people have been manipulating their environment to create shelter. Humans collected and shaped thatch, mud, wood, stone, and other natural materials into domiciles to protect themselves from the elements, wild animals, and each other. Today's wondrous variety of buildings, rooms, and domestic accoutrements comes from our instinctive nesting urge, and the many shelters we inhabit today each has a unique history. The chapter is divided into six sections— Buildings, Houses, Rooms, Elements, Appliances, and Backyard. Within these you'll find a wide range of entries. Under Buildings you can learn about the origins of barns as well as skyscrapers, and you'll discover the inventions that made the latter possible, inventions that we consider commonplace today. In Houses you'll learn the significant differences between apartments and condominiums, as well as when and how trailers came to have a bad reputation. The Rooms sections covers everything from the front porch—which evolved from the shaded verandas of the Renaissance—to the bathroom. You might be surprised to find that the earliest flush toilets were made thousands of years ago, long before the open cesspools and outhouses of more recent vintage. Dip into the Elements section and trace glass windows back to the 4,500-year-old invention of glassmaking. Some fixtures of modern homes have unexpectedly long histories, while others are curiously short—central heat goes back to the Roman hypocausts (underground furnace-and-flue systems), whereas doorbells date only from the 1830s. Under Appliances, learn how an 1890s Illinois socialite made washing dishes easier for us all, and in Backyard you'll find out about the Great Bath, a 12-meter pool in ancient Mohenjo Daro. How we live our lives shapes—and in turn is shaped by—the building spaces we inhabit, and the history of those spaces helps us understand the larger history of where we came from.

Buildings

Today's buildings allow us to live, work, shop, learn, and heal. Buildings like high-rises, skyscrapers, department stores, schools, and hospitals are specifically designed to accommodate these functions. Most people will be suprised to learn that the first apartment buildings were built in the first century B.C., and that skyscrapers are far from 20th-century inventions. Usually, form follows function—e.g., lack of real estate forces builders to look up—but sometimes it's the other way around, as when teachers adapt to limited space when a box-shaped schoolhouse is all a town can afford.

Apartment Building

FROM LATIN, MEANING "TO SEPARATE"
FIRST APARTMENTS: FIRST CENTURY B.C.
ALSO KNOWN AS: FLAT (BRITISH ENGLISH)

Apartment buildings were originally invented for the same reason they're necessary today: people want to live in cities, and cities have boundaries. Ancient Rome, like most cities back then, had walls around it. If people wanted to stay within those walls, they had to build up higher in order to have living space, but for many years the city ordinance forbade buildings taller than 50 feet. An example of the first *insulae,* or apartments, dates back to Trajan's reign. Three stories high, the timber and mud-brick structures included six to eight living units that faced a courtyard, with shops on the first level. They became so popular that by the fourth century A.D., apartments outnumbered *domi* (single-family homes) 25 to 1.

Apartment buildings remained an option rather than a necessity in many places until the industrial revolution, when manufacturing jobs brought people to cities in droves. The communal housing that then sprang up was tenements, either in row house form or in the form of apartment blocks that were overcrowded, underventilated, and sometimes downright dangerous, depending on exits and building materials. Additionally, people were not accustomed to living alone. Most people stayed with nuclear and extended families. It took a while for the idea of "flats" to catch on, but by the end of the 19th century, many men and even women had begun to live singly or with just one or two other people. The solitude and choices afforded by apartment living caught on both in Europe and the United States.

Today elevators, steel-beam construction, and a higher population density have led to more people living in apartment buildings than ever before, and

UNCOMMONLY KNOWN...

Duplex A detached home divided into two living spaces, much like a row of town houses but with only two homes, is known as a duplex. The two owners or tenants share at least one wall. Duplex homes can be either side by side or stacked one on top of the other. Each living space of the duplex operates as a fully functional, independent home.

in more places than ever before. There are apartment buildings in India, Africa, and Russia that didn't exist even a decade ago, in areas that had never before seen apartments.

Barn

FROM OLD ENGLISH, "BERKEM"
IDIOMATIC: "CLOSE THE BARN DOOR AFTER THE HORSE HAS BOLTED" (TAKING ACTION TOO LATE)

B arn is such a common, plain word for common, plain structures that we often forget these buildings have a rich heritage dating back to ancient times. The earliest barns were probably simple stables that kept livestock separate from humans. Eventually, barns evolved to hold both livestock and their feed, including hay. As humans became increasingly agrarian, they needed larger barns to accommodate herds of cattle and other animals.

Since most barns were and are made to last, some from centuries ago, like the Barley Barn at Cressing Temple in Essex, England, still stand. Built by the Order of the Knights Templar in the 12th century, it is regarded as one of the finest timber-framed barns.

Many Americans, if asked to visualize a barn, imagine a structure with red siding (ferrous oxide was cheap and plentiful), white trim, and a rounded roof known as a gambrel (storage area for hay). This common barn, often called a prairie barn because of its proliferation in the Midwest and West, has been used in many illustrations and photographs.

However, many other barn types have been used in the United States, including Dutch barns, round barns, Finnish log barns, and crib barns. Barn construction depended on more than ancestry; even topography could affect the kind of barn erected in any particular place. For example, "bank barns" were a clever use of a hillside. By building into a hill, a farmer could have ground-level access to both stories of a two-floor barn.

Of course, there are also barns that are designed around a particular crop, such as apple barns, rice barns, and hop barns, with conical silos built into the structure. The most American of these was the tobacco barn, with special ventilation and "cladding" boards, both of which allowed the broad leaves of the tobacco plant to dry as quickly as possible.

Skyscraper

TERM "SKYSCRAPER" FIRST USED IN U.S., 1880s
EARLIEST: TOWER HOUSES OF SHIBAM, YEMEN (1500s)
WORLD'S TALLEST: BURJ DUBAI, U.A.E. | 2,684 FEET

T he word *skyscraper* derives from the nautical term for a tall mast, and as early multistory buildings went up in American cities, people compared their lofty profile to that of sailing ships (previously the highest points in most cities' skylines). Although many skyscrapers now tower well over 100 floors, there is no particular height required for a building to be called a skyscraper; that depends on the average height of other buildings in a city or area.

We now think of skyscrapers, with their gleaming metal and glass, as being a relatively late human innovation. However, a quick look at two different times and places will show that people have long been interested in the possibilities offered by building "up": The tower houses of Shibam, Yemen, constructed in the 16th century, were built up to 11 stories high to foil Bedouin attacks, while "Maltings," fabricated of iron, was built in Shrewsbury, England, in 1797.

Every building relies on different materials and different innovations, but the skyscraper could not have existed without several materials and innovations being used together for the first time. First came steel-beam structure, pioneered by George Fuller, whose 1889 Tacoma Building was the first constructed so that the weight was supported by a steel cage rather than outside load-bearing walls. Several 10- to 20-story buildings were finished before the first Fuller-built structure in Manhattan, the wedge-shaped Flatiron Building at Broadway and 23rd Street. Manhattan is, of course, now legendary for its skyscraper-loaded skyline.

Second came safe elevators, made possible in 1853 by an invention from Elisha Graves Otis that prevented an elevator from plummeting down its shaft if its cable broke. Of equal importance to making the elevator a more common transport device for humans was the development of the pump as a transport device for water, which enabled skyscrapers to have safe, effective modern plumbing all the way to the top.

UNCOMMONLY KNOWN . . .
Elevators These lifts are important for freight, boats, autos, and even food—dumbwaiters for the latter are now usually motorized. One type of elevator that still exists but is rarely manufactured anymore is the European paternoster, named the "Our Father" for the way its constant looping resembles a chain of rosary beads.

Hospital

FROM LATIN "HOSPES" (HOST)
FIRST NORTH AMERICAN HOSPITAL: MEXICO CITY, 1524
NUMBER OF HOSPITALS IN U.S.: 7,569

We have no way of knowing exactly when cultures began to try to care for and heal ill people in a systematic way. Although the ancient Egyptians did have temples dedicated to the healing arts, these places were more about praying to the gods for a cure.

The first institution dedicated to using available means and science to heal the sick was the Sinhalese Buddhist Mihintale Hospital, begun by King Pandukabhaya in the fourth century B.C. Around 200 B.C., Princess Macha established the Broin Bearg ("House of Sorrow") in Ireland. The first practice of using state funds for hospitals rather than royal patronage dates to first century A.D. China, and the first teaching hospital was the Academy of Gundishapur, founded in the sixth century A.D. in the Persian Empire.

It's important to recognize disparate traditions and centuries in the creation of the hospital, because many assume that the Christian imperative to offer hospitality to strangers and to the sick means that Christianity invented the hospital. While this is not so, Christian thought helped transform the hospital from a place where the ill were believed to be stricken by malevolent deities into a place where disease was viewed as something physical and potentially treatable. Early medieval hospitals were often staffed and run by the religious, a tradition that continues even in some parts of the United Kingdom, where secular nurses are addressed as "Sister."

The two first hospitals in North America were in Mexico City (1524) and Quebec City (1639), both run by "hospitalers," meaning members of the "hospital orders" that were meant to combine the compassion of the religious with the discipline of the military. During the 18th century, William Penn founded one of the first nonprofit hospitals in Philadelphia. However, hospital care and administration in the U.S. did not see much progress until the Civil War, when clean, organized, and regulated pavilion hospitals led to better postbellum hospitals.

Schoolhouse

ONE-ROOM STYLE POPULAR TILL LATE 19TH CENTURY
ONE-ROOM ATTENDEES: CHILDREN OF ALL AGES
"TRUANT": IN MIDDLE ENGLISH MEANT "IDLER," "VAGABOND"

Today schools are built with multiple classrooms for multiple ages, but in an earlier era where there were fewer schools, fewer methods of long-distance transportation, and children who needed to return home in the afternoon for farm chores,

Civil War Hospitals

When the Civil War began, the Army Medical Corps included the surgeon general, 30 surgeons, and 83 assistant surgeons. By the war's end, thousands of doctors had been called into service. The very scale of the conflict's demand on medicine and sanitation forced Edwin M. Stanton, President Abraham Lincoln's second secretary of war, to form a team of medical inspectors. He also called for the makeshift hospitals to be regulated and turned into pavilion hospitals, buildings that were constructed with a medical purpose in mind. Inspired by Englishwoman Florence Nightingale's work in cleaning up field hospitals during the Crimean War, Stanton's new commission also added a corps of female nurses to the Army under the command of Dorothea Dix.

Patients recovering in the ward of a northern hospital during the American Civil War.

one-room schoolhouses worked. One-room schoolhouses are interesting in and of themselves, but they are also interesting as a way of looking at how colonial interests and opportunities can change. Just like in the United States, there were many one-room schoolhouses in Ireland, Canada, Australia, and South Africa, all former British colonies whose school systems have now become far larger and more complex—but still have ties to the schoolhouse culture from which they came.

Architecturally, one-room schoolhouses were almost always spare and simple, usually rectangular clapboard structures with peaked roofs. This wasn't simply a matter of style; some isolated schools, like one in Pocahontas County, Iowa (now a museum in Cedar Falls), were erected from builder's plans, and busy farming communities had little time to think about embellishments like bell towers, second stories, or porches for their schools. Communities in the new colonies had little on which to base their schools, since the Old World model was of education for the upper classes and apprenticeship for the lower classes. The schoolhouse, despite its hardships, was seen as a vital force in communities. Since many students left before or during their teens, having all grades and age groups in one place was practical; teachers did not have to waste time and materials, but could switch their focus to younger students easily.

Schoolhouses usually closed as communities grew and there was more need for larger schools with teachers who knew a great deal about one or two subjects, instead of a little about seven, eight, or even more. While a few one-room schoolhouses are still active (mainly in Amish and Mennonite communities in the U.S.), most surviving ones have been preserved as museums. The Old West Street Schoolhouse in Southington, Connecticut, dates from 1750 and is definitely one of the oldest American schoolhouses.

Department Store

FIRST IN U.S.: "MARBLE PALACE," NEW YORK CITY (1846)
WORLD'S LARGEST: MACY'S FLAGSHIP, NEW YORK CITY
DESCENDANTS: INDOOR SHOPPING MALLS, STRIP MALLS

Considering how good the French are with fashion and appearances, it should come as no surprise that the first department store was founded in Paris in 1838.

Aristide Boucicaut's Le Bon Marché offered many different departments of goods, including trimmings, linen (modern undergarments), and colognes, all under one roof, and with each item at a fixed price. The latter practice might be the most revolutionary; while some large shopping emporiums already existed, like Saint Petersburg's Gostiny Dvor, for hundreds of years consumers had been accustomed to negotiating for and/or haggling over the cost of goods.

The department store caught on rapidly, with La Samaritaine in Paris, Delany's New Mart in Dublin, and Lewis's in England. The first department store in the U.S. was Alexander Turney Stewart's "Marble Palace," which opened in New York City in 1846. Before long, lower Broadway had become "Ladies' Mile," and included Macy's, Lord & Taylor, B. Altman, and many others. The industrial revolution was in full swing, and these emporiums offering lots and lots of goods were a manufacturer's dream. By 1876, when John Wanamaker opened his eponymous Philadelphia "New Kind of Store," it was a consumer's dream, too: People didn't have to visit multiple shops to find the things they needed, and the large stores became destinations. "Meet me under the eagle at Wanamaker's" was a popular saying, while across the Atlantic, shoppers were in awe of the luxurious things available at Harrods of Knightsbridge.

Department stores continued to proliferate and flourish in the U.S. until the 1960s, when the seeds of new "shopping centers" that urban planners had dreamed up during the postwar 1950s began to take root. As shopping centers turned into shopping malls (the latter were completely enclosed, for the most part), consumers once again began buying shoes at one store, clothing at another, and housewares somewhere else.

House of Worship

TYPES: CHURCH, CATHEDRAL, SYNAGOGUE,
MOSQUE, DUOMO, BASILICA, TEMPLE, SHRINE,
MEETINGHOUSE, CHAPEL, SANCTUARY

Perhaps no other building on this list takes so many and various forms as the "house of worship," which can refer to a temple, a church, a mosque, a shrine, a meetinghouse, a cathedral, a chapel, a synagogue, a basilica, and more. Discussing these forms would fill a separate volume, and so it's more practical (and interesting) to consider the human genesis of worship spaces and how they're used.

A house of worship can be loosely defined as any space in which a group of people come together to perform religious rituals, usually of praise and devotion. The members of congregations, their location, their faith and practices, and their resources all figure into what form a house of worship will take. Earlier cultures, like the Sumerians and the Egyptians, believed that the gods actually lived in these places, or *temenos,* while modern humans generally view places of worship as containing godly qualities because of the good intentions of the people gathered there.

Although a medieval European basilica, a modern Hindu temple, and a 19th-century New England church may have very little in common in style, use, and materials, many houses of worship around the world share at least one characteristic: reaching toward the sky. Spires, domes, towers, and minarets can be humble or grand, literally lofty or figuratively pointed. Additionally, the structure itself can incorporate religious symbolism, as in the rose windows of great cathedrals.

New houses of worship are built all the time, while old ones continue to be used, too. These buildings express a nearly universal human desire to explore meaning. Because houses of worship are so symbolic in their very structure, their preservation is of particular historic importance, and many organizations now exist to help keep these places from crumbling or being demolished.

Nowadays, many independent churches form without a building of their own, members gathering in any space possible—from a crude shelter to someone's private home—in order to be with like-minded individuals and express their beliefs. Some modern congregations have found themselves permanent tenants of school gymnasiums, auditoriums, former storefronts, and even existing church buildings. In the end, the structure matters less than people's desire to congregate.

PARALLEL HISTORY

Shopping Centers and Malls

People all over the world have been constructing covered shopping areas for centuries, like Esfahan's Grand Bazaar and Tehran's Grand Bazaar, both in Iran, and Istanbul's Grand Bazaar in Turkey. Some older covered shopping centers are, like the latter, still in use. In the West, Oxford Covered Market in England dates back to 1774. These convenient and practical arcades allowed many merchants to keep their wares sheltered from the elements while capturing the attention of consumers who were also protected from the same. An early indoor shopping mall in the U.S. was built in 1915 in Duluth, Minnesota.

Houses

Perhaps the most remarkable characteristic of modern homes is that they are designed for the use of a single family, rather than several. From the log cabin to the split-level, people want homes under their control. Sometimes, as in the case of the trailer, they want rooms of their own that they can take wherever they go. However, in most cases a domicile is one of the longest-lasting and most significant items in a person's life. That's why visionary architects like R. Buckminster Fuller tried (and today continue to try) to develop homes that work with the resources readily available. After all, the biggest home of all is planet Earth.

Log Cabin

BROUGHT TO AMERICA FROM SCANDINAVIA
BIRTHPLACE OF ABRAHAM LINCOLN
LINCOLN LOGS: POPULAR CHILDREN'S TOY

Perhaps no other sheltering structure is as closely identified by Americans with American history as the log cabin, but like almost everything else in the United States, the log cabin came from somewhere else. Don't imagine that there were log cabins in Jamestown or at Plymouth; while the Jamestown settlers sometimes used halved logs, they relied more on filling the spaces between the logs with tightly packed clay rather than tightly notching them together. The Puritans who came to Plymouth imitated the clapboard sides and thatched roofs of their native England. Early Dutch settlers favored stone houses, gambrel roofs, and clapboard.

The earliest true log cabins in the American colonies were built during the 17th and 18th centuries by Swedish immigrants to the Delaware Bay area. The Swedes were accustomed to plentiful lumber

PARALLEL HISTORY

Geodesic Dome

Contrary to popular belief, visionary American architect R. Buckminster Fuller did not invent the geodesic dome, although he did help to evangelize and develop it. A geodesic dome is a sphere constructed of intersecting great circles that form triangles at their intersections; it is the only man-made structure that increases in strength as it increases in size. Because there is no standard design for a geodesic dome, and because domes react differently to external stresses than traditional construction forms do, they have not gained widespread popularity.

Architect R. Buckminster Fuller stands with his geodesic dome at the 1967 World's Fair.

and the need to build shelter quickly, in order to escape snow and ice. A fine example of a Swedish log house is the Nothnagle House in Gibbstown, New Jersey, which dates from around 1637. Why is this so significant? Because log houses (and later, cabins) could be constructed without using nails or other joining materials; the notched logs simply fitted one into another, with mud or other filler between the cracks. These houses didn't need internal support structures, either.

They were beautifully suited to an unsettled land that had many large, uniform trees to cut down, especially as pioneers began to move farther and farther west and wanted houses that were sturdy but easily replicated as a family moved from woods to prairie to valley. They were fast and easy to erect, but they were also dark and easy to burn down—residents had to be very careful about their hearth fires. Solid, plain, practical, and humble, the log cabin embodied many of the qualities the growing nation wanted to, and during the election of 1839 Whig presidential hopeful William Henry Harrison ran as the "log cabin candidate" after an opponent tried to belittle him as living in one.

Trailer

FIRST MASS-PRODUCED TRAILER HOME: 1930
ALSO: MOBILE HOME, CAMPER, RV, CARAVAN
FIRST USED AS LONG-TERM HOUSING IN 1950s

The trailer home, also known as a mobile home, doesn't have too many variations in modern life. These affordable living

---

UNCOMMONLY KNOWN...

Camper A "camper" is an American word for a type of trailer that is meant for temporary accommodations, rather than as a permanent dwelling. Two popular types of campers are Winnebagos and Airstreams, the latter having achieved a sort of kitsch icon status. Some campers, called "recreational vehicles" or "RVs," incorporate vehicle and trailer in one.

spaces are usually constructed on concrete slabs and clustered in "trailer parks" that offer rental on the slab as well as utilities like gas, water, and sewage for monthly fees. Trailers are always mobile homes, but mobile homes aren't always trailers—a "trailer" is specifically a mobile home that can be hitched onto another vehicle and taken to a new place. (Mobile homes, sometimes quite elaborate, can usually be moved, but not by trailer hitch.)

Trailers and trailer parks became common in the U.S. during the 1920s, when a growing number of automobiles and highways were making travel different and easier than ever before. Minnesotan Arthur Sherman is credited with inventing the first affordable, mass-produced trailer home in 1930, which he called the Covered Wagon. His year's sales were $56,000. Sherman became the major travel-trailer manufacturer.

Trailers, which long ago would have been wheeled, wooden Gypsy caravans, enjoyed a 1940s heyday, housing war workers and returning GIs in the Washington, D.C., and other metropolitan areas. This may also have been, however, the period in which trailers got their bad reputation. FBI director J. Edgar Hoover called them "dens of vice and corruption," and since the homes were often poorly constructed, there wasn't much to recommend them to solid, upright citizens.

Today, trailer parks have a newly respectable aura, with many upper-class people (even celebrities) seeing them as a great alternative to buying a waterfront home. However, there's still a big drawback to mobile-home or trailer park living. Hurricanes and tornadoes often cause the worst damage to people living in trailer homes. Newer models do have more safety features, but a movable home will never be as sturdy as a permanent one.

Split-level House

CONCEPT BORROWED FROM FRANK LLOYD WRIGHT
HOME DIVIDED INTO LEVELS FOR LIVING AND SLEEPING
POPULAR IN U.S. 1960s-1970s

You may never have visited a split-level home, but you've probably seen one on TV, especially if you've ever watched an American television show recorded during the 1960s or 1970s. Also known as "split foyers," these houses have internal stairs that allow the main entrance to reach both a sleeping level and an entertainment level. Because of a high demand for this kind of "sequestered" living in the 1950s and later, many of these houses were built quickly and cheaply.

The concept of a split level derives from legendary architect Frank Lloyd Wright's idea of houses with "half floors" that would blend more naturally with the surrounding landscape. The method behind split-level mania is that a house with a stacked floor plan does not require a level lot. Like "bank barns," split-levels could be built into, against, or even on a hill.

Split-level houses come in various forms. In some, you enter and see two parallel sets of stairs—one going up, one going down. In others, the staircases are set slightly to the left or right to accommodate a small entryway. There are others, but the main thing to realize is that each of these is a variation on the low, ground-hugging ranch-style house, also popularized by Wright.

In fact, so many modern suburban homes involve some kind of split-level design that people probably don't recognize that they're living in a split-level at all. The stairs can be at the back of the house, at the front of the house, or in the middle of the house. There can be two floors, three floors, or more, depending on the plot, the surrounding vegetation, and the budget. Also, many people who moved into split-level homes have renovated them over the years so that they appear from the front to be Cape Cods or bungalows.

Town House

TYPES: ROW HOUSE, TERRACE HOUSE, CONDOMINIUM
SHARED-WALL HOME DATES TO ANCIENT EGYPT
FIRST APPEARANCE IN U.S.: COLONIAL ERA

Town houses are multilevel homes, sharing at least one wall with an adjoining neighbor. An early illustration of a three-story town house can be found in the tomb of Djehutinefer, royal scribe and treasurer for Amenhotep II. In this spacious and bustling drawing, it is clear that ancient Egyptian town houses often allowed their owners to combine private life with commerce.

UNCOMMONLY KNOWN...
Ranch House The long, low ranch house profile, a popular style in American architecture, was developed out of a wish for a house design that would be as informal and casual as the postwar lifestyle. Ranch houses have very little exterior adornment and owe a great deal to Spanish colonial architecture in the country's Southwest.

With much the same intent, town houses originated in the early modern mind in the United Kingdom. Peers of the realm and other aristocrats often had large country estates but wanted to be "in town" during "the season," which meant London when Parliament was in session. Like ancient walled Rome with its courtyard apartment buildings, London had limited space, so tall, narrow houses made the most of small amounts of real estate. Of these, the elegantly furnished homes of the very rich or well connected were called town houses, while the majority of their middle-class counterparts were referred to as terraced houses, a more pedestrian description of their shared side walls. The terms "terraced housing" and "town house" have flip-flopped in the United Kingdom, with the latter now being preferred.

However, in the U.S., the term "town house" has always been used for this type of city dwelling, and that use has been long. The first town houses in the colonies were built in Manhattan; Boston; Williamsburg and Alexandria, Virginia; and Philadelphia. From the start, American town houses were the province of the wealthy. Poorer people might rent one floor or just a few rooms of a landlord-owned town house, but they rarely owned an entire attached house.

A town house is sometimes also a condominium, meaning the owners jointly own and manage the common walls, utilities, and shared outdoor space (such as gardens, walks, or pools), with all decisions about maintenance and repair managed by an elected board of directors, usually composed of resident volunteers.

Town houses are perennially popular for their benefits, such as allowing for conveniences of high-density living and minimal lawn maintenance.

Condominium

FROM THE LATIN "CON" (TOGETHER) AND
"DOMINIUM" (RIGHT OF OWNERSHIP)
FIRST USE: 1960S

Technically, a condominium is not a type of architecture, but a legal construct. A "condominium" is any type of dwelling in which there is some degree of joint ownership. The units can be apartments, town houses, or even separate dwellings. The difference between a condominium and any other privately owned residence is that a condominium owner has sole legal title to everything within the walls of the home, but everything else—hallways, walkways, common room, recreation areas—is jointly held by the owners and usually by a homeowners association. While there isn't always as much autonomy in making landscaping decisions, for example, this kind of arrangement can be much more convenient, especially for those who don't have time or the inclination to oversee external maintenance issues. Also, in many dense urban areas—anywhere where high-rises are the primary residence type, condos and co-ops are the norm in terms of home ownership.

Another popular modern form of condominium ownership is in planned or gated communities, such as those with golf courses. Owners live in single-family detached homes, with gardens and yards that are maintained by staff hired through the association of owners.

Rooms

A room of one's own is a fine thing, but a room that works for what one needs is even better. Everyone needs access to a kitchen and a bathroom and some form of bedroom, but even the add-ons like porches, garages, and attics can be found at many different socioeconomic levels in different parts of the world. Even more interesting is the fact that certain rooms have been very important at one time, only to lose their significance in another age. For example, the vestibule was once a place in which to practice diplomacy while weeding out good business from bad. Now it's simply a decorative and ceremonial area.

Vestibule

FROM THE LATIN "VESTIBULUM" (ENTRANCE COURT)
DENOTES SPACE WHERE ONE PASSES FROM OUTSIDE TO INSIDE
ALSO ANATOMICAL TERM FOR BEGINNING OF A CANAL

The Latin *vestibulum* means "entrance court," and be it ever so humble, there are few homes entirely without one. Even many tents include a small vestibule, for removing shoes, preventing bug entry into the main tent, and keeping heat inside. A vestibule in a home is the area between the entrance and the interior, and it can be as small as a welcome mat or quite large.

Before discussing the architecture of vestibules, it's worth noting that thresholds and vestibules have long held spiritual significance for different religious traditions and cultures. Crossing from outside to inside is considered a liminal, or transitional, state that can signify changing from child to adult, from single person to married person, from slave to freeman, and from onlooker to participant. Sometimes vestibules are actually waiting areas; neither the transformation nor the action is complete until a person is invited to the other side. A doctor's waiting area is the perfect example of this kind of vestibule.

Vestibules can be large or small, plain or ornate, but they do signal to would-be entrants that they are moving into an interior space. A private home might have a hallway filled with areas for family members to place their belongings, while a public institution might have a separate room decorated with awards and milestones to remind a visitor what he or she is about to experience.

Sometimes people whose homes are grand, or who believe their homes are grand, refer to their hallway or vestibule as a foyer. This is not technically incorrect, but is best used when a vestibule

UNCOMMONLY KNOWN . . .

Staircase Stairs allow users to traverse a vertical distance, such as between floors of a house, without resorting to ropes and pulleys. They always consist of treads for the feet with risers in between and usually some sort of support on the sides, but they can otherwise take many forms, including spiral, alternating-tread, and floating stairs.

has several rooms opening off of it—for example, a library, a sitting room or living room, and a powder room. In opulent, expansive places like opera houses and museums, a foyer might itself be a complex of rooms where spectators can check belongings, rest, and be served refreshments.

Living Room

ALSO: PARLOR, SITTING ROOM, FRONT ROOM, SALON
PLACE FOR: RELAXING, WATCHING TV, ENTERTAINING
"LIVING ROOM WAR": WAR COVERED BY LIVE TELEVISION

When people began to distinguish between public and private life, they also began to designate certain spaces for each. Outer and inner chambers that had different functions are mentioned in ancient writings. At first these rooms were part of temples. As it was necessary for clerics to receive and entertain guests, the rooms probably became more elaborate and comfortable as time progressed. Certainly every monastery and convent in the medieval era had a designated "vistors' parlor" that allowed the dedicated religious not to sully their holy places with outsiders.

The word *parlor* derives from the French verb *parler,* "to speak," which describes what people did in these front chambers: held audiences. Interestingly, in the West these chambers nearly always formed part of another building, while in the East they might be entirely separate: the Turkish "kiosk," which is used in the West solely for information or vending, was originally a sort of gazebo or belvedere

where a conversation could take place away from private spaces.

Parlors, or sitting rooms, became quite popular in England and France in the late 18th and early 19th centuries. Depending on a family's income, they might be quite small, but they were still considered the proper place for receiving visitors. Early American houses often did not have parlors, but as houses grew larger and the nation's manners became more set, proper families made sure they had "front rooms" filled with their finest possessions: upholstered furniture, portraits, fine needlework, sterling silver, and often a piano.

Because these rooms were usually clean, closed off, and quite formal, people often used them when someone died as a place to lay out the body and allow funeral visits. Since home parlors have been largely replaced by funeral parlors, front rooms have become living rooms, where residents of a house conduct their day-to-day activities such as reading, talking on the telephone, talking with each other, and reviewing mail.

Kitchen

FROM OLD ENGLISH "CYCENE" AND
LATIN "COQUERE" (TO COOK)
INFORMAL: PERCUSSION SECTION OF ORCHESTRA

In terms of rooms, the kitchen may actually be the world's oldest. The original kitchen was the space around a fire where humans cooked their meat, and that salient feature has never changed. The one defining commonality

PARALLEL HISTORY

Julia Child's Kitchen

In 2002, The Smithsonian Institution painstakingly moved and exhibited every item of Julia Child's Cambridge, Massachusetts, home kitchen of 45 years, right down to her massive, professional-grade Garland gas stove. Credited as the person who renewed Americans' interest in fine cooking, Child had a series called "The French Chef" on Boston public television. Her easygoing demeanor reflected the fact that this California-raised, Smith College-educated, OSS-trained woman was not a rigid chef. She started cooking in her late 30s while living in Paris. Julia Child equipped the kitchen, and husband Paul designed its layout, blue-and-green palette, and pegboards that accommodate each beloved pot and pan.

of kitchens around the world is that they contain some sort of place that allows raw ingredients to be heated. The first "home improvement" may have been simply clearing a circle of debris and surrounding it with stones to better contain the fire.

The ancient Romans might have had a hearth for warmth in their private homes, but unless they were nobility, they had to do their cooking in public kitchens. In early medieval Europe, communal cooking fires were vented through a hole in the roof, much as in Native American longhouses. The main challenge with all early cooking methods was to contain, dispel, or avoid wood smoke. Since many homes could not separate the kitchen from living areas, the smoke could make life quite grim.

At last, in the early 19th century, inventors began creating stoves like the Rumford and the Oberlin that held the fire and helped to make the heat flow more efficiently. Previously, the only fixed point in kitchens were the hearths, sometimes open, sometimes enclosed within brick or tile walls. Everything else—table, worktops, dressers, shelves—was placed for the convenience of the cook or cooks and could be moved or discarded as necessary.

However, as the enclosed stoves made kitchens cleaner, more could be accomplished in them, and people found that they wanted more cabinets and drawers for equipment. When efficient indoor plumbing made kitchen sinks possible for the first time, people then wanted enclosures for

the pipes. Soon after, when home refrigerators allowed cooks to keep perishables close at hand, they wanted more counter space for meal preparations. These wishes led to our modern "fitted" kitchens, where appliances are slotted in between trim, matching cabinets.

Bathroom

IN AMERICAN ENGLISH, PRIMARILY INDICATES LAVATORY
OTHER CULTURES: TOILET IS SEPARATE FROM BATHING ROOM
BATH HOUSES FIRST USED FOR SPIRITUAL CLEANSING

Americans are so used to saying "I'm going to the bathroom" that many have forgotten that there's a difference between an actual bathroom, containing a toilet, a sink, and a shower and/or bathtub, and a restroom or washroom with just the toilet and sink.

A bathroom, in other words, allows for both elimination and bathing. Most North American homes have bathrooms where everything is in one room together; some homes also have a "half bath" or "powder room," too. However, in other countries (e.g., France, Japan), the toilet is in a completely separate room from the sink and bathing area. This is considered more hygienic and courteous, as bad smells and sounds can be confined.

Toilets are fixtures connected to a building's sewage plumbing and designed for the evacuation of human waste. In modern Western homes, toilets are usually in the form of a seat, made out of industrial porcelain, but in some countries toilets consist of little more than a hole in the floor.

Bathrooms as places to clean the human body have a long history; in ancient civilizations, cleanliness really was considered next to godliness. People didn't bathe to please others or to stay healthy; they bathed because they believed they needed to be purified in order to worship. This tradition survives to the present day in many different forms, including Christian baptisms (infant and adult), Hindu mass bathing in the sacred Ganges, the Jewish *mikvah* bath, and American Indian sweat lodges.

Eventually bathing became pleasurable in its own right, and the virtues of cleanliness were celebrated, too. Although many people think our forebears avoided bathing, it was really only during the Renaissance and afterward that Europeans eschewed it, believing that water spread disease. They were right, of course, but they didn't understand that soap could prevent that. However, this attitude hastened the end of public baths in western Europe and led to the rise of private bathrooms. Many cultures, including Japanese and Russian, continued to use public baths. It's now possible, in New York City, to visit Russian, Turkish, Japanese, and Korean bathhouses. And some U.S. retailers have made a fortune selling everything you need for a relaxing and cleansing bath.

Whether you combine several functions into one room, or build several rooms to suit different functions, indoor bathrooms with plumbing are a weclome and convenient invention.

PARALLEL HISTORY

Harappan Flush Toilets

Excavations at Lothal in western India's Gujarat province uncovered the unexpected: the remains of what were once fully functioning indoor toilets. They belonged to the Harappan civilization, which originated in what is now present-day Pakistan, and had exceptionally well-organized cities and systems. Their toilets date back to about 2,700 years ago and included vertical chutes for waste to be sent to cesspits. The toilets and bathing areas were quite sturdy, as they were constructed of bricks. More important, however, is that the sewage system was fully connected and plumbed, keeping the city and its individual dwellings free of open drains.

Basement

FROM THE DUTCH WORD FOR FOUNDATION
DESCENDED FROM THE DIRT-WALLED CELLAR
MODERN BASEMENTS FIRST POPULAR IN 1950s SUBURBS

Cellars and subspaces have been used in human domiciles for thousands of years, but the term "basement" in the U.S. is recent. In the post–World War II era, many new suburban developments were built, like Long Island's well-known "Levittown," made of concrete slabs with no basements. Some of these developments were grander than others, but what they all reflected was a homeowner desire for storage space.

Suburban basements were usually built of concrete blocks on top of the concrete slab that served as the house foundation. Before this, American homes might have a cellar (often with packed-dirt walls reinforced with beams) where food and canned goods were stored and where families in tornado states took shelter during storms. Used during the 20th century, a newly revitalized postwar economy and a culture of accumulation made basements even more valuable as storage space.

Families wanted and purchased bicycles, toboggans, sports equipment, and hobby materials, and acquired items from parents and other relatives. More important, however, was the fact that basements offered a place for the water heater, furnace, laundry appliances, and other bulky necessities of modern life to be housed without intruding on active living space.

However, homeowners soon found that these "bonus spaces" had problems sometimes, too. Because warm air rises, basements are generally cooler than the rest of a house, and that means damper, too. Mildew and mold that grow in cool, damp conditions can damage things kept there, as well as inflict allergies and breathing problems on the people who live in the home. Drainage problems are frequent, too, causing both flooding risks and sewer gas leaks.

Attic

ARCHITECTURAL TERM FROM 17TH CENTURY
SIGNIFICANT ELEMENT OF RENAISSANCE FACADE
TODAY USED FOR STORAGE OR "BONUS ROOMS"

Some words carry a wealth of connotations; in the case of a house's attic, the connotations are rivaled only by the amount of stuff that some people manage to cram in. Defined as the space between the top floor's ceiling and the pinnacle of a pitched roof, attics conjure up the past, history, baggage, knowledge, mystery, antiques, and surplus. Further adding to these associations is the fact that most attics are difficult to access, oddly shaped, and full of dark spaces that might harbor spiders or rats or worse.

Of course, while attics are full of things unseen, they also serve a purpose, which is to keep a mass of warm air at the top of the house. The unmoving warm air blanket helps to hold a home's temperature steady and comfortable. It also keeps the attic warm and dry, which is why so many people over the centuries have chosen attics as repositories. If you stored your papers, textiles, and furnishings in a basement, they would be subject to mildew and mold. In the attic, the threats are different and can be contained more easily. Mothballs and mousetraps do the trick, most of the time, although homeowners do have to remember not to overfill attics and make them firetraps.

Attics are completely enclosed, and may be accessible via a normal staircase, or pull-down stairs through the top-floor ceiling (in order to preserve more living space). The normal staircases leading to attics in older homes made it easier for guests' luggage to be stored in the attic, out of the way of bedrooms and hallways. This was particularly important for life on large estates, where visitors often arrived for stays lasting weeks and requiring multiple changes of clothes; their trunks and cases had to be stowed somewhere.

Front Porch

FROM GREEK "PORTICO" (TEMPLE ENTRANCE)
FIXTURE OF AMERICAN SOUTHERN ARCHITECTURE
DESCENDANTS: DECKS, BACKYARD PATIOS

Many architectural periods have included porchlike structures and features, from the Greek temple peristyle to the Italian loggia, all of them providing a way station between outside and inside. The word *porch* comes from the Latin *porticus* or Greek *portico,* both signifying the entrance to a temple.

Porticos evolved into vestibules, and later, during the Renaissance, people began to deliberately build shaded verandas that allowed relief from the sun while letting breezes blow freely. These were the precursors of, but not the only influence on, the American front porch.

Most of America's first immigrants were from Europe, and few architectural traditions there included porches. Some of the first porches came from somewhere else entirely: Africa. West African houses included the "shotgun," three to five rooms without a hallway and containing an attached front porch. While in 18th- and 19th–century America, African slaves were held in northern and southern states, the porch tradition grew more quickly in the South, probably because of the heat and humidity in those states.

By the late 19th century, porches had become a unique feature of American architecture, regardless of a house's style. The leisure time afforded by new kinds of labor and labor-saving devices contributed to the rise in a culture where people "sat out" in comfortable weather, watching and interacting with their neighbors. Porches connected people and communities, allowing visitors to stop by for casual exchanges, seniors to stay connected to the neighborhood activity, and parents to keep an eye on their children while relaxing from a day's work. The porch was an extension of Americans' connection to nature, while at the same time sheltering them from it.

The front porch was also part of a walking culture, and as automobiles grew more popular and more widely available, front porches became less important to new-home construction than things like garages and backyard patios.

Garage

FROM THE FRENCH "GARER" (TO SHELTER)
DESCENDED FROM THE CARRIAGE HOUSE
FIRST CARPORT: W. B. SLOANE HOUSE, ELMHURST, IL

Today garages are often used for human comfort: They keep cars cool in hot climates, and they allow for storage of tools, car maintenance items, and anything else that doesn't fit in the basement, attic, or spare bedroom. However, they were created for the care and keeping of automobiles. Early autos weren't airtight, watertight, or particularly sturdy. When they weren't cruising down bumpy roads at blazing speeds of 15 mph, these horseless carriages needed to be kept inside.

Of course, carriage houses had been around for hundreds of years before automobiles, for many of the same reasons. However, autos had the added challenge of mechanical parts. If a carriage was rained on, it might require some oiling; if a Model T was rained on, it might need an entirely new engine.

Like carriage houses, home garages were at first entirely separate, or "detached" from houses. Attached garages, which offer the convenience of avoiding rain, wind, snow, and heat, grew in popularity during the 1960s and 1970s, after car ownership became common. Another method of car protection is the carport, which is really a simple version of the older carriage houses.

Elements

Even the simplest clay hut has a door. Just as people learned to tailor their buildings to communal purpose and their rooms to individual need, they figured out early that if a space doesn't work with the human body, it won't ever be used. Doorknobs work with hands, indoor lighting allows eyes to see after the sun sets, and heating and cooling make enclosed spaces bearable. These and other elements make buildings work with and for us, and in moving more and more tasks indoors, these elements have also affected human industry and progress.

Glass Windows

FIRST MANUFACTURED GLASS: 2500 B.C.
IN ANCIENT ARCHITECTURE, WINDOWS FILLED WITH
IRON OR WOOD GRATES, MICA, OR PAPER

Before people learned to make glass, they could see it. There were two kinds of natural glass: Fulgurites were slender tubes that could result when lightning hit sand. After a volcanic eruption, survivors might see a dark glass known as obsidian that early cultures often used for knives, arrowheads, and jewelry. We know people have been making glass for thousands of years, with the first known manufactured glass dating from around 2500 B.C. Around 50 B.C., the blow pipe was invented by the

PARALLEL HISTORY

English Window Tax

A beautiful English country house with a facade full of windows might be making not an aesthetic statement, but an economic one, especially if it dates from the 17th or 18th century. Many rich landowners ostentatiously added windows to demonstrate that they were able to pay the government-imposed "window tax" that was supposed to circumvent the popular opposition to income tax. In some places in England, there are still bricked-over windows that resulted from owners who opposed or could not afford the tax, levied according to the number of windows in a home.

Windows no longer incur taxes on this street in England.

Phoenicians, allowing artists to manipulate glass into myriad shapes. For many centuries, elaborate and beautiful glass vessels were created.

After the casting process was developed in the 17th century, glass came into more common use—but there was still no way to make consistently smooth sheets of glass to be used in windows. Stained-glass windows, which give medieval churches and cathedrals a mystical glamour, were quite practical: Instead of making many small blown panes, glassworkers could create mosaics of smaller bits.

In the early 19th century, window glass was called crown glass, made by blowing a bubble of glass, then spinning it until it was flat and leaving a sheet of glass with a bumpy "crown" in the center. This was replaced by "cylinder" glass that was flattened to form window panes. In the 1840s, plate glass was made by casting a large quantity of molten glass. After the glass was cooled, it was polished on both sides. Later in the 19th century, a mechanized process was developed that finally made windows affordable for the middle class.

Doorknob

FIRST PATENTER: OSBOURN DORSEY
FIRST PATENTED: DECEMBER 10, 1878
"DOOR-HOLDING DEVICE" U.S. PATENT NO.: #210,764

B efore they had doors, people didn't need doorknobs, which is to say that the humble doorknob's history follows that of private life. Opening early doors might have been as simple as pushing them, or using a key

to unlock them, or using a latchstring looped around the door's bar to keep it closed from the inside. Doors might also fold, slide, or roll back.

There were many kinds of door latches, handles, and other hardware, including doorknobs, used worldwide for centuries before the doorknob was "invented" in 1878 by Osbourn Dorsey.

Despite the fact that round or oval (egg-shaped) knobs had been used since colonial times, Dorsey's U.S. patent for a doorknob changed the way most Americans opened and closed their doors. What Dorsey "invented" was a compression casting method that made it easier and faster to make uniform doorknobs that were highly ornamented. In the early 20th century, ball bearings were put into the knobs' shanks that made them turn much more smoothly.

Most doorknobs are around two inches wide and are made up of a knob rose, shank, spindle, and knob top (also known as plate, stem, shaft, and actual knob). Most doorknobs have a locking device built in since machine processes for steel locks were introduced in the late 19th century. A common locking doorknob today is the push-button type that operates from the knob's center to control a bolt to a spring lock.

While the majority of doorknobs are simple and plain, at different times there have been fashions for elaborate and beautiful knobs. Mid-19th-century glass doorknobs can be particularly elaborate and interesting to collect.

Just as some of the most ornamental doorknobs can be entirely functional, some of the simplest doorknobs can be awfully flimsy. Doorknobs benefit less from design and more from engineering. Smooth bearings and durable materials mean graceful exits and entrances, less chance for breakage, and more security for one's possessions.

Peephole

ALSO KNOWN AS DOOR SCOPE
ALLOWS HOMEOWNER TO SAFELY SURVEY EXTERIOR
FEATURE OF MODERN PROTECTIVE DOORS

Peepholes are used for privacy and for propriety, but one of their most important historical uses has been for protection from other people. A solid door forms a barrier against those who might want to steal or invade property, to cause harm, or to establish some kind of dominance or headquarters. When a knock comes at an unexpected time, inhabitants often want to know who is standing on the other side before they open the door.

Early doors that may have consisted of a simple screen of branches or an animal hide didn't offer much security, and people began to attempt to make more permanent barriers. These ancient doors were often carved out of heavy stone and opened or closed on pivots at the top and bottom—effective at keeping intruders out, but not easy to manipulate just to check if there's a delivery arriving. Every kind of door has some kind of advantage and disadvantage. Some are easy to open but hard to keep closed. Some let in the light but also let in unwanted views.

The peephole is one way of trying to make a sturdy, protective door more useful. In its earliest form, the peephole was probably a slit. When people realized

that dangerous things could go through slits (fire, poison, arrows), they chose instead to cut tiny doors at eye level through which to "peep." Of course, if harm was really meant, while one of these peepholes was open, a predator could inflict harm, too.

A window in the door was a partial solution, but what if people didn't want to have a visitor know if anyone was behind the door? The peephole, or door scope, was the solution, allowing a homeowner to see who was ringing the doorbell without being seen.

Indoor Lighting

EDISON'S INDOOR LIGHTING SYSTEM: 1882, NEW YORK CITY
BY 1993, LIGHTING ACCOUNTED FOR 9.4 PERCENT OF
U.S. HOUSEHOLD ELECTRICITY CONSUMPTION

One of the most difficult things for modern people to imagine is how dark houses were before the advent of electricity. And not just dark, even with oil lamps and candles, but dark and quiet and still. Without electricity, there were no automatic central air systems, refrigerators, radios, washing machines, or other appliances. The old proverb "Early to bed and early to rise makes a man healthy, wealthy, and wise" was written when people could not do certain things after sunset without having to use candles for lighting. Thus, going to bed not only saved resources and prevented fire hazards, but also made the most of morning light.

However, it was the desire for indoor lighting that spurred inventors to find electricity, and it was electricity and the electrical grid that allowed those other things to be connected. In 1879, Thomas Alva Edison developed the first working lightbulb in his Menlo Park, New Jersey, laboratory. People leaped at the chance to extend their days both earlier and later with the aid of indoor lighting. Lightbulbs seemed like such a simple and magical thing: screw them into a lamp, plug the lamp into the wall, and you have light. Small electrical stations sprang up as homeowners started buying lighting devices, but they couldn't power more than a few city blocks, and many people in outlying areas couldn't get electricity even though it existed.

President Frankin D. Roosevelt's Rural Electrification Administration (REA) was founded in 1935 to build the power grid that would allow all Americans access to indoor lighting. The electric lamp changed more than just household rhythms. Indoor lighting meant that factories and other businesses could operate at any hours they pleased.

Since Edison's incandescent bulbs came on the scene, Americans have used them freely at home, preferring their soft glow to fluorescent lighting. Fluorescent lights often used in office buildings give off harsh light that is hard on the eyes and unappealing in residences. However, in the 21st century, people are beginning to change their incandescent, energy-hogging bulbs for a new kind of fluorescent bulb made specifically for home use and lasting much longer than incandescents. These new compact fluorescents save energy and also reduce waste and packaging.

Air-Conditioning

FIRST FULLY AIR-CONDITIONED OFFICE BUILDING:
MILAM BUILDING, SAN ANTONIO, TEXAS, LATE 1920s
FIRST MASS-PRODUCED INDIVIDUAL AC UNITS: LATE 1940s

Imagine a hot, humid summer day. You're stuck in your car in the middle of a traffic jam, and there's no snowflake button your dashboard. You've got no air-conditioning!

That scenario is difficult to imagine for the millions whose lives are made comfortable by air-conditioning in cars, at home, at the office, and in places like schools, supermarkets, waiting rooms, and places of worship.

What did we do before we had air-conditioning? Buildings were constructed differently, for one thing. Homes had porches, high ceilings, and wide eaves under the roofs that allowed the hottest air to rise away from the lower floors. Before that, buildings had water circulating through walls (ancient Romans), water-powered fan wheels (China), cisterns and wind towers (Persia), and ventilators (medieval Egypt). People have always wanted to be cool, after all.

Modern mechanized air-conditioning was made possible by British scientist Michael Faraday's 1820 discovery that compressed, liquefied ammonia could chill the air around it while it evaporated. In 1842, Dr. John Gorrie used compression to cool air in an Apalachicola, Florida, ward of malaria and yellow fever patients.

The term "air-conditioning" was coined in 1906 by textile manufacturer Stuart W. Cramer of Charlotte, North Carolina, who was accustomed to using the phrase "water conditioning" when talking about certain processes. Besides cooling and ventilating the air, like his contemporary air-conditioning innovator Willis Haviland Carrier, Cramer wanted to control its moisture content, an important step toward modern air conditioner technology. The advent of air-conditioning for cars and homes changed the way Americans lived.

Central Heat

EARLY PROTOTYPES: COAL FURNACES AND WOODSTOVES
HEAT TRANSMITTED BY: CONVECTION OR RADIATION
MOST HOMES HEATED WITH NATURAL GAS OR ELECTRICITY

For thousands of years, "central heating" meant having a fire in the middle of a house. Around A.D. 100, the Romans, who had already centralized things like plumbing with aqueducts, came up with the hypocaust, which used air heated by furnaces under floors and behind walls to heat all of the rooms in a house. In Korea, a central heating system called *ondol* was in use at about the same time, and worked on the same principle: excess heat from stoves did not have to be wasted.

In the 18th century, European engineers discovered that water could be used to conduct heat. Sealed water-circulation systems combined with steam provided such steady heat that some of their earliest uses were for hothouses.

U.S. homes were mostly heated by wood until the late 19th century, when coal became the preferred fuel. Coal-fired basement boilers delivered hot water or steam to cheap cast-iron radiators, and the earliest coal furnaces (invented by Dave Lennox in 1885) worked by convection. In the mid-20th century, electric fans were added for more efficient distribution of the furnace-heated air throughout a home's ductwork.

Gas and oil-fired forced air furnaces were not far behind, and made it much easier for homeowners to avoid having to stoke fires, carry coal hods, and keep dirty and spacehogging bins of coal in basements. Today most American homes are heating with gas-fired forced-air furnaces (FAUs), and a few with oil-fired FAUs, while homes in warmer climates often feature "heat pumps" that supply energy for both heating and cooling the air. Gas-fired furnaces are more efficient than others, and that is becoming more important as people consider the environmental impact of home heating and cooling options.

PARALLEL HISTORY

History of Air Conditioning etc.

The modern air conditioner owes its efficiency to American engineer Willis Carrier, who in 1902 built "An Apparatus for Treating Air" for the Sackett-Wilhelms Lithographing and Publishing Company of Brooklyn. Chilled coils cooled air and lowered humidity to 55 percent. Carrier's invention was a huge success, and the first air-conditioned home was in Minneapolis in 1914 and belonged to Charles Gates. In 1922, Carrier made two new innovations: He replaced the ammonia in the coils with a coolant called dielene and added a central compressor that made the units smaller. When Carrier sold his air conditioner to movie theaters, they became even more popular—now people could escape the summer heat along with their workaday cares. Soon air-conditioning units were being installed in office buildings, department stores, and many other places.

Appliances

M odern people might not consider appliances such as a refrigerator an "extra," but it really isn't an essential, such as adequate food and shelter. That's the key to understanding the introduction and development of the (mostly electric) appliances in this section. Not only did they make life easier; technology began making them easier, too. Before the advent of the kitchen range, cooking meant managing a fire. Before the advent of the dishwasher, implements had to be washed by hand (before that, they had to be hauled to the nearest water source, or scoured with sand).

Clock

FIRST CLOCKS: SUNDIALS
FIRST MECHANICAL CLOCKS MADE 14TH CENTURY
OTHER TYPES: GRANDFATHER, ATOMIC, DIGITAL, OGEE

A clock measures time, that age-old human construct for measuring life's events such as changing seasons, births, deaths, duration of activities or situations, and aging. Some of these things are easily quantifiable and others less so. Early human beings, faced with these events, tried to make sense of them. For example, they wanted to measure the movement from day to night, asking the question "How do we get from a place where there is light to a place where there is dark?" Just try to respond to a question like this without using the word *time* or terms of time's measurement, and you'll see how important this concept is to the human mind.

The oldest way to divide light from dark was the sun clock or sundial, in the form of huge obelisks used by the Egyptians, around 3500 B.C. The sundial was a disk with lines arrayed so that when sunlight hit one, people would know if it was early or midmorning, noon or later. Of course, sundials work only when the sun is shining, which limited their usefulness. The next major horological development was the Egyptian water clock, or clepsydra, which used steadily dripping water to mark passages in the day. Its advantage was that it could be used after dark as well.

The first mechanical clocks appeared in the 14th century, and the early ones weren't very accurate. This wasn't simply a matter of someone making it to a big meeting; the race to create an accurate marine chronometer was deadly serious, since the more

---

UNCOMMONLY KNOWN...

Wristwatch Watches have been used since the 17th century, but they were in pockets and not on wrists. The first watches with mechanisms small enough to make them wrist-ready on a large scale began to be made in the early 20th century. The "Santos," designed by Louis Cartier for flight pioneer Alberto Santos-Dumont, was square and fixed to a leather strap.

accurate it was, the better longitude could be calculated. And the better longitude could be measured, the better cartograhers could map the globe.

While modern humans often marvel at the scientific mistakes of their ancestors, some ancient cultures made remarkable strides in establishng time measurements—innovations that have, in some cases, not been surpassed today. For example, the Greeks divided the year into 12 equal passages called "months"—a word that comes from moon and indicates the distance it takes for the moon to fully change. But it was their earlier counterparts, the Egyptians and the Babylonians, who divided their days into 24 equal parts called "hours."

Refrigerator

FIRST ARTIFICIAL REFRIGERATION DEMONSTRATED 1748
FIRST COMMERCIAL REFRIGERATION: 1856
FIRST PERSONAL FRIDGE PRODUCER: GENERAL ELECTRIC

The impact of home refrigerators on people's lifestyles is much larger than most of us think. If you took away a kitchen

stove, food could still be cooked on a grill or in a fire. If you took away a dishwasher, pot and plates could still be rinsed in a water source. But taking away a household's refrigerator would seriously affect the ability of its residents to store perishable foods. The residents might begin to buy just enough for each day, or buy larger amounts of nonperishable groceries, or relearn the art of food preservation such as canning, salting, and drying.

Long ago, cultures had to harvest and store snow and ice in order to have the option of cooling food down during hotter months. Soon the places where they stored them became known as icehouses and could be placed near lakes so that hauling fresh ice up from the surface wasn't too difficult. Icehouses were the forerunner of household ice boxes, which usually had hollow, metal-lined walls and a place for a large block of ice near the top. There really were icemen who came to replace those blocks, which steadily melted from day to day, the water draining into a pan that had to be emptied from day to day, too.

Before discussing the advent of modern mechanical refrigerators, it's important to note that refrigeration, unlike most food-preservation methods, does not change the taste of foods. Salting, drying, pickling, smoking, brining, and canning all affect fresh foods' texture and taste, which refrigeration does not. Still, it took time for refrigerators to catch on, due both to their significant cost and their toxic chemicals. The first refrigerators were created in the 19th century and used for commercial applications; the first widespread use of home refrigerators occurred in the 1920s and consisted of a round compressor above the cabinet that used sulfur dioxide or methyl formate. By the 1930s, the toxic stuff had been replaced with Freon, the price had gone down, and a new generation was ready for refrigeration.

Kitchen Range

EARLY KITCHEN STOVES HEATED BY COAL OR WOOD
19TH-CENT. STOVES: FRANKLIN, POT-BELLIED, RUMFORD
TODAY'S RANGES HEATED BY: GAS OR ELECTRIC

T he earliest kitchen was a cook fire, and that also would be the earliest example of a kitchen stove. While all cookers are stoves, not all stoves are cookers; a "stove" can also be a device that heats a room.

Therefore, while many Americans talk about their "kitchen stove," they're not really accurate. The "kitchen range" is a modern term that describes a combination of burners, oven, heating elements (the stove part), and smoke-removing hood that is designed to fit in with the other appliances and cabinets in the kitchen. Although a range can make a kitchen very warm, particularly during summer, very few American homes include stoves for heat in their kitchens.

Cooking stoves began to evolve in the 18th century, as people became frustrated with the amount of smoke given off by their cooking fires. Building a semi-enclosed space, ventilated by a chimney,

was far more practical than trying to fan away black fumes. Early metal stoves, often heavy cast iron, began to change as natural gas and electricity became options for heating them instead of coal.

The kitchen "range" by its name lets us know that it can accommodate more than one kind of cooking. On the cooktop you can sauté, boil, fry, grill, and simmer; in the oven you can bake, braise, roast, and broil. Some modern ranges also include an attached microwave oven. Still others, like England's celebrated Aga cooker, offer continuous heat: This gas range is always on, and different parts of it are heated to different temperatures, so you can boil the kettle for tea and keep a plate warmed at the same time.

Ranges are gas or electric, for the most part, but many professional cooks prefer gas for the cooktop burners and electric for the oven. One of the most interesting trends in the past two decades has been the installation of professional-grade kitchen ranges, some with six to eight burners, in private homes.

Vaccum Cleaner

JAMES MURRAY SPANGLER
JUNE 2, 1908 | U.S. PATENT NO. 889,823
PATENT "CARPET SWEEPER AND CLEANER"

I f you've ever watched a movie set before the birth of the vacuum cleaner, you may have viewed scenes of servants whacking the dirt and debris out of rugs with "carpet beaters," long-handled paddles made of cane or bamboo. Floors could be swept, but even very stiff brooms couldn't penetrate the fibers of thick wool carpets favored in cold northern climates to keep some warmth underfoot.

Some early 20th-century inventors came up with carpet sweepers and industrial, multi-tubed suction machines, but in an era that saw more people moving into smaller homes and apartments, an easier and more effective solution was needed. Enter James Murray Spangler, a Canton, Ohio, department store janitor, who in 1907 patched together a portable vacuum-powered cleaner from an old fan motor, a soapbox, and a broom handle. A year later, Spangler received a patent for a more finished design and sold one of his first machines to a cousin named William H. Hoover.

The rest, as they say, is history. "Hoover" is now so synonymous with vacuum cleaners that it's a colloquial expression for the act of vacuum cleaning in the United Kingdom. The first Hoover model on the market was the O. The Hoover's most notable feature was its "beater bar," which inspired its once catchy slogan, "It beats as it sweeps as it cleans."

Although Hoover captured the initial brand recognition, it soon had competition from companies like Electrolux, Kirby, and Eureka. All of this competition means that every year vacuum cleaner companies tout some new feature, power level, safety mechanism, or technology that they hope will compel consumers to replace their existing machines as quickly as possible. The latest vacuums are automatic and self-operating, such as the Roomba, a motorized, robotic vacuum cleaner that looks like a thick, oversize Frisbee.

Unfortunately, the Roomba can't lift rugs or reach cobwebs—yet. For the short term, most vacuums are only as good as effort exerted by the people operating them.

UNCOMMONLY KNOWN...

Brooms This ancient cleaning tool has stiff, clustered bristles that allow a person to sweep a level surface, like a wooden or tiled floor, clean of debris and dirt. Long associated with witches, in recent years, brooms gained new popularity as the preferred conveyance for the fictional game of Quidditch in the Harry Potter series. Perhaps also due to their association with witches, brooms, or besoms, are now symbolic elements of Wiccan ritual.

Clocks Through Time

N o one knows exactly when or how humans began keeping track of time, but it must have been early on in history, since a world with regular light and dark, hot and cold, and growth and death would be sensible to track. Nevertheless, it took thousands of years before people were able to track time accurately and consistently. This wasn't because they couldn't figure out the cycles and rhythms of the natural world, but because technological innovation couldn't keep pace with that previously gained knowledge. Even now, some of the earliest clocks, including water clocks and sundials, are remarkably accurate timekeepers up to certain increments. It was the need to be more accurate, more specific, more precise that drove people to figure out a timepiece that would remain accurate and consistent throughout a sea voyage so that the measure of the globe could be taken. Although it took a long time to mass-produce clocks and watches, besides being one of the most essential elements of any house or building, they help us understand the pace of history.

PREHISTORY
Shadow stick A stick placed in the ground with markers around it to show the sun's position at different moments in the day. Shadows grew shorter toward midday and longer toward night.

2000 B.C.
Sundial The stick or gnomon of a simple shadow clock was angled for greater accuracy. Brass sun-dials like this one were used through the European Renaissance.

Dishwasher

JOSEPHINE GARIS COCHRANE
DECEMBER 28, 1886 | U.S. PATENT NO. 355,139
PATENT "GARIS-COCHRANE MACHINE"

For millennia, the word *dishwasher* meant a person who washed dishes and nothing more. Cleaning pots, pans, plates, and flatware was the lowest form of kitchen labor, and while it might be fatiguing, it was a very simple process as long as there were enough people involved.

There was and is a drawback to hand washing dishes, however, and that is human clumsiness. In a sink full of soapy water and slippery plates and glasses, it's easy to break things. Shelbyville, Illinois, socialite Josephine Garis Cochrane found in 1886 that she'd had enough of her servants chipping her fine bone china. Cochrane hated to wash dishes herself, so she began mulling over possible inventions to handle the work.

Evidently inventing ran in her genes. This granddaughter of John Fitch, inventor of the steamboat, wasn't afraid of a little engineering. She constructed a prototype of a machine with racks that held the dishes in place as they were shot with water jets from above and below. Her hand-operated device was the hit of the 1893 World's Columbian Exposition. She was able to patent her device and sell it to many outlets. Eventually her company became known as KitchenAid, which is still in business today as part of Whirlpool.

Dishwashers for home use were not readily available until the 1950s, but by the 1970s most middle-class home had one installed, often in avocado green or gold to coordinate with the other appliances.

A.D. 200
Hourglass We don't have a recorded use of an hourglass until 1300, but we know that people in Alexandria were said to have carried small versions with them centuries earlier.

1500
Pocket watch Earliest versions were actually meant to be worn around the neck; they were far too bulky to fit in a pocket. Streamlined versions, sometimes cased, began to show up toward the end of the 16th century.

1980
Digital clock Modern digital clocks can be very helpful for dyslexics since there is no need to read the display; the numerals are right there, in proper order.

1200
Mechanical clock Early versions ran on water, falling weights, or gears. Many innovations were made by Arabic inventors, partially driven by the need for a way to mark prayer times.

1800
Grandfather clock Most longcase clocks are weight driven with pendulums. They strike the time on the hour and half hour, and some chime quarter hours as well.

Backyard

hen humankind finally settled under a roof and had figured out how to bring things like light, air, and water inside, irony struck. Of course people began longing for gardens, open-air terraces, and other outdoor spaces attached to houses and buildings. Experiencing the connection between indoors and outdoors via tents, decks, gardens, and lawns became quite common, and once again the "extras" came into play, too. If you're worrying about getting enough to eat, you grow cabbage, rather than orchids. If you're worried about having enough water to drink, you haul buckets rather than putting in a pool.

Lawn

FROM OLD FRENCH "LAUNDE" (HEATH, MOOR)
ALSO KNOWN AS: YARD
LAWN PARTY: U.S. VERSION OF GARDEN PARTY

lthough a green lawn is now as symbolic of the American good life as a white picket fence or a brand-new car, at one time a large lawn was considered frivolous and only for the rich. Step out the door of most American homes before the mid-20th century, and you'd probably find a kitchen garden, packed dirt, or a path to an outbuilding.

While many Americans yearned for the kinds of rolling fields and lawns found back in England, much of the New World climate wasn't suitable for nurturing grass. People tried and failed to grow English grass seeds in the U.S., but it didn't work.

Nothing did, until in 1915 an association whose activity depended on even grass, the U.S. Golf Association, teamed up with the U.S. government to create a combination of grasses that would work.

While the result of those efforts paid off, it wasn't the end of the story. English lawns are watered by a humid, rainy climate; American lawns would largely need to be watered, regularly and sometimes during droughts. English lawns at the time were kept low by scything or grazing (one reason President Woodrow Wilson kept a herd of sheep on the South Lawn of the White House during his tenure). American lawns remained few and far between until the garden house and the rotary lawn mower became available. After World War II they became standard features of one's property.

Lawns aren't always purely ornamental. They provide play space for young children; foundation for outdoor sports like croquet, bowls, and soccer; and may also be places for gardens and social events. However, lawn maintenance can be costly and time-consuming, with people who neglect this upkeep receiving pressure from their neigh-

---

UNCOMMONLY KNOWN...

Trellis A structure meant to support climbing plants, such as roses, sweet peas, and ivy, a trellis can form the sides of a pergola (a walkway through a garden, or a plant-covered passage between two buildings). Trellises can be made of inexpensive, natural materials or more ornately constructed from materials such as painted wood, cast iron, and aluminum.

bors to get their grounds in shape. Today many environmental activists believe that resource-draining grass lawns should be replaced with xeriscaping, a process by which local, drought-resistant plants are used to surround a home or other structure.

Patio

FROM SPANISH FOR "INNER OPEN TO THE SKY"
RELATED: VERANDA, GAZEBO, DECK, PORCH
BLENDS INTERIOR AND EXTERIOR SPACES OF HOME

The word *patio* comes to us from Spain, but it might as well have been coined by 20th-century Americans, considering its ubiquity in suburban backyards across the nation. The modern patio is part and parcel of the yard and garden.

Who first had gardens? There were definitely cultivated gardens in ancient Egypt and in ancient Persia, Darius the Great had a "paradise garden." The Hanging Gardens of Babylon were one of the Seven Wonders of the World, and Ptolemy's gardens at Alexandria were also celebrated.

The wealthiest ancient Romans built gardens like those at the ruins of Hadrian's Villa. After the fall of the Roman Empire, many traditions of that civilization were kept alive in the East, and gardening continued in Byzantium and Moorish Spain. It was in the latter that patios began to thrive. Beautifully tiled walkways and sitting areas helped to blend inside and outside. Attempts to make the transition between interior

PARALLEL HISTORY

Empress Josephine's Malmaison Roses

When Empress Josephine Bonaparte began planting and tending her garden at Malmaison, (the Bonapartes' chateau, just west of Paris) in 1799, she was already interested in collecting seeds and plants, many of which she paid to have transported from overseas. Her husband, Napoleon, soon came to enjoy the place as much as she did, even if it did have the name Malmaison, which means "bad house" in French. In her years there, Empress Josephine collected 200 rose specimens, sparking a "rose renaissance" that made France a leading grower and exporter of 2,500 varieties by 1830.

Josephine Bonaparte, who was also known as Rose, held many elaborate parties at Malmaison.

and exterior seamless were also being made in China and then Japan, where Zen gardens were meant to foster meditation.

In Europe, gardening was revived in France and Italy during the later Middle Ages, with a renewed interest in adding places for entertaining and experience of the outdoors. Patios, verandas, gazebos, and decks were all used in England, France, Italy, and the U.S. from the 18th century on, taking different forms depending on the style of the times and materials available.

Simply put, a veranda has a roof, and a patio does not—but many Americans now use the terms interchangeably. Since the 1970s, many homes have decks rather than patios as their primary access between house and yard, often because it's easier to build a deck when the yard isn't level. Regardless of what form these outdoor living areas take, they're more popular for entertaining and relaxing than they have ever been.

Tent

FROM LATIN "TENDERE" (TO STRETCH)
PUP TENT: SMALL TRIANGULAR TENT, SHELTER FOR TWO
"BIG TENT": POLITICAL TERM FOR INCLUDING A RANGE OF VIEWS

A backyard tent set up and stocked with sleeping bags, stuffed animals, comic books, and snacks is a quintessential symbol of American childhood. Tents are always made out of some kind of fabric, and are always temporary: Even the sturdiest of them can be taken down without an extraordinary level of effort.

Originally, all peoples were nomads. The Semitic word Arab means "nomad," and referred to the Bedouins who ranged freely through the Near East. They cultivated no crops and owned no land, so their preferred residences were tents divided into separate areas for public and private life. Tents were not seen as flimsy or temporary; Moses and the Jews received the Ark of the Covenant in a tent. As well as being homes and temples, tents were headquarters and supply depots for military campaigns.

These tents weren't necessarily flimsy. Several Roman garrisons in England were so well outfitted

with tents for different uses that troops stayed and cities grew up in their stead. Ottoman sultans may have taken the tent to its highest aesthetic level, Ceremonial tents were decorated with colored silks and had a peaked roof over an interior filled with carpets, seat pillows, and the sultan's favorite posessions. Once Europeans had seen these ceremonial tents, they adapted them to less nomadic uses.

Home camping tents, like those in countless American yards, owe something to each kind of tent. They can be set up and taken down quickly, like those of nomads; they signal a sort of ceremony, the sleepover; and like military tents, they have a purpose as shelter. Tents were traditionally put up with ropes and stakes, but modern innovations include tents that pop together with interior flexible poles and inflatable beams.

Swimming Pool

PROTOTYPES DATE TO 3000 B.C.
IN ANCIENT TIMES, USED FOR SPIRITUAL CLEANSING
FIRST PUBLIC RECREATIONAL POOLS: MID-19TH CENTURY

The great ancestor of swimming pools is the "Great Bath" at Mohenjo Daro in what is now Pakistan. The bath dates back to 3000 B.C., and was about 40 feet by 26 feet, sealed with tar. Since many ancient bathing places were about religious rituals, this one too might have acted as a purification center. However, Mohenjo Daro, a center of Indus Valley civilization, was unusually advanced in many ways, so it may have been used for recreation, too.

The ancient Sinhalese had far more elaborate pools known as the Kuttam Pokuna, built in the fourth century B.C., which were stepped and tiled and employed underground ducts and a filtering system. These twin pools were truly a herald of modern swimming pools. Ancient Greeks and Romans built swimming pools that they used for athletics and for military training. Our modern word *pool* comes from the Latin *piscina,* or "fish pond," since Romans kept stocked ponds. The first heated pool was also a Roman innovation, built by the wealthy Gaius Maecenas in the first century B.C.

For hundreds of years, swimming pools remained rare, but they gained popularity in England in the mid-19th century after six indoor pools with diving boards were built in London in 1837. One big push in promoting swimming as a sport for the masses was the first inclusion of a swimming race in the Olympic Games in 1896.

Public swimming pools proliferated in the United Kingdom and the United States in the early 20th century, but after World War II as well as the polio epidemic, those who could afford to, began building backyard swimming pools, especially in states with hot climates like Arizona and Florida. Private pools are usually smaller and less suited to lap and competitive swimming, although some people are constructing continuous-current pools that allow swimming for exercise and athletic training.

Nowadays, the modern country with the greatest number of swimming pools and hot tubs per capita is New Zealand, which may be due in part to the mild year-round climate in much of the country, especially on its northern island. Weather extremes in many other parts of the world make backyard pools impractible and virtually unusable.

Tree House

FAMOUS EXAMPLES:
SWISS FAMILY ROBINSON TREE HOUSE (FILM),
"WORLD FAMOUS TREE HOUSE" (LEGGETT, CA, REDWOOD)

While a backyard tree house for play is the envy of most suburban children, tree houses actually have a long history as permanent dwellings. In Southeast Asia and the South Pacific, tree house homes were once common, and made sense in thick jungle areas where it was difficult to access light and air otherwise. In the 17th century Captain Cook saw inhabited tree houses in Tasmania. As Cook and his fellow explorers reported back on tree houses, they became fashionable as playhouses and retreats for the rich and royal. While Italy's Medicis competed to construct the finest marble tree house, Queen Elizabeth I of England was dining in a lime tree that contained a three-story tree house with a second floor large enough to accommodate 100 people. There was even a French street lined with chestnut trees that had several tree house restaurants. The best thing about a backyard tree house? You feel like royalty, even if you aren't.

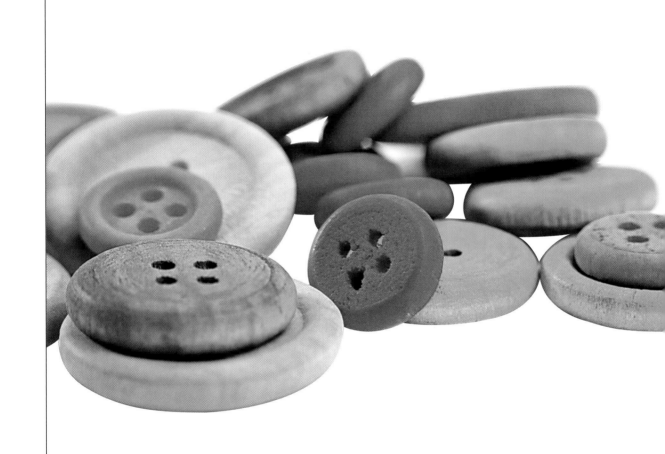

Fashion fades, only style remains the same.
—GABRIELLE "COCO" CHANEL (1883-1971)

Garments & Accessories

People have clothed themselves for millennia, at first with animal skins and then, with increasing ingenuity, in cloth made of fur or plant fibers. With machining came better, quicker ways for people to sew garments and then to mass-produce cloth and clothing. The history of clothing and accessories, as with all the histories here, gives us a clearer picture of how people lived at various periods in the past—the stuff of their everyday life both dictated, and was dictated by, how and where they lived. In our fluid, prosperous times, the giant fashion and clothing industries turn out apparel for all occasions and climates; a glance backward helps us appreciate what we wear. The essays in this chapter cover undergarments and outer garments, from head to toe. Many of our everyday clothes have colorful histories, and we attempt to provide as many highlights as possible. Straight pins, for example, date back to ancient Sumeria, but they have popped up throughout history—as a metaphor for economist Adam Smith's 1776 "division of labor" thesis, as a product of 1830s manufacturing, and elsewhere. The umbrella opens its history in Egypt, provides shade to the Greeks, and goes widespread in 19th-century London. The iron, the belt, and many other items have similarly long and detailed histories. When you put on your bra or boxers in the morning, it's somehow nice to know that people have been doing the same thing for thousands of years. And with today's silky fabrics, you can only imagine what it was like wearing a leather loincloth or a steel corset. King Tut was wealthy enough to wear linen, and was buried with more than 100 linen loincloths. Abraham Lincoln made famous the stovepipe variant of the top hat. And there's lots more trivia and useful information here: the names and layers of 19th-century women's clothing, the origins of the suit and the necktie, the story behind the penny loafer, how pockets were invented to foil thieves, and the answer to that burning question—which came first, the socks or the shoes?

Clothing

Some say clothes make the man (and woman, too), but man and woman first have to make the clothes. A piece of clothing can be as simple as a draped cloth and as fussy as a Saville Row suit. While the things we put on top of our body have come a long way from fig leaves, some of them, like the bikini bathing suit, are of a similar size and shape to fig leaves. Of course, making a bikini involves design skills, sewing skills, and fabric technology. In this section, every garment offers some insight into how we've learned to cover our body creatively, comfortably, and cannily.

Blue Jeans

JEANS: FROM "GÊNES" (GENOA), PLACE OF FIRST PRODUCTION
DENIM: FROM "DE NÎMES" (AS IN, FABRIC OF NÎMES)
FIRST AMERICAN BLUE JEANS MADE BY LEVI STRAUSS

The story of blue jeans involves a purpose from India, a style from Italy, a fabric from France, and a business idea from California. During the 16th century, sailors would buy a thick cotton indigo-dyed cloth near the Dongarii Fort near Bombay, which is where we got the word *dungarees* for work pants.

These sailors brought the fabric back to Italy, and supposedly its manufacture near, and export

from, the city of Genoa led to a new name, *bleu de Gênes*—Genoa blue, and again for some, the origin of the term "blue jeans."

Complicating all of this is serge de Nîmes, a fabric named after but not necessarily made in the French port of Nîmes, since sometimes a fabric made elsewhere but in the same manner would be given the "de Nîmes" appellation. The one thing that historians can say with certainty is that "jean" fabric had two threads, warp and woof, of the same color, while "denim" fabric had one blue thread and one white thread.

Eventually, "jeans" would come to mean the style of trousers, which were loose and comfortable for working and often had pockets, while "denim" would become the fabric of choice for making jeans. That was due, in no small part, to a German

Off-the-Rack Clothing

For centuries, people made their own clothes. If they had enough money, they called in a professional tailor or seamstress, but the clothes were customized to each individual's measurements. The military was one of the forces behind ready-to-wear clothing; since many soldiers needed to be measured, and some of those measurements tended to be similar (for example, chest circumference), patterns could be standardized and clothing made in larger quantities. This was called off the rack, since a shopper could simply pull a coat or trousers in his or her size from a display and take it home, without the time-consuming and more costly fittings that had previously been the norm.

immigrant named Levi Strauss. Strauss went to San Francisco during the gold rush era and opened a dry-goods store. One of his customers, a tailor named Jacob Davis, had come up with the idea of placing copper rivets at stress points on work pants to keep them from ripping. He asked Strauss to go into business with him, and their "waist overalls" proved a huge hit with the laborers. But there was one problem: the canvas that Strauss and Davis first used chafed. When they tried the same pants in denim, workers breathed sighs of relief.

Suits

FIGURATIVE: SUIT YOURSELF, SUIT UP
COLLOQUIAL USE OF SUIT (NOUN): SOMEONE WHO WORKS
IN A LARGE CORPORATION

The word *suit* derives from the French verb *suivre*, "to follow," and applies to items that are meant to be used together. Although they look nothing alike, today's suits are the progeny of medieval armor. Since these garments were created specifically for individual wearers, it was important that they have some look or marks to identify them and make them suits.

It was King Charles II during the Restoration in 1666 who established a new standard of court dress consisting of a coat, waistcoat, and knee breeches in the same material. At first the breeches were full, in the French style, but by 1670 they were trim and fitted. Tailoring had been introduced in western Europe in the late 13th century, and this new style required more of it; tailoring became an established and in-demand craft.

The new suits weren't perfect for the English lifestyle, which centered on riding, hunting, walking, and estate management. A few of the modifications the English gentry made—including shortening the jacket front and using plainer, sturdy cloth that withstood wear better than embroidered silks—made horseback riding easier.

Suiting material changed even more drastically to eventually become the generally sober fabrics we see today. After George Bryan Brummel entered the London scene in the late early 1800s, "Beau" Brummel befriended the Prince of Wales (the future George IV) and encouraged his tailors to mold cloth to the body. Brummel was not an aristocrat, and he understood that quieter colors and weaves would stand the test of time, as well as make people look richer than they actually were.

Until the 20th century, gentlemen's wear usually consisted of a frock or "morning" coat with striped trousers. Coats and trousers of matched cloth were for the country or the lower classes. This changed in the 20th century, when the easier-fitting "lounge suit" (business suit) became the norm in England and the United States. Today business suits can vary in terms of lapel width, jacket venting, pants styles (pleats or no pleats, cuffs or no cuffs), but the idea that a "suit" involves at least two garments cut from the same cloth hasn't. A man's suit has changed very little since the mid-20th century.

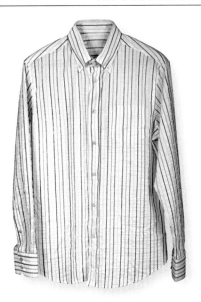

Shirt

RELATED TO GERMANIC WORDS FOR SKIRT AND SHORT
ORIGINALLY WORN AS AN UNDERGARMENT FOR COMFORT
SHIRT OFF ONE'S BACK: LAST REMAINING POSSESSIONS

The first men's shirts were really glorified undergarments. It's not easy to wash an animal-skin tunic, and it's not always comfortable to wear one, either; a garment made of cloth that could be worn beneath a heavy tunic not only made the wearer more comfortable, it could be cleaned, too. Roman men wore a *subucula,* a kind of primary tunic, under their outer tunic. Both layers were then covered by a toga outdoors. This garment was worn, we know, by Charlemagne. These extremely simple garments were not meant to be seen.

In the 13th century, overgarments were deliberately cut to show glimpses of shirts at wrist, neck, and hip. During the 15th century, this titillating fashion led to the addition of collars at the neck and cuffs at the wrists.

Of course, those are two places that can get soiled quickly. By the 1600s, separate collars and cuffs that allowed more frequent cleaning were used. The stylish upside to this was the main body of the shirt could remain soft while the collar and cuffs that were "seen" could be starched

and shaped in many ways. The Elizabethan ruff, with its multiple rows off scalloped fabric, is an extreme example.

As laundry methods changed and the industrial revolution made shirts cheaper to produce, men began buying shirts with attached collar and cuffs. Of course, lighter-colored shirts need to be cleaned more often, and so they were more often worn by men in office jobs, while men who did physical labor wore darker colors that wouldn't show dirt and grease as easily. This led to the terms "white collar" and "blue collar" to define economic classes.

Dress

FROM OLD FRENCH "DRESSER" (ARRANGE, PREPARE)
TODAY, PRIMARILY A WOMAN'S GARMENT, BUT TERM ALSO
REFERS TO ANYTHING WORN BY THE HUMAN BODY

For thousands of years, everyone wore some form of dress, if we define "dress" as a one-piece garment ending in a skirt. Chitons, togas, tunics, frocks, and robes were all forms of the dress. Although trouserlike garments were worn at least as far back as the fourth century B.C., it wasn't until the 16th century in Europe that men began to wear pants or trousers, leaving dresses to women.

Although women's dresses of this period could be quite elaborate, men's fashions were, too. It wasn't until the late 18th century that men's clothing became more subdued, and thus the dress became the canvas for most clothing design. At the beginning of the 19th century, the Empire style, with the waistline just under the bust, was made fashionable by France's Empress Josephine, By mid-century, waists were a bit lower. Throughout, however, dresses remained long, often having multiple petticoats and crinolines and hoops and bustles added.

The 20th century saw some shifts in dress style (in fact, some of them could be called radical shifts). The early 20th-century suffragette movement with its message of female independence inspired slimmer silhouettes in gowns and suits, and led to the straight, unstructured flapper dresses of the 1920s that had hemlines ranging from short to scandalous. Wartime dresses were cut close to conserve material, while in the 1950s designer Christan Dior's "New Look" inspired full skirts with crinolines again—only this time, the hemlines were much higher.

During the 20th century, too, a distinction was made between "dresses" and "gowns," the latter becoming floor-length, formal garments that were often quite elaborate in their materials and/or decoration. "Dresses" were shorter and worn during the day. Women still wear dresses, but in the 1960s and 1970s they began wearing trousers, jeans, and pants much more frequently. The dress lost its place as women's only "look."

Bathing Suit

ALSO SWIMSUIT

FIRST USE: 19TH CENT., WITH ADVENT OF BEACH VACATIONS

FIRST BIKINI: 1947

The bathing suit appeared during the Greco-Roman era (Pompeian murals depict women with fabric around their breasts and hips), and then disappeared, resurfacing in the late 19th century. Bathing costumes in the 19th cenury were a far cry from the modern maillot or bikini (pictured here). For Victorian women, a "two-piece bathing suit" meant a shortened, long-sleeved dress worn over a pair of leggings. When this was not enough coverage, "bathing machines," enclosed wooden carts, were rolled into the water. The occupant would then, away from all prying eyes, be able to exit from a door straight into and under the water.

However, as Victorians became Edwardians and Edwardians became flappers, the bathing suit began shrinking. First came the legs: During the 1920s, the typical one-piece unisex suit of heavy wool knit had a tank top and brief shorts. World War II fabric rationing meant that the midriff of women's suits disappeared, too.

The world was ready, then, when Louis Reard of France introduced his two-piece, skimpy bathing suit with an "explosive" name: the bikini, named after Bikini Atoll, which was bombed to smithereens by the Allies in 1946.

Underwear

O riginally humans wore no undergarments, but they eventually adopted them for warmth, hygiene, and protection. For exmaple, we know the Otzi "Iceman" wore a loincloth beneath his grass cloak 5,300 years ago. Over time, undergarments have become increasingly sophisticated. People learned that more layers trap air, and thinner fabrics dry more quickly. That sounds eminently practical, yet some of the garments listed here have had permutations that are anything but, from frothy petticoats designed to fill out skirts and bustles to lacy nylon stockings that enhance a leg.

Boxers

NAMED FOR: LIKENESS TO SHORTS WORN IN BOXING
PREDECESSORS: LOINCLOTHS, "BRAIES," CODPIECE
OFTEN-ASKED QUESTION: "BOXERS OR BRIEFS?"

W hether from shame or practical considerations, since ancient times many cultures have fashioned loincloths and other coverings for the lower body out of skins, furs, and cloths.

For example, Otzi, the 5,300-year-old Iceman discovered in Europe's Schnalstal Glacier, wore a leather loincloth beneath his woven grass cloak.

King Tutankhamun of Egypt had 145 linen loincloths buried with him in his tomb. These were shaped like an isosceles triangle, with the point facing downward and strings attached to the top two angles. The strings would be tied around the waist from back to front, and then the triangle would be pulled between the legs and secured in the waist tie. While he or his contemporaries might have worn these solo at times, we also know that the pharaohs and other noblemen would have worn them beneath robes and skirts, too.

Teutons wore loose-fitting, short, double-legged garments known as *braies*. Romans wore a simple loincloth called a *subligaculum*. The development of these early coverings did not follow a linear path. First, there was a trend toward more fitted, thicker undergarments necessitated by medieval suits of armor and warfare on horseback. Second came the early Renaissance development of the codpiece, a stiff and sometimes stuffed gusset for the front of men's tights that some believe was invented by England's Henry VIII. Third, knitted, one- or two-piece underwear was made possible by new manufacturing methods. Perhaps named for boxer John L. Sullivan who wore them frequently, they came to be known as long johns.

UNCOMMONLY KNOWN . . .
Briefs In 1935, Coopers, Inc. began making men's briefs. They called the style "jockey," because they offered the support of a jockstrap in a one-piece garment. Thirty thousand pairs sold in just three months. But the innovation that truly made history was the same company's "Y-fronts," with their diagonal front vents.

These three fitted undergarments evolved to become men's briefs, men's jockstraps, and boxer shorts, respectively. The last of these, boxer shorts, came into being when World War I soldiers were issued button-front "shorts" with ties that allowed their fit to be adjusted for field wear. The soldiers liked them so much, they wanted to wear them after the war, too. Nowadays, "boxer briefs" combine the close fit of briefs, with the length of boxer shorts.

Brassiere

FROM THE FRENCH "BRASSIERE" (BODICE)
PREDECESSORS: CORSETS, BINDING CLOTHS, BODICES
CREDIT FOR INVENTION: AMERICAN MARY PHELPS JACOB

Women may have burned their bras during the heyday of the women's liberation movement, but for previous generations who had had to support their breasts with stays, corsets, and other constricting foundation garments, the simple 20th-century brassiere might have seemed a godsend.

The first women to try a bosom-enhancing garment were ancient Minoans, who devised a sort of bikini top that lifted their breasts out of their robes. Their Greek and Roman counterparts preferred a stealth approach, binding their breasts with strips of cloth. During the Dark and Middle Ages, women wore soft corsets that were more often than not a sort of vest that went over their shifts.

The trouble with foundation garments came with Catherine de Medici's arrival at the French court as the wife of Henry II. Queen Catherine could not abide thick waists, and she decreed that all women at court must wear steel corsets. For several centuries following the queen's cruel lead, women forced their waist in and their breasts up.

Change finally arrived in the early 20th century, when a straighter silhouette occasioned less restrictive corsets. With the waist not pulled in so tightly, breasts needed something different if they were going to remain supported, since they naturally sag as women age. Some brassiere-like bodices were invented, with designers taking the name "brassiere" from the French term for upper-arm support. (In France, the term for what we call a brassiere is *soutien-gorge*, literally "throat support.")

In 1889, French corsetmaker Hermionie Cadolle made a great change for women when she patented her "le Bien-Être" (Well-Being) device that supported the breasts from the shoulders down rather than the waist up, as the corset did. A few years later

PARALLEL HISTORY

Corsets and Women's Health

At one time, people believed that corsets, cinching foundation garments, were essential to women's fragile physiques. Unfortunately, corsets did little to help and much to hurt women's bodies. Harder stays and tighter lacing limited the wearer's ability to breathe, sit, and stand without discomfort, while the unnatural hourglass shape of the most restrictive corsets forced internal organs into unnatural positions. Corsets probably did not result in "hysteria," but they did cause fainting, indigestion, constipation, and back pain. Although some women and doctors did call for an end to rigid corsets, the most effective end came with World War I, when the war effort called for an end to excess uses of steel.

Corsets were often named after divine beauties, such as the Leda, "the queen of corsets."

Marie Tucek added separate pockets for each breast and shoulder straps fastened with hooks and eyes.

However, it may be an American socialite, Mary Phelps Jacob, who changed things most dramatically for breasts around the world. In the early 1900s, looking for the right foundation to wear with a sheer evening dress, she took two silk handkerchiefs and fastened them together with ribbon and cord to make suitable support. The modern bra was born.

Petticoat

ORIG. MIDDLE ENGLISH | LITERALLY, "SMALL COAT"
GARMENT FIRST WORN BY MEN UNDER COATS OR DOUBLETS
DESCENDANT: THE SILK SLIP

In modern parlance, the petticoat or slip is considered an undergarment that's not meant to be seen. Though slips have become far less common than they were even 20 years ago, they've left their mark on American idioms. A woman might let a friend know that her slip is showing so that she can adjust her clothing to hide it; now the phrase "your slip is showing" has come to mean that a person has made some kind of gaffe.

However, in the petticoat's early days, it was meant to be seen. A woman would wear it with a gown, bed gown, jacket, or bodice. The petticoat might match the skirt or gown, or be made of different material, and it was one of the ways that women had to stretch their wardrobe.

Petticoats also gave outer garments shape. They could be soft or stiff, as fashion dictated. The waltz craze of the 1800s inspired large, sweeping skirts that needed more petticoats, so they were often stiffened. Petticoats made out of horsehair fabric were known as crinolines, and yet even these crinolines could not support skirts that grew bigger and bigger. Women began sewing rings of cane or whalebone to the bottoms of their petticoats, and when that proved insufficient, patented "cage" crinolines were invented. These were not just bulky and ungainly (sitting in them gracefully was nearly impossible) but also dangerous if the wearer need to make a hasty exit.

The full crinoline fell out of fashion in the mid to late 19th century, but petticoats remained de rigueur for women's skirts. Crinolines with petticoats enjoyed a brief renaissance during the 1950s, but women soon chose single petticoats and slips, which are worn between body and garment to help dresses and skirts hang smoothly, as well as to prevent itchiness and chafing from coarse fabrics like wool. In the modern Western world, unless a garment is particularly sheer, most women do not feel required to wear a slip. In India, on the other hand, a slip worn beneath an Indian sari is still known as a petticoat and is usually made of cotton that coordinates with the sari silk.

UNCOMMONLY KNOWN . . .

Panty Hose They may be women's bane now, but when Allen Gant, Sr., of Glen Raven Mills, North Carolina, invented and first marketed one-piece "panty hose" in 1959, women were relieved to find a stretchy, convenient alternative to wearing garter belt and stockings. While most often made of nylon and spandex, panty hose can even contain moisturizers for smooth skin, or caffeine to eliminate cellulite.

Nylon Stockings

EARLY STOCKINGS MADE FROM COTTON, WOOL, OR SILK
NYLON: FABRIC INVENTED BY THE DUPONT CO.
ALSO CALLED: HOSIERY, PANTY HOSE, TIGHTS

In 1935, "Fiber 66," the world's first totally synthetic fiber, was born in a DuPont company laboratory—and immediately made into toothbrush bristles. It wasn't until 1939 that scientists were able to spin this fiber finely enough that, renamed "nylon," it could be made into women's stockings that mimicked the qualities of silk.

Silk stockings were luxurious to wear but expensive to make and buy and prone to snags and fiber runs. Scientists at DuPont under the direction of Wallace Hume Carothers had long been working on the makeup of filaments in fibers, and when one of them, Julian Hill, discovered a sheer filament that looked like silk, everyone was excited. Hill had placed a heated rod into a solution of coal tar, water, and alcohol. Drawing it out, he saw a fine skein stretching between rod and solution.

The name "nylon" does not stand for "New York and London," as some once thought. It's an invented word that the DuPont executives created, and it doesn't really mean anything. The name

mattered little to women; they cleared the shelves of the new nylons the very day they went on sale in New York City on May 15, 1940.

Unfortunately for women, nylon was co-opted for the war effort and was taken off of the shelves almost as soon as it had appeared. Since early nylon stockings, like the silk and wool predecessors, were made in one piece and seamed at the back, people had become accustomed to the curves of women's legs being accentuated by thin seams. Women in the U.S. and the U.K. made do without their newly beloved nylon stockings by drawing fake seams up the backs of their legs with eyebrow pencils. Once World War II was over, women had their nylon stockings back, and in the late 1950s, DuPont invented another fiber called Lycra that could stretch up to seven times its length without breaking, and return to its original shape. This made nylon stockings stretchier and easier to wear.

Pajamas

FROM PERSIAN "PAE" (FOOT, LEG) AND "JAMAHS" (CLOTHING)
STYLE BORROWED FROM INDIA BY BRITISH COLONIALISTS
REFERS TODAY TO ANY BEDTIME GARMENT

People have been wearing nightclothes for centuries, which in Europe meant a nightgown for women and a nightshirt for men. These garments were actually very similar in shape, though the women's version was longer than the men's. Both versions were actually a type of undergarment that was worn all day next to the skin (men tucked the long ends of theirs into their trousers).

When laundry methods became more modern in the late 19th century, people began changing their nightclothes more frequently. British officers in India had already picked up on a style popular for centuries with Portuguese colonists: loose, baggy trousers with a drawstring waist. These were "pyjamas," a Hindustani word derived from a Persian word for "leg garments." The Portuguese in Goa seem to have worn the drawstring trousers without adopting the usually matching tunic that makes up a *salwar kameez,* but it is impossible to know for sure. When English merchants began to sell pyjamas in 1898, they were generally in sets, with the same fabric used for trousers and shirt.

During subsequent years, American and European men wore pajamas, while women wore nightgowns. However, as styles changed and women began wearing trousers, they began wearing pajamas, often in silk, satin, and other luxury fabrics. For a time in the 1920s and 1930s evening pajamas were considered the height of glamour, popularized by maverick designer Coco Chanel. Casual style in the 1970s and 1980s meant that a T-shirt and boxer shorts might be considered pajamas, and today both men and women wear pajamas that are long, short, woven, knit, cotton, wool, linen, silk, and more.

As a side note, footed pajamas, which are very popular today for young children, may have originated as an anti-pestilence device. The "Hobson-Jobson," a compendium of British colonial terms, includes this quote: "The late Mr. B—, tailor in Jermyn Street, some 40 years ago, in reply to a question why pyjammas [sic] had feet sewn on to them (as was sometimes the case with those furnished by London outfitters) answered: 'I believe, Sir, it is because of the white ants.'"

Undershirt

WHITE IN COLOR
GENERALLY MADE OF COTTON OR COTTON BLEND
ORIGINALLY MEN'S UNDERGARMENT; NOW WORN EXTERNALLY

B elieve it or not, the undershirt, so strongly identified with men, began as a woman's garment. It was introduced in the mid-19th century in England as a way to protect ladies' health during sports. The "vest," as it was known, was usually made of wool. It wasn't until the mid-20th century that white cotton undershirts became a masculine staple.

Several factors contributed to the white, short-sleeved cotton undershirt's rise to clothing classic. In World War I, British soldiers were already wearing lightweight cotton "undershirts" beneath their wool uniforms that helped keep sweat and scratchiness at bay. Soon U.S. service members were sporting the stretchy, crewnecked shirts for comfort and to conceal their chest hair while in uniform. When both military and civilian laborers were photographed wearing just undershirts, these shirts became seen as manly. Finally, in the 1947 film *A Streetcar Named Desire,* Marlon Brando's character, Stanley Kowalski, exuded such raw power in his plain white undershirt that the garment became sexy, too. Today undershirts are often outershirts, but they still provide a clean, smooth line beneath dress shirts for men.

Headwear

W hile hats are now rarely worn by professional, urban people in their working lives, they still denote purpose in a way no other garment can. Someone wearing a top hat is as unlikely to be roping bulls as someone wearing a cowboy hat is to be at a formal daytime wedding. Some headwear is quite functional, like bandannas and ski caps; others are all about pomp and circumstance, like top hats and crowns. Even if we don't wear hats all the time, nearly all of us wear one at some point. Hats and headwear keep us warm, protect us from the sun, absorb perspiration, and serve as decoration.

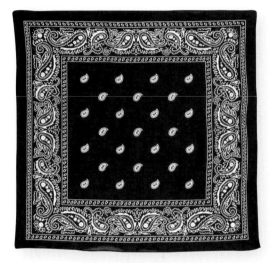

Bandanna

FROM HINDUSTANI OR BENGALI "TO TIE"
INITIALLY MADE FROM IMPORTED INDIAN TEXTILES
SIMILAR TO: KERCHIEF, SCARF, HEAD WRAP

A red or blue bandanna, knotted around a cowboy's throat, tied over an athlete's head, or wrapped around a teenager's wrist, seems like a long-lived, all-American accessory. However, the humble, practical bandanna originated not on the western plains or in some colonial workshop, but across the seas as an Indian textile.

Bandanna or *bandhana* actually means "to tie," either in Hindustani or Bengali (no one is entirely sure), and began to stand as a kind of shorthand for lengths of silk imported from Murshidabad, India. Each printed length made seven to ten square handkerchiefs, which were cut, hemmed, and sold by the importers. The earliest fragment of a bandanna in the U.S. dates from a circa 1750 Charleston, South Carolina, excavation.

The use of these cloths as "kerchiefs" ties the bandanna to a long history of head coverings. *Kerchief* derives from the French *couvre-chef,* or "head covering." Unlike veils with religious or spiritual intents (e.g., the Roman Catholic mantilla or the Indian *dupatta*), bandannas as head coverings owe more to the Japanese *hachimaki,* a headband whose donning signals "time to get to work," or the Russian babushka-style kerchief with its connotations of hardship and struggle.

Over the years, Americans began manufacturing their own bandannas using the most readily available textile: cotton. Since bandannas were used primarily by servants and laborers, for many decades they did not become fancier, remaining just red or blue with black-and-white designs printed on them.

Bandannas are used for head coverings, for sweat bands, and for handkerchiefs—even as a hobo's luggage, knotted at the end of a stick. Because outlaws sometimes tied a bandanna over their face when attempting robberies, bandannas also gained a reputation with the wrong side of the law, which is unfortunately alive today in some urban gang activity. However, most bandannas—now manufactured in all sorts of sizes and colors—are still used for their humble, practical purposes.

Cowboy Hat

ORIGINAL DESIGN DEBATED: EITHER CHRISTY'S HATS
OF ENGLAND OR AMERICAN JOHN BATTERSON STETSON
MADE FROM: STRAW, LEATHER, FELT

We may never know if the "Boss of the Plains" hat that began selling in Colorado in 1865 was an invention of Christy's Hats of Bristol, England, or of John Batterson Stetson, an Easterner who went west to pan for gold and breathe drier air for his health. Christy's did make fur felt hats for sugar plantations in the West Indies that resembled the hat Stetson ultimately manufactured in Philadelphia.

Though Stetson lost a patent case to Christy's, in the name game, Stetson won. Most people now think of Stetsons as iconic cowboy hats, and they may even know of, and believe, the story of its origin: how he made the first one on a hunting trip to demonstrate that he could make felted fabric from animal fur.

The precursor of the "Boss of the Plains" was worn by the *vaqueros* or Mexican cowboys (incidentally, the word vaqueros led to the American term "buckaroos"). Lower-class cowboys wore sombreros, while upper-class ranch managers and owners wore *galans*. The phrase "tan galan" meant "so gallant," and its corruption probably led to the "ten-gallon hat," since a hat that could actually hold ten gallons would be unwearable by a human. Of course, there's another story behind this, too: *Galón* referred to a braid worn around a sombrero-like hat's crown, which attested

to the vaquero's skill. A ten-galón hat, therefore, evinced his prowess with its many braids.

Felt, perhaps the oldest human-made textile, has been fashioned for centuries from wool, fur, and beaver. Although modern cowboy hats can be made from straw, leather, and other fibers, including synthetics, the fur felt Stetson-type hats are often preferred for aesthetic reasons. (Stetsons are also part of the modern-day uniform of the Royal Canadian Mounted Police and the U.S. Army First Cavalry Division.)

Top Hat

19TH CENTURY: "THE CENTURY OF THE TOP HAT"
U.S. RELATIVE: STOVEPIPE HAT
TOP HAT: 1935 FILM WITH FRED ASTAIRE AND GINGER ROGERS

The top hat is scarcely worn anymore, but it still stands for a kind of refinement and elegance that people revere. Therefore, it's ironic that on its first appearance in London streets, women supposedly fainted and children screamed to see a man sporting such a tall, shiny chapeau.

The man wearing the top hat was supposedly hatmaker John Hetherington, and it took from his first sortie in 1797 about 20 years for top hats to truly catch on as the preferred headgear of gentleman. This wasn't because of the hats' height (although collapsible versions, known as *chapeaux claques,* were available early in the 19th century). While many men clung to their beaver hats, rather than wear silk ones, when Royal Consort Prince Albert began in 1850 to wear a top hat made of "hatter's plush" (a fine silk shag), things changed quickly. The new trend put an end to the North American beaver-pelt industry.

In the U.S., the stovepipe hat, which we associate with Abraham Lincoln, was a popular alternative to the top hat. The stovepipe had straight sides except for one slightly convex area referred to as the "chimneypot," and a small brim, unlike the curved top hat with its sometimes ornately curled brim. While the stovepipe was worn erect, the top hat was meant to be tipped forward and slightly to one side—no more than ten degrees in any direction! While that rule might seem silly, its effect was one of class and sophistication, epitomized in John Singer Sargent's 1902 portrait of Thomas Lister, Lord Ribblesdale.

The 19th century is sometimes called "the century of the top hat," although real top hats fell from manufacturing favor quickly as more easily produced bowlers and fedoras became fashionable. Since sewing top hats required time and skill, they were made by fewer and fewer hatmakers, and those catered mainly to those who could afford fine handmade goods.

Since the the top hat was supplanted by the homburg and bowler and then the fedora, the iconic head cover has remained a symbol of glamour, high life, sophistication, refined manners and attention to detail. This was epitomized by Fred Astaire's elegant and graceful performance in the 1935 classic Top Hat. While there are a few opera-going gentlemen who still have collapsible versions in their wardrobes, these toppers are now mostly worn at formal weddings and by spectators at Ascot.

Ski Cap

FROM OLD ENGLISH "CÆPPE" (CLOAK, CAPE)
RELATED: CANADIAN TUQUE, RUSSIAN "USHANKA"
PROTOTYPE: GREEK "PILOS" (FELT SAILING HAT)

The ski cap, a close-fitting cold-weather hat that is now nearly always knitted, has ancient associations that predate the human ability to twist yarn. Two archaeological finds—"Tollund Man" (dating to the fourth century B.C.) and the 5,300-year-old "Iceman"—wore versions of what must be the oldest human head covering: a skull cap. It seems that modern man's soft, warm sports hats share a lineage with this simple one.

The Greek sailor *pilos,* a kind of cap made of black felt, is the earliest name we have for skull caps. These hats, which were copied by the Romans, who called them *pileus,* were known as pilos because this term

---

PARALLEL HISTORY

Mad Hatters

The term "mad as a hatter," made famous by Lewis Carroll's 1865 novel "Alice's Adventures in Wonderland," came about because hatters usually acquired a physical disorder after working for too long with the mercury solution used in the felting process. Breathing in the mercury fumes caused damage to the lungs, but it also affected the central nervous system and brain, eventually resulting in paralysis, memory loss, dementia, and death. In the U.S. "mad hatter's disease" was known as "the Danbury shakes," since most top hats were manufactured in that Connecticut town. In 1864, at least one country—the U.K.—decided to relieve the problem by implementing the Factory Act, which mandated proper ventilation in all workshops.

signifies "topper" or "head pile" and comes from a much old Indo-European word for hair, *pilo*. Besides Greek sailors, other wearers of these early skullcaps included Roman commoners and freed slaves. They were also worn in many places where it wouldn't immediately seem there was a need for head warmth, like the Middle East. However, skullcaps contributed more than warmth. They were mostly worn by men, who experience hair loss and/or baldness more frequently than women do, and whose resulting bare scalp may otherwise have burned from exposure to the strong sun or been uncomfortably pelted by rain. Skullcaps were useful in many different climates.

One of the cousins of the skullcap was the Peruvian "winter skullcap," made with pointed crown and affixed with earflaps to guard against the cold. Another must have been the Laplanders' scalloped cap with huge pom-pom, which made it easy to pick someone out against the snow. Designs knitted into the cap made it easy to identify a person's family and tribe, as well.

Fast-forward several centuries, and welcome to Canada, home of the *tuque,* the French-Canadian word for a knit ski cap. This is not actually the same as a *toque,* the French word for the nearly brimless women's hat of the 16th century, although the mix-up is so common that the spellings are now considered interchangeable. Tuques are tapered, often have earflaps, and also often have pom-poms on top. With their Nordic-inspired designs and materials that now range from wool to synthetic fibers, tuques have become Canada's national hat.

In the United States, a classic tuque might be called a ski cap, a stocking cap, or a watch cap. Just as in Canada, people wear them for much more than skiing; they're considered a cold-weather essential.

Crown

DESCENDED FROM LATIN "CORONA" (WREATH)
TERM ALSO REFERS FIGURATIVELY TO MONARCHY
RELATED: TIARA, DIADEM

Headgear has been used for thousands of years to denote status; for example, indigenous tribes in the Americas would often make special head adornments for leaders out of feathers. In ancient Egypt, a number of crowns were used, including the White Crown or *hedjet.* While these were not necessarily made of precious materials, they were highly formal and symbolized both a pharaoh's divine lineage and earthly dominion.

Tiaras and diadems are among the oldest forms of crowns. The tiara was originally a high, pointed hat, made of leather and/or metal and richly ornamented, used by the peoples of Mesopotamia. The diadem, used in the early Persian Empire, was adapted by Constantine I as the crown of the Roman emperors.

Crowns can be used for coronations or state occasion and to connect the monarch with his or her consort. The most famous crown may be England's St. Edward's Crown, which is still used at coronations of the British monarchs. St. Edward's Crown supposedly contains gold from the crown of St. Edward the Confessor, the "last" Anglo-Saxon king. The crown was destroyed by Oliver Cromwell.

In popular U.S. culture, tiaras are worn by beauty pageant winners and sometimes brides.

Footwear

Going barefoot feels wonderful on cool grass or warm sand, but when the grass is wet or the sand is scorching, a layer between skin and ground can be even more wonderful. The earliest shoes were probably designed for this kind of protection. However, even the earliest shoes known (see timeline) were crafted skillfully. Whether it's because we can all look down and see our feet or for another reason entirely, shoes have long captured the human impulse for design. The items in this section show how widely footwear can vary, from socks to high heels.

Socks

IN ANCIENT TIMES, MADE FROM LEATHER OR CLOTH
INFORMAL: "KNOCK SOMEONE'S SOCKS OFF" (IMPRESS)
"PUT A SOCK IN IT" (STOP TALKING)

Socks have been around for longer than shoes. While the first socks may have been strips of hide or cloth wrapped around the feet and legs, knitted socks have been found in Egyptian tombs at Antinoe. The ancient Greeks made socks of matted animal hair that they referred to as *piloi*.

As time went on, the Romans adapted these loose-fitting items as *soccus,* crafting similar pieces from leather and woven fibers. In the first centuries B.C., Romans used woven material to make socks that they called *udones,* which were the first socks pulled on over the foot rather than fastened on it. After the fall of Rome, Anglo-Saxons took over Britain, and their fashions influenced those of many centuries to come: the loose tunics, tight-fitting breeches, and a short foot covering known as a *socque (stocc).*

As breeches loosened, tightened, lengthened, and shortened, the socks and hose worn with them changed, too. At first these were often made of fabric or hide and were loose "tubes" pulled over foot and leg, and fastened with ties or garters at the top. While some hose were knitted, for most, stretch was provided by cutting materials on the bias.

In 1589, the Reverend Dr. William Lee invented a knitting machine. Queen Elizabeth I refused him a patent for his invention, it was said, because of her concern that it would put hand knitters out of business. However, before long she and her contemporaries had been converted to machine-knit stockings, which could be manufactured six times faster than those of hand knitters.

Wool, silk, and cotton were used for centuries as sock materials, until the 20th-century invention of nylon and Lycra, both of which made socks more comfortable and durable than ever before.

Given the humble nature of this article of clothing, the word "sock" has given rise to a surprising number of English idioms. As early as about 1700, sock was used as a verb to mean "to hit" or "to strike," and in its noun form, it meant a punch. Later, the slang phrase "to sock away" signified saving money, presumably hidden in a sock.

Loafers

BASED ON: NORWEGIAN CATTLE LOAFING SHOES
RELATED TO: MOCCASINS
PENNY LOAFER: TREND OF PLACING COINS IN SLOT OF SHOE

Ethnic clothing styles often inspire fashion trends, and in the 1930s when *Esquire* magazine showed photos of a Norwegian farmer wearing slip-on leather shoes in a cattle loafing (gathering) area, a new style was in demand. The Norwegian shoes were something like moccasins but had a broad, flat heel attached to the sole and no laces at all. Shortly thereafter, American shoemakers began producing what one called "loafers" and another called "Weejuns," their shorthand for "Norwegian."

Another shoe style also gained popularity: slip-on leather shoes with no laces and heels. They were known as "Venetian loafers" because their shape supposedly mimicked the Venetian bark, a type of boat. (Other shoe styles have been compared to boats; see chopine under "High-Heeled shoes.") Unlike Bass Weejuns, Venetian loafers didn't have a strap across the vamp.

Strap or no strap, loafers were aptly named, since these easy-on, easy-off, comfortable shoes had nothing to do with hard labor (ironic, considering how hard those Norwegian cattle farmers probably worked; their "loafers" made it easier for them to move between barn and pen). Loafers came to be the sign of a 20th-century leisure class who could wear unsupportive shoes without socks and incur no pain.

The Bass Weejun's strap had a funny scallop on its top that supposedly stood for the "kiss" Mrs. Bass gave each shoe on its way out the door. Teenagers began putting coins in the opening of this mouth in the middle of the strap, which is how the shoes became known as "penny loafers." Loafers have come a long way from the penny. They're now available in many different styles, and have decorations that range from tassels to buckles to horse snaffle-bits, such as on the classic Gucci version. Although they are still considered a staple of preppy attire, people of all ages have a variety of different types of loafer slip-on shoes in their wardrobes.

High-Heeled Shoes

ORIGINALLY WORN BY WOMEN AND MEN
POPULARIZED BY CATHERINE DE MEDICI
ONCE FORBIDDEN BY MASSACHUSETTS BAY COLONY

A shoe is meant to protect the foot and allow a human to walk more comfortably; if it doesn't do either of those things, it's probably a high-heeled shoe. High heels can benefit the wearer by giving her extra height to look taller people directly in the eye and by enhancing her figure by elongating her legs and flexing her calf muscles.

But high heels were not always worn to enhance allure and were not always the province of women. Some of the first high heels were made for purely practical reasons. For example, Roman *kothorni* from approximately 200 B.C. were worn by actors and no doubt meant to adjust their height relative to their roles. Another reason for wearing high heels was to avoid refuse or dirt; Egyptian butchers wore high heels to keep their feet out of the blood on the floor, and medieval Europeans wore wooden platforms called pattens (see Uncommonly Known) when walking through the streets, both to keep their indoor shoes clean and to avoid sinking into puddles of night soil (a euphemism for human waste).

However, even with these useful applications, others recognized the erotic appeal of a leg elongated by a high heel. Roman prostitutes wore heels, and Venetian noblewomen favored a type of overshoe known as a *chopine* which could be higher than 24 inches. The heights of these overshoes— more like stilts—meant the women couldn't really move anywhere on their own and needed assistance for the simplest task.

A big step forward for the high heel was Catherine de Medici's arrival at the French court in the 16th century. The petite and fashionable queen wore heels to enhance her authority as well as her allure, which helped cement heels' place as a privilege of nobles. During this time straight through to the French Revolution, high heels were worn by men as often as women, with the elaborately painted "Louis heels" of King Louis XIV (the "Sun King") the envy of many a courtier.

In the U.S., high heels didn't catch on until well into the 20th century, perhaps because the Puritans of the Massachusetts Bay Colony originally forbade girls and women from wearing them and associated them with witches. Today, however, high heels can be found in any number of bewitching styles, and despite the physical discomfort they cause, women continue to buy and wear them happily.

Sneakers

INSPIRED BY 19TH-CENT. NEED FOR RECREATION SHOE
ORIGINALLY CALLED "PLIMSOLLS" (BOATING TERM)
MADE FROM: CANVAS, RUBBER, LEATHER, SYNTHETICS

Nineteenth-century railways allowed the English middle and lower classes to easily enjoy a day trip to the seaside, where stout leather boots seemed out of place. To better enjoy the shore terrain, people began wearing simple canvas "sand shoes" instead. The New Liverpool Rubber Company introduced a canvas shoe with a rubber bottom and a band holding the two parts together. By 1876 people called them "plimsolls" after the "plimsoll line" on boats that indicated a safe-water mark for harbor entry.

Plimsolls, which looked like the most simple, basic version of what we now call "tennis shoes," were popular and affordable and proved remarkably versatile. Different styles were adapted for croquet and lawn tennis; eventually, explorers and the military services began to use them, too. A pair was even found with the remains of Captain Robert F. Scott, who perished during his last, doomed Antarctic expedition. The big breakthrough for these shoes was the introduction of a process called "vulcanization." Vulcanized rubber could be melded to cloth, making the manufacturing process much faster and cheaper. This groundbreaking technology had been licensed to Charles Goodyear.

For a couple of decades, the manufacturers of these casual shoes made their own, differently named versions. However, in 1916 they consolidated

Shoelaces Since the 1991 discovery of the nearly 5,300-year-old Otzi the Iceman in Europe's Schnalstal Glacier, we know that humans have been using some rough form of shoelaces for at least that long. There is no definitive date for the invention of shoelaces, but they became widely used in the 20th century. The small plastic or metal sheath on the ends of the lace is called an aglet.

under the brand name Keds. The more general term for these shoes—"sneakers"—originated when an advertising agent named Henry Nelson McKinney noted that the rubber sole made the shoes virtually silent.

Since those early days, "sneakers" have metamorphosized into "athletic shoes," with different styles and features for every purpose from running to basketball to yoga to tennis to wrestling to speed walking. Status, particularly for teenagers, can hinge on having the right pair. However, whether they are some of the most sought-after and stylish "athletic shoes" or plain old "sneakers," with canvas tops, rubber soles, and simple laces, these shoes have made major inroads into current fashion.

Cowboy Boots

POINTED TOE: EASES MOVEMENT IN AND OUT OF STIRRUP
TALL HEEL: PREVENTS FOOT FROM SLIDING THROUGH STIRRUP IF RIDER IS KNOCKED OFF HORSE

Almost every feature of a modern cowboy boot has a practical purpose, and those that don't, like exotic leather

Shoes

Shoes are the closest thing between us and the earth, yet they are also the one item of clothing that is most consistently frivolous and comes in more shapes and styles than even the greatest shoe fanatic could count. Early shoes might have been made with simple materials like reeds, bark, wood, and metals, but they were not necessarily simply made. Even as people contemplated different shapes and colors (Attila the Hun was famous for sporting red-heeled boots), they had to consider where and how the shoes might be worn. Wooden clogs and pattens were durable and easily replaced, so they became the workingman's shoe of choice in heavily forested areas like northern Europe. Meanwhile, high heels became popular as a way for courtiers to demonstrate that they didn't have to walk behind a plow; even today, stiletto heels are mostly worn by women only when they don't have to do much walking. The swashbuckling style of the cavalier boot was eclipsed by its functionality, and it became the forerunner of the Army boot.

1ST CENTURY A.D. Roman sandal The Romans wore sandals made of leather for all occasions. The sandals of gladiators, warriors, and athletes had long straps that wound around the lower leg.

PREHISTORY Bast shoes Pliable bast fibers, from the inner bark of certain plants and trees, were used as far back as prehistoric times to weave shoes such as these.

inlays and intricate decorative stitching, have interesting histories.

Several different cultures contributed to the boots we now identify with the American cowboy. These different cultures and groups influenced the evolution of these boots, including their high heels, their pieced construction, and their unique shape. Soldiers, herders, and other workers on horseback began wearing heeled boots at least as early as the 16th century, although there are reports that Mongols wore boots with red heels. Stuart cavaliers, many of whom immigrated to the U.S. during Cromwell's Interregnum (1649-60), were known for boots with particularly high heels. After Napoleon's defeat at Waterloo, the Duke of Wellington's four-piece boots gained popularity; these boots had low heels and calf-high tops. The shape of American cowboy boots was heavily influenced by a type of riding boot worn by 18th-century Hessian cavalry officers, who favored a tall boot with a V cut in the top center and decorative tassels.

During the 19th century, American military boots continued to develop along the lines of these European styles, and many early pioneers and ranch workers were discharged soldiers who simply took their boots with them when they left service. Old photos show early cowboys in the saddle wearing laced boots. However, they soon found that laces could be lethal; an unseated cowboy was safer being able to slide out of his boots.

Practical and workmanlike, cowboy boots were fairly plain until the 1920s and '30s, when moving pictures and Hollywood idealized rugged, self-reliant cowboys like Roy Rogers and Gene Autry. Just as they prettied up their shirts and lassoes, they gussied up the men's boots, too. Soon, artisan bootmakers like Tony Lucchese were stitching everything from horseshoes to presidential monograms onto the shafts of custom-made kicks.

Although cowboy boots can be found in fancy form, especially in venues such as country and western dance halls, their practical purpose has not disappeared. Plenty of farmers and ranchers around the U.S. (and other countries, too) wear cowboy boots every day as they ride, rope, plant, and plow. The durable boots are even more valued as they become broken in and worn down.

1200
Japanese geta Originating during the Heian Period (794-1192), these shoes became part of ritual dress later in the Middles Ages. Geta or zori sandals set on high wooden platforms were often worn with special socks, "tabi."

1600
Cavalier boots The English cavaliers were part of the Restoration, and their boots developed in popularity over the next few centuries as cobblers became more adept at leatherwork.

1950
Stilettos The at-first dangerous stiletto heel, which punched holes in hardwood floors and sidewalks, was later modified during its pinnacle in the 1960s.

1400
Chopines These wooden platforms elevated people as high as 24 inches above the muck of the streets. The downside was that the wearer sometimes required an assistant to help maintain balance.

1660
Louis heels Named after the French King Louis XIV, these curved and splayed heels were combined with shoes on which highly decorative buckles and brocaded tops were made to coordinate with court dress.

1900
Ballet slippers/ Ballet flats Simple satin dance slippers without heels were popular during the 19th and early 20th centuries. They were deliberately plain, as fancier fabrics were considered "indecent" in the Victorian era.

Fasteners

Clothing doesn't require fastening. After all, a piece of cloth can simply be draped on the body, in the manner of a toga or a sari. However, fasteners (including sewing, which is covered later) do allow clothing to be fitted and made fancier, and to stay on more securely. Early fasteners were ties, slashes, and loops; as humans became more adept, these grew to include metal clasps, buttons, and hooks. For centuries, buttons (and buttonholes) were the most reliable way to make clothes fit closely, but during the 20th century, along came the metal zipper, and clothes could fit even more snugly.

Button

FROM OLD FRENCH "BOUTON"
BOTH DECORATIVE ELEMENT AND PRACTICAL CLOSURE
IDIOMATIC: "PUSH SOMEONE'S BUTTONS" (ANNOY)

The button dates back to prehistoric times, but until the Roman Empire seems to have functioned more as a decorative element on clothing than an actual fastener. The Romans fashioned a loop of material to go over a button and hold a piece of clothing closed.

Buttons and buttonholes seem like a natural combination, but it took returning Crusaders to bring it back to the West from the Turks and Mongols (who were, ironically, at that time also known as "barbarians").

It will surprise no one that the first Button Makers Guild was formed in clothing-conscious France, in 1250. Members of the guild produced buttons so exquisite they were truly tiny pieces of jewelry—and often contained jewels. The catch to this, of course, was that the peasantry was forbidden to own or use buttons made of anything but plain cloth or thread.

However, buttons did not simply change the decoration of clothing; they changed the entire shape of clothing. Buttons came along at a time when there were no zippers, hooks, or Velcro fasteners. Clothing could not be tailored properly without buttons. With buttons, clothes could be made to emphasize the human form. This worked with the Renaissance emphasis on humanism. Just as other disciplines and professions became more highly specialized, so did the tailor's profession.

PARALLEL HISTORY

Mourning Buttons

The indomitable, long-reigning Queen Victoria of England started an enduring fashion trend with her decision to wear buttons made of jet (an ancient ornamental stone) on all of her mourning dresses when her beloved husband Prince Albert died in 1861. Many of these glinting buttons bore her VR (Victoria Regina) monogram. Jet is a naturally occurring mineraloid that can be polished to a high sheen, so that it is regarded as a semiprecious stone (ironic, since jet's closest mineral relative is lowly coal). After Queen Victoria demonstrated her fondness for jet buttons and other ornaments, her subjects began to imitate her and create jet jewelry for mourning wear.

Buttons (from the French *bouton*) were for centuries disks with a shank on the back that people sewed to cloth. This meant that a button could have any sort of decoration, from carving, to embroidery, to painting. In the early 20th century, men began to prefer the four-hole button. While this type of button allowed a firmer closure, it meant that there were fewer decorative buttons produced. Of course, other kinds of fasteners would also weaken the button's hold on the market, but it remains an important element of clothing to this day.

Zipper

GIDEON SUNDBACK, INVENTOR:
"HOOKLESS FASTENER" (1913), "FASTENER NO. 2" (1917)
TERM "ZIPPER" COINED BY B. F. GOODRICH CO.

I magine having a stiff back and a pair of shoes with a dozen buttons that needed to be done up before you could leave the house. That's the dilemma a friend of Whitcomb Judson's had, and so Judson, an inventor, decided to invent a fastener that would be easier to close. His "clasp locker" was a good attempt, but it wasn't until Judson's Swedish-American employee Gideon Sundback tried his hand at the fastener that it became a viable object. Sund-back's innovation, which took him months to develop, was to make the fastener elements resemble small interlocking scoops, rather than hooks and eyes.

Sundback invented the "Hookless Fastener" in 1913, and the "Separable Fastener No. 2" in 1917. It took a while to get the final "zipper" to market because entirely new machinery had to be created to make it; there's no way to make a true zipper by hand.

One of the first customers was the US Army. It applied zippers to the clothing and gear of the troops of World War I. When the B. F. Goodrich Company decided to market galoshes with Sundback's fasteners, the product became popular. These new galoshes could be fastened with a single zip of the hand. A Goodrich executive is said to have slid the fastener up and down on the boot and exclaimed, "Zip 'er up," echoing the sound made by this clever device, and the fasteners came to be called zippers.

Registered in 1925, "zipper" was originally a B. F. Goodrich trademark for overshoes with fasteners. As the fastener that "zipped" came to be used in other articles, its name was used as well. B. F. Goodrich sued to protect its trademark but was allowed to retain proprietary rights only over Zipper Boots. Zipper itself had moved into the world of common nouns.

Pins

TYPES: STRAIGHT PINS, SAFETY PINS
CAN ALSO BE DECORATIVE, AS IN BROOCHES
IDIOMATIC: "ON PINS AND NEEDLES" (ANXIOUS, EXCITED)

S traight pins, used to fasten documents, hold garments closed, and pin clothing patterns to fabric, are extremely humble items that are also indispensable. Perhaps that's why economist Adam Smith used straight pins to illustrate his "division of labor" principle.

In his 1776 *Wealth of Nations,* Smith described a process (the precursor of the modern assembly line) in which one worker drew wire, another straightened it, a third cut it, and a fourth sharpened its end, before the fifth ground the opposite end down in order to attach the head. The importance of this example was that a single worker performing all of these steps could produce just a few pins in one day, while the team of workers could produce thousands.

While pins had been in existence since ancient Sumeria, figuring out how to replicate the technology took thousands of years. American John Ireland Howe was the first person to patent a pin-making machine. His 1835 Howe Manufacturing Company turned out 70,000 pins each day, but it took until 1843 for the company to activate a machine to crimp and fill the pin papers.

One of the worst problems with pins is that the iron would rust. Although electroplating was invented in the mid-1800s, the nickel coating would flake off and the pins would rust anyway. Tailors and seamstresses cleaned the rusted pins by pushing them back and forth into a bag of emery grit, which became known as a "pin cushion." Even though pins are now rustproof, pincushions are considered one of the most sensible ways to hold, store, and use pins, especially for dressmaking.

Pins are now commonplace and inexpensive, but they are still indispensable and available in many forms. While no one but Old Order Amish still use pins as clothing fasteners, a few spare straight pins can save the day if a hemline comes unstitched. Safety pins can extend a waistband, hold a button in place, or close a diaper, too, all without poking delicate skin.

UNCOMMONLY KNOWN...

Safety Pins What we call a safety pin the Mycenaeans called a "fibula." These spring-catch brooches and fasteners were used for centuries, then disappeared in the late Middle Ages. It wasn't until 1849 that the ancient fibula was "reinvented" as an unadorned "safety pin" by an American named Walter Hunt. Hunt, who was a prolific inventor, didn't think much of his new pin and sold its rights for just $400.

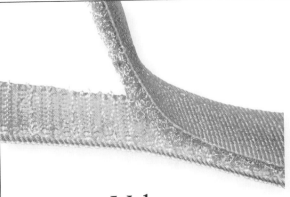

Velcro

INVENTOR GEORGE DE MESTRAL NAMED VELCRO FROM FRENCH "VELOURS" (VELVET) AND "CROCHET" (HOOK)
PATENTED 1955

D on't call that piece of hook-and-loop fastening on your sneaker, pillow, or jacket Velcro. According to the Velcro Corporation, that's the name of a company and a product's brand name, but it is not what you call the actual product. Not even employees are allowed to make that gaffe.

Though the patent expired in 1978, you might be protective of your product's name too, if it had taken you over two decades to get your invention developed and manufactured. George de Mestral, a Swiss engineer, thought of the idea for a micro hook-and-loop fastener in 1941 after coming back from a day's shooting with his dog and examining the cockleburs stuck to the hound's fur. He observed that the burrs hooked themselves into the hairs, and decided to create a prototype of this action. He called it "Velcro" after the French words *velours* ("velvet") and *crochet* ("hook").

De Mestral worked on his idea for nearly ten years, and didn't receive a patent until 1955. It took several more years for his fasteners to find a natural home, but when they did, they really took off: It was the space industry that first realized the practical uses of this easily opened and closed system. NASA uses Velcro brand hook-and-loop fasteners throughout uniforms and spaceships, even including a small patch of the hook material inside helmets for use as a nose scratcher.

Accessories

A n "accessory" helps out, and that's what the items here do for clothing and outfits. Some accessories are entirely optional: no one is required to wear a pocket square. However, most accessories serve a purpose, and it's only when their material and/or manufacture get to be too luxurious that they're optional. Many people need a handbag to carry things like money and identification; no one actually needs a handbag that costs $12,000. Similarly, gloves are vital in cold weather, but eelskin gloves lined with alpaca do not accomplish anything more in terms of warmth than knitted sheep's wool.

Gloves

USES: WORK, SPORT, FORMAL DRESS, GARDENING
IDIOMATIC: "FITS LIKE A GLOVE";
"THROW DOWN THE GLOVE" (GAUNTLET)

G loves have served humans both as garment and as fashion accessory. While many climates do not require gloves against cold, there are now so many different protective gloves for sports and other activities that the garment use is more important than ever. And while for several centuries gloves were vital accessories, their use as decorative and ceremonial items has dwindled to just a few places and occasions.

Prehistoric man made clumsy glove coverings for his hands, and the ancient Greeks and Romans reference gloves in their literature—for example, Homer describes Laertes as wearing gloves in his garden to avoid brambles. However, not much else is recorded about gloves until in the 11th thorough the 13th centuries they became part of women's fashion. They also took on talismanic properties: a "gauntlet" might be thrown down in challenge, or a lady might give a knight her glove as a token of admiration.

Queen Elizabeth I was so fond of using gloves as a prop to show off her beautiful hands that she owned more than 2,000 pairs. She was also fond of perfuming her gloves, and *maitres gantiers parfumeurs* (master glovemakers and perfumers) became the fashion both in England and France.

Gloves remained an essential part of a lady's wardrobe until late in the 20th century. During the 19th century, women preferred to wear their gloves at least one size too small, to emphasize the delicacy of their hands and to keep them curved in a ladylike position. It could take an hour or more of effort and powder for a lady's maid to stretch kidskin gloves over hands that were oversize.

One of the most important innovations in gloves was the invention of the latex glove for medical purposes. Latex gloves allow nurses to administer vaccinations, doctors to make examinations, and lab technicians to process samples, all without contaminating anything.

Purse

FROM GREEK "BURSA" (HIDE, LEATHER)
ALSO: HANDBAG, BAG, POCKETBOOK
OTHER USES: SUM OF PRIZE MONEY IN SPORTING CONTEST

P urses began as small carried sacks, turned into small hidden sacks, then became pockets, and finally wound up as handbags. That's a simplistic summary, but it helps to show that the history of these carryalls is of both practical considerations (size, security) and aesthetic concerns (decoration, proportion).

The "pockets" that men carried in early times might contain nothing more than a few coins. Of course, this depended on the society in which a person lived; a peasant might carry seeds or food, while a city dweller might carry some sweet-smelling herbs to hold against bad smells.

The forerunner of modern purses and handbags arrived in the late Middle Ages, when both men and women began carrying larger, more decorated pockets. By the 17th century, women were wearing their pockets beneath their skirts, and soon men's clothing had started gaining sewn-in pockets. The transition to the "purse" as a woman's accessory had begun, and it was cemented when women only began carrying their bags outside of their clothes once more when the slim "Empire" gown became fashionable in the early 19th century.

These new visible purses were called by such names as "reticules" and "chatelaines," depending on where and how they were carried; for example,

the chatelaine was usually attached to a waistband or belt. Purses had always been decorated, but now that they were always on display and the industrial revolution was in full sway, purses might be elaborately beaded or made of chain metal.

In the early 20th century, purses became larger and had more features, including small mirrors, pouches for spectacles, and outside pockets. Different kinds of leathers and hides were more durable than delicate embroidered silks and velvets for these carryalls. While wartime and technology would affect the materials of women's purses and handbags, their purpose was secure: A woman could now carry her own necessities and not rely on an accompanying male.

Pocket

DESCENDED FROM EXTERNAL, TIE-ON POUCH
EVOLVED INTO PURSES (PRIMARILY FOR WOMEN)
FROM ANGLO-NORMAN "POKETE" (LITTLE BAG, SACK)

T he first pockets were small pouches that hung from a belt or waist where a person might keep small valuables. They were separate from clothing, and since the Old English word for "pocket," *pocca*, is the same as the one for "purse," at one time these items must have been quite similar.

Of course, as any woman who has ever had her purse snatched will tell you, carrying valuables on the outside of one's clothing can be a perilous practice. Thieves and "cutpurses" were common in early modern Europe, and people began to find new ways to carry their money and possessions. Since they already had their separate pockets, they cut slits in their clothing so that they could wear the pockets beneath a shirt, skirt, or trousers.

This meant that the pocket itself had to change size and shape, becoming flatter and easier to reach into. Rather than a pouch, the pocket became a two-piece sack with a long slit in its front and a deep bottom. In the late 18th century as men's jackets and breeches became more fitted, there was no room to tie a pocket beneath, so smaller versions of the two-sided pockets were sewn into seams for them.

However, women continued to use tie-on pockets beneath their voluminous skirts, between their shift or underpetticoat and their top petticoat. Wearing a pocket meant that a woman might keep personal items (letters, a journal), tools (scissors, needles, a pen), and even toilet articles (smelling salts, eau de cologne) on her person. At first these interior pockets were quite plain, but many later pockets are richly decorated with different types of embroidery.

While men and their tailors continued to find new places for pockets—breast pockets, watch pockets, and coin pockets, among others—when women ceased to use pockets because of their own more fitted fashions, they began once again to carry outside pockets—or "purses."

UNCOMMONLY KNOWN...
Handkerchief Pieces of linen used to wipe the nose have been used since Roman times for this practical purpose, but over the centuries handkerchiefs have just as often been purely decorative and ornamental, waved during a joust or tucked in a dapper pocket. Pocket handkerchiefs have been largely supplanted by facial tissues but are still used at ceremonial occasions like weddings and funerals.

Belt

REPLACED SUSPENDERS IN EARLY 1900S
FIRST USED IN MILITARY ATTIRE
DESCENDED FROM: ROPE OR WOVEN TIES

Different forms of "girdles" (as they were once called) and belts have been worn for thousands of years, but the current most common use of them, to hold up men's trousers other than decoratively, is quite recent. Men have been wearing belts with their trousers only since the 1920s.

Before that, most men used suspenders (or "braces" in the U.K.), straps that go over the shoulders and button onto trousers at front and back. Leather belts were almost exclusively the province of the military and security forces. In the former, especially during the 19th and early 20th centuries, belts were part of creating a trim, uniform line. However, belt wearing in the military developed from practical considerations. A belt over one's tunic was where you hung your sword guard or your pistol holster. Even after military personnel no longer kept weapons at hand, police forces used utility belts to carry holsters and other tools like handcuffs.

Men wear belts and suspenders because their waist and hips are often equal; without some form of support, their trousers would fall. Women are shaped quite differently, and rarely require a belt for support; instead, women wear belts as fashion accessories. Men's belts are usually made of plain leather with metal buckles, but women's belts run the gamut from leather to fabric to plastic and metal, adorned with everything from beading to rhinestones to chains.

The oldest forms of belts are sashes made of rope and fabric. Nearly all of the world's religions use some form of this ancient belt in their clerical garb, from the simple obi-like bands on Buddhist monks' robes, to the cinched ropes worn by Roman Catholic priests. These belts are variously meant to remind the religious of the vows that bind them to the divine, of their chastity, of the need to pray, and of the parts of a creed.

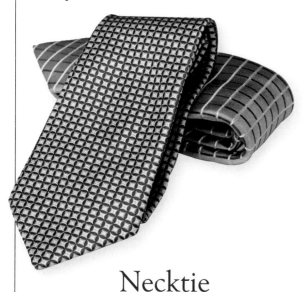

Necktie

DESCENDED FROM: NECKCLOTHS, KNOTTED KERCHIEFS
EARLY PROTOTYPE: "CRAVAT," WORN BY KING CHARLES
MODERN TIE: DESIGNED 1924, JESSIE LANGSDORF (N.Y.)

No one knows why the earliest neckties found were worn, but they were numerous: many of the more than 7,000 life-size terra-cotta soldiers built to guard the 210 B.C. tomb of Shih Huang-Ti, the first Chinese emperor, wore silk neckcloths. There is written evidence of Roman *fascalia*, neckcloths worn to keep an orator's vocal cords warm. In A.D. 113, the Roman emperor Trajan built a monument celebrating a victory of the Dacians (modern Romanians), with 2,500 figures who each wore three different types of neckwear: a short necktie, a neckcloth, and a

---

UNCOMMONLY KNOWN . . .
Scarves Called "sudarium" (sweat cloths) in ancient Rome and used to indicate rank in medieval China, lengths of woven fabric wrapped around the neck have a long history. The first knitted version may have been invented by the third Duke of Krakow, who in 1783 got a chilled, stiff neck. His physician recommended a neck wrap, and the crafty duke knitted himself one.

---

knotted kerchief. It's not just modern men who find it important to display their "colors."

The first modern necktie was the cravat, which was named after silk kerchiefs worn by Croatian mercenaries who came to the French court in 1660 to be thanked for service to King Louis XIV. The "Sun King" was so taken with their colorful neckwear that "cravats," which may or may not be a corruption of "Croat," became the rage.

In 1660, England's King Charles II (whose sister Henrietta married Louis XIV's brother) was restored to the throne, and brought elaborate lace cravats into fashion. Known as the Merry Monarch, he presided over the period known in English history as the Restoration.

As time went on, ties became a way to declare allegiance to a particular group. The first "sporting colors" as a flag were created by the I Zingari Cricket Club at Cambridge University in 1845, and in 1880, Oxford University's Exeter College Rowing Club took their ribboned hatbands and tied them around their necks, creating the first "old school tie." As the British military abandoned its colored uniforms, they retained the colors in regimental ties.

One of the most important developments in modern neckwear was New York tailor Jessie Langsdorf's patented 1924 design of cloth cut on a bias and divided into three parts, which became the world standard. After hitting a sales peak in 1995, tie sales and wear declined. In mid-2008, the Men's Dress Furnishings Association, which represented men's fashion accessories, shut down after 60 years.

For a brief time in the 1980s, women entering traditionally male professions like investment banking and law wore floppy silk ties in an effort to fit in with their colleagues.

Umbrella

FROM LATIN "UMBRA" (SHADE)
FIRST USED BY NOBILITY AS PROTECTION FROM SUN
TELESCOPIC UMBRELLA CREATOR: HANS HAUPT (1920s)

The umbrella's name comes from the Latin word for shade, *umbra* (Greek: *ombros*). From its earliest appearances in the ancient Assyrian city of Nineveh to its 19th-century fashion triumph in the form of a parasol, this shielding apparatus was primarily used to denote status, provide comfort, and protect the skin from the sun's effects.

The Egyptians held umbrellas over nobles to signify the authority of those being shaded, and over members of the royalty to symbolize the "vault of heaven" protecting them. Ancient Greeks also used the umbrella to denote their deities, but in both Greece and Rome, the device soon became more popular as a shade provider.

The Western Roman Catholic Church also used the umbrella in its liturgy, which may be one reason why commoners did not begin to use umbrellas until the early Renaissance. Portuguese colonists brought umbrellas back with them from Asia and Africa, and their use soon spread to French and English royalty (both Catherine de Medici and Mary, Queen of Scots had parasols). It took much longer for the umbrella to catch on as rain protection among Europeans than it did for them to adopt it as a sunshade. Stylish Persian traveler Jonas Hanway used his umbrella while walking through the streets of England in the mid-18th century, popularizing it with men. By 1800, the umbrella coexisted with the parasol.

The first all-umbrella shop, James Smith and Sons, opened in London in 1830 and is still in operation today. Its early products were made of wood or whalebone and usually covered with oiled canvas. The major step forward was loommaker Samuel Fox's 1852 steel-rib design for umbrella works.

The next breakthrough in umbrella design was the telescopic umbrella, which allowed users to carry a more compact version of the otherwise unwieldy accessory. In the 1920s German engineer Hans Haupt discovered how to make the steel-rib umbrella more portable and started a new company called Knirps to market his collapsible product.

In recent years the diminishing ozone layer has increased people's concern about the effects of the sun. For a few decades, people relied on sunscreen and sunblock creams and lotions to block harmful rays, but as we learn more about different types of rays, the use of parasols and umbrellas to block the sun is gaining popularity once more. Parasols of silk, paper, lace, and natural fibers can be used for parties, parades, and long walks and, of course, on the beach. Beach and backyard umbrellas are more popular and widely used than ever.

PARALLEL HISTORY

Designer Items

One of the earliest sources of designer goods was the luggagemaker Louis Vuitton, whose flat-topped trunks, cases, and custom-made items like bookcases and campaign desks revolutionized global travel. Close on Vuitton's heels was the equestrian leather goods house of Hermès, which began making expensive handbags in the 1900s when Mme. Hermès complained she could not find any to her taste. Around this time revolutionary designer Coco Chanel created her iconic leather handbag swinging from a chain, and soon people were hooked on anything with a logo or monogram. Today there are hundreds of designer bags, belts, sunglasses, and more; the most difficult choice is knowing whether something is genuine or counterfeit.

Laundry

Clothes endure many different conditions. The body is dirty, and so is most of the world. Between sweat, smoke, dirt, and food, clothing gets dirty, and although disposable socks and underwear have gained fans in the travel industry, most clothing must be cleaned. Tools of the laundry trade are so much easier to use than they once were. A modern electric clothes-washing machine requires only pressing buttons; in contrast, as late as the mid-20th century, most people were still heating water and putting clothes in a washtub through an ungainly and sometimes dangerous mangle.

Clothespin

SECURES LAUNDERED CLOTHING TO CLOTHESLINE TO DRY
CAN BE ONE PIECE OR TWO PIECES (WITH SPRING)
COMEBACK IN 21ST CENT. AS ECO-FRIENDLY OPTION

The "spring-clamp for clotheslines" was patented in 1853 by David M. Smith of Springfield, Vermont. Despite nearly 200 later 19th-century patents and dozens of late 20th-century "improvements," the simple wooden clothespin remains useful.

While Smith improved the humble clothespin, wooden clamps for clothes drying had been around for a few decades already. People may have gotten the idea from returning sailors used to hang their drenched garments in the rigging to dry. Hanging clothes from a raised line made more sense than draping them over branches and hedges, which often left wet fabric full of debris and even the occasional critter.

Once upon a time, Richwood, Virginia, produced the greatest number of clothespins, but by 2001, only Vermont's National Clothespin Company in Montpelier was still producing the small clamps. After it shut down that same year, wooden clothespins could still be purchased in the U.S.—but they were all manufactured in China. Several factors led to the decline of the clothespin, including home washing machines and clothes dryers, but one of the biggest may have been the introduction of disposable diapers. Even after homemakers began using clothes dryers for shirts, dresses, and other items, bulky cloth diapers were best dried on a line both because of their frequent use and their heavy material. Once people could simply toss a disposable diaper into a pail, the need for clothespins severely decreased (although using a clothespin placed gently on the nose to avoid bad smells still works quite well).

While it might actually seem that clotheslines and clothespins would be enjoying a renaissance due to eco-friendly trends, it's not as simple as it sounds to

---

UNCOMMONLY KNOWN...

Line-drying Hanging clothes in the sun is the oldest form of clothes drying, and despite a hiatus with the advent of the electric clothes dryer, it's making a resurgence. Green laundry practices, including line-drying, result in savings of hundreds of thousands of megawatts of energy per year. Removing clothes promptly from the washing machine and shaking wrinkles out before hanging on the clothes line reduces the need for ironing, which can use up to 1800 watts of energy.

get modern Americans to use them: Many neighborhoods and homeowners associations bar the use of clothes lines. Perhaps inventors should spend less time on new, improved plastic clothespins and focus on developing an attractive clothes line or rack for backyard use.

Clothes Iron

DESCENDED FROM FLAT PIECES OF IRON HEATED IN FIRE
ELECTRIC IRON: PATENTED BY HENRY W. SEELY (1882)
ALSO USED TO MAKE DECORATIVE PLEATS OR CREASES

The clothes iron is used to press wrinkles out of, and pleats into, clothes. An iron is now plugged in and heats up, and then a person moves it back and forth over a piece of clothing that rests on a firm ironing board.

People have used heat and pressure both singly and together to dewrinkle fabric for many years in many cultures, and it wasn't simply to make clothes look smooth. For the many centuries when clothing wasn't heated in the drying process, hot irons killed parasites (fleas, lice), bacteria, and mildew in fabrics.

One of the earliest irons was the "goffer," a round bar heated by Greeks and used to create pleats in linen. The Roman "hand mangle" was used to beat fabric, although the Romans also used a clothes press known as a *prelum*. The ancient Chinese favored the pan iron, its flat bottom and coal-holding top quite similar to 19th-century clothes irons. By about the tenth century, Scandinavian Vikings were employing glass linen smoothers that may or may not have been used with water.

In the 14th century, the flatiron appeared in Europe. It was a thin piece of iron with a handle attached that could be heated in the fire and used until it was cool. An "ironing cloth" was usually placed between the flatiron and the garment being pressed to prevent soot stains. The next iron was the box iron, so called because its hollow metal bottom could be filled with coals, eliminating need for a cloth.

Box irons were used until the 19th century, when gas irons and electric irons supplanted them. The first electric iron was patented by Henry W. Seely in 1882, and while it heated on a stand and cooled quickly, it was a big improvement over previous irons. Steam irons in the 1920s and nonrusting soleplates in the 1930s were innovations that further increased the usefulness of clothes irons.

Sewing Machine

SHIFTED PRODUCTION FROM TAILORS TO FACTORIES
DESIGN PATENTED BY ELIAS HOWE (1846) AFTER DISPUTES
WITH LARGEST MANUFACTURER, ISAAC SINGER

Sewing needles are one of the most ancient human tools that can be verified, since archaeologists have found needles dating back 20,000 years. The earliest needles were made of bone and horn and included a sharply pointed end and an "eye." They were used for rudimentary forms of sewing; humans understood early on that attaching hides and skins was the best way to make warm coverings for the body and utensils to hold food and supplies.

Iron needles came on the scene much later, sometime in the 1300s. Machines to replicate the sewing motion wouldn't be realized until just over 200 years ago, when British inventor Thomas Saint made the first workable sewing machine. It was workable but evidently not practical enough to go into production.

There were several other attempts at a sewing machine before a French tailor named Barthelemy Thimonnier made a working model in 1830 with one thread and a hooked needle that mimicked embroidery's chain stitch. His machine so enraged his colleagues, who feared unemployment, that they burned down his premises.

However, real progress in a sewing machine came in 1846 when American Elias Howe gained a patent for a machine that used thread from two sources instead of one. Combined with this lockstitch process, Isaac Singer's up-and-down mechanism and Allen Wilson's rotary hook made a modern sewing machine a reality.

While Howe and Singer subsequently became embroiled in patent struggles (Howe eventually won), Singer's successful manufacturing enterprise remains strong to this day. The new machines made it possible not only for home seamstresses to work more quickly, but for garment factories to produce far more than they ever had before, employing scores of women crammed shoulder to shoulder at machines doing piecework. Unfortunately, these "sweatshops" were both common and hidden from public view.

By the early 1900s, electric sewing machines were widely available, and this is when they started to become a fixture of domestic life. People no longer had to rely on tailors and seamstresses for large sewing projects; they could make curtains, hem several pairs of trousers, or finish a dress at home.

Companies like Singer began making machines that were smaller and could fit more easily into a "sewing room," as well as making machines that were built into or on top of attractive cabinets that would fit in well with a family's other furnishings. Modern sewing machines improve with each technological development: many now have computers built in that offer hundreds of stitch options and embroidery patterns.

PARALLEL HISTORY

Triangle Shirtwaist Factory Fire

On March 25, 1911, 146 women were killed when the Triangle Shirtwaist Factory on the eighth, ninth, and tenth floors of the Asch Building in lower Manhattan caught fire. With some as young as 12, the poor immigrant women and girls from Germany, Italy, and eastern Europe were working on a Saturday because they needed extra money. Their bosses, Max Blanck and Isaac Harris, both escaped the blaze by going to the roof. Unable to get out, because proper exits were not accessible, many women jumped to their death. This fire is considered a turning point in labor reform in the U.S., since once it had happened, the government could no longer stand by and allow businesses to regulate workers' conditions.

Firefighters douse flames coming from the Asch Building, during the fire of 1911.

Clothes Washer

DESCENDED FROM: WASHBOARDS, REVOLVING DRUMS
FIRST ELECTRIC MACHINE PATENTED ALVA FISHER, 1910
POST-WORLD WAR II, INTRODUCED LEISURE TO HOUSEHOLDS

Two methods of washing clothes endured for thousands of years: pounding clothes against rocks by a river, or dragging bagged clothes through seawater behind a boat. Humans knew that getting cloth clean required something to force water and soap through the fibers, but they didn't have many different ways of doing so. Even into the early decades of the 20th century, laundry remained a labor-intensive task that required water toting and manual operation (spinning a large tub or hand-scrubbing) to complete.

The earliest washing machine was the 1797 washboard, which provided people with a hard, ribbed surface against which to scrub their clothes. The first washing machine was a cage with wooden rods that caught the clothes and a handle for turning; it was designed in 1782 by Henry Sidgier of Great Britain. Once paddles had been implemented, James King developed the revolving drum, in 1851, and Hamilton Smith brought out the revolving drum with reversing action in 1858.

The washing machine went electric in the early 20th century, with one of the first made by Alva J. Fisher. It took until the 1930s for engineers to design a case to enclose the works so that water wouldn't splash and short the motor out or harm the person operating the machine. Fully automated machines in the 1930s and 1940s were followed by fully automated machines with spin cycles that eliminated the need for wringers on top of them.

Another laundry challenge that washing machines solved was a water source. Before homes had internal plumbing, laundry might require as much as 50 gallons or 400 pounds of water. Once running water was available, early automatic washing machine models could be connected temporarily, as needed, to sink taps. As machines became more sophisticated, homes were constructed with permanent hot and cold taps for the washing machine.

You might think that after thousands of years with nothing but rocks and water, a mechanical clothes-washing machine would remain in one form for some time—but modern technology has moved so fast that this has not been the case. Like sewing machines and refrigerators, washing machines are subject to all sorts of innovations: digital instrument panel displays, stronger motors, and built-in computers that allow for combinations of functions that previously might have taken a person hours to complete.

Today's washing machines are either "top-loaders" or "front-loaders." Most American washing machines operate with an agitation system: the inner cylinder moves back and forth while paddles in the washer's drum lift clothes. The front-loading machines use less water and are more energy efficient. Other features can include steam heat, a delicate cycle for fabrics like silk and linen, and wrinkle removal.

While most modern homes in the U.S. include washing machines and clothes dryers as basic appliances, Laundromats that contain anywhere from a few to scores of each machine still exist and are used by apartment dwellers, students, and others when their machines are temporarily out of service.

UNCOMMONLY KNOWN . . .

Clothes Dryer Early clothes dryers from 1800 or thereabouts were called "ventilators" and looked like barrels; they were turned in front of a fire and actually operated on the same principle as modern electric clothes dryers, which use heat and rotary action to remove water from clothes. Without a heat source, the best method of getting clothes dry involved using a mangle, a machine that squeezed fabric between two rollers, and then hanging the garments outside to dry.

It's actually the spirit helping the spirit;
it is the doctor, the bed, the potion.
—FRANZ GRILLPARZER (1791-1872)

Medications & Potions

Everything has a history, and some of the most interesting history relates to the stuff we find in our bathrooms and medicine cabinets. Soap, nail polish, laxatives, and aspirin are such common items that we rarely consider anything other than their price and effectiveness. But versions of these were available to consumers several millennia ago. Written records from the cradles of Western civilization—Egypt, Greece, and Rome—are filled with references to potions and medicaments similar to those we use today. Our knowledge of earlier use is limited by the fact that recorded history goes back only some 6,000 years before the present. One common theme that emerges is that while our predecessors often were on to the right thing with their natural remedies and nostrums, just as often they were not. This hit or miss approach many times resulted in harmful substances—makeup that would poison the blood so slowly it was not suspected as a killer, toothpastes that destroyed tooth enamel, depilatories that left scars. On the other hand, nature's pharmacy sometimes yielded effective remedies—willow bark extract, which acts like aspirin, was used as a painkiller by the Romans. Many potions and medicines used long ago may have worked, but we would not want to use them today. Iron Age men used pine resin for hair gel; Romans rinsed their mouth with urine; cavemen shaved with volcanic glass. In short, people did the best they could with what they had. People wanted to shave (or, along the Nile, felt they had to for health reasons), so they fashioned the articles they had at hand. Improvements came with advances in technology. Not until the mid-19th century, with the sciences of chemistry and medicine firmly established, did modern potion-making begin to take shape, and not until the 20th century did big industry take over.

Hygiene

This is one section sure to be an eye-opener to just about everybody. Soap, deodorant, toothpaste, shaving cream—those bathroom products that we depend upon every day to make us feel clean and fresh have been around in one form or another for a long time. True, toilet paper was not widely used until the late 19th century, but there were various substitutes that we might consider a tad unpleasant today. The most basic hygiene product, soap has been with us since the earliest civilizations, its chemistry improved on only in the last 150 years.

Soap

INGREDIENTS THEN AND NOW:
600 B.C.: GOAT TALLOW AND WOOD ASHES
TODAY: VEGETABLE OILS, GLYCERIN, SODIUM HYDROXIDE

It seems to possess magical properties, a bar of soap. We rub our dirty hands on it and they come away clean, and so, miraculously, does the bar of soap—ready for the next grimy customer. The need to clean oneself seems instinctive, and it's not surprising that the first cleansing agents came from plants. In the second millennium B.C., the Hittites of Asia Minor washed themselves with water and ashes from the soapwort plant, which contains a natural cleansing agent called saponin. Ashes from this and other plants form soluble salts called alkalis that have cleaning properties.

But actual soap came along in about 600 B.C., thanks to the seafaring Mediterranean people known as the Phoenicians. Soap is made not only of alkalis (such as potassium carbonate) but also fats—the two react together under heat to create an emulsifying product that is both hydrophilic and hydrophobic. Molecules of soapy water will thus attach themselves to whatever isn't water—e.g., dirt—and then suspend the dirt within the suds so that it can be rinsed away. Without understanding the chemistry, the Phoenicians developed a soap made by boiling ashes, water, and goat fat. What remained after evaporation was a waxy substance—soap.

By about A.D. 800 soapmaking had become a European craft, with Spain one of the preeminent

PARALLEL HISTORY

Detergents

The creation of synthetic cleaning agents occurred in 1916 when German scientist Fritz Gunther developed a synthetic surfactant (surface-acting substance) for use as a cleaner. He may have benefited from experiments by German chemists from the 1890s who mixed alcohol with a soap solution and achieved a lathery substance. Gunther's product was too harsh for home use, but by the 1930s both homes and industries were using detergents. The advantage over soap was that detergents left no scummy residue. The reason? Soap binds with minerals that occur in water, forming molecules that won't dissolve and wash away; detergents don't. "Detergent," by the way, has come to mean synthetic surfactant, but it's the generic term for any cleansing agent, including soap.

manufacturers. The saponification process was still essentially the same as that of the Phoenicians. Makers also added various scents and colors. The price of soap dropped considerably in the late 18th century after French chemist Nicholas Leblanc discovered a way to make lye (an alkaline substance) from table salt. The popular floating Ivory soap was invented by accident in 1879 when a worker at Harley Procter's soap factory forgot to turn off a mixing vat—too much air was added to the soap, but the product was a huge hit.

the Middle East in the 13th century, courtesy of the Crusaders. The first modern deodorant in the U.S. came out in 1888 in Philadelphia. Called Mum, it was an underarm cream with a zinc compound. But all of these early deodorants simply hid body odor with a more pleasant one.

In 1903, the first commercial antiperspirant, Everyday, made its appearance, getting to the root of the problem. By this point a less irritating compound of aluminum chloride was substituted for zinc. Scientists then and now are uncertain how these drying agents work; they may block sweat glands, temporarily preventing them from secreting perspiration. Spray-on antiperspirants appeared in the 1960s. Pump-release and stick deodorants became popular in the 1980s when criticism arose over the ozone depletion caused by chlorofluorocarbons (CFCs) in aerosol sprays.

Deodorant

FIRST ANTIPERSPIRANT INTRODUCED IN 1888
ROLL-ON ANTIPERSPIRANT FIRST SOLD IN 1952
MOST ANTIPERSPIRANTS ALSO CONTAIN DEODORANT

Efforts to mask natural human body odors appear to have been around as long as civilization. The Sumerians of the fourth millennium B.C., who developed one of the earliest written languages, left records of their deodorants. Ancient Egyptians used perfumed oils, mixtures of cinnamon and citrus, and a kind of time-release device—a cone of perfumed fat that slowly melted in the heat. The Egyptians even went a step further by removing their underarm hair. It worked because odor is produced not by perspiration but by colonies of bacteria that break down in perspiration; they thrive in warm, damp areas such as the underarms, genitals, and feet. Greeks and Romans used perfumed oils. Alcohol-based perfumes came to Europe from

Shampoo

FROM A HINDI WORD MEANING TO PRESS OR MASSAGE
EARLY SHAMPOOS: SOAP AND CITRUS EXTRACTS
DRY SHAMPOO: POWDER THAT ABSORBS OIL

Products for cleaning the hair date from as far back as soap, and the ancients probably knew as well as we that soap just didn't wash. The problem is not so much to get rid of the dirt but the sebum, an oil produced by glands in the skin. Also, soap leaves a dull film on the hair. The early Egyptians came up with a clever solution—they washed their hair with a mixture of citrus juice and a little soap. The citric acid cuts through the sebum. By the Middle Ages a more refined hair product had been developed by combining soap with soda (sodium carbonate) or potash (potassium carbonate), from which soap itself is often made. The resulting preparation has a high number of negatively charged hydroxyl ions, as do modern shampoos.

By the late 18th century posh British salons were offering customers a hair-washing massage called a "shampoo," the word borrowed from the Hindi for "massage." One such establishment, Mahomed's Indian Vapour Baths, operated by a Bengali businessman in Brighton, offered customers a therapeutic massage or a *champi* (shampoo). By the late 1900s such salons were commonplace; hairstylists used special preparations of shaved soap boiled with aromatic herbs such as jasmine and sandalwood.

Also by the end of the century, German chemists were coming up with nonsoap, synthetic surfactants known as detergents (see Parallel History, p. 192) that would clean without leaving soapy residues. It took until after World War I for manufacturers to bottle a soft, nonabrasive, commercially viable detergent for the hair. A Massachusetts entrepreneur named John Breck began marketing a shampoo in 1930 after a failed search for a baldness cure; his business would for a while become the nation's top shampoo producer.

Today shampoo comes in every scent and formula imaginable. Many manufacturers are touting all-natural blends, with increasingly specialized products for different types of hair, such as oils for super-curly locks.

UNCOMMONLY KNOWN...

Hair Gel Possibly the earliest known use of hair gel occurred on an Iron Age man living in central Ireland in the third to fourth century B.C. His preserved body was recovered from a peat bog and revealed that he coiffed his hair—possibly to compensate for shortness—with a gel of plant oil and pine resin from trees that grew in Spain and southwestern France.

Toothbrush

EARLY MODELS: ANCIENT EGYPTIAN CHEWSTICK, CHINESE HOG-HAIR BRUSHES
FIRST MODERN TOOTHBRUSH: DUPONT, 1938

Modern dental hygiene has greatly extended the life and health of the teeth and gums, but it wasn't as though earlier societies didn't try. At least as far back as 3500 B.C., people were cleaning their mouth; the Babylonians of that era rubbed their teeth with chewsticks—pencil-length twigs frayed at one end. Chewsticks have been found in Egyptian tombs from 3000 B.C., and are still used in some tropical areas, the sticks taken from such trees as *Garcinia kola*, *Salvadora persica,* and *Gouania lupiloides.* The chewing released a mouth freshener and an aromatic odor, and the non-frayed end could be used as a toothpick.

The first real toothbrushes were invented by the Chinese in the 15th century. The bristles were plucked from the necks of Siberian hogs and fastened to handles made of bamboo or bone. About 300 years later such toothbrushes had made their way to Europe, where many people found them too hard on their gums. By this point the few Europeans who were brushing were using softer horsehair toothbrushes, or simply picking their teeth with toothpicks—made of gold or silver if they could afford it.

A pioneering dentist, Frenchman Pierre Fauchard recommended in a 1728 publication that people rub their teeth and gums daily with a piece of natural sponge. Gradually the idea that regular dental hygiene was beneficial took hold, and by the early 1800s, toothbrushing had caught on. The next breakthrough occurred in 1938, when the DuPont company introduced the nylon toothbrush. The bristles held better to the brush than hog hair, but they were just as stiff. In the early 1950s the company rolled out a softer nylon toothbrush. The first electric toothbrush was invented in Switzerland in 1939; by 1960 you could buy one called the Broxodent in the United States.

Toothpaste

EARLY TEETH CLEANERS: PUMICE STONE, URINE
EARLY WHITENER: NITRIC ACID
FIRST COLLAPSIBLE TUBE OF TOOTHPASTE: 1892

The Egyptians of 2000 B.C. used a toothpaste made of powdered pumice stone and vinegar. For the next 3,000 years this formula—or variations on it—were deemed good enough. The pumice whitened the theeth, never mind that in abrading the enamel it promoted tooth decay. The Romans used urine instead of vinegar; its ammonia (an ingredient in some modern toothpaste) cleaned the teeth. The Greeks and Romans tried other abrasives—crushed bones and shells worked well; adding powered charcoal and bark freshened the breath. The toothpaste was probably applied with a chewstick. The Romans also liked urine as a mouthwash; the wealthy imported theirs from Portugal.

Around the year A.D. 1000, the Persians were cautioning toothpaste users against harsh abrasives. They favored burnt horn, crushed snail shells, gypsum, flint, and honey. Europeans in the Middle Ages went to barber-surgeons to have their teeth filed and painted with nitric acid, which ate the enamel; the

---

result was beautifully white teeth that had a short life. Later toothpastes of brick dust, china, and cuttlefish had similar effects.

Not until the 1800s did a toothpaste come out that actually did more good than harm. British chemists added bicarbonate of soda (nonabrasive whitener) and strontium (strengthener) to toothpaste. In 1802 doctors in Naples, Italy, noticed that though their patients had stained teeth, they also had few cavities, and guessed it was the result of high fluoride concentration in the local water. In the 1940s fluoride was added to drinking water, and in 1956 Procter & Gamble first put it in toothpaste, advertising Crest "with Fluoristan!" Collapsible toothpaste tubes were introduced in 1892 in Connecticut with Dr. Washington Sheffield's Creme Dentifrice.

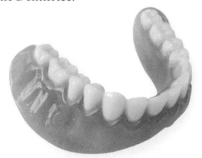

Dentures

EARLY DENTURES MADE FROM:
IVORY, BONE, HUMAN TEETH, PORCELAIN
GOLD, VULCANIZED RUBBER (1864)

The first known false teeth appeared in Egypt around 4,500 years ago. The art of denture making flowered 1,800 years later among the Etruscans. Living in present-day Tuscany, they fashioned false teeth of ivory or bone and secured them with intricate gold-wire bridgework. Only the wealthy could afford the expensive dental surgery. After the decline of the Roman Empire in the third century A.D., good dentures were hard to come by.

Well-to-do women of the 16th century endured having their gums pierced so that dentures could be secured with wires. Queen Elizabeth I (1533-1603) simply relied on bits of cloth to plug gaps in her teeth. In the 17th century dentists tried securing sets of false teeth with springs. Strong muscles were required to keep the mouth closed; sometimes one's jaw would suddenly open and the teeth would plop out. Dentures continued to be hand-carved from ivory and bone, but they often rotted and smelled bad. Human teeth offered a somewhat better substitute—they were harvested from freshly dead soldiers or, if teeth sellers could get away with it, from soldiers not quite dead. Barrels of "Civil War" dentures were shipped to Europe. Poor people would sell healthy teeth, and slaves were sometimes forced to endure extractions. George Washington wore a set of dentures crafted probably from ivory (of hippopotamus teeth). In the late 18th century the French began making teeth of porcelain, the best denture material until the advent of plastics, in the 20th century.

Razors

ANCIENT RAZORS: SHELLS, GLASS, SHARKS' TEETH
EARLY BLADES: SINGLE, BRONZE, COPPER, GOLD
FIRST T-SHAPED RAZOR: 1847

P rehistoric cave paintings and archaeological evidence indicate that people were shaving some 30,000 years ago, using sharp-edged shells, flint, volcanic glass, and even

sharks' teeth. Over the millennia, facial hair has come in and out of fashion. A smooth face was a status symbol among the ancient Egyptians, and the highborn were often buried with their bronze razors. Other cultures fashioned razors from copper and gold. The Greeks and Romans hammered iron into razor-sharp cutting implements. Roman soldiers began shaving routinely in the sixth century B.C., possibly as a health regulation, but daily shaving was still hundreds of years away. Roman women also used razors, as well as tweezers and pumice stones.

What the Greeks and Romans used for those early razors was the same design carried forward until the late 19th century—the straight, or cut-throat, razor. It was a long, single-sided blade with a handle. Nicks and cuts by all but the most skilled barber were a potential hazard. Experiments with safety razors started with the French in the 18th century. Early models had guards that prevented deep cuts in the skin but were impractical because the guard constantly had to be removed so the blade could be sharpened. The solution was to shrink the size of the blade, make it disposable, and reorient the handle to a T-shape so that it could be dragged across the face like a hoe. The shape was the easiest of these innovations, devised in 1847 by an Englishman.

The disposable blade took years of effort, culminating in a 1903 product marketed by a man named King Camp Gillette (see Parallel History).

PARALLEL HISTORY

Gillette

I n the late 19th century an eccentric, indefatigable traveling salesman named King Camp Gillette asked a friend how to make a fortune. The friend, William Painter, had invented the disposable bottle cap and suggested making something that would always need replacing. After years of peddling his idea for a disposable razor, Gillette persuaded an MIT professor to help him employ the technology to produce a cheap, thin, throwaway steel blade. Gillette's persistence paid off when, in 1903, the first disposable razor blades rolled out. By the time of World War I his invention had caught on, and the U.S. government contracted him to supply razors for the Army.

Shaving Cream

FIRST BRUSHLESS SHAVING CREAM:
BURMA-SHAVE, 1919
FIRST SHAVING CREAM IN SPRAY CAN: 1950

The word *barber* comes from a Latin word, *barba,* for "beard," and the early Roman barbers knew that you couldn't simply take a razor to a beard and get a good, clean shave. Facial hair is wiry and stiff, and in order to cut it without causing pain it needs to be wet and lubricated. Soap and water worked for hundreds of years. The soap could be churned up to a good, thick lather that held the moisture in place and eased the passage of the razor over the skin.

By the early 1800s special soaps for shaving were being marketed. One of the first widely available was Vroom and Fowler's Walnut Oil Military Shaving Soap, a foaming tablet introduced in 1840. The viscosity and moisture-retaining properties of foam made it especially suitable as a shaving aid. The soap was placed in a cup to which water was added; a brush was used to stir up a lather, which was then applied to the face. The first successful brushless shaving cream was a product called Burma-Shave, which debuted in the early 20th century. It was applied to the face with the hand, but it was mostly known, from the 1920s to the 1960s, for its successful advertising campaign—series of highway bill-

boards that sequentially doled out rhyming verses: "Within this vale / of toil / and sin / your head grows bald / but not your chin—use / Burma-Shave."

Aerosol spray cans were first used for dispensing insecticides during World War II. The first shaving cream in a spray can came out in 1950, and pressurized foam soon became the most popular shaving cream. Canned shaving creams are about 80 percent water; other ingredients include such soap fats as stearic acid and glycerol. With concern beginning in the 1980s over aerosols as pollutants, shaving soaps and hand-applied creams have made a modest comeback. Because soaps penetrate the beard better than airy foams, they can actually provide a closer and smoother shave.

Petroleum Jelly

VASELINE: FROM GERMAN "WASSER" (WATER)
AND GREEK " ELAION" (OLIVE OIL)
DISCOVERED DURING 1850s IN TITUSVILLE, PA

Locals from the small lumber town of Titusville, Pennsylvania, had long known about the "rock oil" that flowed there. The pungent petroleum had been bottled for medicine; experiments proved its potential as fuel. But extracting enough from the ground seemed impossible.

Then in 1857 a well driller went to work; it took two years and a 67-foot hole until oil began to flow. During the drilling, a New York chemist named Robert A. Chesebrough, interested in moneymaking opportunities, came out to have a look. What drew his attention was a strange, viscous stuff that kept seizing up the rig equipment. The workers called it rod wax and used it as a liniment on their cuts and burns. Chesebrough developed it into a jelly-like product, patented with a name he created from the German *Wasser* for "water" and the Greek *elaion* for "olive oil." Thus trademarked as Vaseline, the product was by the late 1880s selling at more than 500,000 jars a year in the United States.

Tissues

ORIGIN: CELLUCOTTON (FROM WOOD FIBERS)
FIRST PRODUCED TISSUE BOX: KIMBERLY-CLARK, 1921
BRAND NAME KLEENEX NOW SYNONYMOUS WITH TISSUE

Toilet Paper

FIRST FACTORY-PRODUCED BRAND: GAYETTY'S
MEDICATED PAPER, 1857
FIRST ROLLS: WALDORF TISSUE (SCOTTISSUE), 1880S

An item we consider a necessity today was unheard of 150 years ago. The use of paper for personal hygiene can be traced to the first century, but it was a rarity until paper became more common around the 18th century. The ancient Romans used sponges on a stick, then replaced them in a bucket of brine. People preferred wool, cotton, or lace but used whatever was handy; early Americans favored the corncob. As paper became widely disseminated, bathrooms and outhouses were generally equipped with old newspapers, flyers, and catalogs. As a result, the first toilet paper, by Joseph Gayetty in 1857, was a flop because people wouldn't buy what they already had for free.

A shortage of cotton during World War I led to the development of an artificial fabric called cellucotton. Made of wood fibers, the material was five times as absorbent as cotton and much less expensive. It was put to use in surgical bandages and gas mask air filters. After the war, the manufacturer, Kimberly-Clark, sought a use for the remaining surplus of cellucotton.

The first repackaging attempt was called Kleenex Kerchiefs, a "Sanitary Cold Cream Remover." It was advertised as a glamour product that celebrities (and, of course, ordinary people) could use for removing makeup. Instead of reusing a facial towel, they could spend 65 cents for a pack of 100 paper "kerchiefs." The product moved off the shelf rapidly. But consumers were finding the Kleenex more useful as a disposable handkerchief. They wrote in to say so, and in 1921 the company started selling Kleenex in a pop-up box called Serv-a-Tissue. A test-marketing campaign in 1930 confirmed that people preferred the tissues for blowing their nose, and new advertising soon doubled sales.

UNCOMMONLY KNOWN . . .

Baby Wipes Nonwoven disposable towelettes were created in the late 1970s, and were soon marketed as, among other things, a means of cleaning infants. Kimberly-Clark (producer of Kleenex and Huggies diapers) and Procter & Gamble (Pampers) were among the first to produce baby wipes; with decreasing costs, other brands became available.

Tampons

FIRST SANITARY NAPKIN: KIMBERLY-CLARK, 1920
FIRST TAMPON: DR. EARLE HAAS; U.S. PATENT 1933
BRAND NAME TAMPAX NOW SYNONYMOUS WITH TAMPON

To absorb menstrual blood, Egyptian women used soft papyrus or pellets of linen held together with gum arabic. In the fifth century B.C., Greek physician Hippocrates wrote that women used lint wrapped around a sliver of wood. The ancient Romans often used wool, the Japanese paper, the Indonesians vegetable fibers, and the equatorial Africans grass. Through the 19th century American women employed whatever came to hand—usually old rags or towels that could be washed and reused.

After World War I the Kimberly-Clark company had stacks of leftover cellucotton (see "Tissues"), an artificial cottonlike fiber. In 1920 the company introduced Kotex disposable sanitary napkins. Advertising was subdued in deference to the modesty of American women. After slow initial sales, knowledge of the product began to spread, and despite its bulky awkwardness, a new market in "feminine hygiene" was born. Other companies began competing for a share and imme-

diately started trying to develop a less bulky alternative. One such inventor was Dr. Earle Haas, who had already invented a flexible contraceptive diaphragm. Although Haas cannot be credited with the idea for the tampon itself, he did invent the collapsible applicator tube and removal string. In 1931 he applied for a patent on his "catamenial [monthly] device" and sold the rights to a Denver group that would become the Tampax Sales Corporation. Again, advertising and sales were sluggish at first but gradually picked up, soon making Tampax tampon a standard item in bathrooms and purses.

PARALLEL HISTORY

Cleopatra

The last ruler of Egypt's Ptolemaic dynasty, Cleopatra, reigned from 51 to 30 B.C. Born in 69 B.C., she and her ten-year-old brother, Ptolemy XIII, became co-regents in 51 B.C. and were married (per Egyptian tradition). Later, Julius Caesar became Cleopatra's lover, and together they had a son named Caesarion. Cleopatra soon returned with Caesar to Rome. After Caesar's 44 B.C. assassination, she returned to Egypt and made her son co-regent with her after Ptolemy XIV died. In 41 B.C., Mark Antony, struggling for Roman leadership with Octavian (Caesar's adopted son), began an affair with Cleopatra that was at least in part to establish a political alliance between the countries. They had two sons and a daughter and fought together against Octavian, who eventually defeated them in 30 B.C. in

Alexandria. According to legend, both Antony and Cleopatra chose suicide over imprisonment. Although her strategic and romantic affairs fascinate modern people, Cleopatra is also remembered for her distinctive glamour, then the height of Egyptian fashion. With kohl-rimmed eyes, a dramatic black wig, and stained lips, Cleopatra's likenesses show us a powerful woman who was also powerfully beautiful and elegant. In the centuries since her death, woman around the world have sought to imitate her dramatic style. Eyeliner, mascara, rouge, lipstick, and foundation all owe a debt to Egyptian cosmetic production.

Cleopatra's makeup and style spawned centuries of imitation.

Beautification

Most of our beautification products were used in some version by the Egyptians and Babylonians, the Greeks and Romans. Often the primitive versions were toxic—lead in early makeup foundations and mercury in rouge preparations could poison the blood. But just as often, the early cosmeticians were quite inventive in finding natural products that safely enhanced beauty, and one wonders how much more vivid an eye shadow of powdered malachite and iridescent beetle shells was than the sterile compounds of today.

Eyeliner

EARLIEST KNOWN: EGYPT, FOURTH MILLENNIUM B.C.
ANCIENT KOHL: LEAD ORE, POWDERED ANTIMONY,
BURNT ALMONDS, CLAY OCHER, AND VARIOUS OXIDES

For untold millennia, men and women have been enhancing their features with cosmetics—for war and religious rituals and for beautification. Precivilization Stone Age men most likely painted their body for camouflage in hunting and battle. Egyptian tombs have been among the richest museums of the practices of early civilizations, and archaeologists have found Egyptian palettes for grinding and mixing eye paint and face powder dating from 6000 B.C.

Within the next two millennia, makeup had become a refined art. Special attention was paid to the eyes, the most revealing part of the face. Heavy eye shadow accented the contours of the eyes. The favorite color for lining both upper and lower eyelids was green, made from powdered malachite. The lashes and eyebrows were darkened with kohl, a black paste of galena (a lead ore); powdered antimony (a silvery element); burnt almonds; clay ocher; and oxides of copper, iron, and manganese. The antimony was probably imported from Persia and Asia Minor; the other ingredients were local. Stored in alabaster vases, the makeup was moistened with saliva and animal fat and applied with wood or ivory sticks. Egyptian and Greek women may have connected their eyebrows with kohl pencils to give the effect of a unibrow. Even eye glitter dates to the Egyptians—made from crushed shells of

PARALLEL HISTORY

Mascara

Using a black makeup called kohl, the Egyptians of 4000 B.C. applied mascara (from the Italian "maschera," or mask) not just to their eyelashes, as do women of today, but to their eyebrows. Both sexes also exaggerated the almond-shaped contours of the eyes by drawing dark ovals around them. The mascara was used not just for beauty but also to ward off the evil eye (see p. 117), and possibly, in the bright desert sunlight, to protect their eyes from glare—in the same way that athletes do today with lines of greasepaint beneath the eyes. Kohl was also used on children to prevent eye diseases.

iridescent beetles, it was mixed in with eye shadow and used by men and women alike.

Gradually the use of eyeliner and makeup in general was moderated. In ancient Greece, only courtesans used it. The original painted woman, Jezebel, was the scheming wife of Israel's King Ahab in about 850 B.C. After painting her face to taunt a contender for the throne, she was put to death. Makeup was never the same. But subtle eyeliner and other cosmetics remain a standard part of a woman's war paint.

Lipstick

EARLIST USE: BABYLONIAN CITY OF UR 3500 B.C.
EGYPTIANS USED RED OCHRE AND OIL OR FAT
ALTERNATIVELY KNOWN IN THE U.K. AS "LIPPY"

The practice of coloring the lips is as old as the art of makeup itself—dating back well into prehistory. Second only to the eyes in expressing emotions, the lips command attention—whether vocalizing, pouting, puckering, sneering, or smiling—and exaggerating them for spiritual or sexual purposes was commonplace.

Henna is a reddish dye that was readily available to many ancient cultures and was most likely one of the earliest lip paints. Possibly the oldest makeup item ever unearthed is a lip color from the Babylonian city of Ur—it dates from 3500 B.C. and was made from a base of white lead. At around the

same time, the Egyptians were dyeing their lips with red ocher mixed with oil or fat. The ancient Greeks were more restrained in their use of makeup than the Middle Easterners and Africans, probably because of their belief in the aesthetic purity of the unadorned body. As with mascara, lipstick was used almost solely by courtesans, which meant that for centuries painting the lips was not part of most women's daily regimens.

The Italian Renaissance ushered in a new period of cosmetic use, and by the Elizabethan period (1558-1603), English ladies had a basic arsenal of white powder, rouge, and lip coloring. Queen Elizabeth herself set the pattern; her lip dye was glazed with egg whites. By the mid-1700s makeup in Europe had reached a peak of extravagance, with lips rouged with carmine (a bright red dye from female cochineal insects) or painted on with colored lipsticks made of ground plaster of paris.

But a backlash occurred in the Victorian era (1837-1901), and the art of makeup again became the mysterious province of courtesans. A step up the social ladder from the demimonde, actresses brought new attention to cosmetics by the turn of the century.

Lipstick, previously sold in paper tubes, began appearing in metal cartridges around 1915. In the 1920s Paris reintroduced vivid lip coloring to the fashion world, and lipstick became the most popular piece of cosmetic equipment for increasingly independent young women on both sides of the Atlantic.

Despite new forms of lip coloring on the market, including glosses, stains, and gels, the traditional tube lipstick remains a staple of women's cosmetic kits around the world.

Rouge

TODAY, SIMULATES NATURAL FLUSH
USED BY MEN AND WOMEN IN ANCIENT GREECE
EARLY INGREDIENTS: MULBERRY, ROOTS, WINE DREGS

Reddening the cheeks with makeup was known even among ancient Greek men, who generally looked down on cosmetics. The early rouges, like other cosmetics, date from several thousands years B.C. They could be applied to cheeks or lips, and were made of mulberry, seaweed, or other vegetation, colored with cinnabar, a red mercuric sulfide. Applied to the lips, the cinnabar could enter the bloodstream, where it could poison the user, who probably made no connection between makeup and early death.

The use of rouge continued unabated, often with such less toxic materials as polderos, a root that Greek women used. Similar to alkanet and henna, the red dye gave non-courtesans one of their few options for beautification. Roman women preferred rouging their cheeks and lips with dye made from red ocher or wine dregs.

During the Middle Ages, very few people indulged in cosmetics of any kind, but by the time of the Renaissance, artistic enhancement of the face was back in vogue. The trend slowly arrived in England during the Elizabethan era. By 1773, an issue of *Ladies* magazine was reporting that "there is no making a decent complexion, unless the rouge is in perfection." And yet in the same decade, an act of Parliament was created to protect men from the false allure of painted women: "All women of whatever age, rank, profession . . . [who] betray into matrimony, any of his Majesty's subjects, by the scents, paints, cosmetic washes . . . shall incur the penalty of the law in force against witchcraft. . . ." A century later, makeup was again almost gone, a victim of its own excesses and the ire of puritans.

Then, in the early 20th century, with the rise of Hollywood idols and the changes wrought by two world wars, rouge returned. The intended effect was of a natural blush.

Foundation

CERUSE: ANCIENT GREEK LEAD-BASED FOUNDATION
LATER MADE FROM BEAR GREASE, HOG LARD, HONEY
ALSO KNOWN AS: PANCAKE MAKEUP

Courtesans of ancient Greece were among the first to apply a foundation to the face as a base for makeup and to accentuate the effects of rouge. A foundation could also cover blemishes and provide a uniform tint to the skin. But these early cover-ups took the form of a white lead-based powder called ceruse. Over time, the lead not only ruined the complexion but could poison the blood. Since the harm was gradual, the practice remained popular in Europe well into Renaissance times. Not only was the powder applied to the face, it whitened the neck and bosom to a fine, milky, stay-indoors pallor sought by the upper classes. The lucky foundation users happened to favor a white powder made from ground alabaster, chalk, or starch and scented with perfume.

By the Elizabethan era there were other, relatively safe substitutions for ceruse. Bear grease was fairly expensive, but hog lard, honey, and beeswax were affordable ingredients for ointments and foundations.

With the return of the natural look in the morally high-toned Victorian age, white powder almost vanished from Europe, along with rouge and lipstick. All these returned in the early 1900s. In 1937, Polish cosmetics impresario Max Factor introduced Pan-Cake makeup as a foundation; its main ingredients were talc and mineral oil. During the lean years of World War II, English women often used vegetable oil as a foundation for facial powder. After the war, companies began marketing foundations for individual skin tones.

Powder Compact

DESCENDED FROM:
17TH-18TH CENT. "PATCH BOX," WHICH HELD
PATCHES THAT COVERED SMALLPOX BLEMISHES

The modern powder compact evolved from an article of similar size called a patch box. In 17th- and 18th-century Europe, beauty patches or spots were worn to disguise disfigurements caused by smallpox. The little silk or velvet stars, crescents, and hearts were coated on one side with an adhe-

sive of glycerin and isinglass (a fish gelatin). The box held extra patches and a mirror in the lid.

Nail Polish

FIRST NAIL PAINT: CHINA, CA 3000 B.C.
NAIL COLOR INDICATED STATUS IN MANY CULTURES
KEY MODERN INGREDIENT: NITROCELLULOSE

Ancient Egyptians dyed their fingernails with henna and other natural plant stains, but the first real paint for the nails was developed in China around 3000 B.C. Made of beeswax, egg white, and vegetable dyes, and sometimes gelatin and gum arabic, the lacquer was color-coded by social rank. At around 600 B.C., gold and silver were sported only by royalty; later, red and black became the top-ranking colors.

Among the Egyptians, bright red was allowed only on the highest classes. Queen Nefertiti in the 14th century B.C. painted her fingernails and toenails ruby red; Cleopatra (first century B.C.) preferred a darker red. Lower ranking men and women also wore nail varnish, but only in pale shades.

A gold manicuring set was uncovered in the royal tombs of Ur in southern Babylonia, indicating that the nobility of 2000 B.C. used well-groomed nails as a way of setting themselves off from the common laborer. Babylonian, Egyptian, and Roman military officers often took great pains with makeup before battle—curling their hair and having their nails and lips painted in matching colors.

In the early 20th century, an innovation in nail polish revolutionized it as a beauty product. Nitrocellulose was invented in the 1830s by European chemists as an explosive. Cellulose (plant fiber) mixed with nitric acid made for a highly combustible product, which chemists were able to turn into guncotton, or smokeless gunpowder. Later, nitrocellulose was used to make celluloid, the basis for film and various hard plastics. After World War I, nitrocellulose lacquers began appearing in a multitude of colors, thanks to a booming automobile industry. By the early 1930s, nail polishes were also available in a variety of shades, giving nails a glossy enamel finish.

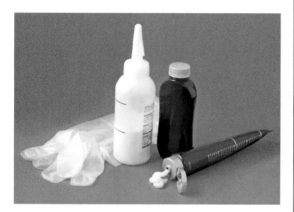

Hair Coloring

EARLY HAIR DYERS: ASSYRIANS, 1500 B.C.
ROMAN MEN DYED THEIR GRAYING HAIR DARKER
FIRST COLOR TREND: ELIZABETH I-INSPIRED RED LOCKS

Coloring the hair, along with painting the face and body, most likely started among primitive cultures long ago. Among early civilizations, the Assyrians of 1500 B.C., living in what is now northern Iraq, were accomplished hairstylists, and dyeing was one of their arts. Several hundred years later, the Greeks had a similar taste for long, curling tresses, and they favored light-colored hair. To achieve golden locks they sprinkled yellow

PARALLEL HISTORY

Men's Hair Dyeing

An Elizabethan recipe for hair coloring reveals the degree of attention a gentleman could lavish on his appearance: "How to colour the head or beard into a Chestnut Colour in half an hour: Take one part of Lead calcined with Sulphur, and one part of quick lime; temper them somewhat thin with water; lay it upon the hair, chafing it well in, and let it dry one quarter of an hour, or thereabout; then wash the same off with fair water divers times; and lastly with sope and water, and it will be a very natural hair colour: The longer it lieth upon the hair, the browner it groweth."

pollen, flour, and gold dust in their hair. Sunlight was also popular for making hair fairer. Athenian playwright Menander (fourth century B.C.) observed that men would wash their hair with a special ointment, then "sit bareheaded in the sun by the hour, waiting for their hair to turn a beautiful golden blond. And it does."

At around the same time, Roman men were happy with dark hair, but if it went gray, they were prepared to dye. A concoction for black hair dye was made of boiled leeks and walnut shells. By the first century A.D., fashions had changed, at least among women, who bleached their hair the flaxen color of the Gauls (French) by washing it with a soap made of beechwood ash and goat tallow. This harsh treatment too often led to hair loss. A typical result may have been Ovid's complaint to his mistress in *Ars amatoria* (circa 1 B.C.): "Did I not say to thee, 'Cease to dye thy hair?' And now thou hast no longer any hair to dye."

Other early societies favored unusual hair colorings. The Saxons sometimes dyed their hair bright red, green, orange, or sky blue. The Gauls, not content to be the envy of the Romans, often tinted their yellow hair a light reddish color.

In 16th-century England, Queen Elizabeth I established a hair color trend with her naturally red hair. The Italian court at the time also influenced a leaning toward yellow and golden hair, from a plant-based dye.

Modern hair color kits revolutionized hair care. Before the 1960s, only about 7 percent of women colored their hair; today, it's 75 percent.

Combs

FROM GREEK "GOMBHOS" (TEETH)
EARLY PROTOTYPES: DRIED FISH SKELETONS
CAN ALSO BE A DECORATIVE HAIR ORNAMENT

A requisite part of the human vanity kit, the comb has been in existence for at least 6,000 years. The earliest combs were probably dried fish skeletons, which are still used in parts of Africa. Egyptian tombs from around 4000 B.C. have held combs, some with a single row of teeth, others with a double row. A creative variation useful on long or stiff hair was a comb with a row of long, thick teeth, and another shorter, thinner row. Egyptian men and women could use combs both for grooming their hair and pinning it.

Almost all early societies availed themselves of the comb. Its simple ergonomic design has changed little from the fish-spine pattern, the word itself, from the Greek *gombhos,* for "teeth," suggesting its design. A notable exception to the use of combs was the early Britons. For unknown reasons, the coastal occupants of the British Isles enjoyed untidy heads of hair. The occupying Romans (first through fifth

centuries), who appreciated the arts of the hair-stylist, brought no change to the Britons' shaggy ideal. A new group of invaders, the Danes spread the doctrine of hair combing in the ninth century. An old sea chantey of unknown origin captures the spirit of those early seaside combers: "Glos'ter girls they have no combs, Heave away, heave away! They comb their hair with codfish bones."

By the 14th century, combs were among many household implements that could be turned into decorative arts. The French made double-sided ivory combs engraved with scenes of lovers frolicking in a garden; teeth on one side were more closely spaced than on the other to give the user a finer comb-through.

Wig

EGYPTIAN WIGS MADE FROM HAIR, WOOL, PALM
ALTERNATIVELY KNOWN AS:
SYRUP OF FIGS (COCKNEY RHYMING SLANG)

When we think of wigs in history, we probably most often think of 18th-century composers and Founding Fathers. But hairpieces have been around since at least 3000 B.C. The Egyptians back then habitually cut their hair short and shaved their body hair for protection against the heat and Nile-borne diseases. They made elaborate wigs of human hair, wool, palm fiber, and flax; these were braided or curled

---

UNCOMMONLY KNOWN...
Churchill on Hair Dyeing At a British society wedding in 1909, Winston Churchill, then president of the Board of Trade, quipped that "seemingly not one woman in ten can do without hair dye." He suggested that a tax on it would "yield a vast income." By the late 1960s almost 70 percent of American women were altering their hair color.

and held in place with beeswax. The rich sometimes put jewelry in their wigs and sported so many piles of tresses they became top-heavy. During ceremonies, the pharaohs also wore plaited false beards.

Among the Romans, blond wigs became the rage in the first century B.C. The material was in ready supply from the large number of fair-haired Gallic prisoners. Not intended to look realistic, the wigs were crimped with curling irons and adorned with ribbons, flowers, or jewelry. It was not long, though, before blond wigs became the hallmark of prostitutes. The lofty would sometimes don a wig to go out on the streets

Hairstyles

Men and women have been playing with their hair for millennia; anything we can try today has been tried before when it comes to cut, color, and style. That doesn't mean the ancients weren't practical; Egyptian men and women often shaved their head for comfort in a hot climate but donned heavy, elaborate wigs for ceremonial occasions. While Greeks and Romans usually followed the fashion of men keeping their hair relatively short and face clean-shaven, the back-and-forth (really, up-and-down) of men's hair fashions is nearly as tumultuous as that of women's. A hairstyle might indicate social class, such as in a Roman hairstyle woven around a wire frame, evidence of financial wealth. It could also show political loyalty, as the Manchu-dictated men's queue did, or religious devotion, as in the monk's tonsure. While monks might eschew hair's glamorous properties, both sexes have long known that hair can be a great accessory and a tool of seduction. Hair "towers" of the 18th century were sometimes more elaborate than court gowns. The "Gibson girl," whose abundant tresses were piled into a perfect nest for elaborate hats, was the forerunner of future pinups. But while some hairstyles are quite serious (dreadlocks, a Sikh's long hair, a soldier's crewcut), others start out seriously but wind up seeming humorous. The long, greased-back ducktail/pompadour popular in the 1940s and 1950s was supposed to show that the man (boy, more often) wearing it was a rebel—but since he didn't often have a cause, the exaggerated style became a caricatured element of a "greaser." Similarly, the first women to pile their hair skyward in a bouffant or "beehive" probably believed that their look was sophisticated. Unfortunately, the more extreme bouffants resembled rocket bombs (hence their nickname of "B-52s") and at times inspired more amusement than amazement. Even more extreme than beehives were the Mohawks (borrowed from Native Americans) and other spiked hairdos favored by 1970s and 1980s punks and New Wave aficionados. Like earlier styles (the ducktail, the bouffant), punk 'dos required copious amounts of hair gel, spray, pomade, and sometimes even Elmer's glue.

500 B.C.
Greek curls Greek men favored curls all over their head, and often used an early form of the curling iron—metal tongs heated in a fire—to achieve this uniform look.

1000 B.C.
Egyptian wigs Both men and women wore wigs in ancient Egypt, although men were more likely to appear bald in public. Wigs came in many styles and were a must for priests, who shaved all of their body hair.

1950
Ducktail Those who sported this popular greased style usually also carried a comb in their back pockets for frequent touch-ups throughout the day.

in disguise—the licentious empress Messalina (circa A.D. 22-48) wore a yellow wig when visiting brothels, as did the mad emperor Caligula (A.D. 12-41).

The Roman Catholic Church did a good job of getting rid of wigs for several hundred years, even excommunicating people who refused to cooperate. But after the Reformation, they began reappearing in France and England. Queen Elizabeth I helped spread the fashion in the late 16th century by wearing a wig to hide her patchy hair. In one year she bought six heads of hair, 12 yards of curl, and 100 other items made of hair. By the 18th century wigs had reached

1600
Chinese queue This hairstyle, with its shaved forehead, was an outward sign of Manchu control over the Han Chinese, and also of submission, since the Han traditionally did not cut or shave their hair at all.

1900
Gibson girl For women whose hair was less than luxuriant, achieving the "Gibson girl" updo required backcombing (teasing), hair "rats," and lots of pins—ironic for what was touted as a "natural" look.

A.D.700
Monastic tonsure Although no one is entirely sure why the tonsure was originally stipulated, it did lead to the wearing of a small cap for head warmth, which today is called the "zuchetto." The pope wears a white one.

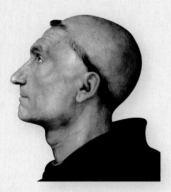

1700
Hair tower Hair towers could require horsehair padding and two hairdressers; some even had ships, birds, tiny houses, and other ornaments built into them.

1960
Bouffant From the French "bouffer" ("to puff out") comes this hairstyle moniker, but it was also known as a beehive, a B-52, or just plain big hair.

1980
Mohawk The wearer must shave the sides of the head, leaving a strip of hair down the middle. Sometimes this lies flat and off to the side, but in modern times it's often made to stand straight up, defiantly.

such a height of popularity that the finest, most expensive ones were often the targets of thieves, who would boldly snatch wigs off the heads of wearers.

Hair Dryer

LATE-19TH CENT. HAIR DRYERS: GAS-POWERED
FIRST DRYERS: ATTACHED TO VACUUM CLEANERS
REPLACED CURLERS AS PRIMARY STYLING TOOL

One of the first attempts to create an artificial hair dryer was by Paris inventor Alexandre Godefroy. In the late 1880s he came up with a salon dryer that was basically a bonnet that delivered hot air via a tube from a gas stove. As late as the 1930s gas dryers were still being used, though many patrons were unhappy with the fumes.

Electricity offered a much better energy source for appliances. Early electrical appliances were often touted for their versatility; thus the first hair dryers were sold as vacuum cleaners. An attachment to the vacuum's exhaust channeled the expelled hot air into a handheld device that served as a hair dryer. An ad for the Pneumatic Cleaner depicted a woman at her vanity, drying her hair with a hose leading to a vacuum exhaust that blew a "current of pure, fresh air." Such multipurpose appliances were sold into the late 1920s, but by then a new device had been invented.

The first electric hair dryer was introduced in Germany in 1899. But it would take two more decades until handheld hair dryers became practical. They needed a small, efficient motor. Such a motor became available in 1920 in Racine, Wisconsin, where inventors were tinkering with an electric blender. The blowing of hot air was an

easy use for the motor, and so the hair dryer beat out the blender by two years. These first hair dryers were heavy and cumbersome and had metal casings that would overheat. In the 1930s and '40s, models appeared with plastic casings and adjustable temperatures. Hair dryers became popular with men in the late 1960s, when long hair was in fashion.

Smaller, portable home "blow dryers" first appeared in the 1970s and are now ubiquitous in health clubs, hotels, and homes everywhere. Blow dryers gave rise to the "blow out" hairstyle, in which volume is added not with hair curlers, but through brushes and heat.

Perfume

FROM LATIN "PER" (THROUGH), "FUMUS" (SMOKE)
DESCENDED FROM: INCENSE
EARLY USE OF SCENTED OILS: BATHING AND EMBALMING

What is now a billion-dollar annual business in the United States started out more than 8,000 years ago with the burning of incense at religious ceremonies. The word *perfume* comes from the Latin *per* ("through") and *fumus* ("smoke"). The fragrant gum resins and woods were often burned to cover the smell of sacrificed animals. Frankincense, myrrh, spikenard, and cassia (a cinnamon bark) were typical ingredients.

By 3000 B.C., the Egyptians and Sumerians (of Mesopotamia) were using scented oils for both embalming and bathing. Essences of iris, jasmine, hyacinth, honeysuckle, and cardamom would be fixed in animal or vegetable oil and applied liberally. The north Egyptian city of Mendes was an important perfume-making center; what they didn't have, they imported from the Middle East and the Greek islands.

The ancient Greeks avoided the use of cosmetics, but perfumes were a different matter. Greek women applied aromatics copiously, as detailed in the writings of the philosopher Theophrastus (fourth century B.C.): "Rose and gillyflower [carnation] perfumes are made from the flowers: so also is the perfume called Susinon … namely lilies: also the perfumes named from bergamot mint and tufted thyme, kypros, and also the saffron perfume." The Romans picked up the lavish use of perfume from the Greeks. After the fall of the Roman Empire, perfume died out in Europe until the Crusaders brought it back from the Middle East in the early 13th century. By the late 1800s, perfumes were being made from artificial ingredients, a saving grace for the deer from the Himalaya and Atlas Mountains from which musk was gathered and the sperm whales that produce ambergris.

Soon cologne became established as a grade of perfume. Eau de perfume was an ethyl alcohol concoction, 25 percent of which was fragrant oils; eau de toilette had about 5 percent fragrant oils; cologne had 3 percent fragrant oils.

UNCOMMONLY KNOWN...

Perms A procedure for creating a long-lasting wave in the hair was invented in 1906 in London. It involved a six-hour visit to the hair salon, where two-pound brass rollers and borax paste did the job. Around the same time, Madame C. J. Walker introduced a method for straightening curly hair; she became one of the first female black millionaires.

Cologne

NAMED FOR A FRANK TOWN ON THE RHINE RIVER
FIRST EAU DE COLOGNE: BOTTLED EARLY 18TH CENT.
DEVELOPED AND SOLD BY ITALIAN JEAN-BAPTISTE FARINA

Eau de cologne ("water of Cologne"), also known simply as cologne, is often considered perfume for men, though it's also used by women. It originated, as might be expected, in the German town for which it was named. It might as easily be known today as agripe.

In A.D. 50 the Romans established a colony in what is now western Germany and called it Colonia Agrippina ("colony of Agrippina"), naming it for the emperor Claudius's wife. After the Franks took over in the fourth century, the name was shortened to Cologne, and the town grew into a lovely Rhine River city, boasting one of the greatest Gothic cathedrals in Europe.

But the cathedral city would become best known for a product conceived by Italian barber Jean-Baptiste Farina, who settled in Cologne in 1709. He created a light, alcohol-based perfume by blending orange bitters, lemon spirits, and oil from the bergamot fruit. Farina named his fragrance eau de Cologne and sold it to great acclaim. French soldiers stationed in Cologne during the Seven Years' War (1756-63) took a liking to the perfume, and soon its reputation was spread far and wide. Members of Farina's family moved to Paris and opened up another prosperous perfumery. And during the Great Exhibition of 1851 in London, cologne made a big splash when it was exhibited along with exotic fragrances from the Middle East and sophisticated scents from Paris: The cologne was spectacularly displayed in a fountain.

Depilatories

FORMS OF HAIR REMOVAL, THEN AND NOW:
TWEEZING, TOXIC CREAMS, ELECTROLYSIS,
"PUNCHING," WAXING, X-RAYING, BLEACHING

How to get rid of unwanted hair is a problem that has plagued mankind for millennia. Unlike other beauty aids, depilatories were invented not to make women more feminine, but less masculine. American Indians, who had little facial hair, sometimes tweezed out their body hair with clam shells. Roman women used tweezers, pumice stones, and depilatory creams laced with quicklime or arsenic; less toxic creams were made from medicinal plants such as bryonia.

Over time, tolerance for female body hair has varied from one culture to another. Leg hair was not appreciated in Israel in the 10th century B.C., but it was accepted in 20th-century Europe. A mild amount of chin or upper lip hair was permissible for middle-aged American women until the mid-19th century. Then things began to change. A battery-powered needle epilator was introduced by a St. Louis doctor in 1869—the needle was inserted into the follicle, where it deadened the hair root. A doctor skilled in electrolysis could remove 30 to 50 hairs in a 45-minute session. The hairs would often grow back, and the procedure sometimes left little pits or black dots.

The American Dermatological Association, formed in 1877, looked at female body hair and saw an opportunity; it coined a word for such hair—hypertrichosis. Various crude and painful procedures were practiced to root out the problem: cauterizing hair follicles, injecting them with carbolic acid, or inserting a barbed needle into the follicle and twisting it. "Punching" was an especially damaging depilatory. A narrow, sharp cylinder was knifed into the skin, and the hair shaft, including the surrounding skin, was gouged out.

More popular in the late 1800s was an early form of waxing, which involved spreading galbanum (a resin) and plaster on a piece of leather, applying it to the offending hairs for three minutes, then yanking it off. After World War I, X-ray depilation was introduced to the public, and it was especially popular in the U.S. among women from Mediterranean countires (Italy, for example)—women who were trying to remove evidence of their ethnicity. It was widely used until the mid-1940s, when the dangers of radiation became more apparent.

During the postwar years, the easiest home depilation wasn't really depilation at all, but bleaching creams that lightened the hair and made it less noticeable. In the 1960s, depilatory creams came onto the market; their convenience outweighed their horrendous smell. Throughout, women used razors, trimmers, and even automated tweezing depilator machines to get rid of body hair. It wasn't until the 1980s that electrolysis, a method of sending electrical current down a hair shaft to kill the root, became a widespread method for hair removal. Today there are home electrolysis machines available, too. In addition, ancient techniques like sugaring, from the Middle East, and threading, from India, are experiencing a trendy resurgence in popularity for removing unwanted hair.

Health

The number of ingenious concoctions we have derived for keeping ourselves healthy says as much about the number of ways we can get sick as it does about our cleverness. This section offers just a few of the many daily soothers and preventive medicines on our bathroom shelves. Laxatives and cough drops go back at least to ancient Egyptian times, while vitamins and insulin go back even farther. Of course, we didn't know what vitamins and insulin were until we discovered that the lack of them caused serious health problems—their discovery in the 20th century revolutionized heatlh.

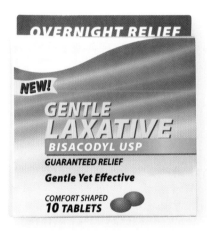

Laxatives

EARLY NATURAL LAXATIVES: HIGH-FIBER DIET, CASTOR BEAN OIL, SALINE SOLUTIONS
EX-LAX (FROM EARLY 1900s): "EXCELLENT LAXATIVE"

The Latin *constipare* ("to pack tight") says it all. Constipation of the bowels has long been a problem, and people have sought laxatives to ease their suffering. Anthropological research suggests that the high-fiber diet of early man—who gathered roots, berries, and grains and ate lean meat—made him less susceptible to bloating and constipation than the higher fat diet of agricultural societies, who fed on livestock and milk. Certainly by the third millennium B.C., people were reaching into nature's medicine cabinet for relief from irregularity.

The Egyptians and Mesopotamians of that time used a cathartic that remained popular until a few generations ago—castor bean oil. This pale, viscous oil was also employed as a skin lotion and a lubricant for pushing stone blocks on rollers. In a similar way, it lubricates the lining of the intestines. The beans themselves are poisonous, and too much oil can make constipation worse.

The Assyrians in the second millennium B.C. were well versed in the science of laxatives. They used bulking agents such as bran; saline solutions to pull water into the intestines (which helps bulk up the stool); and motility stimulants to create the bowel contractions that move waste through the system. These three approaches are still used today—leafy vegetables and cereals, Epsom salts, and motility drugs. Another time-tested remedy is drinking copious amounts of water.

In the early 1900s the first chemical laxative was brought out by Hungarian immigrant Max Kiss. After moving to New York, he experimented with

---

UNCOMMONLY KNOWN...

Linus Pauling In 1971 Nobel-winning chemist Linus Pauling published a paper, "Vitamin C and the Common Cold." He later hailed the vitamin as an anti-cancer agent, recommending up to 200 times the daily recommended dose of 60 mg. Human ancestors, he wrote, lost the ability to make vitamin C, prompting the necessity for getting it from an outside source. Its collagen-making role helps prevent illness by strengthening skin and blood vessels.

combinations of chocolate and phenolphthalein, an additive in wines. He came up with Ex-Lax, an abbreviation for "excellent laxative." Castor oil was soon demoted.

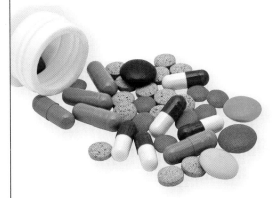

Vitamins

"VITA" (LIFE) + "AMINE" (ORGANIC COMPOUND)
FIRST BREAKTHROUGHS: STUDY OF SCURVY
13 VITAMINS HAVE BEEN IDENTIFIED AND ISOLATED

Almost all animals use vitamins, whether they are aware of it or not. Organic compounds essential for metabolism, vitamins are either consumed in the diet or manufactured in the body. The need for vitamins becomes apparent when the body isn't getting enough. Vitamins were unknown when Scottish physician James Lind studied scurvy among sailors in the 1740s. The wasting disease, marked by weak gums and bleeding in the skin, was killing more sailors than battle. Observing thousands of cases, and remarking on the habits of Dutch sailors of the 1500s, he recommended that lemon juice and citrus fruits be consumed on long voyages. It was not until 1795 that the Royal Navy adopted this simple fix; when it did so, scurvy disappeared "as if by magic."

Lind had vanquished an ancient disorder. What he didn't know was that the citrus supplied one vital, missing nutrient—ascorbic acid, or vitamin C. Dietary science slowly came to life. A Japanese physician, Kanehiro Takaki, similarly cured sailors' beriberi with supplements of meat and vegetables

Got B_{12}?

Cyanocobalamin, vitamin B_{12}, was not isolated until 1948, but in the previous decade American medical scientist W. B. Castle did isolate what he called an "intrinsic factor." It was found in normal gastric secretions, but not in the secretions of people suffering from pernicious anemia. He also noticed that anemia patients who ate lots of liver improved. Further study showed that there was an "extrinsic factor" that somehow got into the liver from outside. It turned out that helpful bacteria interacted with gastric juices to synthesize a protein substance that aided in digestion. These bacteria contained extrinsic factor, now known as vitamin B_{12}.

in 1882. The disease was caused by lack of thiamine, vitamin B_1. In 1897 Dutch pathologist Christiaan Eijkman showed that unpolished (unhulled) rice protected against beriberi. But when Casimir Funk, a Polish biochemist, tried in 1912 to isolate the "antiberiberi factor" from the hulls, he failed. He called the substance vitamine, an amine (organic compound) vital to life.

Scientists persisted in trying to isolate these accessory food factors—substances not in the basic fats, carbohydrates, proteins, minerals, and water. At first they believed there were only two vitamins—one water soluble, the other fat soluble. The first vitamin isolated in pure form was thiamine, in 1926. A total of 13 vitamins have now been identified, the most recent was vitamin B_{12} in 1948.

Cough Drops

EARLY USE: 1200 B.C. EGYPT
ALTERNATIVELY KNOWN AS:
"ATTRACTIVE WOMAN" (SOUTH AFRICA)

Medicines to suppress coughs by relaxing the throat date back to about 1200 B.C. Egypt in the form of hard candies in flavors such as elm bark and citrus. The cough drop that we know was not packaged until the mid-1800s. At that time, one of the first mass-produced troches, or lozenges, was that of the Smith Brothers of Poughkeepsie, New York. According to company lore, their father, confectioner James Smith, bought a cough-candy formula from a passing customer and whipped up a batch in his kitchen. The drops were an instant hit. He began advertising in 1852, and his sons went to work moving the product on the chilly streets of Poughkeepsie. By 1872 there were so many imitators that the bearded Smith brothers came out with a trademarked box bearing their likenesses. Luden's Throat Drops appeared a few years later in Reading, Pennsylvania, in boxes lined with wax paper. Luden's lozenges were flavored with an alcohol of mint oil called menthol, which has a mild numbing effect.

By the end of the century, chemists had derived heroin from morphine (which had been produced from opium earlier in the century). Both these narcotics were put in cough drops for several years—one under the brand name Glyco-Heroin—until their addictive properties were understood.

Insulin

FROM THE LATIN "INSULA" (ISLAND)
IDENTIFIED 1921, FREDERICK G. BANTING AND CHARLES BEST
TREATS TYPE 1 DIABETES

I nsulin is a pancreatic hormone that controls the body's blood sugar level. Before its discovery in 1921, people who suffered

---

UNCOMMONLY KNOWN...
Insulin Biotechnology In the mid-1950s scientists decoded the chemical structure of human insulin. They then located the gene for insulin at the top of chromosome 11. In 1977 a team of researchers announced that they had produced human insulin by splicing a rat gene into an insulin-making bacterium. Five years later the Eli Lilly Corporation made the first genetically engineered pharmaceutical insulin.

---

from the autoimmune deficiency type 1 diabetes faced a bleak future. Without proper levels of insulin, those suffering from diabetes experience increased thirst, excessive urine, itching, hunger, weight loss, and weakness. Under these conditions, the body does not metabolize carbohydrates and eventually develops ketosis and malaise, followed by nausea, vomiting, dizziness, coma, and death. The sufferer slowly wastes away.

But progress in finding a cure was being made. In 1889 two German physicians, Oscar Minkowski and Joseph von Mering, proved by experimenting on dogs that the pancreas secretes a blood-regulating substance. Then in 1921 Frederick G. Banting, a young orthopedic surgeon from Ontario, zeroed in on the islets of Langerhans (named for another German physician), the groups of cells that do the secreting. He and a student named Charles Best removed the pancreases of dogs to make them diabetic. They then succeeded in isolating a pancreatic extract that when injected into the dogs reduced their blood sugar level. They had found the magic substance. It was named insulin from the Latin *insula* ("island"), for the islets of Langerhans.

The next step researchers took was to find a way to make insulin release more slowly in the blood. By adding a protein from fish sperm, they achieved this breakthrough in 1936. Various modifications followed over the next few decades; along the way, in 1923, Banting received the Nobel Prize. Diabetics used insulin purified from cattle and pigs into the early 1980s, and since the structure is similar to human insulin, there were few allergic reactions.

Type 2 diabetes is more common and is known as adult-onset diabetes. It is insulin resistant.

First Aid

What happens when we cut ourselves, get a headache, or experience indigestion? Often we do what people did thousands of years ago. First aid items from the forest include an aspirin-related compound from the willow tree, an astringent of witch hazel distillate, and a time-honored formula for antacid that was good enough for the Sumerians and works about as well as anything today. We also include here the history of vaccination, which, while not generally a first aid treatment, is now a first line of defense against all kinds of diseases.

Aspirin

COMMON NAME FOR: ACETYLSALICYLIC ACID
DESCENDED FROM: SALICYLIC COMPOUND IN WILLOWS
DEVELOPED INTO MODERN MEDICINE 1890S

The world's best known medication, aspirin is the common name for acetylsalicylic acid. It was not created in the laboratory until the 1830s, but a related salicylic compound found in nature has been used for thousands of years.

Prescriptions on the 4,000-year-old Sumerian tablet of Nippur bear the cuneiform sign of the white willow. The Ebers Papyrus from 1500 B.C. Egypt lists a willow decoction—probably from the bark or twigs—which was mixed with figs, frankincense, and beer and "boiled, strained, and taken for four days to cause the stomach to receive bread."

Hippocrates (circa 460-circa 377 B.C.), the Greek father of medicine, knew about the effects of this plant and prescribed a tea made from its leaves.

When 19th-century science began probing the mysteries of natural medications, one of the first plants investigated was willow. A French chemist named Leroux extracted the active substance in the bark and called it salicin. In 1853 another French chemist, Charles-Frédéric Gerhardt, produced acetylsalicylic acid, but the process was difficult, and Gerhardt didn't think it a great improvement over salicin for reducing pain and fever. Not until the 1890s did Felix Hoffman, a chemist with Friedrich Bayer and Company near Cologne, Germany, rediscover acetylsalicylic acid. He was looking for a drug to help his arthritic father, and the new product did the trick. Instead of using willow, he extracted salicin from meadowsweet (genus *Spriaea*).

PARALLEL HISTORY

Classic Painkiller

Aspirin's forerunner, willow, has long been lauded. Specific observations on its analgesic properties were made by Pedanius Dioscorides, surgeon and botanist to the Roman Emperor Nero in the first century A.D. Using the Latin name "Salix" for willow, he remarked upon its painkilling and anti-inflammatory qualities: "the juice out of the leaves and bark . . . doth help the griefs of the ears . . . and the decoction of them is an excellent fomentation for the gout." In the next century, famous Greek physician Galen recommended willow-bark extract for cleansing and healing eyes that were inflamed or infected.

It was first marketed in 1899 as a powder called Aspirin. Bayer Aspirin tablets came out in 1915. After World War I Germany surrendered the brand name, and a U.S. Supreme Court decision in 1921 ruled that since the drug's name was so widely known, no company could claim it. It became simply aspirin.

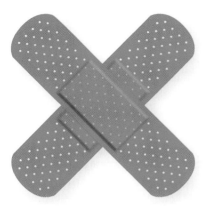

Adhesive Bandages

STERILE BANDAGES FIRST DEVELOPED LATE 19TH CENT.
BY JOHNSON BROTHERS (JOHNSON & JOHNSON)
FIRST ADHESIVES: 1920

Before the acceptance of the germ theory of medicine in the late 1800s, surgical bandages were made from rags, pressed sawdust, and other unsterile materials. English surgeon Joseph Lister changed all that with his studies on antisepsis. He presented his findings to the Philadelphia Medical Congress in 1876; Brooklyn pharmacist Robert Johnson was in the audience, paying close attention.

Johnson and his two brothers partnered and began packaging sterile dressings of gauze and cotton. Calling their company Johnson & Johnson (for some reason referring to only two brothers), they also came up with a zinc oxide adhesive tape and other products in the 1890s. Their most famous and successful product was invented in 1920 by an employee, Earle Dickson, whose wife was continually nicking herself in the kitchen. He prepared several ready-made bandages by placing pieces of gauze along a strip of adhesive tape. To keep the tape sticky, he put crinoline on it. When a bandage

was needed, his wife simply had to cut one off and peel away the crinoline. Dickson demonstrated the first aid item to James Johnson, and the company began making Band-Aids.

The product sold slowly at first. But after the company gave away huge numbers of Band-Aids to Boy Scouts and butchers, people began taking notice. By the late 1920s, the adhesive strips were being sold in various sizes and with aeration holes in the gauze pads to promote healing. Dickson went on to become a company vice president and member of the board of directors.

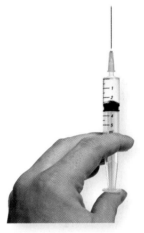

Vaccines

FIRST VACCINE: SMALLPOX, EDWARD JENNER, 1796;
PATIENTS INOCULATED WITH COWPOX
VACCINE THUS NAMED FROM LATIN "VACCA" (COW)

The idea of injecting a disease into a healthy person as a defense against that very disease took a leap of faith. Smallpox was such a deadly scourge that people were willing to take the risk. Caused by the *Variola major* virus, smallpox may have existed in Mesopotamia some 7,000 years ago. Pustules on the mummy of Egyptian pharaoh Ramses V resemble those of smallpox victims. By the 16th century, smallpox had likely surpassed plague as the most dreaded pestilence in Europe. Highly contagious, it could devastate entire communities. Victims suffered severe headaches, fever, and red rashes that left disfiguring scars; up to 40 percent of victims died.

UNCOMMONLY KNOWN...

Polio Beaten An infectious disease of the nervous system, poliomyelitis once spread fear throughout communities—outbreaks in the 1940s and 1950s left many children paralyzed. Epidemics were brought to an abrupt halt by the introduction of two vaccines: an inactivated, or killed, vaccine developed by Dr. Jonas Salk in 1953, and a live, oral vaccine, by Dr. Albert Sabin in the early 1960s.

Then in 1796 English physician Edward Jenner took a calculated risk by purposely infecting a boy with material from skin lesions on the hand of a milkmaid with cowpox, a relatively innocuous disease caused by a near relative of the virus that causes smallpox. He had observed that dairy workers infected with cowpox seemed immune to smallpox. After the boy recovered from a mild infection of cowpox, Jenner inoculated him with smallpox, and the boy had no ill effects. Based on this discovery, Jenner coined the term "vaccine" from the Latin word *vacca*, which means "cow." Another 87 years would go by before the next vaccines were developed, for plague and rabies (see Parallel History). The 20th century saw a steady advancement in the field of immunization, including vaccines for cholera and typhoid, tetanus, polio, measles, and hepatitis A.

Antacids

USE OF SODIUM BICARBONATE ORIGINATED WITH SUMERIANS
EARLY AMERICAN ANTACIDS: MILK OF MAGNESIA (1873),
PEPTO-BISMOL (1901), ALKA-SELTZER (1931)

Sumerians from 6,000 years ago used medicines to settle their stomach—milk, peppermint leaves, and carbonates proved useful tonics for indigestion. People living farther back and eating a good deal of raw food may well have used similar remedies for neutralizing the acids in their stomach.

The best antacid in the Sumerians' medicine chest—and the best treatment for centuries afterward—was sodium bicarbonate. Also known as bicarbonate of soda, or baking soda, this white crystalline substance is a gentle alkaline salt that interacts with the stomach's hydrochloric acid. Even today, with an endless array of laboratory-produced treatments available, baking soda dissolved in water is still widely used to relieve heartburn, acid indigestion, and sour or upset stomach.

Early popular American brand-name antacids start in 1873 with the introduction of Phillips' Milk of Magnesia. The milky, metallic-tasting medicine in the blue bottle was the output of a Connecticut candlemaker named Charles Phillips. The magnesium hydroxide, suspended in water, acted as both an antacid and mild laxative. In 1901 a New York physician invented a formula to help children suffering from diarrhea and vomiting. He mixed pepsin, bismuth salicylate, zinc salts, oil of wintergreen, and pink coloring. Instead of selling it, he gave it to a pharmaceutical company, which sold it under the name Bismosal: Mixture Cholera Infantum. To sell it to adults, it changed the name in 1919 to Pepto-Bismol.

In 1931 a new antacid came out that not only relieved indigestion, it also helped cure headaches and other pains. This novel medicine combined aspirin with antacid ingredients into an effervescent tablet called Alka-Seltzer. A number of highly successful advertising campaigns followed. One airing in 1954 had a cartoon character named Speedy singing, "Down, down, down the stomach through / Round, round, round the system too / With Alka-Seltzer you're sure to say / Relief is just a swallow away."

Other popular antacids, like Tums, come in rolls or pop-top dispensers for quick relief from heartburn or stomach acid distress. Even with today's over-the-counter swallowable pills, some people still prefer chewing the chalky tablets.

Witch Hazel

POPULAR WITH EIGHTH-CENTURY ANGLO-SAXONS
ONCE THOUGHT TO HAVE MAGICAL PROPERTIES
COMMON USES: ANTISEPTIC, CLEANSER, PAINKILLER

D istillates of witch hazel bark have long been used as an ingredient in astringent and soothing lotions. The Anglo-Saxons of the eighth century and beyond used the leaves and bark from this shrubby tree to make alcohol for cleaning cuts and burns. The witch hazel is unusual in that it flowers in late fall. The thin-petaled yellow blossoms have a spidery, gnarled look, and they often cling to the bare limbs into the winter. Another odd trait is that the fruit capsules, after contracting in the autumn, eject their seeds as far as 30 feet away.

The aromatic tree must have seemed possessed to those early dwellers of the British Isles. And so they ascribed magical properties to it. They believed a priest could use a witch hazel twig to locate a criminal in a crowd. A forked branch was employed as a divining rod—the forks were held in the hands, and the long end would dip down where there was underground water. In North America, natives long knew of its healing properties. In the

UNCOMMONLY KNOWN...

Historic Jingle Ad slogans shortened in the late 20th century. Alka-Seltzer's 1969 "Mama mia, that's a spicy meatball" was followed three years later with "I can't believe I ate the whole thing." And in 1979, one of the most famous commercial jingles began airing: "Plop, plop, fizz, fizz. Oh, what a relief it is."

PARALLEL HISTORY

Rabies Vaccine

A fter Edward Jenner's landmark smallpox vaccine in 1796, another 89 years would elapse before a breakthrough in rabies immunizations. The scientist was Louis Pasteur, founder of microbiology. After years of groundbreaking work with various animal diseases, Pasteur turned his attention to the deadly disease of rabies. During experiments with dogs, he found that by using dried tissue from infected animals he was able to isolate weakened viruses. In 1885, he used a solution of these viruses to save the life of a boy, nine years old, who had been bitten by a rabid dog. The boy developed no serious symptoms.

French microbiologist Louis Pasteur invented vaccines for rabies, anthrax, and chicken cholera.

early 1600s, Native Americans taught the Pilgrims in Massachusetts a way to brew witch hazel bark for a topical lotion to soothe aches, bruises, and abrasions. In succeeding generations, Americans used native *Hamamelis virginiana* witch hazel preparations for a variety of purposes—as an anti-inflammatory, painkiller, antiseptic, deodorant, facial cleanser, and cosmetic foundation. One of the first commercial packagings of witch hazel was by New England clergyman Thomas Dickinson, who began selling a preparation in the 1860s. Sold to pharmacies in kegs, it was then bottled for sale to individuals.

Witch hazel has become a medicine chest standby. Its antiseptic tingle on a cotton pad is, for many American women, a standard skin-care routine step, and a bottle of witch hazel sits in many home cabinets next to the hydrogen peroxide and the rubbing alcohol.

Fun is good.

Toys & Games

Many of the toys and games that occupy our free hours today have histories extending well back into ancient times. Some obvious playthings, such as marbles and tops, were found in a number of different cultures. And some amusements once had more serious purposes—cards were used for soothsaying, kites for signaling. Anthropologists believe that the oldest toys probably mimicked tools and weapons used for surviving daily life. Thus a club, stick, or spear could be converted into an object of play, and our modern stick games—hockey, golf, baseball—derive from earlier forms of battle- or work-related sports. Early games were imitative of more serious struggles and also instructive: Primitive football and other war-type games prepared young warriors by making them physically fit and cohesive as a team. Leadership skills and strategic planning made early sports good training for the arts of war. Balls, marbles, dolls, toy animals, tops, and wheeled carts were among the oldest of toys, found alike in ancient Africa, Greece, and Rome. By the early 1900s, handmade playthings were being replaced by manufactured games and toys. Board games have been around since at least 3000 B.C., and the 20th century saw an explosion of interest in new board games, the most popular of which was Monopoly. The origins of any of the games and toys included here could make for a full-length study—and in most cases already has. By 1900 there were hundreds of books devoted to the then wildly popular game of checkers. The classic games and toys and popular sports that this chapter comprises have been selected for their prevalence and familiarity. Each of them has a fascinating history, whether it's thousands of years or only a few decades. And we've thrown in several other amusements as well—merry-go-rounds and fireworks, for instance—not all of which started out as amusements.

Old-fashioned Fun

What could be a more basic toy than a marble? The fact that marbles have been found in children's graves from 5,000 years ago indicates that the ancients had similar ideas of fun. What's interesting is that some of the early toys and games were once used as divination tools by adults. Children at some point must have been curious and, just as today, began playing with grown-up things when grown-ups weren't around. Later—perhaps when the objects were no longer considered sacred—toy versions were made specifically for children.

Marbles

NAME ORIGINS: IN 17TH CENTURY, BALLS WERE MADE
FROM MARBLE CHIPS
EARLIER, MADE OF SEA PEBBLES, NUTS, PITS, BONES

A children's toy for millennia, marbles have been discovered in prehistoric caves. These baked clay marbles were of uncertain purpose, but it is known that adults in almost every early culture used marbles for augury. They appear to have evolved from religious objects into toys. Marbles made of the knucklebones of dogs and sheep were used for divination in the Near East centuries before they were being placed in the tombs of Egyptian children. The earliest of these presumed toy marbles were unearthed from a grave dating to 3000 B.C.

Minoan children on the Greek island of Crete played with brightly polished jasper and agate marbles. The Romans made marbles of clear glass (from silica and ash), as well as from sea-washed pebbles and even oak galls. It is unknown what games they played, but the emperor Augustus sometimes disembarked from his litter to join youths shooting marbles in the streets of Rome.

Marbles in other cultures were made of simpler materials. Celtic, Saxon, and African tribes had plenty of marbles, but they were often made of easily fashioned organic matter, such as olives, chestnuts, hazelnuts, and fruit pits. Burial mounds of American Indians have yielded engraved marbles. And firsthand evidence of primitive cultures using marbles as toys comes from early settlers, who observed Indian children playing marble games. In a game from 17th-century England, a player had to shoot from the exact place where his marble landed, thus often requiring that he use

PARALLEL HISTORY

Jump Rope

Not only did the ancient Egyptians use vines for hoops, they also used them for jump ropes. It's unclear when rope jumping started, though primitive societies have long enjoyed the game. Double Dutch jumping took hold after World War II among African-American girls. Starting with clothes lines on the streets of New York, they evolved the game into a complex, multi-person athletic activity in which two ropes are swung in opposite directions. Jumpers improvise a series of skips, one-legged hops, and trick moves, often executed against a background of chanted rhymes. Skilled jumpers bounce balls between jumps, or do flips while the rope passes twice beneath them.

his knuckles for support. The term "to knuckle down," meaning to apply oneself diligently to a task, most likely comes from this game.

Tops

FIRST-KNOWN TOPS: 3500 B.C., CITY OF UR
ENJOYED BY ANCIENT CHINESE, GREEKS, AND ROMANS
MADE OUT OF WOOD, STONE, CLAY, BONE, SHELLS

The spinning motion of a conical object has held the fascination of many a child and adult for ages. Acorns or nuts were probably the first such objects to be spun. Actual clay tops were found in the city of Ur (in present-day Iraq), dating from about 3500 B.C. Etched with animal and human figures that were discernible as the rotation slowed, they were found in children's graves and thus were most likely toys.

By 1250 B.C. the Chinese had invented a whip top that could be kept in motion by means of a small whip; the top was made of wood or stone. The early Greeks and Romans had a variety of tops; some of the Roman tops were made of bone, while the Greeks used fired clay. One of the earliest figurative uses of the top comes from the Greek poet Homer, who relates the fall of Troy in the *Iliad* (circa ninth century B.C.): "...reels like a top staggering to its last turnings."

For many centuries Japanese children have played with intricately painted *koma asobi* clay tops, some of which were pierced with holes around the edge to make a whistling or humming sound. The Maori of New Zealand also made humming tops; these

potaka takiri were fashioned from gourds and often used in mourning ceremonies.

From the 14th to the 16th centuries, it was not uncommon for European towns to have a large top spinning continually in the square; known as a village or parish top, the gyre provided exercise to those who kept it going. The Chinese *Ko-en-gen* top became the rage in 18th-century Europe. In a game called diablo, the whipped top was spun into the air and caught on another player's whip.

Hula Hoop

"HULA" ADDED TO HOOP IN EARLY 19TH CENT.,
REFERENCES HAWAIIAN HULA DANCING
HEIGHT OF U.S. HULA HOOPING FAD: LATE 1950S

The first people to swing a hoop around their midriff were probably the Egyptians of 1000 B.C., who used dried grapevines for hoops. These multi-purpose toys were rolled over the ground with sticks, or swirled around the waist like a modern hula hoop. Children in Greece and Rome later caught on to the same game.

A hoop craze swept England in the 14th century. Both adults and children were taken with the fad of spinning metal or wooden hoops, and doctors attributed many dislocated backs, heart attacks, and various other aches and pains to hooping. "Hoops kill" was the pronouncement of the medical establishment, a reference to an earlier British game called "kill the hoop" in which darts were thrown through rolling hoops.

In the early 1800s the toy became known as the hula hoop when British sailors to the Hawaiian Islands observed the similarity between hooping and hula dancing. A sensuous Polynesian dance, the hula was performed by topless women wearing short skirts and men wearing loincloths, accompanied by chants and rhythmic drumming. With undulating hips, the dancers would honor their gods and praise fecundity, using a rich vocabulary of highly stylized gestures of the arms, hands, fingers, and face to tell a story.

Yo-yo

OLDEST SURVIVING YO-YO: 550 B.C.
FIRST U.S. YO-YO FACTORY: SANTA BARBARA, 1928
EARLY: "BANDALORES," "EMIGRETTES," "JOUJOUS"

The perennially popular spinning disk on a string probably originated in China. The first mention in history was in Greece around the fifth century B.C. The toys were simply called disks and were made of wood, metal, or painted terra cotta. A vase from this period depicts a youth playing with a yo-yo.

In the late 1700s the French nobility had yo-yos made of glass or ivory; when they fled during the revolution they became emigrants, and the spinning toys they took became known as *emigrettes*.

During this same time, French troops played with yo-yos to relieve the stresses of army life. The toy was also called the "*joujou* (plaything) *de Normandie*," a possible origin for the term "yo-yo."

A more likely origin for the word is from the Tagalog, the language of the Filipinos, who in the 17th century had a weapon called a *yo-yo*. The weapon was a disk that was hurled at prey and then retrieved by a piece of attached twine. Through the 19th century the toy, known then as a *bandalore* or *quiz*, grew in popularity in Europe and the United States. The Filipinos became especially good at carving and using what they called yo-yos, and in the 1920s a Filipino named Pedro Flores started a yo-yo company in California. His yo-yos—strings looping the axle—revolutionized the pastime, by opening up an infinite number of possible tricks.

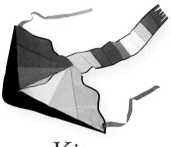

Kite

ORIGINATED AS MILITARY SIGNAL AND SPY SATELLITE
KITE-FIGHTING COMPETITION: LAST KITE FLYING WINS
KITE LOVERS: BENJAMIN FRANKLIN, LEONARDO DA VINCI

Now used mostly for recreation, kites have enjoyed a rich history in military, religious, scientific, and industrial efforts. They probably originated in China around 1000 B.C. as military signals—colors, painted patterns, and flight maneuvers could all be used as codes to nearby troops. During the Han dynasty (202 B.C.-A.D. 220), kites were fitted with bamboo pipes; flown over the enemy, they made a terrifying whistling sound. The ancient Chinese also constructed large, lightweight kites of bamboo and paper capable of bearing a man aloft to spy on the enemy. How many people died in this high-risk job is unknown. Traveler Marco Polo saw prisoners being flown from the decks of Chinese ships in the 13th century.

From China, kites spread to India, Japan, and Europe. The fourth-century Greek scientist Archytus of Tarentum experimented with kites, and Romans flew wind socks (used today at airfields to indicate wind direction) as regimental standards. Buddhist missionaries brought kites to Japan around A.D. 700. Possibly religious symbols at first, kites were used by the Japanese to carry materials to workers in elevated places.

In the meantime, children were flying kites for fun as well. Ancient Chinese prints and woodcuts show children flying elaborately designed kites with weighted tails. The sport of kite fighting developed in the Far East; kite strings were coated with bits of glass and pottery, and fliers tried to cut each other's strings. From about the 12th century, European children were flying whistling kites, the sound produced by holes in the fabric.

Kites continued to be used for scientific purposes: Leonardo da Vinci in the 15th century theorized kites' role in building bridges. In 1749, before Franklin's experiment (see below), Scottish meteorologist Alexander Wilson measured high-altitude temperatures by flying thermometers up on kites.

PARALLEL HISTORY
Franklin's Kite

One day in 1752 American statesman and scientist Benjamin Franklin went out to a field during a thunderstorm with his son. They began flying a kite in the rain. Near the end of the string Franklin tied a little metal key. While lightning raged around, he kept touching the key to see if it gave him a shock. They were about ready to quit and go home when they noticed that fibers on the kite string were standing on end. Franklin touched the key and, as he'd suspected, he felt a little jolt. He'd proved that lightning was electricity. Many attempting to repeat the experiment have been electrocuted.

Ring-Around-the-Rosy

FIRST PRINT APPEARANCE: 1881 "MOTHER GOOSE"
ALLEGEDLY, THE RHYME REFERS TO THE
GREAT PLAGUE OF LONDON, 1664-65

Small children to this day play a nursery rhyme game in which they join hands and circle while chanting, "Ring around the rosy / a pocket full of posies / ashes, ashes / we all fall down." They then collapse in laughter. The author of the rhyme is unknown, but the first appearance in print is in the 1881 book *Mother Goose*. As a children's tradition it is much older and has its origins in a very dark period in history.

During the Great Plague of London in 1664-65, some 70,000 people—about one out of every seven persons in the city—died. An early symptom of bubonic plague, or black death, is a ring-shaped skin rash. The poem's first line ("ring-a-ring o' roses" in an earlier version) refers to this rash. One of the commonly held defenses against plague was a posy of aromatic herbs or flowers. The second line refers to the belief that diseases were spread by effluvia, and thus a sweet smell could serve as protection. Finally, "ashes, ashes / we all fall down" relates to the practice of cremating plague victims. An earlier version substitutes "a-tishoo! a-tishoo!" for "ashes, ashes," referring to the violent sneezes made by sufferers.

Classic Games

A half dozen of the most popular games in recent history are included in this section, with accounts of how they came to be. It may be no surprise to learn that Monopoly dates from the Great Depression, but the story of how its clever inventor went about selling it may be new to many. Chess and checkers both have long and distinguished histories, while Parcheesi has a kinky, male-dominant twist. The card games of poker and bridge went through a number of evolutions, the former game tinged with the smoke of New Orleans back rooms and bordellos and Civil War camps.

Monopoly

CREATED BY CHARLES B. DARROW, 1930S
DEBUT COINCIDED WITH GREAT DEPRESSION
MONOPOLY REAL ESTATE BASED ON ATLANTIC CITY, NJ

The best-selling board game in history, Monopoly has been sold in 103 countries and produced in 37 languages. Since the game's introduction in 1935, more than 200 million sets have been purchased.

A number of related games were invented in the decades leading up to the release of Monopoly. In 1904 a woman named Lizzie Magie patented a game called The Landlord's Game, based on the theories of American political economist Henry George, an anti-monopolist who believed that only real estate should be taxed. Her game was devised to show how landlords profit at the expense of tenants. A few sets were produced, and homemade spin-offs were played by university students and others.

The game was known as Monopoly by the time Charles B. Darrow played it in 1933. An unemployed engineer from Germantown, Pennsylvania, Darrow spent countless hours playing and refining the game of high-stakes real estate investment. During the Depression of the 1930s, papers were full of news about foreclosures, bankruptcies, and mortgages. Darrow included these ideas in the game, as well as deed names from resorts he had known in Atlantic City, New Jersey. In 1934 he approached the Massachusetts game firm of Parker Brothers. The company turned him down, citing design errors, complex rules, and general slowness of action.

Instead of giving up, Darrow borrowed money and printed up 5,000 sets of Monopoly. He delivered them to a Philadelphia department store, where they sold quickly. Depression-era players loved the fantasy of making a pile of cash on a throw of the dice and cleverness. Suddenly Parker Brothers was

---

UNCOMMONLY KNOWN ...
Chaturanga A forerunner of chess, the Indian game of "chaturanga" (or "shaturanga") was adapted around the sixth century A.D. or earlier from a race-type game played on a 64-square board. Each of the four players had eight pieces—a rajah, elephant, horse, boat, and four pawns or foot soldiers. Players with red and black pieces were allied against those with yellow and green.

interested, and in 1935 it copyrighted the game. As a precaution, the firm bought out Magie's patent for $500, as well as a similar game called Finance. Darrow was shrewd enough to get a royalties deal and ended up a millionaire.

Chess

FROM OLD FRENCH "ESCHES" (CHECK)
FIRST AMERICAN WORLD CHAMP: BOBBY FISCHER, 1972
MOST POWERFUL CHESS PIECE: QUEEN

One of the oldest board games still being played, chess is believed to have its origins in a Hindustan game called *chaturanga* played in the sixth century A.D. or earlier. The name refers to the four parts of the army—elephants, horses, chariots (or boats), and foot soldiers. It was a four-handed dice game that made its way from India to Persia. By the time it was introduced to the West in the seventh or early eighth century, it had more or less taken on the format known today—a two-player game, each with 16 pieces that are moved, according to type, across a 64-square board to checkmate (capture) the opponent's king.

Muslims took the game of chess to Spain; the Byzantines brought it to Italy; and by the year 1000, it had spread throughout Europe as far north as Scandinavia. The aristocracy especially liked the game, with its simulation of the strategies of war; it thus earned the nickname the Royal Game.

Over the next few centuries, the rules and moves of chess altered somewhat. Most notably, by the mid-15th century the queen went from being the weakest piece (capable of moving only one diagonal square at a time) to being the most powerful piece. Along the way, it also changed sex from counselor or general to queen. The bishop likewise gained power—formerly moving only two diagonal squares. This piece was known by the Persians as a *pil,* or elephant. The rook (castle) is a stylized version of the Indian chariot, which protected the army's flanks.

An 18th-century Frenchman named Philidor is considered the first world champion chess player. In 1972 Bobby Fischer became the first American world championship winner by defeating Boris Spassky of the Soviet Union.

PARALLEL HISTORY

Backgammon Backstory

Forerunners of the game of backgammon are among the oldest of known board games. The Babylonian tombs of Ur held gaming boards dating from 3000 B.C. Each player had seven game pieces, which were controlled by six pyramidal dice. The rules have not survived, though the earliest board games may have served as equipment for mystics and soothsayers. A thousand years later the Egyptians were playing a similar game of 30 squares. Then the ancient Romans invented a version called "ludus duodecim scriptorum" (game of 12 lines). A first-century variant called "tabula," with two rows of spaces, was almost identical to today's game of backgammon.

A 17th-century carving of an after-dinner game of backgammon in the garden.

Checkers

ORIGIN: ANCIENT EGYPTIAN GAME "ALQUERQUE"
SHARES SAME BOARD AS GAME OF CHESS
FROM FRENCH "ESCHEC" (KING)

The game of checkers (draughts in Britain) originated in an ancient Egyptian game called *alquerque*. The oldest known alquerque boards date to about 1400 B.C. Each player had 12 pieces, which were placed on a five-by-five board. One space was left blank so that play could begin. As in checkers, jumps over enemy pieces resulted in the capture of those pieces, and multiple jumps were permitted.

By the year A.D. 1100, the French adapted alquerque to the chessboard, which had been in existence for about seven centuries. The game still began with 12 pieces for each player, but they were placed on squares of the same color. Pieces advanced diagonally forward. When a piece reached the far side of the board it was crowned and could then move forward or backward. In the 16th century the rule of compulsory capture was added, and the modern game of checkers was born. Under this rule, if you have a jump, you must make it, or else your opponent can huff (take) that piece. The French called this game Jeu Force, and the older version Le Jeu Plaisant de Dames, or simply Les Dames, meaning that it was a social amusement for women.

From France, the game spread to Spain, England, and America. Spaniard Antonio de Torquemada published the first book on the subject in 1547. English mathematician William Payne penned

Introduction to the Game of Draughts in 1756, with a dedication by writer and avid draughts-player Samuel Johnson. In 1847 the first world championship games were held. Checkers became so popular that by the turn of the century there were hundreds of books about the game, and newspapers held analyses of game moves and reports on matches. The word "checker" is a 14th-century word for "chessboard," deriving from the French *eschec* ("king").

Parcheesi

ORIGINS: INDIAN GAME OF "PACHISI"
PLAYED IN COURTYARD WITH HAREM GIRLS AS PIECES
U.S. GAME: TRADEMARKED BY SELCHOW & RIGHTER, 1874

One of the best-selling board games in the United States, Parcheesi comes from a royal Indian diversion known as *pachisi*. The Mogul emperors of the 16th and 17th centuries designed their courtyards as elaborate pachisi boards with inlaid marble; the game pieces were 16 beautiful harem girls, each dressed a different color. The players sat on a four-foot-high central dais and threw cowrie shells for dice. The girls moved among the lush gardens according to the throw—advancing one place for each shell that landed with its mouth up. A pachisi courtyard at the Agra palace survives today.

Laid out in the form of a cross, the game had a number of precedent race-type games played on crosses or circles. The track for the Korean game of *nyout* is a cross within a circle; the game dates from about A.D. 300. American Indians had several similar games. In the early 16th century the Spanish observed the Aztec nobles playing *patolli* on a cross-shaped double track; game pieces were semiprecious stones and dice were beans.

In the Victorian era, a scaled-down form of pachisi made its way to England, and a patented version called Ludo (Latin for "I play") came out in the late 1800s. A winding pathway and ivory pawns replaced the courtyard and harem girls. The American company Selchow & Righter trademarked the game of Parcheesi in 1874. Among devoted players were President Calvin Coolidge, inventor Thomas Edison, and actress Clara Bow. Pawns advance to the board's center, the "home" space that represents the courtyard's central dais. In 1952 Selchow & Righter bought the rights to a crossword puzzle game. Known as Scrabble, the game would eventually eclipse Parcheesi in sales, pushing Parcheesi into third place among best-selling games in America. Neither could top the big-money game of Monopoly.

Poker

FROM FRENCH "POQUE" (BLUFFING GAME)
POPULARIZED IN NEW ORLEANS, 19TH CENTURY
HIGHEST SCORING HAND: ROYAL FLUSH

Although poker originated in Europe, it became established and popularized in the United States, and then spread back across the Atlantic. Card games similar to poker

> **UNCOMMONLY KNOWN...**
> **Playing Cards** Playing cards probably came from China in the seventh to tenth centuries. Earlier cards with symbols may have been used for centuries as divination tools. From China, cards traveled to Europe in the 13th century, possibly through Venice in the hands of famous father-and-son travelers Niccolò and Marco Polo.

were developed by the 1520s. The Spanish three-card game *primero* (Italian: *primiera,* French: *la prime*) included betting on high hands—three of a kind, a pair, and a *flux* (flush), or three of the same suit.

By the year 1700 there were a number of five-card games that not only involved betting but also bluffing—betting on a bad hand to trick others into folding, or dropping out. The English game brag, the German *pochen,* and the French *poque* all refer to this underlying principle that with any hand a player must calculate not only the strength of his cards, he must also guess his opponents' ability to bluff or to read his own bluff. The word *poker* derives from poque, which itself is a corruption of pochen ("to bluff"). Good players develop a "poker face," or unreadable bluff.

French colonists brought poque into the Louisiana Territory, and from New Orleans it spread up the Mississippi River. The first reference to poker was made in 1829 by a touring English actor. The Civil War (1861-65) was probably the greatest spur to poker, the game giving soldiers relief from the strains of battle and camp life. Two main forms of the game evolved—draw (cards dealt facedown) and stud (some cards dealt faceup).

In 1870 Col. Jacob Schenck, U.S. Ambassador to Great Britain, taught poker to members of the court of Queen Victoria. The queen herself became interested in the game, and Schenck wrote up a set of rules for her. Not until after World War I did the rest of Europe catch on to the game, which was imported by American soldiers.

Since the advent of the Internet, poker has gone online big time. Besides online lessons, message boards, and strategy sites, professional and amateur players compete virtually for real stakes in global, real-time competitions.

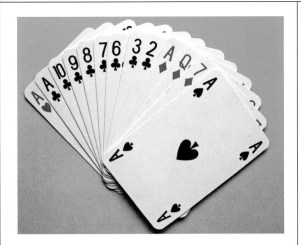

Bridge

DESCENDED FROM "BIRITCH," BRITISH WHIST
VARIANTS: CONTRACT, AUCTION
REQUIRES FOUR PLAYERS, 52-CARD DECK

The four-player card game of bridge developed from an early 17th-century game called whist, or whisk. British poet John Taylor refers to the game in a 1621 poem, and another poet, Charles Cotton, details it in his 1674 *Compleat Gamester*: "Ruff and Honours, [alias slamm] and Whist are games so commonly known in England in all parts thereof, that every child almost of eight years old hath a competent knowledg [sic] in that recreation."

Whist started out as a game played mostly by the lower classes, but by the early 1700s it had caught on in the fashionable world and spread from England to the rest of Europe and across the Atlantic, where it prospered in colonial taverns and homes. Two partners sat facing each other, and all the cards were dealt out. Teams then vied to win the most tricks (round of four cards), which were then "whisked" away by the winner. It was the card game of choice until being dethroned in the late 1800s by bridge.

In the 1870s European aristocrats on holiday gathered in the salons of the French Riviera for card games. One of the most popular was the Turkish game of *khedive,* or *biritch.* It was like whist except the dealer could name the trump suit (the outranking suit), or extend this privilege to his or her

partner. By the 1880s the game was known as bridge, though a few years later it was called bridge whist to distinguish it from a new variation known as auction bridge. Then, in 1926, champion yachtsman Harold S. Vanderbilt, great grandson of railroad tycoon Cornelius Vanderbilt, invented the game of contract bridge while voyaging from the West Coast to New York. The Whist Club of New York liked the new rules, and by the end of the decade contract bridge reigned.

One of the reasons contract bridge won and has retained (at least some) popularity is that it is based on partnership. During the 1920s to the 1960s, there were fewer at-home distractions like television, VCR and DVD players, video games, and music choices; a bridge foursome was not simply an opportunity to match wits, but an opportunity to catch up on news, gossip, and connections. In contract bridge, pairs of players have to communicate to bid and share the same score on each deal.

However, contract bridge is not confined to foursomes gathered around baize-topped tables in suburban living rooms. An advantage to this form of bridge is that it can be played in tournaments, with any number of participants. From the Bermuda Bowl, founded in 1950, to the World Olympiads, avid bridge players have lots of possible competitions to enter if they so choose.

Bridge began losing its cachet in the 1970s, as people explored other ways to spend their evenings. Like poker, the game has expanded into cyberculture; bridge aficionados from all over the world can meet, share strategies, and play online. Internet bridge also allows those who are immobile or unable to find local bridge-playing friends to enjoy the game, with the real-time convenience of a virtual card salon in which players have great flexibility over when, how long, and by what rules to play.

Sports

The histories of our major sports provide a glimpse into the leisure life of a number of early societies. Equestrian events in Roman times were as multi-layered and thrilling as today, with all the attendant complexities of breeding and wagering. When the medieval Brits wanted to get out their aggressions, they indulged in a football antecedent that makes the NFL look almost quaint. Look to 15th-century Scotland for golf, and find out how the game insinuated itself despite opposition. The most recent major sport, basketball (just over 100 years old), is traceable to an imaginative PE teacher.

Horse Racing

HELD IN ANCIENT GREEK OLYMPICS, 700-40 B.C.
MODERN: HARNESS RACING, STEEPLECHASE, HURDLES
TRIPLE CROWN: BELMONT, PREAKNESS, KENTUCKY DERBY

The sport of horse racing may well extend into the prehistoric beginnings of the horse's domestication. Man's close relation to the horse as a main mode of transportation made racing—and wagering on the outcome—as natural as car racing today. By around 1500 B.C., Assyrian kings were keeping stables of professionally trained race horses. Chariot races became a fixture at the Greek Olympic Games in the seventh century B.C., and a few decades later, races between mounted riders were added.

Chariot and mounted racing were also sports of the Roman Empire. In one type of race, a rider stood on two side-by-side horses. Champion horses were buried with a stela that listed their accomplishments, one of them chalking up 1,300 wins. Breeders consulted public records of equine bloodlines. During the reign of the emperor Augustus (27 B.C.-A.D. 14), there were 12 races a day; by the end of the first century, there were 100. As in today's sport, Roman races were full of drama, with betting (on- and off-track), accusations of doping, legal disputes, and rioting.

The Romans carried horse racing to Great Britain, where it became known as "the sport of kings." Among those kings was Richard the Lion-Heart (1157-99), a Crusader who liked Arabian horses. During his reign one of the first purses was offered—mounted knights raced a three-mile course for 40 pounds in gold. Charles II (1630-85), himself a racer, established Newmarket as the center for horse racing.

Across the Atlantic, one of the first American racetracks, New Market, was laid out near what is now Long Island, New York, in 1665. By the 1890s horse racing had reached a pinnacle, with more

---

UNCOMMONLY KNOWN . . .

Steeplechasing Racing horses over jumps and obstacles started as far back as ancient Greece, where historian Xenophon (ca431-ca352 B.C.) expounded on cross-country horsemanship. The modern steeplechase began as an exercise for cavalry officers and a contest for British foxhunters, who in the early 1800s used a village steeple as a landmark.

PARALLEL HISTORY

Polo

The fast-paced, mallet-and-ball horseback game of polo was being played by Persians in the first century, and possibly much earlier. The original games served as training exercises for the king's guard and other mounted soldiers; sometimes up to 200 players would take the field in what must have been extremely rough contests. The game spread to China, where after a game in 910, a disappointed emperor ordered the players beheaded. In the 1860s British officers stationed in India learned the sport from tribal horsemen, and by the next decade polo had become popular in the United States.

than 300 thoroughbred tracks in the United States. Anti-gambling sentiment reduced that number to a mere 25 by 1908, but the sport came roaring back in the 1930s.

Gymnastics

DATES TO ANCIENT GREEK OLYMPICS
SURGE IN POPULARITY IN EUROPE IN 19TH CENTURY
MODERN EVENTS: FLOOR, VAULT, BEAM, RINGS, BARS

Gymnastics originated from the same platform that has popularized the sport in modern times—the Olympic Games. By the 13th century B.C., five centuries before the first Olympics (see Parallel History, opposite), the Greeks were holding public athletic contests in conjunction with funeral ceremonies and later as part of religious festivals. Gymnastics were at first training exercises for the competitive sports. Then,

during the early Greek Olympic Games, a primitive form of gymnastics developed as its own sport. With the end of the ancient games in the fourth century A.D., all sports fell into a long period of decline. Local athletic events were still held, mostly during holidays, but a number of laws regulated or banned sports.

It was not until the 19th century that organized sports began to reappear on a large scale. Gymnastics as a systematic and disciplined training of the body was one of the first sports to reemerge. Gymnastics societies sprang up in Germany and Bohemia, then in France and Switzerland, the latter country creating a unison gymnastics performed by a group. These societies offered classes for children as young as five, and gymnastics became one of the few early sports for both girls and boys.

By the mid-1800s Sweden had developed a system of rhythmic floor exercises that made its way to England in 1879. A tide of immigrants brought gymnastics to the United States in the 1880s, where the sport began to proliferate in schools and universities. Meanwhile, Germany was creating various apparatus exercises that emphasized strength. Not until the 1920s did the gymnastics world combine the fluency of the Swedish model with the static motions of the German.

Baseball

DESCENDED FROM: ROUNDERS (BRITISH GAME)
FIRST PRO TEAM: CINCINNATI RED STOCKINGS, 1869
U.S. MAJOR LEAGUE TODAY: 30 TEAMS, 2 DIVISIONS

America's national pastime, baseball has its origins in a 17th-century British game called rounders. As in baseball, players hit a ball with a bat and ran around bases. One of the big differences, though, was that an out was made when a fielder threw a ball and hit a runner. This feature of the game was known as "plugging" or "soaking" the runner, and it naturally precluded the use of hard balls, though one wonders how soft the balls were and how many injuries occurred.

American colonists played rounders in the early 1700s, calling it by such names as "town ball," the "Massachusetts game," and "base ball." By the 1740s, in both England and America, the word "base-ball" appeared in print. It was an informal game, and rules varied from one location to another. The first published reference to organized baseball was in an 1825 New York newspaper. Around 1840, the practice of plugging was dropped and tagging for outs was adopted. This paved the way for the use of a hard ball and thus a larger field. Professional baseball began in 1869 when the Cincinnati Red Stockings, one of many amateur teams, decided to pay its players.

The history of baseball took an interesting turn in the early 1900s. A commission made up of a U.S. senator, sporting-goods maker A. G. Spalding, and various investigators looked into the origins of what had become a great American game. Solid evidence pointed to rounders, yet the 1908 official report on the history of baseball concluded that the game was invented in Cooperstown, New York, in 1839 by Gen. Abner Doubleday (later a Civil War

The Olympics

The Olympic Games were the most important of four festivals that took place in ancient Greece. The first Olympics on record were held in Olympia in 776 B.C. The contestants, all men, were nude, and the only event was the "stadion," a 210-yard dash. Koroibos, a cook from Elis, was the winner. The games were then held every four years, an interval of time that became known as an Olympiad. In 708 B.C., wrestling was added, as well as a pentathlon of running, jumping, wrestling, discus, and javelin. The Romans banned the Olympics in A.D. 393. In the 1870s, after excavations of the old stadium and temples of Olympia, a movement grew to restart the games, and the first modern Olympics were held in 1896–in Athens, Greece.

UNCOMMONLY KNOWN...

Softball Gym of the Farragut Boat Club, Chicago, Thanksgiving Day, 1887: Some 20 young men gather to learn the outcome of the Harvard-Yale football game. The winner is announced, bets are paid, rowdiness ensues, and George Hancock, a reporter for the Chicago Board of Trade, shouts, "Let's play ball!" The sport of "indoor baseball" is born; it later moves outside and becomes known as softball.

hero). Not until 1939 did the claim begin to be refuted, though for decades many people clung to the Doubleday theory.

Basketball

INVENTED BY JAMES NAISMITH, 1891, MA
FIVE-ON-A-SIDE RULE MADE OFFICIAL: 1897
FIRST UNIV. GAME: U. OF CHICAGO VS. U. OF IOWA, 1896

James Naismith was a 29-year-old physical education instructor at the International Y.M.C.A. Training School (afterward Springfield College) in Massachusetts when he came up with a novel game in December 1891. His class was bored with endless calisthenics and Indian club tossing. To put the young men's rebellious energy to use, he nailed two peach baskets ten feet high on the gymnasium balcony, took a soccer ball, and laid out some basic rules. His game was to be an indoor activity that combined elements of soccer, rugby, and hockey. There were nine players on a side (so everyone in the class could play). The first game ended 1-0; the janitor climbed a ladder to retrieve the ball.

The popularity of basketball quickly spread. In spite of Naismith's rule against physical contact, early games often broke out into wild melees. The main problem was the variable number of players. In order to include as many people as possible, games could involve up to 100 players at a time. Y.M.C.A.'s had to ban the sport. But basketball had become too well liked—by both players and spectators—to die. The game was such a success that within five years it had become a college and professional sport. Most of Naismith's original rules were kept, though court sizes were standardized and only five players on a side were allowed. Baskets evolved into a hammock-type net that could be opened with a chain, and then around 1913 to simply a bottomless net.

Among outstanding early teams, the Original Celtics of New York City won 91 percent of their games from 1921 to 1928. Dominant all-black teams of the 1920s and 1930s included the New York Renaissance and the Harlem Globetrotters. In the 1950s college and professional teams began to integrate black players into all-white squads.

Football

FROM MIDDLE AGES "MELLAYS," OR BRAWLS
GAME EVOLVED INTO FOOTBALL, SOCCER, AND RUGBY
BALLS ORIGINALLY MADE FROM PIG BLADDERS

The sport of American football, as hard-hitting as it is, evolved from sports even more hazardous to life and limb. Ancient Egyptian fertility rites involved team games with the object of carrying or kicking a ball to one side of a field. The Chinese of around 300 B.C. were playing a football-like game, as were the Greeks and the conquering Romans, whose game of *harpastum* consisted of teams throwing a ball and advancing it to opposite sides. The Romans probably introduced the game to the British. By the Middle Ages, the British were playing games called "mellays" (or *mêlées*) with large numbers of people trying to punch, throw, or carry an air-filled animal bladder. Shrove Tuesday festival games became highly popular, with inter-parish contests involving hundreds of men. Goals were about half a mile apart, and play would continue for hours until a goal was scored.

These brawling football matches continued into the 19th century. Though somewhat less violent, they were still dangerous, as witnessed by a writer in 1801: "... the players kick each other's shins without the least ceremony, and some of them are overthrown at the hazard of their limbs." In the 1820s, football broke into two separate sports—one like today's soccer, the other like rugby (see Parallel History). The two sports would re-combine in America.

In 1874 the Harvard football team hosted a team from Montreal's McGill University. They agreed to play two games, the first by Harvard's soccer-like rules and the second under McGill's rugby style of play. Both games allowed for ball-carrying and for kicking the ball through the goalposts, but rugby used an egg-shaped ball and allowed for tackling. After the series, Harvard became so enamored of rugby-style football that it spread the gospel to other colleges. By 1900 football was well established. Since players wore little padding and no helmets, serious injuries often occurred. President Theodore Roosevelt in 1905 pushed for rule changes to make football safer.

Skiing

EARLIEST-KNOWN SKIS DATE TO 8000-7000 B.C.
FIRST WRITTEN RECORD: HAN DYNASTY (200-25 B.C.)
MODERN: ALPINE (DOWNHILL), NORDIC (CROSS-COUNTRY)

What we generally think of as a fun wintertime sport has for thousands of years been an essential mode of transportation for Scandinavians. Skis dating from 4,000 to 5,000 years ago have been found in bogs in Sweden and Finland, and a petroglyph near the Arctic Circle in Norway clearly depicts a figure on long skis holding some sort of pole—it dates to around 2000 B.C. In Norse mythology, the god Ull, stepson of Thor, was known for his skiing prowess.

The ease with which skis enabled people to move through snow-covered terrain has naturally been exploited by the military. Since at least the year 1200, when the Norse were fighting the Vikings, ski troops have been deployed at various times by Norway, Sweden, Finland, Poland, and Russia. In World War II, Finnish ski patrols were used to stop a Russian invasion, and the U.S. Army Tenth Mountain Division employed skis battling the Germans in the Italian Alps.

Skiing had begun as a sport long before the 20th century. One of the first organized competitions was a cross-country race in Tromsø, Norway, in 1843.

Then, around 1860, a revolution in skiing took place when Norwegian skier Sondre Nordheim developed a new kind of binding that not only held the toe but also wrapped around the heel. He went on to develop long, sweeping turns—the Christiana and Telemark (named for his region)—which were possible with the new equipment. Within the same decade, competitive downhill skiing began in California—with 12-foot-long skis and leather toe straps.

The first Winter Olympics were held in Chamonix, France, in 1924 and featured only Nordic (cross-country) skiing. Alpine (downhill) events joined the Olympics roster in 1936 in Garmisch-Partenkirchen, Germany.

Swimming

TRAINING FOR GREEK AND ROMAN WARRIORS
EARLIEST SWIM MEETS: JAPAN, FIRST CENTURY B.C.
MODERN STROKES DEVELOPED IN MID-LATE 19TH CENT.

Most mammals can swim at least a little bit—even cats, if they have to. The fact that movement through the water is much slower than on land did not stop early man from learning how to feel safe and comfortable in an environment from which he drew sustenance.

The early Egyptians, Assyrians, Greeks, and Romans knew the value of swimming; ancient soldiers honed their strength and stamina in the water. Swimming competitions were held in Japan dating as far back as 36 B.C., during the time of Emperor Sujin.

In the Middle Ages, swimming became one of the least popular sports because of a widespread—and not incorrect—belief that many diseases were waterborne. But by the mid-1800s, aquatics had returned to favor, and organized swim meets began taking place. The main stroke at that time was the breaststroke, which had been described as early as 1696 in a book by French writer M. Thevenot called *Art de Nager* (Art of Swimming). Not until the late 19th century did the crawl develop. This more demanding but faster stroke may have been used by South Pacific islanders before it was introduced in Australia around 1893. It was actually an adaptation of the sidestroke, which was faster than the breaststroke because one arm recovered above water, thus lessening resistance. Swimmers tried a modified, double-overarm sidestroke with the body rolling from side to side.

Soon after the crawl emerged it became the most popular stroke. In 1896 men's swimming was one of nine events at the first modern Olympic Games (along with cycling, fencing, gymnastics, lawn tennis, shooting, track and field, weight lifting, and wrestling). Women's competitive swimming events were added at the 1912 Olympics.

Mark Spitz held a longtime record for most gold medals won in a single Olympic competition—seven, at the 1972 Munich Games. His record was shattered in 2008 by fellow U.S. swimmer Michael Phelps, who won eight and broke several records.

Tennis

OLD FRENCH "TENEZ" (TAKE); SHOUTED BEFORE SERVE
FROM FRENCH GAME "JEU DE PAUME" (PALM GAME)
COURTS: GRASS, CLAY, HARD SURFACE (SYNTHETIC)

Tennis began as an indoor game called *jeu de paume* (palm game) in medieval France. It was a version of handball and probably first played by priests in cathedral cloisters. The word *tennis* most likely derives from the French *tenez* (take), which was shouted before a serve. By 1292 there were no fewer than 13 makers of tennis balls in the city of Paris; most balls were made of wool covered by sheepskin. By the mid-16th century rackets were being used to hit the ball instead of hands. Balls were hardened by wadding together bits of wet rags, wrapping them with string, then covering the whole in white cloth.

The game grew in popularity, becoming a favorite pastime of many kings and their courts. Francis I (king of France 1515-47) was so dedicated to the sport that he had a court built on a ship, which disappointingly sank.

From France, tennis spread across Europe; it took firm hold in England in the 16th and 17th centuries. In 1873 a Welshman named Maj. Walter Wingfield invented an outdoor version of the game and called it *sphairistikè* (Greek for "playing ball"), or lawn tennis. At around the same time, rubber balls came into use, making it possible for a ball to bounce off a grass surface. By 1875 lawn tennis had become so popular that the All England Croquet Club dedicated one of its courts at Wimbledon to tennis; the next year the club became known as the All England Lawn Tennis Croquet and Club. The first Wimbledon tennis tournament was held there in 1877.

The scoring still used today dates from medieval times. A clock face may have been used to keep score; thus the four points needed to win a game were quarters of 60—15, 30, 40 (abbreviated from 45), and game. Saying "love" instead of "zero" was either a corruption of the French *l'oeuf* ("egg," which represents zero) or referred to the concept that a person who fails to score is playing for love of the game.

Golf

PRO GOLF ASSOCIATIONS: PGA (MEN), LPGA (WOMEN)
FIRST U.S. CLUB: ST. ANDREW'S GOLF CLUB, NY
DOMINANT PLAYER: TIGER WOODS

The Romans, during their occupation of Britain (A.D. 40s-early 400s), played *pagan-ica,* a golflike street game using a bent stick and a leather ball stuffed with feathers. The

Belgians played *chole,* a game in which players tried to hit targets in the fewest number of strokes. And the Dutch had *kolven* or *kolf,* a similar game in a walled court.

But actual golf came into existence on the craggy hills and moors of Scotland in around the 15th century. The first reference to the sport was a royal reproof from King James II in 1457. Apparently such games were interfering with archery practice, and so he decreed that "Fute-ball and Golfe be utterly cryed downe." Yet clearly golf would not let go of the popular imagination, because a few decades later James IV tried to ban the game. He must have realized how futile, and wrong-headed, such a law was, for he later became a golfer. His account books include payments for "golf clubbis and ballis." In 1565, Mary Queen of Scots became the first woman golfer of record when she was found playing just days after the murder of her husband. The addiction of the game was simply too much to resist.

In 1744 "several Gentlemen of Honour skillful in the ancient and healthfull exercise of Golf" organized to play a tournament on the links of Leith outside Edinburgh. From that union came the first golfing club, now known as the Honourable Company of Edinburgh Golfers. Several clubs are reputed to be the first in the U.S., including Vermont's Dorset Field Club, Pennsylvania's Foxburg Country Club, and the St. Andrews Golf Club in Hastings-on-Hudson, New York. They were all founded in the 1880s.

PARALLEL HISTORY

Miniature Golf

The first smaller-scale course, "The Himalayas," at St. Andrews, Scotland, was built in 1867 for the Ladies' Putting Club. According to the dictates of the time, women were not supposed to swing a golf club over a shoulder. While that was a decorous form of regulation golf, the miniaturized form enjoyed today came into play with several gentlemen. James Barber in 1916 built "Thistle Dhu," a miniaturized golf course on his private estate in Pinehurst, North Carolina. In the early 1920s Englishman Thomas McCulloch Fairborn developed an artificial surface for a miniature golf course. Garnet Carter's 1920s "Tom Thumb Golf" empire swept the U.S.

Classic Toys

T he toys of our youth—where did they come from? Tinkertoys and Lincoln Logs have been around since the 1910s, the Frisbee since the 1950s. Silly Putty and the Slinky, both from the 1940s, were the result of failed scientific experiments. All of these classic toys were invented by people who had to put in months, and sometimes years, of work to bring their product successfully to market. Rattles and dolls, as you might expect, go back to ancient history, but modern versions—Barbies, for instance—were again the brainchild of one very determined inventor.

Tinkertoys

INVENTOR: CHARLES H. PAJEAU, ROBERT PETTIT, 1914
CANISTER CONTAINED WOOD STICKS, WHEELS, PEGS
USED IN CONSTRUCTION OF 1998 CORNELL UNIV. ROBOT

C ommuting by train to work one day in around 1914, Chicago stonemason Charles H. Pajeau met trader Robert Pettit. Both were bored with their day jobs and wanted to do something creative and original. Pajeau had an idea. He had noticed children playing with pencils, spools of thread, and other objects; fitting the pencils into the spools and making structures provided hours of amusement. Pettit liked the idea. The two men agreed to make up some construction sets and try to sell them.

Pajeau came up with a simple concept to create an interlocking building toy. The linking objects were small wooden spools or hubs, drilled with holes around the side and one through the center. These hubs would serve as the basic unit to which sticks of various lengths could be attached. An unlimited number of frameworks and designs could thus be created, including towers, ships, and moving Ferris wheels. Pajeau and Pettit established the Toy Tinkers company, the name referring to the fiddling around that their new toy inspired. Finding a niche in an already crowded toy market proved difficult at first, but the business partners were persistant. They began setting up displays in department store windows, including a brilliant Christmastime publicity stunt: In a store window, hired midget actors dressed as Santa's elves busily assembled brightly colored "Tinker Toys."

Word spread quickly, and within a year almost a million sets had been sold. A plastic version of Tinkertoys came out in 1992, but eight years later Nostalgia won out and the traditional wood version was reprised by popular demand.

UNCOMMONLY KNOWN...

Lincoln Logs The interlocking toy logs, used in old-fashioned cabin construction by generations of children, were the brainchild of John Lloyd Wright, son of architect Frank Lloyd Wright. He claimed to have been inspired watching the foundation-laying of the earthquake-proof Imperial Hotel in Tokyo. Lincoln Logs came out in 1916.

Frisbee

DESCENDED FROM DISCUS
MODERN VERSION DATES TO 1950s
ORIGINALLY MADE OF METAL; CALLED "FLYIN' SAUCERS"

The ancient Greeks threw the discus as part of the Olympic pentathlon, but the heavy clay disk was only for throwing, not catching. No doubt children over the intervening centuries found any number of round objects they could spin through the air, but the actual Frisbee dates only from the 1940s.

The disk-flying craze started on college campuses, independently on the East and West Coasts. Students at those bastions of intellectual rigor Harvard and Yale amused themselves by flinging empty pie tins from the William R. Frisbie bakery. The Bridgeport, Connecticut, establishment had been in business since 1870, so it's possible that the shallow tin pans had been sent flying by earlier generations. Since the pans most likely were unstable in the air, they would have been difficult to throw and catch with any degree of reliability. An inventor was needed.

Such a man presented himself in California in the 1950s. Walter Frederick Morrison was the son of the inventor of sealed-beam automobile headlights. He was fascinated with flying saucers and the possibility of aliens from outer space, concepts much in vogue then. To mimic the shape and hovering ability of a flying saucer, Morrison invented a lightweight toy

metal disk. He later switched to plastic and marketed his product to the Wham-O company in San Gabriel. In 1957 the first "Flyin' Saucers" made their appearance in West Coast stores.

The saucers proved popular right away, but only in southern California. Wham-O's president, Richard Knerr, then went on a promotional tour of East Coast colleges, handing out free saucers to create a buzz. He was amazed to find Ivy Leaguers already throwing disks—pie tins that they called Frisbies. Knerr changed the name of his toy to Frisbee, trademarked it in 1959, and started a national mania.

Rattle

OLDEST KNOWN: EGYPTIAN, 14TH CENTURY B.C.
FIRST MADE OF CLAY, WOOD, GOURDS, SHELLS
ALSO USED IN HEALING RITUALS AND MUSIC

Among a baby's first toys, rattles date far back in human history. Primitive cultures continue to use rattling seed pods as toys, musical instruments, and devices to ward off evil spirits. Tribal priests rattled during precarious times in a person's life—birth, illness, and death—to smooth the transition to or from the spirit world.

The oldest known rattles were made in Egypt, near the dawn of the New Kingdom in the 14th century B.C. Several of them are held by Egypt's Horniman Museum. Filled with pebbles, the rattles are variously shaped and sized. Some are elaborately painted and carved to represent bears, pigs, or birds. Materials included clay, earthenware, and wood, often covered with a protective layer of silk. The lack of sharp objects showed concern for child safety on the part of the maker: Ears were flat to the head, and birds had no feet or beaks. Many such rattles were found in children's tombs. The British Museum holds a clay, owl-shaped rattle from Cyprus, dating to about 1200 B.C. The ancient Greeks also had a number of animal rattles, including those bearing the forms of animals such as ducks, turtles, and rabbits. And Roman children were not without rattles, as indicated by discoveries in the ruins of Pompeii, which was destroyed by the eruption of Mount Vesuvius in A.D. 79. In the catacombs of Rome, children's graves have yielded a number of archaeological treasures, including rattles.

Rattle construction varied according to the available materials, and if an object in nature needed little fashioning, its rattling potential was realized. Thus seaside cultures have used shells filled with pebbles, while inland cultures have used gourds or hollowed-out bamboo and other tube-shaped plants.

Teddy Bear

NAMED FOR PRESIDENT TEDDY ROOSEVELT
FIRST CREATED BY TOY SALESMAN MORRIS MICHTOM
RELATED: STEIFF BEARS, BY GERMAN MARGARET STEIFF

C uddly stuffed bears have been a standard child's toy for more than 100 years. The teddy bear story began on a hunting trip taken by President Theodore Roosevelt in 1902. The President having failed to bag a trophy, his gracious Mississippi hosts caught and tied up a bear for him to shoot. Good sportsman that he was, Roosevelt declared, "Spare the bear! I will not shoot a tethered animal." The incident was nicely captured in a cartoon by Clifford Berryman in the *Washington Star*: the President turns his back on a cowering cub. The caption, referring to a state border dispute, reads: "Drawing the line in Mississippi."

The image was reprinted in papers across the nation, and a Brooklyn toy salesman named Morris Michtom got an idea. The 32-year-old Russian immigrant made a stuffed animal, called it "Teddy's Bear," and put it and the cartoon in his store window. Customers were not just attracted to his store, they wanted to buy a Teddy's Bear. Michtom started manufacturing Teddy's Bears, with button eyes, and in 1903 founded the Ideal Novelty and Toy Company, which netted him a fortune.

At the same time, over in Germany, seamstress Margaret Steiff, who had been making a variety of hand-sewn felt animals—including bears—since the 1880s, was given a copy of the Roosevelt cartoon. She decided to turn out her own line of bears, which premiered at the 1904 Leipzig Fair. Steiff was a wheelchair-bound polio victim with an enviable amount of energy; swamped with orders for bears, she satisfied customers' demands. Up to the eve of World War I, she sold millions of stuffed bears.

Teddy bears off all sorts have remained popular, while Steiff bears have become collector's items. In 1994, a 1904 cinnamon Steiff bear sold at auction in London to Yoshihiro Sekiguchi, founder of the Teddy Bear Museum in Izu, Japan, for £110,000.

PARALLEL HISTORY

Crayons

T he word "crayon" is French for chalk or pencil, but when an American mentions "crayons," others know that she's referring to the colorful wax writing instruments perfected by entrepreneurs Edwin Binney and Harold Smith in the late 19th century. Binney & Smith first produced deep red pigments for barns and country buildings but soon began manufacturing slate pencils, and then dustless chalk for teachers. While traveling to schools for that product, the pair saw a need for reliable colored drawing implements, and their combo of paraffin wax and pigment went on the market for the first time in 1903 as Crayola, a name that signifies "oily chalk."

Silly Putty

CREATED BY JAMES WRIGHT, GE ENGINEER (1943)
LATER BOUGHT, SOLD BY STORE OWNER PAUL HODGSON
RETAINS FORM: STRETCHED, BOUNCED, HEATED, COOLED

During World War II, the U.S. War Production Board asked General Electric to come up with a cheap, synthetic, all-purpose rubber that could be mass-produced and used in jeep and airplane tires, gas masks, and other military gear. The company passed the job on to engineer James Wright.

Wright went into his lab in New Haven, Connecticut, and began mixing. A compound of boric acid and silicone oil had a rubbery consistency, as well as many unique characteristics. The gooey substance rebounded 25 percent more than a good rubber ball, it stretched farther, would not mold or decay, could be heated or cooled without effect, and, perhaps most striking of all, it could be flattened across a printed page and then, when peeled off, would reveal a mirror image of the print.

Wright's synthetic rubber was not, alas, quite what the War Production Board had in mind. But it sure was fun. The engineers called it "nutty putty" and enjoyed showing off its novel properties to visitors. They even sent samples to engineers around the world, soliciting practical uses for the product, but to no avail.

At a New Haven party, some nutty putty was brought out. One of the guests was an ad copywriter and toy store owner named Paul Hodgson. Not only was he fascinated with the wad of nutty putty, he was aware that it kept the group entertained for hours. He later approached GE and bought a blob of the putty for $147. Then he and a Yale student packaged one-ounce balls into colored plastic eggs. In 1949 Hodgson's store offered Silly Putty for sale; by year's end it had outsold everything else in the store. An even more spectacular rubber called "flying rubber" or "flubber" was imagined for the 1961 Disney hit movie *The Absent-Minded Professor*, starring Fred MacMurray.

Slinky

CREATED BY RICHARD JAMES, MARINE ENGINEER
DEBUTED AS TOY IN PHILADELPHIA, 1945
MADE OF STEEL RIBBON OR PLASTIC

The coiled metal toy that walks down stairs began life, as did Silly Putty, as a failed scientific endeavor. Marine engineer Richard James was trying to create an anti-vibration mechanism for ship instruments in the early 1940s. He was using tension, or torsion, springs that would quickly counter the effects of waves at sea. One day he knocked over a delicate experimental spring and watched in amazement as it crept, its coils fountaining, down a stack of books, onto a table, then to the floor. He found that it was especially good at descending steps.

Seeing the spring as more than a passing curiosity, James and his wife borrowed $500 and started a production company for a toy they called Slinky. Using a homemade machine, they coiled 80-foot sections of steel ribbon into the first Slinkys, and during Christmas 1945 debuted the toy at Gimbels department store in Philadelphia. Nervous about how the toy would sell, James lined up a friend to buy the first one. He needn't have worried—within 90 minutes he had sold 400 Slinkys.

Since then, more than 300 million Slinkys have been sold. Though they started as a scientific failure, the flip-flopping toys have proved useful in a number of ways. The Slinky is the perfect device for illustrating wave motion in physics classes; soldiers in Vietnam used Slinkys as radio antennas; and a Slinky was part of a space shuttle experiment that tested the mechanics of springs in zero gravity.

The inventor's life spiraled in a different direction from his toy. Suffering a midlife crisis, he left his family in 1960 and joined a religious cult in Bolivia, donations to which nearly sank the company. He died in 1974 at age 60.

Dolls

EARLIEST: EGYPTIAN PADDLE DOLLS, 2000-3000 B.C.
DOLLMAKING POPULARIZED IN RENAISSANCE
BARBIE DOLL: FIRST INTRODUCED 1959, MATTEL

For perhaps tens of thousands of years, people have sculpted human likenesses; the perishable material used in prehistoric times,

Barbie & Ken

Ruth Handler was a secretary at Paramount Studios in Los Angeles in the early 1950s. She was also a mother of young children, and she noticed that her daughter preferred playing with paper cutouts of teenagers more than infant dolls. Her husband was a founder of the Mattel toy company. When she approached the company with an idea for a grown-up doll with clothing and accessories, they were unimpressed. Handler persisted, and in 1959 the new Barbie doll appeared, named for Handler's daughter. The immediate success of Barbie called for a sequel; in 1961 Mattel brought out a boyfriend named Ken, after Handler's son.

Barbie and Ken stand by while a girl sings along with a 7-inch record called "Barbie Sings."

though, has not survived. The oldest known dolls are Egyptian paddle dolls, dating from 2000 to 3000 B.C. Carved from flat pieces of wood, the dolls were painted with geometrical patterns and given hair of clay or wooden beads. The earliest dolls were idols with a religious significance and were buried with the dead. At some indefinable point they became playthings—yet, instead of representing babies, the dolls were miniature adults with exaggerated hips, breasts, and genitals.

By about 500 B.C. the Greeks and Romans had wood and clay dolls with movable arms and legs, using pins for joints. Fancier dolls were made of bone or ivory. Girls typically played with dolls until they were of marriageable age, then they symbolically deposited the dolls on the altar of Diana (Roman) or Artemis (Greek), goddesses of childbirth. By the third century B.C., the Greeks had infant dolls that nested in the arms of mother dolls; eventually the baby dolls became more popular. The oldest surviving cloth dolls, dating from the sixth and seventh centuries, were found in Egypt in the graves of a Christian sect called the Copts. Other than these, few dolls have survived from the Middle Ages.

Not until the Renaissance did dolls and other toys have a resurgence. By the early 1400s there were doll-makers, *Dochenmacher,* in Nürnberg, Germany, the center of European dollmaking through the 1700s. Paris was also a leading doll manufacturer during this time, producing dolls dressed in the latest fashions.

manipulated those knobs to draw everything from a single line to complicated portraits. For a plaything so closely identified with American childhood, the Etch-a-Sketch has surprising Gallic roots: Frenchman Arthur Granjean first showed what he called *L'Ecran Magique* (Magic Screen) at a German toy expo in 1955. Ohio Art executives bought the rights to Granjean's device, and released it several years later as U.S. patent #3,760,505. The Etch-a-Sketch works with elegant simplicity: The glass screen's underside is coated with a mix of aluminum powder and plastic beads. Aluminum powder will cling to almost anything, and the beads help make it movable. The knobs control a stylus that can move in any direction to make lines in the powder/bead mixture. If it were just a grid making machine, the Etch-a-Sketch would not have lasted this long as a toy that's still bought and used. With coordination and quick manipulation of the knobs, a person can create curved lines—the catch is that the line has to keep going as you draw. If you stop and reverse direction, or try to head to a different point in the picture, your creation will be finished. This challenge makes the Etch-a-Sketch fun and engaging. Over the years there have been different models, colors, and sizes of Etch-a-Sketch, including one with buttons to mimic a computer console, but the only one that has lasted is the original red, white, and gray. The toy's inner workings remain the same, too. The aluminum powder and plastic beads have not been swapped out for some space-age synthetic material, and the metal stylus is still made and rigged exactly as it was in 1959. While the original Etch-a-Sketch is still going strong, several other toys in its category are also worth mentioning for their approach to

Etch-a-Sketch

DEVELOPED BY ARTHER GRANJEAN, LATE 1950S
BOUGHT AND SOLD BY OHIO TOY COMPANY, 1960
INSIDE: FINE ALUMINUM POWDER AND BEADS

With its bright-red frame, gray screen, and white plastic knobs, the Etch-a-Sketch toy is a 20th-century toy icon. Millions of kids around the world have

mess-free, reusable, and portable drawing. The Magic Slate is a simple cardboard rectangle topped with a slightly sticky board that has a piece of thin, peelable plastic attached. With an included plastic stylus, a child can draw simple figures, as well as write messages or math equations. A flick of the

plastic, and the drawing is erased. Two popular drawing toys are based on magnets. The first dates back to 1955: Smethport Specialty Company's "Woolly Willy." Don and Jim Herzog, brothers whose father, Ralph, owned Smethport, used metal shavings left over from production and a vacuum

Dolls

L ike other toys, dolls are playthings. But unlike a spinning top or a Frisbee, which might mimic movements needed later in life (for instance, for hunting or labor), dolls are often a very realistic toy that mimics relationships built later in life (like that of a mother-child bond, friendships, caregiving relationships). Dolls are sometimes not toys at all; for example, those of high craftsmanship with elaborate costumes may be intended for display only. One of the other remarkable things about dolls is that they are made to look like humans, and throughout history they have been stand-ins for humans as religious icons or totems, as companions, and as decoration. The earliest Egyptian dolls, found in numerous tombs, were made from wood (or pottery, for the rich). While their presence in tombs indicates that they must have been important possessions, no one is completely sure whether they were toys, or used for rituals. The latter purpose was served by fertility dolls, which existed in many cultures; our examples are African. Hopi Kachina dolls were also religious icons. The role of dolls as toys became more pronounced with Greek and Roman graves; the graves found to include dolls were primarily those of children. While most Greco-Roman dolls were clay or wood, a few were made of bone, ivory, or wax, and it is during this period that people first begin making dolls with articulated limbs. For many centuries, the most popular and best produced dolls were made out of wood and created in Europe. Although wood could be manipulated into many different shapes, it was time-consuming and expensive for a woodcarver to make a lifelike doll. "Composition dolls," made from pulped wood leavings and glue or more often from papier-mâché (paper cut into strips, dipped in liquefied plaster, tucked around a mold, and dried), became popular because they were much cheaper. While later dolls were made of everything from rag to vegetable matter to plastic, wax and porcelain were next in line for doll duplication (one of the first baby dolls was made of wax) and are still used for many dolls, especially high-end ones today. As mass production gave rise to an increasing number and variety of products, so did the number and variety of dolls multiply. If we are to judge by the myriad doll crazes of the 20th century shown here, this ancient symbol, icon, and toy will be around for plenty of millennia to come.

2000 B.C.
Egyptian wooden In some tombs, many wooden "dolls" are found; some ancient Egyptians believed that groups of them would be called to life by Osiris.

A.D. 150
European ivory Ivory doll modeled after Faustina the Elder and Faustina the Younger, who lived during the second century A.D.

1959
Barbie doll Introduced in 1959, this teenage fashion doll was named after inventor Ruth Handler's daughter Barbara. Handler based Barbie on a German doll, Bild Lilli, inspired by a comic strip about a young working woman.

dome to create a toy that is still manufactured and sold in its original as well as new forms. Basically, a child could take a metal "magic wand" to gather up the polarized shavings and move them to different places on "Willy's" face (the simple, silly visage was drawn by artist Leonard Mackowski).

The Magna Doodle, first released in 1974, is a natural meld of the Etch-a-Sketch, the Magic Slate, and Woolly Willy: It combines the frame construction of the first, the stylus function of the second, and the magnet science of the third to make a durable and very adaptable drawing surface.

1820
German Bisque Dolls with heads made of glazed porcelain (Dresden) or unfired bisque (ceramic) became popular in the early 19th century.

1890
Matryoshka
Matryoshka wooden nesting dolls look rustic, as they're meant to, but they aren't an age-old handcraft. They were first made in the late 19th century during a folklore revival in Russia.

1870
Fertility
"Akua'ma," like these from the Asante people of Ghana, were carved wooden dolls believed to help with pregnancy and childbirth. A priest would bless the doll for the expectant mother, who often dressed and treated it as she would a future infant.

1900
Kachina These Native American religious items are usually carved from cottonwood and carefully detailed to resemble mythological figures, like the chief Hopi deities Eototo and Ahola.

1983
Cabbage Patch Kids
Co-inventors Xavier Roberts and Debbie Morehead have never referred to their soft, stuffed creations as dolls. Cabbage Patch Kids were each different, supposedly individuals with unique personalities, bolstered by "birth certificates" for their "adoptions."

1991
American Girl
The "American Girl Dolls" are made by Pleasant Company, founded by Pleasant T. Rowland. Some of the dolls carry backstories from different eras of American history such as colonial Williamsburg, while others are customizable by hair and eye color.

Other Pastimes

In this catchall section we've included a number of popular amusements—carnival rides, fireworks, musical instruments, and mental puzzles. One of the most interesting histories is that of the circus, which in its modern incarnation goes back only to the 18th century. But for centuries, traveling bands of entertainers have set up shop in a village or town for a few days, then moved on. The word *circus* derives from a stationary place of entertainment, the great racecourse of ancient Rome. The Roman Colosseum, though, held spectacles closer in spirit to our circus, albeit of a more barbaric nature.

Sledding

MODERN SLED DESCENDED FROM TOBOGGAN
RIDDEN DOWNHILL OR PULLED BY HORSES OR DOGS
FAMOUS SLED: CITIZEN KANE'S ROSEBUD

Long a children's recreation in parts of the world where it snows, sledding most likely began on small sledges that were used to haul cargo. The modern sport developed from two different sources in the 19th century—tobogganing in North America and skeleton sledding in Europe.

Algonquian hunters built *odabaggans* to pull their game and supplies across the snow. These early toboggans were made of long, thin strips of birch or hickory, joined together with crosspieces. The Inuit often made their toboggans of whalebone. The front end was curved up and the bottom had a smooth, highly polished surface. Later Indians had a canoe-shaped toboggan, outfitted with wooden runners. Early children's sleds in the United States were probably adapted to some degree from toboggans. The Pilgrims were known to have sledded on boxes equipped with runners.

After about 1870 the coasting, or clipper, sled became common on the snow-covered slopes of American villages. They were built low and long, with round steel rods for runners. The girls' sled was lighter and shorter and had high, rimmed sides and wide, flat runners. By the 1880s, the sport of coasting had become quite a popular activity, especially in the fashionable resorts of Switzerland, where it was known, interestingly, as tobogganing. Sledding runs were built; the most acclaimed was the curving, three-quarter-mile-long Cresta at St. Moritz. Competitions at Cresta evolved into the sport of skeleton, in which the racer lies prone, headfirst on a ribbed-frame sled. Skeleton was a winter Olympic event in St. Moritz in 1928 and 1948 before becoming a permanent event in 2002.

In the meantime, children in the United States had been sledding on Flexible Flyers, since their

---

UNCOMMONLY KNOWN...
Bobsledding Bobsledding dates to the late 1870s in Switzerland when a steering wheel was added to a toboggan; the name came from the way sledders bobbed their body back and forth to gain speed. The first competition was held in 1897 on the Cresta run in St. Moritz. The Winter Olympics in 1932 had four-man and two-man bobsled events.

introduction in Pennsylvania in 1889. These and similar sleds featured two steel runners which responded to a steering bar.

Crossword Puzzles

INVENTOR: ARTHUR WYNNE
DECEMBER 21, 1913, NY "WORLD" SUNDAY SUPPLEMENT
NOTEWORTHY DESCENDANT: SCRABBLE

The word puzzles that are featured in many daily newspapers date back only to December 21, 1913, when the first one appeared in the New York *World*'s Sunday supplement, *Fun*. The creator was journalist Arthur Wynne. He had grown up in Victorian-era England, where children's puzzle books and other periodicals printed word squares—groups of words arranged so that they read alike both horizontally and vertically. Wynne's grandfather had shown him a very basic puzzle, Magic Square. The words necessary to complete the puzzle were given.

Wynne's innovation was to give clues instead of words. The first crossword puzzle appeared along with several other "mental exercises," and featured simple clues to familiar words. The public liked solving the puzzle, and by the early 1920s almost all the major newspapers were carrying crosswords. The puzzles began growing in sophistication and complexity, their interlocking words often taking hours instead of minutes to complete. In 1924 crossword puzzle books claimed the top four spots on the national best-seller list. Dictionaries began selling better than ever.

The crossword fad spread back to England in the mid-1920s and then into almost every other alphabet-based language. So popular were the puzzles that women's fashions in the 1930s often featured crossword designs. Today's challenging puzzles have been hailed as vocabulary builders, entertainment, and a way to keep mentally sharp.

Merry-Go-Round

ALSO KNOWN AS CAROUSEL, ROUNDABOUT
EARLIEST KNOWN: A.D. 500, BYZANTINE EMPIRE
TALLEST: HIMMELSKIBET (TIVOLI GARDENS, DENMARK)

A primitive sort of merry-go-round may have existed as far back as A.D. 500, the date of a Byzantine etching of riders in baskets swinging around a center pole. In the 12th century, Italian and Spanish Crusaders observed Arabian horsemen throwing and catching clay balls filled with perfume—those who missed were scented for days. The Italians called the game *garosello* (little war) and brought it back to Europe, where the French, calling it *carrousel,* turned it into a grand equestrian pageant. In one event, riders rode full tilt and tried to spear dangling rings with their lances. In the late 17th century, young knights sometimes practiced for the tournaments on a mechanical device that featured a wooden horse attached to an arm extending from a center pole that was powered by a mule or servant.

These early carousels became popular with women and children, and by the mid-19th century they had developed into hand-cranked machines with various wooden animals on wheels or arms extending from a rotating center post. Instead of skewering a ring, riders could reach for one, hence the expression "grabbing the brass ring." The stage was set for a breakthrough in carousel design.

In 1870 English engineer-manufacturer Frederick Savage devised an efficient way to turn a carousel by steam power. Gone were the mules and hand cranks. A few years later another Englishman invented a device for making the animals move up and down, as though galloping. Soon carousels were built that could hold two or three rows of animals. Elaborately carved and painted carousels, playing spirited band and calliope music, began appearing at fairs and seaside resorts.

The late 1800s was a golden age of carousel making on both sides of the Atlantic. Two immigrant woodworkers, Gustav Dentzel of Germany and Charles Looff of Denmark, built a number of elegant carousels on the East Coast, featuring a menagerie of colorful painted animals.

PARALLEL HISTORY

Sudoku

Immensely popular in recent years, Sudoku dates as far back as 1783, when Swiss mathematician Leonhard Euler created Latin Squares. In Euler's puzzle every number or symbol had to appear only once in each row or column of a grid. In the late 1970s Dell puzzle magazines began publishing a nine-by-nine grid puzzle called Number Place. Then, in the 1980s, a Japanese publisher refined the game and called it Sudoku, combining *su* (number) and *doku* (unique). Sudoku came back West when a retired judge from New Zealand saw a puzzle in a Japanese bookshop in 1997, developed a computer program to create Sudoku, and in 2004 persuaded The "Times" of London to publish them.

Circus

ORIGIN: ANCIENT ROME, CIRCUS MAXIMUS
FIRST U.S. CIRCUS: PHILADELPHIA, 1793
TOP ACTS: JUGGLING, TRAPEZE, TIGHTROPE, STILTS

Circuses have always been crowd-pleasing spectacles. Yet little else remains in common with the oldest circuses. Whereas today's acrobats and showmen work in close harmony together, the performers in ancient Rome engaged in contests that often ended in death.

The original and largest Roman circus was a racecourse called the Circus Maximus, built under Julius Caesar in the first century B.C. Holding up to 150,000 seats, this tremendous structure was modeled after the Greeks' hippodrome, an oval racetrack. By the fourth century A.D. its length was seven times that of a modern football field. The seven-lap chariot races held here were the main event, though bloodier exhibitions often took place as well. Admission was free, but you could buy wines and pastries, and make arrangements with bookies or prostitutes. The place to go for the best blood sports was an amphitheater, of which the Colosseum was the largest. Up to 50,000 at a time could watch executioners torturing Christians, wild animals tearing apart criminals, and gladiators battling to the death. In one pageant, 2,000 gladiators and 230 beasts were scheduled to die. By the sixth century the Roman spectacles were over.

During the Middle Ages, occasional itinerant troupes of tumblers, jugglers, and animal trainers played at country fairs. But the modern circus got its start in 1768 with a show put on by British impresario and trick horseback rider Philip Astley. To musical accompaniment, Astley galloped in a tight circle standing on a horse, affixed by centrifugal force. He later included acrobats, ropedancers on tightrope, and a clown, all performing within the circular structure that became known as Astley's Circus.

A similar circus opened in Philadelphia in 1793, the first in America. By the 1870s traveling circuses had become well established—elephants and colorful wagons would parade through a town to draw attention to the show.

Roller Coasters

MADE OF WOOD OR STEEL
FIRST STEEL COASTER: DISNEYLAND, 1959
FIRST 360-DEGREE ROLL: KNOTT'S BERRY FARM, 1975

Among the most popular rides in modern amusement parks, roller coasters originated with giant ice slides in 16th- and 17th-century Russia. Soaring up to 70 feet high, the steep wooden slides were slick with ice; riders descended on blocks of wood or ice and landed in sandpiles. By 1817 the French had two roller coasters on wheels. The one known as the Russian Mountains of Belleville had carts with axles that fit into a groove in the track. A looping roller coaster was built in Paris in around 1846, the 13-foot-diameter loop besting a 6.5-foot loop ride in England.

The forerunner to American roller coasters were narrow gauge railways that had carried coal over the mountains. One of the earliest, the Mauch Chunk Switchback Railway in Pennsylvania, was refitted to carry passengers on scenic tours for a dollar a ride. The first real American roller coaster was built in 1884 on Coney Island in New York City. Passengers paid five cents, then walked up a 50-foot-high stairway to get in the car. Facing sideways, they descended a gentle, undulating track for 600 feet until gravity stopped the ride. By the 1920s North America had some 2,000 roller coasters. That number dropped considerably during and after the Great Depression years, but the 1970s and '80s saw a resurgence of coaster building; tubular steel was used in the construction of twisting loops, sharp drop-offs, and other scream-worthy designs.

The oldest roller coaster still in existence is the 1902 Leap-the-Dips coaster, designed and built by the Edward Joy Morris Company for Lakemont Park in Altoona, Pennsylvania. Restored in 1999, the national historic landmark ride in the shape of a figure eight features an oak track and dips of no greater than nine feet. With modern coasters capable of exceeding 120 miles an hour, Leap-the-Dip's ten-mile-an-hour average harks back to a tamer age.

Country Club

OLDEST: THE COUNTRY CLUB, BROOKLINE, MA (1882)
EARLY ACTIVITIES: FOXHUNTING, ICE SKATING,
TENNIS, HORSEBACK RIDING, GOLF

After the Civil War, wealthy families who wanted to escape the cities during the summer needed a convenient place to socialize with their peers and enjoy outdoor recreation. In 1882, Bostonian J. Murray Forbes organized a group of his elite friends to purchase a tract of rolling land in the suburb of Brookline, southwest of Boston. They converted a farmhouse into a clubhouse, with rooms for dining, playing cards and billiards, and spending the night. Eventually they added a bowling alley, grass tennis courts, a golf course, polo fields, and a horseracing track. There was also skeet shooting and afternoon concerts. All these activities cost members $50 a year (about $1,000 in today's money).

Called The Country Club, the Brookline institution became a model for similar clubs throughout the United States. The spread of trolley and train lines made movement out to the suburbs much easier, and since gentlemen's downtown clubs offered no amenities for women and children, the new country clubs filled a growing need. While they were inclusive of families, part of the attraction of the clubs was their exclusivity. Membership was by invitation only. Money was important, but not a guarantee of an invitation. Until the late 20th century, blacks, Jews, and sometimes Catholics were excluded from the most prominent country clubs.

In the early days of The Country Club, members did not always see eye to eye. Golf was a new sport, and many equestrians thought it a nuisance that interfered with their own activities. One rider said that golfers were "idiots intent on chasing a Quinine pill around a cow pasture." On one occasion some 30 golfers were arrested for playing on Sunday, in defiance of state blue laws. The game only grew in popularity, as did country clubs—by the turn of the century there were more than 1,000.

UNCOMMONLY KNOWN ...

Fireworks A tenth-century Chinese cook accidentally mixed saltpeter (a preservative), sulfur (a heat intensifier), and charcoal (fuel). The resulting explosion started an industry. Loaded into bamboo, the explosives would shoot up. These "flying arrows of fire" soon became an integral part of New Year's, weddings, and other celebrations.

Piano

FROM ITALIAN "PIANOFORTE" (SOFT-LOUD)
BARTOLOMEO CRISTOFORI, FLORENCE, 1709
STANDARD MODERN PIANO: 88 KEYS, 3 PEDALS

Devilishly hard to master but unrivaled for learning the elements of music, the piano has become a standard piece of American furniture. The instrument dates from the early 1700s, but there were several forerunners. The dulcimer, a stringed instrument played with hammers, was probably of ancient Middle Eastern origin. By the 1400s, Europeans were playing a keyboard called the clavichord, which had metal blades called tangents that struck the strings. Since the tangent stayed against the string until the key was released, the player could alter the pitch. More widespread was the harpsichord, which appeared in the 14th century and remained popular through the 18th. On the harpsichord, leather picks called plectra pluck the strings, giving a tinny sound of uniform volume.

In the first decade of the 18th century, Italian harpsichord builder Bartolomeo Cristofori invented what he called an *arpicembalo che fà il piano e il forte* (harpsichord that can play quietly and loudly). His innovation was a mechanism that gave the player control over the volume—strike the key more forcefully, and a louder tone results. After the note was struck, its hammer withdrew so that it could be played again immediately. At last there was a keyboard that gave the player an almost full range of musical expression.

In the late 1700s and early 1800s, several improvements were made on the pianoforte, as it was called. The action (keyboard mechanism) contained several thousand parts. A fuller and richer sound resulted, and most of the major composers by then were writing works for the piano. The most famous American pianomaker, Henry Englehard Steinway (1797-1871), emigrated from Germany and founded a company that made high-quality pianos with large cast-iron frames and bass strings strung diagonally over others.

American-made instruments gained more respect when a Baldwin grand became the first one to win the Grand Prix Award at the 1900 Paris International Exposition. The social culture of the piano in America has been significant. A stringed or woodwind instrument requires training to play in tune, but a piano's keys do not need to be adjusted constantly during performance, making it an ideal instrument to have in a home. Of course, the strings of a piano, struck again and again by its felt-covered hammers, do need to be tuned from time to time, which is a task done solely by the professional piano tuner, rarely by an individual owner. In the home, multiple players could take lessons on a single piano, and as they progressed, play hymns, popular songs, and many other compositions.

The piano was considered proper for young women to learn, but its presence and playing also provided entertainment that, in the 18th, 19th, and early 20th centuries, had not been supplanted by radio, TV, or the Internet. Since so many Western families wanted their children to become proficient piano players, a number of teaching methods sprang up: for example, the Lethko-Palmer Method is still published under the Alfred's Basic Piano Library series.

The first "electric" pianos were made by Harold Rhodes, who called them "electronified," in the 1940s. Rhodes operated a 40-studio piano chain, then gave piano lessons to his fellow soliders while serving in World War II. He even rigged up a partially electric piano for USO events. The instrument that came out of this, the Fender Rhodes piano, became an important part of late 20th-century music, including jazz, rock, and funk.

PARALLEL HISTORY

Kennedy Center

The U.S. Congress passed legislation in 1958 creating a national center for the performing arts in Washington, D.C., although the Kennedy Center, dedicated to the memory of assassinated President John F. Kennedy, wasn't completed until 1971. It marked the first time the government allocated federal monies to this cause, and the unique combination of public and private stewardship has made the performing arts center world famous. Designed by architect Edward Durrell Stone, the white marble building on the Potomac near the Watergate complex opened on September 8, 1971, with a performance of Leonard Bernstein's "Mass" dedicated to Kennedy's memory.

An amazing invention—but who would ever want to use one?

−RUTHERFORD B. HAYES (1822-93), ON THE INVENTION OF THE TELEPHONE

Tools & Innovations

From the first shapers of stone and wood tools up to the computer scientists and biotech wizards of today, people have been inventing things to improve their lives or to gain an advantage over other people. Sometimes, as with guns or nuclear devices, the original purpose (warfare) might be adapted for a different use (hunting, electrical energy). Often, an inventor works simply out of curiosity, the thrill of creating something new. Though inventions and innovations have sprung up throughout human history, some periods have been especially fruitful. During the Renaissance a demand for books almost forced the invention of a European printing press, one of the key moments in civilization. The industrial revolution brought together science and industry to create life-altering inventions in transportation, communication, and other fields. By the mid-19th century, the industrial world was producing a host of new products using interchangeable, machine-made parts. American inventors such as Alexander Graham Bell and Thomas Edison patented all kinds of machines that we find indispensable today, and their work proves a key point. It has never been enough for an inventor simply to have a good idea—seeing it through the patenting process and into market takes another kind of talent and persistence. Ideas are in the air at any given moment, but few people have the commercial savvy to make them into sellable products. Another interesting concept arises from these short histories—the dead end. Many seemingly great inventions were either ahead of their time (e.g., the 1890s battery-operated car) or they were simply replaced by better inventions—thus the steam car gave way to the gas-powered car, the telegram faded with the rise of the fax, and mechanical television had no future compared with electronic TV.

Tools

Among the oldest of tools, the ax and plow date well back into the Stone Age. With the Bronze and Iron Ages, agricultural and other tools became more effective and durable. Not until the Industrial Age of the 18th and 19th centuries did a major shift begin taking place. With a ready supply of steel and a proliferation of small, mechanized parts, factories began cranking out new machinery and improved versions of old implements. Advances in chemistry and other sciences helped refine toolmaking; gradually steam, gasoline, and electric motors took over from hand tools.

Matches

PRE-19TH-CENTURY FIRES WERE MADE FROM:
STRIKING FLINT AGAINST STEEL, RUBBING STICKS
KEY INGREDIENT IN MODERN MATCH: PHOSPHORUS

Until the early 19th century, the standard way to create fire was to strike flint against steel. In 1680 British chemist Robert Boyle made fire by drawing a sulfur-tipped splinter of wood through a piece of paper coated with phosphorus. But phosphorus was a newly discovered and expensive element, and more than 100 years would go by until scientists turned their attention to household matches.

As early as 1805 French chemists began making "ethereal matches"—splinters tipped with potassium chlorate (an oxidizing salt), sugar, and gum arabic. The matches were dipped into a bottle of sulfuric acid; when pulled out, the match tip combusted. Another variation, the Promethean, was a match tipped with an acid-containing glass bead; the user would break the glass, exposing the treated tip to air, and the match would ignite.

The real breakthrough came by accident in 1826. English pharmacist John Walker was stirring a mixture of antimony sulfide, potassium chlorate, sulfur, and gum. To clean the stirrer off, he scraped it on the stone floor and it caught fire. Walker had just invented the friction match. Though Walker did not patent his invention, three-inch matches called lucifers soon hit the market. Lit by drawing them through folded sandpaper, they showered the user with sparks and gave off such a pungent odor that warnings were printed on the box for people whose lungs were delicate.

Manufacturers began tipping matches in phosphorus, which made it possible to strike them on any rough surface. The phosphorus created another health hazard (see Parallel History, opposite), and there was still the problem of unwanted sparks. The safety match came along in 1844, the product of Swedish chemist Gustave Pasch, who removed some of the igniting ingredients from the match and put them in the striking surface. A new industry was born; well into the 20th century the Swedish Match Company supplied most of the world's matches.

Candles

DESCENDED FROM: TORCHES, OIL LAMPS
EARLY WAX: ANIMAL FAT, BEESWAX, SPERM WHALE OIL
19TH CENTURY POPULARIZED PETROLEUM-BASED WAX

According to many sources, candles have been around since at least 3000 B.C. Used in Egypt and Crete, these candles had no wicks. They were torches, or rushlights, made by soaking the cores of reeds in tallow, a tasteless solid rendering from animal or vegetable fat. By the first century A.D., the Romans had developed candles with wicks. The tallow was generally made from the fat of cattle or sheep. Wicks of paper or cotton would draw up melting wax, which vaporized as it burned and thus produced light. But oil lamps were still preferred; candles were smoky and acrid and gave off low illumination, and the wicks constantly had to be trimmed so that the tallow burned efficiently.

During the Middle Ages, beeswax was substituted for tallow, and candles improved greatly—wax burned brighter and without a smoky flame. But the expense of wax candles made them affordable only by the wealthy. Tallow continued in use throughout the candle age, which lasted until the rise of gaslights in the early 19th century. Wick trimming was such a demanding job that large households had "snuff servants" who maintained the candles. A castle might go through hundreds of candles in a week, keeping snuffers constantly busy. Trimming a wick often put out the flame, hence the word *snuff* came to mean "extinguish."

By the 18th century, candle use reached a peak. A new, longer burning wax was made from the oil of sperm whales, and in North America bayberry wax, though time-consuming to extract, produced a sweet-smelling candle. In 1784, Benjamin Franklin estimated that Parisians in the wintertime burned their candles for seven hours every night, consuming a half pound of wax or tallow per hour. By the mid-1800s paraffin wax (from petroleum) and stearic acid became the main ingredients of candles.

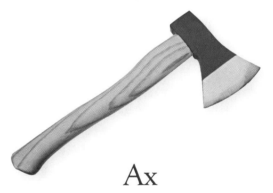

Ax

DATES TO STONE AGE
BLADE MADE FIRST FROM BRONZE, THEN IRON, STEEL
USES: CLEARING FORESTS, SPLITTING WOOD FOR FIRES

Among the oldest and most useful of tools, the ax dates back well into prehistory. Stone Age toolmakers were fashioning axes with wooden or bone handles around 30,000 years ago. The heads were lashed

---

PARALLEL HISTORY

Phossy Jaw

The spread of easy-to-light phosphorus-tipped matches in the 1830s led to a debilitating condition known as phossy jaw. Fumes from white phosphorus can cause necrosis of the bones, especially in the jaw. Factory workers were particularly susceptible, and as the industry grew, hundreds of people were affected; many died. Babies who sucked on match heads developed deformed skeletons. The problem only escalated through the century. Then in 1900 the Diamond Match Company bought a French patent for a nonpoisonous flame-starting chemical called phosphorus sesquisulfide. The formula failed to work in the U.S. climate, but in 1911 an engineer appropriately named William Fairburn adjusted it, and phossy jaw flamed out.

onto the handles with whatever fibrous material was available; a split in the wood was often used as the point of attachment. By about 4000 B.C., the beginning of the Bronze Age, Egyptians began making ax blades of bronze. These were followed sometime before 1000 B.C. by iron axes.

The problem with iron axes was that they were hard to hone to a sharp edge. Welding steel onto the blade helped solve the problem, since steel could hold its edge better under stress. But until the late 19th century steel—a refined iron with low carbon content—was rare and expensive. Small amounts had been made by the Haya of eastern Africa and people in southern India as far back as 300 B.C. In the Middle Ages, Europeans made some steel in special furnaces, but a great deal of time and labor was spent to produce a small quantity of steel. Furthermore, steel blades would often bend or twist unless the ax wielder consistently struck with even blows.

Nevertheless, iron or steel axes did the monumental work of clearing the great forests of Europe and the Americas for agriculture starting in the Middle Ages. In the 18th century, polled axes became standard in America. The poll was a projecting blunt end opposite the blade. It made the ax heavier and thus more powerful, and it balanced the ax by shifting the center of gravity farther away from the blade. By the 1880s, manufacturers were selling more than 100 varieties of felling ax, with such names as Kentucky, Main, Turpentine, and Fire Engine.

Jefferson's Plow

In 1788 Thomas Jefferson, while serving as U.S. minister to France, designed what he called a "mouldboard of least resistance." Though he never patented it, he had several built and sent to friends. Whether his invention influenced future plow design is unclear, but Jefferson declared that a plow with his iron moldboard was "so light that the two small horses or mules draw it with less labor than I have ever before seen necessary. It does beautiful work and is approved by everyone." Furthermore, they were easy to make "by the coarsest workman, by a process so exact, that its form shall never be varied by a single hair's breadth."

Plow

EARLY PLOWS PULLED BY MAN, OXEN, OR HORSES
WHEELED PLOW: INTRODUCED MIDDLE AGES, EUROPE
20TH-CENTURY PLOW POWER: STEAM, LATER GAS

Prehistoric people discovered that seeds planted in loosened soil fared better than those that had merely been pushed into holes in the ground. The digging stick became one of the first agricultural implements. The first plows, dating back some 8,000 years, most likely were forked branches. One person pulled the branch so that a sharpened end dragged along the ground; another person pushed down on the other, raised fork. By the second millennium B.C., the Egyptians were breaking their topsoil with wooden plows pulled by harnessed oxen. The Romans added iron shares (blades) to plows, but they found that these plows were too light to handle the stiffer soils of northern Europe.

The development of the wheeled plow, dragged by oxen and then horses, in the early Middle Ages made possible the spread of agriculture throughout Europe. Appearing around the 16th century, moldboards were a major step forward. A curved plate attached over a plowshare, the moldboard would lift and turn a slice of furrowed ground, thus more thoroughly churning the soil.

Plow design changed little until the 19th century, when American ingenuity faced the task of cultivating vast tracts of untilled land. In 1837 a Vermont inventor named John Deere made a steel plow that would function well in the prairie sod. His smooth moldboards cut cleanly through the sticky soil. Within 20 years he was selling 10,000 plows a year. Deere and other makers began turning out sulky plows, which permitted a farmer to ride and thus gain better control. The first steam-powered plows came along in the early 1900s.

Wheelbarrow

INVENTED IN ABOUT A.D. 200 IN CHINA
DESCENDED FROM CHINESE RICE PADDY CARTS
CHINESE MODEL INTRODUCED TO EUROPE IN 17TH CENT.

A one-wheeled cart seems like such an obvious tool that it may come as a surprise that it was not invented until around A.D. 200. The Chinese before that time were using two-wheeled carts in their rice paddies. But the carts were always slipping off the narrow impoundment walls that bordered the flooded fields. Somebody had the idea of putting one big wheel under the cart; suddenly the embankments were easier to negotiate. The Chinese military then began using the wheelbarrow—which they called "wooden ox" or "gliding horse"—to transport supplies and dead and wounded soldiers.

Chinese wheelbarrows were unknown in Europe when medieval miners and construction workers came up with a novel solution for carrying loads through narrow passageways. They were accustomed to hauling things in a two-man hod—a long trough with handles in the front and rear. Someone had the ingenious idea of replacing one set of

handles with a wheel, thus making it possible for one man to do the work of two.

The new European wheelbarrow, though, was not as well designed as the Chinese model. With the wheel out front instead of directly beneath the cart, the carrier still had a large burden to lift and push; with the Chinese wheelbarrow the weight was borne by the cart. European laborers got along well enough, hauling stones for the great castles and cathedrals of the 12th to 15th centuries. Finally, during the 17th century, with increased trade between Europe and China, word arrived of a marvelous Chinese wheelbarrow. Soon wheelbarrows began appearing in Europe with the cart over the wheel.

Cotton Gin

INVENTED BY: ELI WHITNEY
WIDELY COPIED DESPITE MARCH 14, 1794, PATENT
REVOLUTIONIZED COTTON INDUSTRY IN U.S. SOUTH

Gins, or engines, for removing the seeds of cotton from the fibers have been in existence in simple form since first appearing in ancient India. Mechanized rollers did the work.

But not all kinds of cotton seeds cooperated. The black-seed, long-staple variety that grew along the United States southern coast could be cleaned by being pressed through a pair of rollers, but not the green-seed, short-staple variety that grew inland. Lots of arable southern land had the potential to feed the European demand for cotton, but the work, even with slaves, was too slow.

A mechanically minded Yale graduate named Eli Whitney was studying law while working in Savannah, Georgia, in 1793, paying for his keep at a plantation house by repairing things. One night some guests were discussing how unprofitable green-seed cotton was. Whitney saw an opportunity and began designing a four-part, hand-cranked gin. A hopper fed the cotton into a revolving cylinder covered with little wire teeth that meshed up with narrow grooves on a breastwork through which the fiber, but not the seeds, could pass; a roller with brushes then removed the fiber from the hooks. The gin did the work of 50 people in one day. Later models would do 50 times the work of the original.

Swiss Army Knife

DESCENDED FROM 15TH-CENTURY FOLDING PENKNIFE
NAMED FOR: MULTI-TOOL KNIFE USED BY SWISS ARMY
TODAY'S MODELS CAN HAVE MORE THAN 30 GADGETS

O ne of the earliest pocketknives, the folding penknife has been around since at least the 15th century. Through the 18th

---

century it came in handy for sharpening the dull end of a quill pen. The longer-bladed, all-purpose jackknife was in existence by the early 1700s.

From about 1886, all soldiers in the Swiss Army were issued a wooden-handled pocketknife. A few years later the army began using a new kind of rifle that could be opened with a screwdriver. So a screwdriver was added to the standard-issue knife, along with an awl, reamer, and can opener. These first, tool-loaded Swiss Army knives were made in Germany, but in 1891 Swiss silverware manufacturer Karl Elsener founded the Swiss Silverware Guild in order to supply his country's army. Among the different kinds of pocketknives he designed, the most popular was the Officer's Knife, a lightweight knife with two blades and four tools, including a corkscrew.

Within a couple of years, Elsener's company had competition from another silverware manufacturer. The Swiss Army diplomatically decided to buy half its knives from each company. After the death of Elsener's mother in 1909, he gave her name, Victoria, to his line of knives. With the appearance of nonrusting stainless steel in the 1920s, the name was changed to Victorinox (the "inox" meaning "does not oxidize"). Today the red-covered Swiss Army knife, with the Swiss cross logo, comes in a number of models, including the Officer's Knife and the SwissChamp, the latter featuring more than 30 gadgets.

Today the celebrated "Officer's Knife" comes in more than 100 different combinations of tools, blades, and sizes and can be found in places ranging from NASA expeditions to the Museum of Modern Art in Manhattan. About 34,000 are made each day at the factory in Porrentruy, Switzerland. The largest Swiss Army knife is the 33-tool/feature "Swisschamp."

Communication

From cave scratchings to the computer, we have come a long way. Prehistoric people used charcoal, the Egyptians had reed pens, medieval readers relied on scribes, and since the 1970s we have had personal computers. Our communication tools today span a wide range of instruments, from the wooden pencil to the digital-signaled television. The journey from ink to keystroke took thousands of years, that from telephone to wireless a mere quarter of a century. The dizzying speed of our breakthroughs in communication technology calls for a look back in history at how we got here so fast.

Pencil

DESCENDED FROM: CHARCOAL WRITING TOOLS
GRAPHITE: FROM GREEK "GRAPHEIN" (TO WRITE)
AMOUNT OF CLAY IN GRAPHITE DETERMINES LEAD SOFTNESS

Prehistoric people discovered that charcoal could be used for drawing on stone or wood; a thinner piece of coal would make a finer mark. But it was not until the 1500s, with the discovery of another form of carbon, that the first real pencils were made. Near Keswick in England's Lake District in about 1564 a mine was found that contained graphite, a less porous carbon material that could be used for writing. The Europeans may not have known that the Aztecs of Central America had been writing with graphite before Hernán Cortés arrived in 1519.

The first pencils were simply sticks of graphite, but since these tended to stain the hand of the user, pencils became encased in rope and then wood. By the early 17th century, both the British and the Germans were making wooden pencils that held rods of graphite, called lead, which it resembled. There was a precedent dating back to the early Greeks for using flat pieces of lead to trace faint lines on paper—the lines served as guide marks they could use for writing in ink. The first pencil factory was founded in Nürnberg, Germany, in 1662.

The Keswick mine yielded the purest graphite ever discovered, and long before it gave out in 1833 people were looking for a way to dilute its graphite and thus keep the pencil industry afloat. Enter French chemist Nicolas-Jacques Conté. In 1795 he mixed powdered graphite with clay; when baked the mixture yielded a smooth, hard pencil lead. Varying the proportions of clay and graphite made the lead harder or softer.

Probably the best known brand of American pencils was started by Bavarian immigrant Eberhard Faber, whose great-grandfather began making pencils in 1761. Moving to New York in 1848 at age 26, Faber sold Bavarian-made pencils until deciding to open his own factory in 1861.

Pen

EARLIEST: INK-FILLED REEDS (EGYPT), 4000 B.C.
QUILL PENS: USED FROM SIXTH CENT. B.C.-19TH CENT.
IDIOMATIC: "THE PEN IS MIGHTIER THAN THE SWORD"

A
s far back as 4000 B.C., the Egyptians were writing with crude pens made of hollowed reeds. What kind of ink they used is unknown, but within 1,500 years they had an ink composed of soot, lamp oil, and gelatin from donkey bones. By the 13th century B.C. the Greeks were using the penlike stylus, but it was really an etching tool for writing on clay or wax tablets. The Chinese in the first millennium B.C. inked characters with brushes made of camel or rat hair.

In the sixth century B.C. a new kind of pen was developed that would serve until the 19th century. Quill pens were made from the wing feathers of such large birds as geese and swans. The shafts were hardened and the points angled and slit; dipped in ink, they drew the liquid up by capillary action. Europeans were using them by the sixth century A.D.; crow feathers were preferred for finer work, such as drawing.

The first steel pens were introduced in London in 1803, and in 1828 the first machine-made metallic pens were rolled out in Birmingham, England. These still operated on the quill principle, requiring constant dipping in ink. Fountain pens, with the

---

UNCOMMONLY KNOWN . . .
Medieval Scribes Before the appearance of the printing press in the 15th century, the only way to create books and articles was by hand. During the Middle Ages, monks laboring in workshops called "scriptoriums" produced the majority of manuscripts. These scribes were the first to use capital letters, punctuation, and spacing between words.

---

ink contained in the pen, had been experimented with since the mid-1600s, but it was not until 1884 that the first practical one was introduced to the public. The inventor was New York insurance salesman Lewis Edson Waterman, who reputedly was inspired when a leaky pen ruined a contract he had prepared for a client. He lost the client but invented a pen that would reliably channel ink from an interior reservoir to the nib.

Printing Press

DESCENDED FROM: ASIAN WOODBLOCK PRINTING
FIRST MOVABLE TYPE: CHINA, CA 1045
FIRST MODERN PRESS: JOHANNES GUTENBERG, 1440s

T
he wonder is that a printing press didn't appear earlier. The technology had long been in existence. By the eighth century the Chinese, Japanese, and Koreans were printing texts on paper with wood blocks. Movable, reusable type appeared in China around 1045 when printer Bi Sheng molded clay characters, but the number of characters necessary made the system unwieldy, and it did not evolve. The Koreans made further progress with typography, one printer having a set of 100,000 cast bronze characters by the early 1400s.

The technology slowly trickled into a Europe awakening from centuries of religious superstition into a cultural Renaissance. Paper began replacing parchment by the 12th century, and wood-block printing began two centuries later. As the demand for books soared, block printing and hand copying could not keep up.

In Germany in the 1440s, Johannes Gutenberg and his associates adapted wine press mechanics to create the first printing press. He put cast metal letters into composing sticks to form lines of a page; these were locked into a metal form, which was attached to a surface called the platen, which hung above the press bed. The type was then inked, paper was placed on the bed, and the platen was lowered and pressed down with a heavy, handle-turned screw to imprint evenly on the paper. Gutenberg's press could crank out 300 pages a day. Copies of the famous Gutenberg Bible came out in about 1455. It was designed to look like manuscript Bibles, with woven text and illuminated initial letters.

PARALLEL HISTORY

Ballpoint Pen

Today's most common writing instrument took decades to develop. A ballpoint pen was patented in 1888, but it was of poor quality (as were many subsequent models), the ink either leaking and smudging or else drying up within the pen. The first successful ballpoint was designed in 1935 by a Hungarian named Ladislas Biro while he was living in Argentina. The cost of the pen was high and the quality imperfect, and French high school dropout Marcel Bich sensed a market. In the late 1940s his new plastic-bodied Bic ballpoints went on sale; by 1952 he was selling 42 million a year.

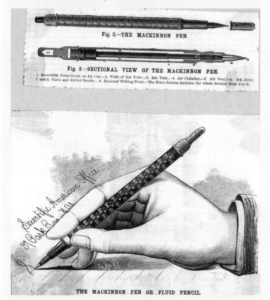

Duncan MacKinnon, Canadian pen inventor, founded the MacKinnon Stylograph Company.

By the early 1500s, more than 100 printing presses had produced nine million copies of some 40,000 works. Until the advent of metal presses in the late 18th century, Gutenberg-type machines held sway. Speed then became the object. German printer Friedrich König's steam-powered cylinder press (1811) printed 1,100 pages an hour. In 1847 American industrialist Richard Hoe invented the rotary, or "lightning," press, capable of a blistering 8,000 sheets an hour.

Typewriter

EARLY: RESEMBLED A PIANO'S SIZE, MECHANISM
FIRST USABLE: CHRISTOPHER LATHAM SHOLES, 1867
ELECTRIC MODELS POPULARIZED 1920s

The first known try at a typewriter was a 1714 British patent for "an Artificial machine or Method for the Impressing or Transcribing of Letters Singly or Progressively one after another, as in Writing, whereby all Writing whatever may be Engrossed in Paper or Parchment so Neat and Exact as not to be distinguished from Print." Whether this thoroughly titled machine was ever made is not known. For the next 153 years various other attempts were made, including models the size of a piano, but they were all slower than handwriting.

In 1867 American inventor Christopher Latham Sholes created the world's first practical typewriter. The next year he patented a second model, and in 1874, under a contract with gunmaker E. Remington and Sons, the first typewriters were marketed. These typewriters included most of the principal features that would remain standard—key levers and wires to move the type bars (metal arms with characters on the end); a semicircular arrangement of type bars, each hitting at the paper's center; an inked ribbon; an escapement, moving the carriage after each keystroke; and a cylinder with both line-spacing and carriage-return mechanisms.

Early typists found that with quick typing the type bars often jammed together. Sholes came up with a system still universal on keyboards today. Known as QWERTY, for the letters on the upper line, the new arrangement of keys separated letters that were most commonly grouped together so that jamming would occur less frequently.

Thomas Edison invented an electric printing-wheel typewriter in 1872, but electric typewriters did not become office equipment until the 1920s. With electrification, typewriters or keyboards could adapt to serve a growing number of communications devices—the ticker tape printer, the teletype machine (from the telegraph), and a computer interface. Despite new applications, the "QWERTY" keyboard remains the most common one used.

UNCOMMONLY KNOWN...

Printed Books The first books were Egyptian papyrus rolls written around 2700 B.C. By 1000 B.C. the Chinese began making books by binding together printed strips of bamboo or wood. Most of the early books were either histories or records of government and business. By around 500 B.C., the Greeks were writing books in the form of papyrus scrolls, as were the Romans a few centuries later.

Writing Instruments

At some point early in human history, men and women realized that the hands they used to pick up and grasp things and to gesture could also be used to make marks for other people to "read." The earliest writing implement was no doubt someone's index finger, marking a spot to remember in dirt or sand. But once we humans realized that we could make marks, language began. The interesting thing about the writing implements pictured here is that while they can be used to form pictures, characters, symbols, and letters in many different systems and languages, the implements themselves can be the same. They change over time, not between cultures. Thus, a reed pen might have been used to copy texts in Latin or Old French, a quill pen documents in English or Spanish. Among the factors causing writing implements to change over time were the availability of materials (reeds, quills, metal) and manufacturing methods (for example, ballpoint pens depend on reliable capsules for a particular "slip" of ink). While very few modern humans use a stylus or a quill pen on a regular basis, each of these methods still works if you want to write something down. The pen may or may not be mightier than the sword, but it's certainly easier to pick up and hold.

8500 B.C.
Stylus The earliest styli were probably twigs used to scratch symbols and markings into clay. The Romans developed metal versions to use on thin wax sheets attached to wooden tablets; when something needed deletion, the blunt end of the stylus could rub it out.

2000 B.C.
Reed pens Reed pens were used for thousands of years, and could be quite sophisticated, with slits for nibs that allowed ink to flow continuously onto a page. Simple yet effective, these pens would have been the instrument of choice at the time the New Testament was written.

Neon

FROM THE GREEK "NEOS" (NEW)
NEON GAS UNDISCOVERED UNTIL 1898
FIRST NEON SIGN: "THE PALACE HAIRDRESSER," PARIS, 1912

By distilling liquid air, British chemists William Ramsay and Morris Travers discovered a new rare gas in 1898. They named it neon for the Greek *neos* (new). The odorless gas had a reddish orange glow, which flamed an intense red when charged with electricity. As far back as 1675, scientists had observed the phenomenon of electric discharge or vapor light. A mercury barometer tube gave off a faint light when shaken. Not until the 19th century was it understood that agitating mercury produced static electricity, which excited the mercury's atoms. More electricity caused mercury to glow blue; charged carbon dioxide gave off white light; helium, gold.

The first person to make a neon light was French physicist Georges Claude, who in 1909 charged neon in an airless glass tube. No filament was necessary; instead, the gas itself created a luminous line between two electrodes. Back in 1855 a German glassblower named Heinrich Geissler had made a mercury vapor light by applying electricity to a glass-filled tube. But Claude's work came at the dawn of the electrical age, so when he

1570
Pencil Since the introduction of a stick of graphite encased by wood in the 16th century, the humble pencil has gained a built-in eraser and comes in various shapes and sizes, with different thicknesses and lead densities.

1935
Ballpoint pen
Ladislas Biro and his brother Georg invented the first working ballpoint pen in 1935 in Budapest, Hungary, and patented it in 1938. The British still refer to ballpoint pens as "biros."

A.D. 700
Quill pens The cartilage in a quill pen dulled quickly with use and needed to be sharpened frequently, which is where we get the term "penknife." Even if sharpened, quill pens lasted only a week with frequent use. The strongest quills come from live birds.

1884
Fountain pen Fountain pens consist of a nib, a barrel, and a feed mechanism. The first self-filling fountain pen with an integrated rubber bladder was patented by American John Jacob Parker in 1831, but early models did not work very well.

illuminated the Grand Palace in Paris with neon light he demonstrated the commercial possibilities of vapor lighting—and in particular, of neon. In 1912, "The Palace Hairdresser" on Boulevard Montmartre blazed its garish red lettering into the Parisian night, becoming the world's first neon sign.

The Packard auto dealership in Los Angeles put up the first neon sign in North America. Costing $24,000, the neon "Packard" caught the eye of the public. Soon the new "liquid fire" was used for everything from casino advertising to airplane beacons—neon light is visible 20 miles away, even in fog.

Computer

FIRST U.S. AUTOMATIC DIGITAL COMPUTER:
HARVARD MARK I (IBM/HARVARD, 1944)
9,445 POUNDS | 530 MILES OF WIRE | 765,299 PARTS

French scientist and philosopher Blaise Pascal invented the first calculating machine in 1642; gear-driven wheels were capable of adding and subtracting up to eight columns of digits. In the early 1670s German mathematician Gottfried Leibniz, who had helped invent calculus, improved Pascal's calculator so that it could multiply, divide, and extract square roots.

The next step toward computers was made by a French weaver, Joseph-Marie Jacquard, who in 1801 invented a loom that turned out patterns based on punched cards. The English mathematician Charles Babbage was among those inspired by Jacquard. In the 1830s he began work on a grandly

conceived project he called the analytical engine. As envisioned, this new machine would be fed punch cards, work out complex computations, and then store the results in a memory system. It would "weave algebraic patterns as the loom weaves flowers and leaves." Though Babbage spent 40 years on it, the engine was too complex for the technology of the time and was never completed, but his ideas were used by future generations.

In 1888 American inventor Herman Hollerith created an electrical tabulating machine that used punched cards. The machine tabulated the results of the 1890 census, and Hollerith's company became the forerunner of International Business Machines Corporation (IBM). Another key development occurred in the mid-19th century when English mathematician George Boole invented Boolean algebra and logic to perform complex math based on the numbers 0 and 1, the binary system.

Now everything was in place for the first electronic digital computer, which was built by U.S. mathematician and physicist John Atanasoff in 1939. The first general purpose computer debuted seven years later. Known as ENIAC (Electronic Numerical Integrator and Computer), it contained 18,000 vacuum tubes and took up 1,500 square feet. Miniaturization followed with the invention of transistors in 1947 and integrated circuits (connected electronic components on a small silicon chip) in the early 1960s.

It would take another two decades for the "personal computer" to enter people's homes. Today

PARALLEL HISTORY

Carbon Paper

Carbon paper first appeared in about 1806 when an English inventor named Ralph Wedgwood patented a device to help the blind learn to write. Since pens had to be dipped constantly, a sightless person had trouble writing with ink. But with a metal stylus applied to a piece of "carbonated paper"–paper soaked in ink and dried–a consistent supply of ink could be printed on underlying paper. Demand for carbon paper was low until the appearance of typewriters in the 1870s. Coated with wax and carbon black (a pigment), the paper became standard in offices until the spread of photocopy machines in the 1960s.

"PC," which stands for "personal computer," is shorthand for any type of home computer that runs on a Windows operating system, while "Mac" ("Macintosh," made by Apple, Inc.) computers have their own; there are others, too, including the popular Linux. The first home computers were quite basic. If a user wanted to do anything besides the basics, she had to write a program. Today, most computers arrive standardized with software that runs applications without an owner doing much beyond plugging in and switching on. In 1977, about 48,000 home computers were sold; in 2008, the worldwide number hit one billion.

Fax Machine

MADE POSSIBLE BY TELEPHONE AND TELEGRAM
EARLY MODEL: ALEXANDER BAIN, 1842
FAX SHORT FOR FACSIMILE, MEANING "TO COPY"

After the invention of the telegraph in the 1830s, it was not long before people thought of sending printed information electronically from one location to another. Scottish physicist Alexander Bain invented a primitive facsimile device in 1842, but it was not until the arrival of the telephone in the 1870s that a practical fax machine could be developed. The invention of the telegram in about 1900 was a step forward, but ultimately along a dead-end path. Telegrams rely on a telegraph system—a

message is typed in, sent via telegraph, and then received by a printer on the other end.

Faxes work differently. A document is inserted into a feeder, where a scanning device creates electrical signals equivalent to the light and dark spots on the page. These signals are then coded and sent through a telephone line to a receiving machine, which prints out a duplicate of the original document. Early fax machines, in the 1930s, were used by news agencies to send photographs. Instead of fax, the method was called "Telephoto" or "Wirephoto," both trade names. By the 1980s, fax machines had become much smaller, cheaper, and faster, making them a widespread business tool. Before the rise of the Internet, faxing was the quickest way to send copies of documents. In the 1970s, "gonzo" journalist Hunter S. Thompson called the fax machine through which he sent stories to *Rolling Stone* magazine "the mojo wire," likening its speed and wondrous capability to magic.

Telephone

ALEXANDER GRAHAM BELL
MARCH 7, 1876 | U.S. PATENT NO. 174,465
FROM THE GREEK "TELE" (FAR) AND "PHONE" (SOUND)

Mr. Watson, come here, I want you." The words were those of Boston inventor Alexander Graham Bell to his assistant on March 10, 1876 after spilling battery acid on himself. Watson rushed into the adjacent room, and the two of them realized the invention they'd been tinkering with—the transmission of the

human voice through an electrical current—worked. Since that time, untold trillions of words have been spoken on hundreds of millions of telephones around the world.

Bell was not the first person with the idea for a telephone (from the Greek for "far" and "sound"). Since the 1830s, scientists had understood that vibrations in iron or steel could be turned into electrical impulses and hence that sound itself could travel over a wire. But it took an inventor who saw the commercial possibilities of telephony to carry out the work. In 1875 Bell noticed that when Watson was trying to fix a metal reed in their experimental harmonic telegraph, he could distinctly hear the sound—the electrical current had mimicked the variations Watson was making. Excited by the prospects, he went on to patent the telephone in less than a year.

Bell then had to sell his idea. It took more than a year of demonstrations before he could interest the public in his newfangled apparatus. He used a telegraph line to show how the device could work over several miles. It was not long before separate telephone lines were being strung. Those earliest lines connected individual phones—each connected to every single one. To cut down on the tangle of wires, centralized switchboards were set up. Until the early 1900s, and in rural areas until the 1950s (and possibly even 1960s, in some remote areas), switchboard operators manually connected all telephone calls.

Just like its service, over the years the form of the telephone has changed. Early models looked like wooden boxes with metal bells attached. As time went on, large dials were developed, and these led to phones with buttons that could be pressed (easier on people's fingers).

Record Player

PHONOGRAPH: INVENTED BY THOMAS EDISON, 1877
FIRST RECORD (DISC) PLAYERS: EARLY 1900s
DISCS: WAX-BASED, THEN SHELLAC/ALUMINUM, VINYL

When Thomas Edison invented the phonograph in 1877, he gave the world the first machine that could record and play back sounds. It featured a diaphragm attached to a vibrating stylus that made grooves in a turning, tinfoil-wrapped cylinder. The depth of the grooves made a record of the sound waves; to play them back, the cylinder was spun again, with the stylus just touching the foil. For the first time in history the human voice could be stored and reproduced.

Subsequent machines would improve upon the sound's fidelity—its likeness to the original. A wax cylinder was the first advance, followed in the late 1880s by a flat disc developed by German inventor Emile Berliner, who called his machine a Gramophone. Edison also began making discs and disc-playing machines, and by about 1915 they had replaced cylinders. The 78-rpm record could hold about 3.5 minutes of sound per side.

Early record players were cranked by hand, and a correct playback could occur only if the record spun at a consistent speed. Electric motors began replacing hand-cranked mechanisms by the late 1800s. The discs themselves evolved from wax (heavy-metal soap with a wax gel) to shellac on an aluminum base to vinyl by the 1940s. In 1948

Columbia brought out its 12-inch long-playing record. With 23 minutes of playing time per side at 33 ⅓ rpm, the LP soon replaced the 78 as the standard record.

Recording on magnetic tape started in the late 1920s with U.S. and German patents for a tape made by coating a strip of paper with magnetic particles. By the late 1950s and early 1960s, recordings in stereo sound were being marketed to the public both on disc and on tape. By the early 1980s, sales of cassette tapes began edging out those of discs.

Radio

FIRST TRANSATLANTIC WIRELESS SIGNAL: 1901
FIRST RADIO BROADCAST OF VOICE AND MUSIC: 1906
FIRST PRESIDENTIAL BROADCAST: WOODROW WILSON, 1919

It had been only 25 years since the world's first telephone conversation when an event even more astounding occurred. Italian inventor Guglielmo Marconi's reception of a transatlantic signal in 1901 marked the beginning of the wireless age.

Marconi had experimented for years with wireless signals, receiving a patent for a wireless telegraph in 1896. He was expanding on the work of others, such as British physicist James Clerk Maxwell, who in 1864 theorized the existence of electromagnetic waves that travel at the speed of light, and German physicist Heinrich Hertz, who two decades later proved Maxwell right. It was then up to an inventor to find a practical use for the science. Marconi's wireless telegraph became a valuable communication tool, especially for ships in distress. Signals sent by sinking ocean liners helped saved thousands of lives.

While Marconi's signals were transmitted in the form of telegraphic code, it was not long before other engineers began figuring out how to send the human voice itself through electromagnetic waves. Marconi's telegraph employed radio waves, or electromagnetic waves with a radio frequency (between audio and infrared on the spectrum). The invention of vacuum tubes in the early 1900s improved the detection and amplification of radio waves, and in 1906 Canadian physicist Reginald Fessenden made the first radio broadcast of voice and music—from Massachusetts to ships in the Atlantic Ocean.

The era of radio had begun. Woodrow Wilson, speaking to his troops in 1919, became the first U.S. President to broadcast on the radio. Commercial radio stations started up in the 1920s, and the middle of that decade saw the beginnings of a golden age of radio broadcasting that was to last until well after World War II. News, family entertainment, and soap operas kept listeners tuning in. Programs featured such popular entertainers as Tommy Dorsey, Benny Goodman, and the comedy duo of George Burns and Gracie Allen.

That was radio's heyday, before the television entered people's living rooms and they could watch their favorite characters move and gesture and see the locations of different shows instead of imagining them. During the second half of the 20th century, radio had a new role playing rock and roll. Top 40 lists, new releases, weather, traffic reports, and interviews became reasons Americans tuned in.

UNCOMMONLY KNOWN...

iPod German engineer Karlheinz Brandenburg began research into audio compression technology in 1977. His efforts came to full fruition in 1998 with the debut of portable MP3 players, which allow for the storage of much more data than CDs. One of the most popular MP3 players, the iPod, was introduced by Apple Computers in 2001.

Camera

FROM LATIN FOR "ARCHED CHAMBER"
DESCENDED FROM: DAVINCI'S CAMERA OBSCURA
FIRST KNOWN PHOTOGRAPH: 1826

The camera obscura was a dark chamber used by Renaissance artists such as Leonardo da Vinci to project images on a canvas to use as a drawing guide. By the early 1800s, experiments were afoot to capture such images on chemically treated, light-sensitive surfaces. The world's first known photograph was taken by French chemist Joseph Niepce in 1826—a view from his attic in Burgundy. He later went into business with theatrical scene painter Louis Daguerre, and in 1839 they introduced daguerreotypes, photographs which were printed on metal plates.

The problem was that daguerreotypes could not be reproduced. Over in England, William Fox Talbot was inventing a solution, and in 1840 he patented a process for producing negative images by exposing photosensitive silver iodide paper in a camera and then developing it in a solution of silver nitrate and gallic acid. He then had to fix it (make it permanent) with sodium thiosulfate. Talbot could then take the resulting ghostly negative and print it multiple times on a silver chloride paper to create positive pictures.

Improved lenses in the 1840s and '50s made landscapes and portraits sharper and more lifelike by gathering more light and thus reducing exposure time to a few minutes. In 1851 a new developing technique was invented by British sculptor F. Scott Archer that dramatically reduced exposure time and sharpened photographic detail. His wet-collodion process involved coating a glass plate with silver salts and a sticky material known as collodion. The wet plate was exposed for only a few seconds, then immediately developed.

Television

FIRST TRANSATLANTIC TELEVISION BROADCAST: 1928
FIRST ALL-ELECTRONIC TV: VLADIMIR ZWORYKIN, 1931
FIRST COLOR TV: RCA, 1954

Several pioneers worked on creating the technology to make possible a system for broadcasting and receiving television signals. The development of radio in the late 1800s was the first step, because it showed that it was possible to communicate through electromagnetic waves. But even before radio broadcasting, German engineer Paul Nipkow designed a scanning disk to send pictures short distances. His 1884 device was a mechanical version of television, the rotating disk producing a pattern of light and shadow that was converted into electrical impulses.

Scottish inventor John Logie Baird picked up on Nipkow's work, which had languished for lack of current technology. His 1925 "Televisor" was still a mechanical system. An unflagging promoter of his work, Baird made the first transatlantic television broadcast in 1928 and the following year persuaded the BBC radio network to make regular broadcasts. He sold a few thousand tiny TV sets, which televised black and orange images.

At the same time, electronic television research was under way and would eventually push Baird's work aside. The key element was the cathode-ray tube, invented by German physicist Karl Braun in 1897. The tube could shoot a beam of high-speed electrons against a screen to produce light and thus images. The technology was now far enough advanced for Russian-born immigrant Vladimir Zworykin to become the father of modern television. His work spanned many long, often frustrating years, and involved blowing his own glass photocells. But his remarkable talent and ingenuity would change the world. Though he invented many things, he is best known for his 1923 iconoscope (camera tube) and 1929 kinescope (cathode-ray tube), which together formed the basis of the first all-electronic television system. By 1960 most U.S. homes had a television set.

Cell Phone

CELLULAR: "CELLS," OR RANGES OF FREQUENCY
CALLED MOBILE PHONE IN EUROPE
FIRST MOBILE PHONE SYSTEM: CHICAGO, 1983

Wireless portable telephones that can be used nearly anywhere are still referred to as "cell phones," although "mobile

phone" is a more accurate term; cellular phones were the early form of networking for communications providers that consisted of multiple base stations that divvied up a region into "cells."

Wireless technology that makes these phones possible owes a great deal to the mid-19th-century work of Michael Faraday, who researched how electricity could travel through space. Two decades later, Dr. Mahlon Loomis of Virginia was the first person to transmit a message via the atmosphere, using a system of kites and copper wires. In 1973, Dr. Martin Cooper of the Motorola Corporation invented the portable handset.

Portable telephones were first developed in the 1940s and first became truly usable in the 1960s, the catch being that they would work only in one discrete area. At this time, some moguls and magnates began to install car phones. In the 1970s, those phones became more practical, since a person could use them during travel. It wasn't until the 1980s that the Federal Communications Commission (FCC) approved a plan for Advanced Digital Phone Service, or "cellular" service. Of course, the early phones approved for use with this plan were huge and bulky, often with battery or power packs larger than the phone itself that had to be carried around with it. The second-generation mobile phones were somewhat smaller, but regardless of their size and style quickly became obsolete when analog networks were replaced with digital networks. Third-generation phones accommodated digital networks, and are capable of many popular functions including texting, taking photos, playing music, etc.

PARALLEL HISTORY

Mathew Brady

New Yorker Mathew Brady (ca 1823-96) learned to take daguerreotypes from artist and inventor Samuel F. B. Morse, and in 1844, at about age 21, opened his own studio. The nascent art of photography had found its first American practitioner. Brady's pictures of the Civil War (1861-65) provide the best pictorial record of the conflict. His eyesight failing, he relied on a staff of 20 photographers for much of the shooting. He was unable to recoup the money he spent on the project, and he died in a hospital charity ward. Since then his presidential portraits and war reportage have been recognized as archival treasures.

Transportation

T he modes of transportation detailed here include only a few of the many devices used for moving people and cargo today. One of the oldest, the sailboat, dates from about 3000 B.C., and until about 150 years ago was the main method of hauling things long distances. By the early 1800s railroads had already begun supplanting ships; airplanes would gain preeminence only a century later. The first horse-drawn carts appeared around 3500 B.C.; automobiles began rolling off assembly lines in 1901, and have become so ingrained in our lives that a replacement does not appear imminent.

Train

DESCENDED FROM: 16TH-CENT. MINING VEHICLES
FIRST STEAM LOCOMOTIVE: 1804
WORLD'S LONGEST LINE: TRANS-SIBERIAN RAILROAD, 1916

A lthough the world's first railroads date back to the advent of horse-drawn mining vehicles in the mid-16th century, rail technology really took off in the early 19th century. English inventor Richard Trevithick presented the first successful steam locomotive in 1804, and by 1830 the world's first steam passenger railroad was in operation, carrying people the 30 miles between the towns of Liverpool and Manchester in England.

It was in the 1830s that rail lines began to spread across the United States. By 1835 the U.S. had more than 1,000 miles of tracks, and by mid-century there were railroads operating or being constructed in every state east of the Mississippi.

With settlers pushing ever westward, the U.S. Congress began granting land for the development of railroads in 1850. During the Civil War (1861-65), the Union's superiority in railroads and locomotives gave it a decided edge over the Confederacy in its ability to transport troops and supplies. In the meantime, work on the first transcontinental railroad began. Chinese and European immigrants, joined by Civil War veterans, pushed the work to completion in May 1869, when west-going tracks from the Union Pacific Railroad met east-going tracks from the Central Pacific at Promontory, Utah. In 1916 the world's longest continuous rail line was completed—the 5,600-mile Trans-Siberian Railroad took 25 years to build.

Engineers were gradually increasing trains' ability to travel fast in the late 1800s. In 1893, the American steam locomotive No. 999 was the first to travel 100 miles an hour. Diesel-electric trains, introduced in the 1920s, increased fuel efficiency; the streamlined diesel-electric Zephyr set sustained speed records on runs between Chicago and Denver, on which it averaged 76 miles an hour.

UNCOMMONLY KNOWN . . .
The General Buster Keaton's classic 1927 film "The General" was based on a famous Civil War incident. A Confederate locomotive named "The General" was captured by Union forces in Georgia. Confederate soldiers gave chase in another engine, finally catching and retaking the locomotive in Tennessee. In the movie, Keaton plays the determined southern engineer.

Subway

FIRST: METROPOLITAN RAILWAY, LONDON, 1863
FIRST ELECTRIC SUBWAY: THE "TUBE," LONDON, 1890
NEW YORK SUBWAY EST. 1904; NOW LARGEST IN WORLD

Electric locomotives were in existence by the early 1800s and high-voltage generators by the mid-1800s, so it would be reasonable to expect that the first underground railway was powered by electricity. A subway system was proposed in London as early as 1843, and construction on the city's Metropolitan Railway began in 1860. But it was not to be an electric system.

The tunneling work was done by a cut-and-cover process, whereby trenches were dug along the streets. The walls were then lined with brick; after the tunnel was covered with an arched brick roof, the road was rebuilt over the top. Running nearly four miles, the railway opened in 1863. The train was pulled by a steam-powered locomotive, fueled with coke and later coal, which belched noxious fumes into the underground tunnel. Yet the subway was a big hit, carrying nearly ten million passengers in its first year. A few years later work began on a deeper railway, the "tube" line. Not until 1890 would engineers master the difficulties of providing power to an underground electric train; that year the tube became the world's first electric subway. The fare was two pence for any destination along the three-mile line.

Budapest would follow London with a 2.5-mile electric subway in 1896. The system used single

cars, which were powered by trolley-type poles (see Uncommonly Known). The first U.S. subway system, built in Boston from 1895-97, also started out with trolley cars along its 1.5-mile line. New York's subway began operating in 1904, and would become the largest system in the world.

Bicycle

EARLY: DRAISIENNE (BARON KARL VON DRAIS, 1817),
VÉLOCIPÈDE (PIERRE AND ERNEST MICHAUX, 1861)
FIRST MODERN BICYCLE: 1885

The first bicycle-like vehicle was the creation of German engineer Baron Karl von Drais. His 1817 *draisienne* looked much like a modern bicycle, except it had no pedals. The wooden machine was propelled by the rider's feet. Scottish blacksmith Kirkpatrick Macmillan put pedals to the draisienne in 1839. Driving cranks attached to the rear axle, the pedal mechanism was too inefficient to catch on.

A much better bicycle came along in 1861, the product of French father and son Pierre and Ernest Michaux. Their *vélocipède* had pedals attached to a large front wheel. Sitting atop this wheel, the rider turned the pedals—one rotation would turn the wheel all the way around. The wheels were made of iron or solid rubber, and gave such a bumpy ride that it was also nicknamed the boneshaker. In England, a similar contraption became known as the penny-farthing (after the penny coin and the much smaller farthing), its front wheel as large as five feet in diameter. It was very unsafe. Falls from the high wheel were common. Attempts to reduce accidents by placing the small wheel in front were unsuccessful.

In 1885 the safety bicycle was introduced by English bicyclemaker J. K. Starley. As on the draisienne, the wheels were the same size. But on the safety bicycle the pedals drove a chain attached to the rear wheel, and the saddle was atop a diamond-shaped frame. The pattern for the modern bicycle was in place. The solid rubber tires were replaced by pneumatic (air-filled) tires in 1887, an innovation by Scottish inventor John Dunlop for his son's bike. By 1890 coaster brakes were added, and millions of people were riding bicycles. Later improvements gave bicycles the distinction of being the most efficient means of self-propulsion ever devised.

Roller Skates

FIRST MANUFACTURED: HOLLAND, AFTER 1760
POPULARIZED LATE 19TH CENTURY
ROLLER DERBY: SPEED-SKATING COMPETITION

The first roller skates appeared in Holland in the early 1700s but were not manufactured until after 1760. The year

---

> **UNCOMMONLY KNOWN . . .**
> **Rollerblades** When Minnesota brothers Scott and Brennan Olsen saw a pair of old in-line skates in a store in 1980, they thought the design could work for a kind of roller skate that would let them practice hockey in the off-season. Working out of their parents' basement they designed the first Rollerblades. The brand name soon became synonomous with in-line skates.

before, an inventive Belgian instrumentmaker named Joseph Merlin designed a pair of skates, each with two in-line wheels that he hoped would function like ice skates. Trying to make a spectacular entrance at a party, he skated in while playing his violin, tried to stop, failed, and crashed into a tall mirror. Despite his lack of practice and the obvious difficulty of turning and stopping on roller skates without a braking mechanism, Merlin's prototype demonstration had made an imapact. Merlin went on to make and sell his skates in London.

Though the technology improved in the next century, roller-skating was still much harder to master than ice-skating because of the unforgiving front-to-back alignment of the wheels. Thus performances involving roller skates were highly appreciated. Such was the case when German composer Giacomo Meyerbeer debuted his opera *Le Prophète* in 1849; an ice-skating scene was performed on roller skates. Word of the spectacle spread, and people flocked to the opera just to witness that scene. Ballets and other performances began featuring the technically difficult art of skating on dry land.

Roller-skating began to take off as a popular pastime in the late 1800s with technology that allowed skaters to mimic the curved strokes of ice-skating. By the 1860s, wheels were positioned side by side. Cushioned wheels allowed for some swivel and thus better turning, and in 1884 ball-bearing wheels proved the best solution for control on turns. Surfaces for roller-skating rinks varied over the years, the best surface being the close-grained wood of the American sugar maple. Eventually in-line skates, or Rollerblades, further advanced skating.

Cars

FIRST INTERNAL COMBUSTION ENGINE VEHICLE: 1885
FIRST U.S. AUTO RACE: NOVEMBER 1895
PIONEERING VEHICLE: FORD'S MODEL T ("TIN LIZZIE")

The invention of the automobile took place over several years, with the involvement of many people working independently. The first steam-powered vehicle appeared in France in 1769, and steam cars would hang on until the demise of the Stanley Motor Carriage Company, manufacturer of the Standly Steamer, in 1924. With their bulky, noisy engines, steam cars were a dead end in automobile evolution. A battery-powered electric car was successfully introduced by American inventor William Morrison in the 1890s. It was quiet and easy to operate and lacked noxious fumes; sadly, its top speed was 20 miles an hour, and it had to be recharged every 50 miles.

What made the automobile industry take off was the invention of the internal combustion engine. When such engines were adapted to carriages by German engineers Karl Benz and Gottlieb Daimler in 1885, the automobile found a road to the future. It was ten years later that the French rubber manufacturer Michelin began selling pneumatic tires (tires with compressed air).

UNCOMMONLY KNOWN ...
Internal Combustion Engine Experiments with exploding gases as far back as the 17th century finally paid off in the 1820s when early gas engines were created in England. In short, they exploded a hydrogen-air mixture in a chamber, which when cooled acted as a vacuum to move a piston.

Now equipped with a gasoline-powered engine and pressurized tires, the automobile was primed for a boom. Two major things happened to spur the industry. First, oil was discovered in Texas in 1901—its abundance meant a ready source of cheap fuel. Next, assembly-line production methods were applied to the manufacture of automobiles by Ransom Olds in 1901 and Henry Ford a few years later; suddenly nearly everyone could afford a car.

The Model T Ford, or Tin Lizzie, was first available in 1908 for $825, but by perfecting mass production Ford was able to drop the price to $290 by 1924. For nearly 20 years the Model T was the best-selling car on the market.

Airplane

DESCENDED FROM: GLIDERS, HOT-AIR BALLOONS
FIRST FLIGHT:
ORVILLE AND WILBUR WRIGHT, KITTY HAWK, N.C., 1903

Several experiments in engine-powered, heavier-than-air flights in the 19th century inched flying technology forward. Samuel Langley's aerodrome came close to flying in late 1903, but it crashed into the Potomac River. That same year the goal of airplane flight would be achieved by Orville and Wilbur Wright. During the 1890s, the brothers had become fascinated with the possibility of flight. Bicycle repairmen in Dayton, Ohio, they used their technical know-how to design gliders and planes. First they built a wind tunnel and began testing various wing designs. Then they took up residence at Kitty Hawk on North Carolina's Outer Banks, where there were high dunes and steady winds. In the fall of 1902 they made more than 1,000 glider flights. By the following year they had built a wooden biplane, the wings covered with cloth.

They mounted a lightweight gasoline engine on the lower wing and put two propellers in front, driven by a bicycle-type chain-and-sprocket rig.

On December 14, 1903, they attempted to fly, but the plane crashed. Three days later Orville launched again and flew 120 feet in 12 seconds. They made three more flights that day; the longest was 852 feet. Since there were no public officials to observe the feat, it took years for their accomplishment to be recognized. Within two years they had devised an airplane that was fully maneuverable and capable of flying for more than 30 minutes at a time. By the end of the decade airplanes were being built on both sides of the Atlantic. In 1909 the Wright brothers earned a contract from the U.S. Army to build the first military plane. That same year French inventor Louis Blériot flew his monoplane 23.5 miles across the English Channel— the world's first international flight.

Sailboat

EARLIEST KNOWN SAILORS: EGYPTIANS, 3000 B.C.
1400S: FIRST 3-MASTED SHIPS USED IN EXPLORATION
1800S: CLIPPER SHIPS SPEED WITH UP TO 35 SAILS

In about 3000 B.C. the Egyptians found that they could capture the power of the wind by attaching a sail to their longboats. Wooden planks for boatbuilding came into use about this time, replacing the standard bundles of reeds. A single rectangular sail and two lines of oarsmen powered the Egyptian yachts. Most of these vessels were lightweight, built for sailing the Nile River.

The first real seafarers were the Minoans of Crete, who plied the eastern Mediterranean in sturdy, square-rigged cargo ships, starting around 2500 B.C. The Greeks later became great sailors, building big two-masted freighters by 500 B.C.; within two centuries they had developed a 100-foot-long, four-sail rig, the most sophisticated sailing ship up to that time.

Sailboats continued to grow in size, but the rigging made few advances until the 1400s, when three-masted ships became popular. It was in these ships that Christopher Columbus and other explorers began charting hitherto unknown corners of the Earth. The most famous ships of the 15th and 16th centuries were the galleons, which were used both for cargo and battle. They featured a high sterncastle and three to four masts, the foremast and mainmast each holding two or three sails.

But the most elaborate sailing ships were yet to come. The glorious clipper ships of the mid-1800s were the pinnacle of sailing technology. These graceful, sleek vessels could carry up to six rows of sails per mast, for a total of up to 35 sails. Built for sailing around the tip of South America to China, they were capable of tremendous speed—a trip from New York to San Francisco could be made in less than 100 days. Sailboat racing was popular by this time. The first America's Cup, held in 1851, was won by the (two-masted) schooner *America*. That race continues today, despite the fact that sailboats mainly have become pleasure craft.

Observation

W̲e have, over the course of history, enhanced our senses, extended our vision and hearing to bring us within miraculous reach of the boundaries of the known cosmos—from the subatomic fabric of matter to the big bang radiation at the edge of the universe. This section delves into the history of the instruments that help us see and hear more of what's out there and in there. Though they may not be everyday objects for most people, the microscope and telescope have perhaps the most interesting histories, because they developed not out of necessity but out of curiosity.

Hearing Aids

EARLY "EAR TRUMPETS" MADE FROM
ANIMAL HORNS, WOOD, SILVER, SHELL, OR BRASS
FIRST ELECTRIC HEARING AIDS: LATE 1800s

D̲evices for amplifying sounds in a listener's ear date back to the ear trumpets of antiquity. Hollowed animal horns were used first, most likely, the small end placed in the ear and the other end directed toward the speaker so that it could collect and funnel sound, acting like a large, maneuverable outer ear. Through the 17th century a wide variety of ear trumpets, or speaking tubes, were in use, made of wood, silver, shell, or horn. By the 18th and 19th centuries, ear trumpets were generally made of brass or other metal, covered with vulcanite (a hard rubber), and painted black to be more inconspicuous. Among famous users of ear trumpets was composer Ludwig van Beethoven (1770-1827), who began suffering from hearing loss at about the age of 28.

The first electric hearing aids came out in the latter 1800s. These bulky devices were of help only to people with minimally defective hearing. Another curious instrument appeared around this time. The acoustic fan was a thin, round piece of vulcanite attached by a wire to a piece of wood, which was gripped by the user's teeth. Sound vibrations would travel from the fan to the teeth, where they were conducted to the jawbone and then the auditory nerves.

Though Alexander Graham Bell did not invent a hearing aid, his experiments in telephony grew out of his work training teachers of the deaf. Bell's technology was used to create the first electronic hearing aids in the 1880s; carbon microphones, transmitters, and batteries converted sound into electrical impulses and then back into sounds.

Hearing aids were finally shrunk to a user-friendly size in the 1950s with the appearance of transistors. The first ones fit onto a pair of eyeglasses; later they were designed for wearing behind the ear.

Eyeglasses

LENS: FROM ITALIAN "LENTICCHIE" (GLASS LENTIL)
CONVEX LENSES FROM LATE 1200S, SALVINO ARMATO
BIOFOCALS: BENJAMIN FRANKLIN INVENTED, 1760S

Italian glassworker and optical physicist Salvino Armato damaged his eyesight around 1280 while experimenting with light refraction. Before the decade was out he had devised a pair of thick convex lenses that enabled him to see close-up again. It was probably in Pisa that Armato introduced the first eyeglasses to the world. These glass disks became known as "glass lentils" for their shape—the Italian *lenticchie* became the origin for "lens." Early glasses gave farsighted people the ability to read, write, sew, and do other close work that had eluded them. Concave lenses for the myopic, or nearsighted, were still more than 100 years away.

Until the 1700s, spectacles had no arms to fit over the ears. People used cords, handles (as on lorgnettes), or simply kept pushing the pince-nez style frames back up the bridge of the nose. And they were uncomfortably heavy, with lenses of real glass and frames of horn, bone, tortoiseshell, or ivory.

Up to the 1760s, people who had lost the ability to see both near and far had to keep switching from one pair of glasses to the other. Benjamin Franklin decided to come up with a more practical solution. He hired a glass cutter to slice a pair of reading lenses and a pair of distance lenses in half and place the distance pair on top. His new bifocals did not catch on with the public until the 19th century, when the cost of glasses went down. A large and growing middle class could now afford the cheaper glasses. No longer a status symbol, they had become a necessity.

> **UNCOMMONLY KNOWN...**
>
> **Contact Lenses** Leonardo da Vinci was the first to dream up contact lenses. In the 16th century he proposed a short water-filled tube, the water end touching the eye. But the first workable lenses came out in Switzerland in the 1880s. The thick, uncomfortable glass lenses covered the entire eyeball. Soft lenses were introduced in 1971.

Microscope

DESCENDED FROM SINGLE-LENS MAGNIFIERS
COMPOUND MICROSCOPE: 1590, ZACHARIAS JANSSEN
20TH-CENT.: ULTRA- AND ELECTRON MICROSCOPES

The earliest known magnifiers were rudimentary lenses from Crete and Asia Minor dating from 2000 B.C., some 1,500 years after the invention of glass in Egypt. The Greek playwright Aristophanes in about 400 B.C. refers to water-filled glass globes, and later Roman engravers may have used the same kind of magnifying glass. It was not until the late 13th century that polished lenses came into being. By the mid-1400s natural philosophers were using simple one-lens microscopes to examine insects.

Dutch spectacle maker Zacharias Janssen invented the compound microscope in 1590 by arranging two or more lenses in a single tube to create a larger image. But chromatic aberrations—fringes of color around the object—meant that compound microscopes were not widely used until the early 19th century, when the distortions were overcome. In the meantime, the most famous early microscopist, another Dutchman, was pushing single-lens technology to great heights. The amateur scientist Antoni van Leeuwenhoek (see Parallel History, below) produced extraordinarily powerful lenses and pioneered the fields of bacteriology and protozoology in the late 17th century. Using lens-grinding and viewing methods that he guarded carefully, he discovered that "in all kinds of water, standing in the open air, animalcules can turn up."

In the 18th century, materials for microscope stands changed from wood and leather to brass, and focusing mechanisms improved. Magnification was enhanced only gradually until the introduction of the ultramicroscope (1903), which by scattering light could see objects smaller than the wavelength of light. The electron microscope (1931)—which shoots high-velocity beams of electrons into a vacuum—made possible the viewing of objects the diameter of an atom.

Telescope

LIGHT REFRACTION PIONEER: EUCLID (3RD CENT. B.C.)
EARLY 1600s: GALILEO USED FIRST TELESCOPES
TO STUDY MOON, PLANETS, AND GALAXIES

With lenses in existence as far back as 2000 B.C. and the study of light reflection and refraction dating at least to Euclid in the third century B.C., there is a good chance that people lined up two lenses and made distant objects appear closer before telescopes were invented. The 11th-century Arab scientist Alhazen wrote treatises on parabolic mirrors and magnifying lenses that influenced European optics researchers. One of the Renaissance scholars to delve into the study of lenses was English philosopher Roger Bacon (circa 1220-circa 1292), who noted "thus from an incredible distance . . . the Sun, Moon, and stars may be made to descend hither in appearance."

The Dutch maker of spectacles Hans Lippershey is often credited with the invention of the telescope in 1608, but he was denied a patent because the device was already known. By the next year there were telescopes all over Europe. A Italian scientist made several telescopes in 1610 and became the first great astronomer to turn this instrument to the heavens. In one year alone Galileo Galilei (1564-1642) discovered that the moon shines with reflected light and has craters and mountains, the Milky Way is filled with stars, Jupiter has four large satellites, and Venus has phases and revolves around the sun. His largest scope was 1.75 inches in diameter and capable of magnifying 33 diameters. With it he turned the notion of an Earth-centered universe on its head.

PARALLEL HISTORY

Leeuwenhoek

Antoni van Leeuwenhoek (1632-1723) started out as a linen draper and haberdasher with an interest in science and a hobby of lens grinding. His hobbies became a passion, and he produced the most refined lenses up to that time, capable of magnifying 270 times. In so doing he opened up vast new worlds. He observed and took notes on bacteria and protozoa ("very little animalcules"), the mouthparts of insects, parthenogenesis in aphids, the minute structure of plants, red blood cells, muscle striations, and the spermatozoa of dogs and man. After examining his own ejaculate he was censured for immorality, but his work proved that sperm cells were not tiny man-shaped homunculi. And he debunked the theory of spontaneous generation, whereby life was bred from dust and corruption.

Weapons

A smattering of the weapons available today are included here, in several broad categories. The kinds of guns on the market now are so many, and yet they all stem from the same root—the guns of 14th-century Europe and the black powder devised in Asia several centuries earlier. The most primitive weapon included is the bow and arrow, used in the early Stone Age, while the bomb (with its nuclear fusion variety) is the latest. It's interesting to note how a new weapon did not necessarily render an old one obsolete—at least not at first.

Gun

GUNPOWDER FIRST USED IN CHINA, TENTH CENT.
FIRST GUNS: EARLY 1300s, WESTERN EUROPE
MUSKET RETAINED POPULARITY THROUGH 19TH CENT.

Before there were guns there had to be something to make them fire. That explosive was black powder—a mixture of saltpeter, charcoal, and sulfur—which was probably used for fireworks by the Chinese as early as the tenth century. Black powder made its way to Arabia and then Europe in the early 14th century, where right away people began devising ways to use it for military purposes. The Arabs had a bamboo and iron gun that shot projectiles. In Europe a possibly legendary German monk and alchemist named Berthold Schwarz is reputed to have made the first brass cannons. At any rate, by 1325 large guns were found throughout western Europe.

During the next 300 years gun technology made slow progress—smoothbore gun barrels and unpredictable powder made gunnery a haphazard affair, and more reliable and accurate weapons such as the longbow continued in use. Europe's conservative outlook also made advances in any field sluggish.

Handguns came into being around the 1400s. These matchlock guns had a metal tube into which a round bullet and black powder were loaded. The user then lit an attached wick ("match"); pulling the trigger brought the match in contact with powder in an open pan. Around the same time, soldiers began shooting muskets, including the harquebus, a long matchlock that was so heavy it often needed a support structure. Early muskets weighed up to 40 pounds and measured six to seven feet in length.

In the 1500s the science of ballistics developed in Italy, and guns became a serious study. Rifling of gun barrels, to give projectiles spin and thus more accuracy, was attempted as early as the 1400s, but these efforts would not succeed until about 1655. Yet because of their convenience, muskets remained in use long after the appearance of accurate rifles.

In contemporary America, handguns require a license. Some states allow their purchase immediately, but others require a registration process with a waiting period.

Bomb

EARLY BOMBS: CANNONBALLS
FIRST MAJOR AERIAL BOMB RAIDS: WORLD WAR II
FIRST NUCLEAR BOMBS USED: JAPAN, 1945

Dating from about the 16th century, the first bombs were gunpowder-filled, cast-iron balls shot by cannons; they would detonate on impact. Timed fuses were added to bombs, and in the late 1700s English artillery officer Henry Shrapnel invented the shrapnel shell, a projectile that would predictably explode in midair. The bomb was filled with lead musket balls and a charge of black powder. When the bomb exploded, the dispersing balls wreaked destruction over a wide area. It was first used successfully in 1804 in Dutch Guiana (Suriname). The word "shrapnel" came to refer to any bomb fragments.

Thanks to the explosive properites of fused bombs, Francis Scott Key was inspired to pen the line "the bombs bursting in air" about the shelling of Fort McHenry during the War of 1812; the line became part of the national anthem.

The first aerial bombing occurred in 1849 during a revolt in the Austrian-occupied city of Venice. The Austrians dropped bombs from hot-air balloons, but most of them exploded high in the air and did little damage. Likewise, bombing in World War I had little impact—both hand-dropped and larger bombs rarely found their targets. Then came World War II and the highly destructive carpet-bombing raids. Both Germany and the Allies devastated cities with incendiary and other kinds of bombs. The Germans developed radio-guided bombs during the war, and Britain created a tremendous 11-ton "Grand Slam" bomb. In total, the United States dropped over 1.5 million tons of bombs on Germany.

With the destruction of Hiroshima and Nagasaki by atomic bombs in 1945, World War II came to an end and the world was blasted into the nuclear age. The 1950s witnessed the creation of the even more deadly hydrogen bomb, which works by nuclear fusion.

PARALLEL HISTORY

Samuel Colt

Born in Hartford, Connecticut, in 1814, Samuel Colt was sent off to sea at age 16. While aboard ship he carved a wooden revolver that he would patent in 1835. Colt's revolver had a cartridge cylinder that rotated with each cock of the hammer. Failing to find a market for his guns, he turned to other inventions, successfully devising the first remote-controlled explosive, a naval mine. He returned to gun manufacture in 1847 after his revolver proved its worth in the Mexican War. Building a huge armory in Hartford and improving on assembly-line methods, he became one of the richest men of his time.

Samuel Colt, 19th-century gun designer and manufacturer, poses with one of his creations.

Bow and Arrow

USE DATES TO PREHISTORIC TIMES
EARLY BOWS MADE FROM WOOD, IVORY, HORN, OR HIDE
ARCHERY POPULAR IN ANCIENT EGYPT AND GREECE

The first archers were Paleolithic people who relied mostly on flint for arrowheads. The earliest recorded use of the bow and arrow was by the ancient Egyptians; some 5,000 years ago they were shooting arrows both for hunting and military purposes. Through the Middle Ages, the bow and arrow was the weapon of choice for Europeans and people living near the Mediterranean; the Chinese and Japanese continued to rely on archery even longer.

The ancient Japanese sometimes made elaborate carvings on their bows—shorter bows were of bone or ivory, and wooden bows measured up to eight feet in length. The North American Indians made bows of wood, reinforced with sinew. Bow strings varied in composition. Sinew, hide, and bamboo were used by primitive cultures; the early Arabs preferred mohair or silk; the medieval English strung their bows with hemp or linen. The English settlers in Jamestown noted in the early 1600s that a Powhatan arrowmaker took about a day to craft a single arrow. Thus, breaking the enemies' captured arrows was a particularly effective warfare tactic.

And, of course, the English were able to establish themselves because they had guns, and the Powhatan did not.

The crossbow, or arbalest (from the Latin *arcus*, "bow," and *ballista*, "arrow"), appeared in Europe around the tenth century, and for a while it was the most feared weapon on the continent. The short, metal bow sometimes had a cranking mechanism for the string, which was then trigger released. Arrows or small missiles shot by a crossbow could penetrate chain mail and travel up to 1,000 feet. The longbow was quicker to use than the crossbow and was in many cases the preferred weapon. In the 1415 Battle of Agincourt, some 5,000 archers with longbows beat a French army of more than 20,000.

Submarine

FIRST: 1620S, DUTCH INVENTOR CORNELIUS DREBBEL
FIRST MAJOR WAR USE: GERMANS, WORLD WAR I
PRIMARY WEAPON: UNDERWATER MISSILE, OR TORPEDO

A submarine is a vessel that can operate independently while completely submerged beneath the surface of water.

From the 16th century on, people have worked on the principles that make an effective submarine. In the 1500s, Englishman William Bourne tried to explain how a floating ship could be made to operate below the surface, though his idea did not result in a successful invention.

The first operable submarine to make an attack on an enemy craft was constructed in 1776 by American David Bushnell. Bushnell's craft, dubbed the *Turtle*, was operated by Sgt. Ezra Lee. Early on September 7, Sergeant Lee tried to maneuver his underwater craft close enough to the H.M.S. *Eagle* (a British craft docked in New York Harbor) so that he could drill a hole in its hull and fill that hole with a keg of gunpowder. While Lee was unable to drill the hole, and had to surface when he became disoriented, his attempt still made history.

It took another century and numerous additional attempts before a fully submerged submarine achieved a blow against an enemy vessel. In 1898, the French *Gustav Zede* actually both worked underwater and successfully torpedoed an anchored battleship. The first major conflict in which submarines played a role was World War I. They became strategically necessary during World War II.

At that point, naval warfare had been changed forever by these new craft. Because of submarines' new importance, new tools and technologies like sonar and radar became familiar words. Submarines are also used for many nonmilitary purposes, including research, tourism, and salvage.

Tank

FIRST USE: WORLD WAR I
FIRST MAJOR TANK INVASION: GERMAN BLITZKRIEG, 1939
PANZER: GERMAN ARMORED UNIT OR TANK DIVISION

A few armed and armored vehicles were built in the early 1900s, including a turreted car made in Austria in 1904. But not until World War I was there an incentive to put an armored fighting vehicle on tracks. With

the onset of massive war came the problems of moving troops and supplies over trenches, rutted ground, and barbed wire. The technology was in place for a new kind of vehicle, and in 1915 Britain hastily welded an armored car body to a tractor chassis. A larger model called "Big Willie" was approved by the British Army, which ordered 100. At the same time, France was building 400 tanks along similar lines.

The first tanks to see action were from a British division in the 1916 Battle of the Somme. Though they were slow (four miles an hour) and ineffective, they were deployed again the following year at Cambrai and made a decisive breakthrough. The age of tanks had begun. By war's end, France had produced some 3,900 tanks; Britain, 2,700. One country had made only 20, and yet within 21 years its tank divisions would begin a series of lightning-fast victories to start World War II.

With 3,200 tanks organized in concentrated panzer divisions, Germany invaded Poland in 1939. The startling blitzkrieg caught the Polish by surprise, and in one month it surrendered. Even quicker victims of blitzkrieg fell the following year—Norway, Denmark, Belgium, Luxembourg, and the Netherlands. But the most shocking victory was against France, which had been one of the world's dominant powers at the beginning of the century. Starting in early May, panzers supported by aircraft pounded their way into France. By mid-June Paris had fallen. In 1941, the Germans nearly pulled off the same feat against Russia. Panzer divisions came roaring in, killing and capturing hundreds of thousands of Soviet troops. In the second of two attempted assaults the Germans advanced to just 18 miles from Moscow's center, but a fierce Russian army forced them back.

Medicine

Visit the doctor's office or hospital today and you will almost certainly be probed by a thermometer, stethoscope, or x-ray machine. These standard devices have been around only since the 17th, 19th, and 20th centuries. Diagnostic and repair surgeries have a much longer history, starting with a strange practice to relieve headaches among Stone Age peoples. While we can only guess at the success rate of those earliest operations, today we can thank pioneers such as Dr. René-Théophile-Hyacinthe Laënnec (father of thoracic medicine) and physicist Wilhelm Röntgen (discoverer of x-rays).

Thermometer

DESCENDED FROM THE THERMOSCOPE
MERCURY THERMOMETER: 1714, GABRIEL FAHRENHEIT
FROM LATIN "THERMO" (OF HEAT), "METRUM" (MEASURE)

Scientists in the 1500s noticed that changes in the volume of a liquid or gas were accompanied by consistent changes in its temperature. To accurately measure these changes they devised thermoscopes, the simplest of which were glass tubes, with one end projecting into a vial of water. Rising temperatures would expand the air in the tube and force the column of water down. Galileo invented a thermoscope in around 1600 using water as the liquid variable. A sealed thermometer with alcohol and degree markings was created by the grand duke of Tuscany in 1641, and in 1664 English scientist Robert Hooke designed a thermometer with zero as the starting point.

A reliable temperature scale had to wait for the work of German physicist Gabriel Fahrenheit, who invented the mercury thermometer in 1714.

He also devised the Fahrenheit scale that we use to this day. He set the freezing point of water at 32 degrees and the boiling point at 180 degrees higher (the number of degrees in a semicircle), or 212 at sea level. He also observed that decreasing atmospheric pressure (as at higher elevations) lowers the boiling point.

Calibrating thermometers with 180 degrees between freezing and boiling made sense for many scientific investigations, but it was awkward for others. A scale with exactly 100 degrees—with 0 for freezing and 100 for boiling—was proposed in 1742 by Swedish astronomer Anders Celsius. The new centigrade, or Celsius, scale was adopted as part of the metric system by France in the late 18th century and by the international scientific community in the 1940s.

PARALLEL HISTORY

Lord Kelvin

One of the most energetic and brilliant scientists of the 19th century, William Thomson, Lord Kelvin (1824-1907), introduced a new temperature scale in 1848. The scale begins with absolute zero (or 0 kelvin), which is the temperature at which the atoms of a substance have no heat or energy. This theoretical temperature, -273.15°C, has never quite been obtained, even in a nearly perfect vacuum using magnetic forces. As an engineer and physicist, Kelvin published more than 600 papers, patented 70 inventions, and oversaw the laying of the first transatlantic cable in 1866. Knighted by Queen Victoria that same year, he was made Baron Kelvin of Largs, Scotland, in 1892.

Stethoscope

FROM GREEK "STETHOS" (CHEST)
INVENTED CA 1819 RENÉ-THÉOPHILE-HYACINTHE LAËNNEC
FIRST MODERN COMBINATION STETHOSCOPES: 1902

W hen most people picture a physician they probably visualize a man or woman in a white lab coat, a stethoscope draped around his or her neck. Still the most useful instrument for diagnosing cardiovascular disease, the stethoscope can also supply information about the intestines, veins, and arteries.

Until the early 1800s the only way to listen to a patient's heart and lungs was to press one's ear to the patient's chest or back. In 1816 French physician René-Théophile-Hyacinthe Laënnec (1781-1826), the father of thoracic medicine, was preparing to examine an obese young woman in the usual way. He hesitated, perhaps embarrassed, or simply concerned that he could not make an accurate auscultation. Taking a sheaf of papers, he rolled them into a cylinder, pressed an ear against one end and applied the other to the woman's bare chest. "I was surprised and pleased to hear the beating of the heart much more clearly than if I had applied my ear directly to the chest," he reported.

Within about three years Laënnec had designed and manufactured a stethoscope (from the Greek *stethos*, "chest") in the form of a foot-long wooden tube. Various monaural stethoscopes followed, and by 1850 there was a binaural stethoscope with rubber tubes leading to the ears, setting the pattern for the modern stethoscope. The first combination stethoscopes appeared in 1902; having both bell and diaphragm contact pieces, they could pick up both low- and high-pitched sounds.

Laënnec went on to publish his studies in the influential *De l'auscultation médiate* (1819). Appointed professor at the Collège de France in 1822, he became a physician at the Hôpital de la Charité in Paris in 1823. He died at age 45 of tuberculosis, a disease on which he was an expert.

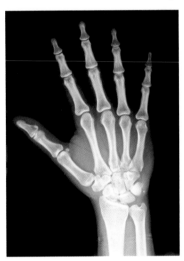

X-ray

ELECTROMAGNETIC RADIATION OF
SHORT WAVELENGTH AND HIGH FREQUENCY
DISCOVERED 1895, WILHELM CONRAD RÖNTGEN

G erman physicist Wilhelm Conrad Röntgen (1845-1923) was experimenting with electric current in a cathode-ray tube in 1895 when he noticed a strange phenomenon. A fluorescent chemical across the room began to glow with light. Electrons formed in the tube were somehow traveling across the room and interacting with the chemical. Furthermore, the electrons could travel not only through glass, but through wood, paper, aluminum, and other materials. Not willing to give a name to something he did not completely understand, he simply called it "X radiation." Since the radiation did not appear to behave like light, he did not at first realize that it was part of the electromagnetic spectrum.

The existence of an electromagnetic spectrum had been theorized only in 1864. Radio waves, discovered in the late 1880s, were the longest wavelength (lowest energy), followed by infrared rays, visible light, and ultraviolet rays. X-rays fit next on the spectrum, with a wavelength shorter than ultraviolet rays. (Having the shortest wavelength, gamma rays would complete the spectrum in 1900.) Like all other electromagnetic energy, or radiation, x-rays come naturally from the sun. Most of this radiation is blocked by the atmosphere. But Röntgen's discovery showed that x-rays could be artificially created, and to useful purpose.

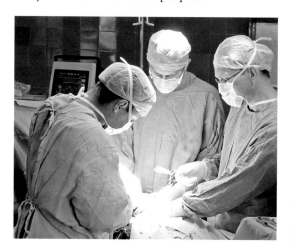

Surgery

ANCIENT SURGICAL PRACTICES: TREPHINING,
SETTING BROKEN BONES, CAUTERIZING WOUNDS
MEDIEVAL SURGEONS DOUBLED AS BARBERS

Among the earliest known kinds of surgeries was the practice among Paleolithic people of trephination—a hole was drilled in the skull, possibly to let out evil spirits causing headaches, epilepsy, and other maladies. Prehistoric people also used splints to set broken bones. Early civilized societies practiced cauterization of wounds and circumcision. Ancient China and Egypt developed the surgical arts, as did Greece, starting about the time of Hippocrates (circa 460-circa 377 B.C.), the father of medicine. And the Hindus performed numerous operations, including plastic surgery on noses and ears sliced off during battle.

During the Middle Ages, until the pope intervened in the 13th century, surgical operations were often performed by priests. After this time, a patient in need of surgery generally visited a barber-surgeon, whose duties ranged from shaving to performing simple operations. One of the main duties of barber-surgeons was bloodletting; a sick patient would have a vein opened and be drained of a pint or two. The practice derived from the ancient Greek idea that illness was caused by an excess of one of the four humors—blood, phlegm, choler (yellow bile), and melancholy (black bile). Physicians in England were sometimes known as leeches (meaning "healers"); the bloodsucking worms they used were named for the healers, not the other way around.

One of the most eminent early surgeons was a Frenchman named Ambroise Paré (1510-90). Physician to four kings, he became known as the father of modern surgery for his many treatises and for introducing the practice of ligature (tying off) of blood vessels instead of cauterization by hot oil, and of cleaning wounds with wine and water. In England, the Company of Barber Surgeons of London was organized in 1540; the guild brought some standardization to surgery and became the precursor to the Royal College of Surgeons of England in the 1700s.

UNCOMMONLY KNOWN . . .

Barber Pole Still a symbol of the barber, the red-and-white-striped pole originated with the barber-surgeons of the Middle Ages. A patient in need of bloodletting gripped a pole to make his veins swell. The pole was painted red so that bloodstains would not show, and posted outside, wrapped with white gauze, as an advertisement.

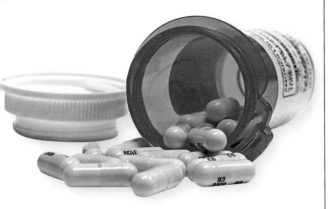

Antibiotic

FIRST PRODUCED ANTIBIOTIC: PENICILLIN, 1941
TREATS BACTERIAL, NOT VIRAL, INFECTIONS
RELATED: ANTIBACTERIAL WASHES AND DETERGENTS

The definition of an antibiotic is simple: it is a chemical substance produced by an organism that is destructive to a different organism. Ancient Egyptians put honey on wounds because not only did the sticky substance form a natural seal that kept bacteria out, but honey also contains hydrogen peroxide, which acts as a healing antibiotic against sepsis. Other cultures used bread or cakes on open wounds, having learned (without knowing entirely why) that the naturally occurring penicillin-like molds that form on yeast-based foods combat bacteria, too.

During the 19th century, scientists made huge strides in understanding the role of germs in disease. In 1871, Englishman Joseph Lister found that urine specimens contaminated with certain molds resisted certain forms of bacteria. But humans didn't understand definitively that diseases could be caused by bacteria until Frenchman Louis Pasteur's 1877 experiments with cultures of *Bacillus anthracis*. The fruit of these findings was Alexander Fleming's 1929 discovery of pencillin, a mold that grew unmolested in a petri dish full of staphylococcus bacteria that the notoriously untidy Scotsman had left out in open air while he was on vacation.

Penicillin was a miracle drug, and is still often highly effective. However, as demand for it grew,

efficacy waned: The changes made in the formula that allowed it to be made in large quantities also caused it to become less effective as bacteria developed resistance to the mold.

All antibiotics can lose their effectiveness as bacteria evolve. During the 1950s and 1960s, many new classes of antibiotics were discovered, including aureomycin, chloromycin, and streptomycin. Although fewer new classes of antibiotic drugs have been found since the mid-20th century, those that exist are still extremely important in the worldwide fight against disease. Scientists continually work to research and develop new antibiotics to counter resistant strains of disease.

Pregnancy Test

PRIMITIVE VERSIONS DATE TO EGYPT, 1350 B.C.
HORMONE TESTS DEVELOPED EARLY 1900s
FIRST HOME PREGNANCY KITS: 1977

Tests for determining whether a woman is pregnant go back to at least 1350 B.C. An Egyptian papyrus from that period describes a pregnancy test in which a woman would urinate on wheat and barley seeds. If the barley grew, she was pregnant with a boy; if the wheat grew, it was a girl; if neither grew, she was not pregnant. A 1963 test of this method showed that it was not simple divination—70 percent of the time, urine of pregnant women helped the plants grow. Other Egyptian diagnostics included examining a woman's skin and nipples for unusual pigmentation, and having a woman drink breast milk from a woman who has borne a son—vomiting would confirm a pregnancy.

In the Middle Ages "piss prophets" foretold pregnancy by examining the color of urine—pale lemon with a cloudy surface meant pregnancy. Another test mixed wine with urine, and since alcohol reacts with some proteins the test may have been mildly useful.

Scientists in the 19th century turned to their microscopes for definitive answers, but it was not until the early 1900s that hormones were identified. Researchers found that human chorionic gonadotropin (hCG) hormone was found only in the urine of pregnant women, and they developed assays to identify it. If urine containing hCG was injected into a rabbit, the animal would ovulate within 48 hours. The only way of determining ovulation was to kill the rabbit, hence the term "the rabbit died." Of course, the rabbit died either way, and so cheaper, more humane tests were developed.

In the 1960s and '70s scientists came up with immunological pregnancy tests—antibodies in the test would react in a specific way with hCG, if present. These tests were refined for greater accuracy, privacy, and simplicity, and in 1977 the first home pregnancy test kits were sold for about ten dollars.

Home pregnancy tests have grown more and more sophisticated and easy to use, as well as faster: Many versions have accurate results within just a few days of conception. Even with home kits, however, most doctors require that their patients have pregnancies confirmed by blood tests, which have very little margin of error.

UNCOMMONLY KNOWN...

Medicine Droppers These handy little devices derive from the ubiquitous laboratory instrument the pipette. A pipette, or dropper, is used to carry a measured amount of liquid from one place to another. In the case of the medicine dropper, with a rubber bulb top, it is used to bring liquid medicine from bottle to cup, or from bottle to mouth.

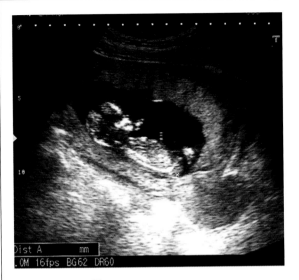

Sonogram

AN IMAGE OF THE BODY'S INTERIOR
PRODUCED BY SOUND WAVES, OR ULTRASOUND
PRIMARILY USED IN PRENATAL CARE

One of the most exciting moments for expectant parents is when they see a sonogram image of their child in utero. The only way to see a growing fetus, sonogram pictures evoke a sense of awe in people.

The sonogram is a readout of an image generated by ultrasound technology. Ultrasound is the energy generated by sound waves vibrating 20,000 or more times per second, far above the frequencies picked up by human ears. An instrument called a transducer picks up the sound waves and relays them back to the ultrasound machine, where they are turned into a digital image that can be "read" by technicians trained in the use and interpretation of these machines and images.

Ultrasound owes a great deal to two systems of measuring distances underwater using sound waves: sonar (sound navigation and ranging) and radar (radio detection and ranging). In effect, an ultrasound machine performs a kind of diagnostic sonar, allowing the technician to "navigate" from place to place in a human body and find spots that "respond" to the machine's signals. Those responses can be displayed because of radar, which allows the ultrasound machine to display those responses through digital imaging in a meaningful way for human interpretation.

Ultrasound technology was first used in the U.S. in the 1940s by Dr. George Ludwig at the National Naval Medical Center in Bethesda, Maryland. However, neither Ludwig nor his contemporaries originally applied ultrasound to pregnancy. Its earliest applications were less about finding and diagnosing (whether that meant tumors or pregnancy) than about using the heat and high-frequency waves to heal damaged muscle tissue and soothe major organs in distress (e.g., for stomach ulcers).

Although the applications to obstetrics are common and widely used, they are not the only modern uses of medical ultrasound. From detecting and even treating tumors, to dental cleaning, to cataract treatment and even liposuction, this technology has many applications. Still, none of them is more exciting and inspiring than a grainy black-and-white picture of a baby's head.

Midwife

PROFESSION DATES TO ANCIENT TIMES
ERADICATED IN MIDDLE AGES, REVIVED IN 17TH CENT.
MIDWIFERY LARGELY REPLACED BY HOSPITAL CARE

The English word *midwife* means "with woman," and ever since there was more than one female alive, women have been helping other woman through the process of labor and delivery. We know that the role was socially and culturally sanctioned: the Bible makes reference to midwives in several places,

and in ancient Greece there was a requirement that a midwife be a woman who had herself already given birth.

While midwives in Paris were required as early as the 1500s to pass an exam, in England this wasn't true until the turn of the 20th century. Like their English counterparts, colonial and later midwives had little or no access to medical texts, training, or proper supplies. When Dr. William Shippen opened the first training course for midwives in Philadelphia in 1765, it was not well attended, for several reasons, the foremost being that many midwives then (and today) believe that childbirth is a natural process learned through experience rather than classroom training.

During the 19th century in both the U.S. and Europe, better medical training and new discoveries (e.g., the link between hygiene and disease prevention) gave trained physicians (almost uniformly men) greater respect and authority.

Midwifery became a victim of scientific advances that were sorely needed but overshadowed the experience and wisdom of many "old-fashioned" practices in childbirth, like allowing a woman to sit, stand, or lean during labor pains instead of being placed in a supine position. Automatic cesarean sections, internal fetal monitoring, and twilight sleep anesthesia were not called into question until relatively late in the 20th century, during the 1970s, when women began to ask for midwives—and new, accredited training courses and groups began to support them.

Economy

oney is a topic that captures the interest of just about everybody. How did we develop the system of currency and credit that we use today? It turns out that our economy has much in common with that of ancient Babylonia—instead of marking clay tablets for barter deals, we swipe plastic cards to record our cash obligations. Electronic transactions have in many instances replaced the exchange of paper and coin, yet the underlying principles have remained the same for thousands of years. Here we explore the origins of money, checks, credit cards, ATMs, and more.

Money

EARLY: METAL, SHELLS, BEADS, BONES, TOOLS
FIRST STANDARDIZED: LYDIA, SEVENTH CENT. B.C.
FIRST PAPER MONEY: CHINA, SEVENTH CENTURY A.D.

efore there was money, people bartered trade goods or services for what they considered equal value. Metal in some form may have been used as far back as 2000 B.C. as a convenient, trusted medium of exchange, just as cowrie shells were used in India, wampum (shell beads) in North America, and whales' teeth in Fiji. But the first standardized, accepted currency were the coins minted in seventh-century B.C. Lydia, an ancient kingdom in what is now western Turkey. They were bean-shaped pieces of electrum, a natural mixture of gold and silver, stamped to indicate a uniform value regardless of weight. Other countries realized the convenience of a money system and started their own currencies.

The Chinese had been using knives, spades, and other tools for currency. Then, as far back as the 12th century B.C., they began trading miniature tools, which evolved into coins. And it was the Chinese who started using paper money, in about the seventh century A.D. Marco Polo's accounts of his travels in China in the 13th century recorded his astonishment at the acceptance of paper for merchandise. It was not until the 17th century that the Europeans began using paper, which seemed too flimsy and of little intrinsic value. Then, some European banks began issuing paper banknotes that could be redeemed for gold or silver. Settlers in North America in the late 17th century sometimes used playing cards for money; not allowed to mint their own money, the settlers had to rely on such currency when cash shipments were held up at sea.

UNCOMMONLY KNOWN . . .
Milling The practice of milling coins—putting a rim or serrated edge around them—dates back to the late 17th century. To get more value from coins, people would sometimes clip the edges or "sweat" coins in a bag—shake them and collect the metallic dust. They would then spend the light coins and sell the heavy ones for their metal. Milling prevented such fraudulent currency debasement.

In the early 18th century, France became the first European government to issue fiat paper money—money that was just money, not a promissory bill convertible to gold or silver.

Credit Cards

EARLY CREDITORS: BABYLONIANS, ROMANS
FIRST CREDIT CARDS: EUROPE, 1880s; U.S., 1920s
COLLOQUIAL: "PLASTIC MONEY" OR "PLASTIC"

Several thousand years ago, the Babylonians extended credit by using clay tablets for barter transactions. A commodity and quantity would be marked, and the tablet could be redeemed for, say, two cows, a bolt of cloth, or whatever was agreed upon. The Romans further developed the arts of borrowing and lending, and by the Middle Ages the concept of credit had come to include bills of exchange issued by banks. From the 17th to 19th centuries, English tallymen sold goods on an installment plan, notching the transactions on a stick, or "tally."

The first credit cards began appearing in Europe around the 1880s, and in the United States by the 1920s. Early credit cards were charge cards, allowing users to delay payment for a time (usually one month), after which the balance had to be paid (as opposed to modern credit cards which can carry balances month to month). These were cards issued by individual merchants—retail stores, oil companies, hotels, and the like—to their customers. It was in 1950 when the first credit cards came out that were usable at a number of locations. Frank McNamara, head of the Hamilton Credit Corporation, was having dinner in New York with his lawyer and a friend. When it came time to pay for the meal, McNamara was embarrassed to discover that he had no cash. Later, the three men formed the Diners' Club—200 customers were issued cards that worked in 27 restaurants. These first credit cards were made of paper; the restaurants had to pay 7 percent for each transaction, and customers paid a three-dollar annual fee. Within two years, the Diners' Club cards had caught on enough for McNamara to sell his interest to his partners for about $200,000. He was far too hasty. What McNamara considered a fad gained more and more ground. In 1958 American Express and BankAmericard (later Visa) came out, and the age of plastic money had arrived.

PARALLEL HISTORY

Checking Account

Merchants and traders in 16th-century Amsterdam, a major shipping center, began safeguarding their cash by depositing it with a Dutch "kassier" (from a word meaning "money box"). These cashiers then acted as middlemen, paying out debts on the order, or written note, of a depositor. Slowly the concept of using written notes both for depositing and receiving cash spread across Europe, arriving in England in the 18th century. The first printed checks were issued by British banker Lawrence Childs in 1762. To prevent forgeries, early bank checks were issued with counterfoils, detachable stubs with serial numbers, so that the notes could be traced or "checked."

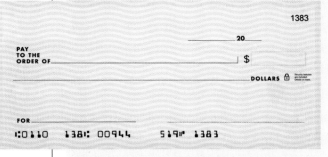

Modern paper check, including the owner's account number and bank routing number.

ATM

FIRST MACHINE: 1967, BARCLAY'S BANK, LONDON
FIRST AUTOMATED TELLER MACHINE (ATM): 1970S
MORE THAN ONE MILLION ATMs WORLDWIDE

Automated teller machines, or ATMs, became part of American banking in the mid-1980s. Investors began testing automated banking machines as far back as the late 1930s; the prototype was actually invented by Luther Simjian in 1939. This not-quite-ready-for-real-world-banking "hole in the wall" (as Simjian called it) was scuttled after a poor test run with Citicorp, and the first cash-dispensing machine went into operation in 1967 at a branch of Barclay's Bank in North London. Invented by John Shepherd-Barron, the machine took paper vouchers encoded with a personal identification number, or PIN, in carbon 14. Within a year, cash machines had appeared in France, Sweden, and Switzerland, and by decade's end they had reached the United States and Japan.

Work toward a more sophisticated banking machine continued on both sides of the Atlantic in the late 1960s, However, it was American Don Wetzel's introduction the following year of the networked ATM that truly brought these machines to the forefront of modern banking. Wetzel and his baggage-handling company, Docutel, were formally recognized in 1995 by the Smithsonian National Museum of American History as the founders of the modern ATM.

Basically, an ATM works by transmitting information from its parent bank via telecommunications. ATMs allow people to be flexible and make spur-of-the-moment purchases, as well as deposit money, transfer funds, and check accounts. Some even allow you to buy postage stamps.

In the early 1970s a Credit Card Automatic Currency Dispenser was debuted by the Docutel Corporation (which also created automated baggage-handling machines) for a branch of Chemical Bank in New York. Although this machine was technically an ATM, the main difference for customers was that it used plastic cards with encrypted magnetic strips. There soon appeared a more advanced ATM, which could dispense cash, accept deposits, and transfer money. The machines were programmed with security keys and changing codes to prevent theft of money and PINs.

The early ATMs were self-contained, off-line machines. In the early 1970s work began on connecting ATMs to their banks' computer systems, as they are now. By the late 1980s there were 100,000 ATMs in existence, and in 1999 there were more than a million all over the world. Today in nearly every major city the only things to prevent you from getting money from an ATM are if the machine is out of cash or not working or you forget your PIN.

UNCOMMONLY KNOWN...

Online Banking Rather than going to a bricks-and-mortar bank, beginning in 1994 consumers were given a new choice: to withdraw, deposit, transfer, invest, apply for loans, and check balances on their financial accounts through secure websites. Stanford Federal Credit Union of California's Stanford University was the first institution in the U.S. to offer these services.

Savings

FIRST U.S. BANK: PHILADELPHIA SAVINGS FUND SOCIETY
FDIC CREATED 1933
MUNICIPAL SAVINGS BANKS DATE TO 18TH CENTURY

For many decades of the 20th century, every American family (and sometimes each and every member of a family) had a passbook in which they faithfully recorded transactions—mainly, if they were lucky, deposits. Having a savings account in a bank was de rigueur and a sign of the Puritan work ethic deeply ingrained in American society.

A savings account is a means of stockpiling money that is not immediately needed in a secure, government-guaranteed environment. Savings accounts earn a certain amount of interest as return; this gives consumers incentive for keeping their money in the bank, and the bank is able to use those monies for other financial interactions and purposes. Some savings account setups require that people keep their money in the bank for a specified, contracted period of time—say six months. Most, however, do not. The money is accessible in its entirety at all times.

Humans have saved money for thousands of years in their pockets and piggybanks and under mattresses. It wasn't until 1778, however, that the first savings bank was founded, in Hamburg, Germany. Early savings banks in Europe and in England were founded to encourage thrift among the lower classes, and were often tied to groups of laborers, such as, ironworkers in England. The first attempt at government regulation of savings banks was in England in 1810.

The first savings bank in the U.S. was the Philadelphia Savings Fund Society, established in 1816 and setting the precedent of these institutions being managed by the participants. The strong influence of savings and loan banks on the public can even be seen in popular culture. For example, in the story of Mary Poppins, a small boy's determination to hold on to his pence sparks a run on the bank resulting in its downfall. In a less fantastical manner, the Frank Capra film *It's a Wonderful Life,* which is based on real-life events following the American stock market crash of 1929, shows hero George Bailey scrambling to personally guarantee bank deposits of Bedford Falls.

In reality, the stock market crash and the Great Depression that followed motivated Congress to enact legislation requiring the federal government to guarantee funds for individual accounts. The result, the Federal Deposit Insurance Corporation (FDIC) created in 1933, guarantees each individual's savings up to $100,000. The FDIC is funded not through taxpayer dollars but through insurance premiums paid by banks as well as through earnings on U.S. Treasury investments. Experts have debated whether modern Americans save enough, but one thing is certain: Americans save a much lower percentage of their post-tax income than people in some other industrialized nations. For example, working Japanese people customarily save 10 to 20 percent of their post-tax income for retirement. In 2002, the American rate was 3.5 percent, and while modern Japanese rates are falling, they are traditionally much higher.

Further Reading

Aveni, Anthony F. *The Book of the Year: A Brief History of Our Seasonal Holidays.* Oxford University Press, 2004.

Brasch, R. *How Did It Begin?* David McKay, 1965.

Brown, David E. *Inventing Modern America: From the Microwave to the Mouse.* Cambridge: MIT Press, 2002.

Bunch, Bryan H. *The History of Science and Technology: A Browser's Guide to the Great Discoveries, Inventions, and the People Who Made Them, From the Dawn of Time to Today.* Boston: Houghton Mifflin, 2004.

Cardwell, Donald. *Wheels, Clocks, and Rockets: A History of Technology.* New York: W. W. Norton, 2001.

Carlisle, Rodney. *Scientific American Inventions and Discoveries: All the Milestones in Ingenuity from the Discovery of Fire to the Invention of the Microwave Oven.* Wiley, 2004.

Carlson, W. Bernard, ed. *Technology in World History* (7 volumes). New York: Oxford University Press, 2005.

Chevalier, Jean, Alain Gheerbrant, and John Buchanan-Brown. *The Penguin Dictionary of Symbols.* New York: Penguin, 1997.

deBono, Edward. *Eureka! An Illustrated History of Inventions from the Wheel to the Computer.* New York: Holt, Rinehart and Winston, 1974.

Forbes, Bruce David. *Christmas: A Candid History.* Univ. of California, 2008.

Hooker, Richard J. *Food and Drink in America: A History.* Indianapolis: Bobbs-Merrill, 1981.

Gunn, Fenja. *The Artificial Face: A History of Cosmetics.* New York: Hippocrene, 1973.

Kolsbun, Ken. *Peace: The Biography of a Symbol.* National Geographic, 2008.

Levy, Joel. *Really Useful: The Origins of Everyday Things.* Willowdale, Ontario: Firefly, 2002.

Macaulay, David. *The New Way Things Work.* Boston: Houghton Mifflin, 1998.

McClellan, James E. *Science and Technology in World History: An Introduction.* Baltimore: Johns Hopkins University Press, 2006.

Norman, Donald A. *The Design of Everyday Things.* New York: Doubleday, 1989.

Pacey, Arnold. *Technology in World History: A Thousand-Year History.* Cambridge: MIT Press, 1990.

Panati, Charles. *Panati's Extraordinary Orgins of Everyday Things.* New York: Harper & Row, 1987.

Petroski, Henry. *The Evolution of Useful Things.* New York: Knopf, 1993.

Porter, Roy. *The Cambridge History of Medicine.* Cambridge Univ., 2006.

Shenk, David. *The Immortal Game: A History of Chess.* Norwell, MA: Anchor, 2007.

Vare, Ethlie Ann and Greg Ptacek. *Mothers of Invention: From the Bra to the Bomb: Forgotten Women and Their Unforgettable Ideas.* New York: William Morrow, 1987.

Credits

2, Objectsforall/Shutterstock; 4, J. Helgason/Shutterstock; 12, Yuri Arcurs/Shutterstock; 14, Danny Smythe/Shutterstock; 15 (LE), Elena Aliaga/Shutterstock; 15 (RT), Rafa Irusta/Shutterstock; 16, Jovan Nikolic/Shutterstock; 17 (LE), Ultimathule/Shutterstock; 17 (RT), Stanislaff/Shutterstock; 18, Charles Shapiro/Shutterstock; 19, Kmitu/Shutterstock; 20 (LE), Elnur/Shutterstock; 20 (RT), Denise Campione/Shutterstock; 20 (LO), Sunny/Shutterstock; 21, Marc Dietrich/Shutterstock; 22, Donald R. Swartz/Shutterstock; 23 (RT), Floortje/iStockphoto.com; 23 (LE), Feng Yu/Shutterstock; 24, Ljupco Smokovski/Shutterstock; 25 (LE), Marc Dietrich/Shutterstock; 25 (RT), Michal Zajac/Shutterstock; 26 (LO), Florin Cirstoc/Shutterstock; 26 (UP), Tim Graham/Getty Images; 27 (UP), Travis Manley/Shutterstock; 27 (LE CTR), Katie Lunzman/Shutterstock; 27 (RT CTR), Karol Kozlowski/Shutterstock; 27 (LO RT), Silberkorn/iStockphoto.com; 27 (LO LE), Vuk Vukmirovic/Shutterstock; 28, Bjorn Heller/Shutterstock; 29 (LE), Ljupco Smokovski/Shutterstock; 30, Steve Cukrov/Shutterstock; 31, Alex Staroseltsev/Shutterstock; 32 (LE), Danny E. Hooks/Shutterstock; 32 (RT), Stanislaff/Shutterstock; 33, Alex Staroseltsev/Shutterstock; 34 (LE), Tootles/Shutterstock; 34 (RT), Joao Virissimo/Shutterstock; 35, Dumitrescu Ciprian-Florin/Shutterstock; 36, Marc Dietrich/Shutterstock; 37, Maksymilian Skolik/Shutterstock; 38 (LE), William Berry/Shutterstock; 38 (RT), Thomas M. Perkins/Shutterstock; 39, Denise Kappa/Shutterstock; 40 (LE), Elena Elisseeva/Shutterstock; 40 (RT), Ronald Sumners/Shutterstock; 41, White Smoke/Shutterstock; 42, Danny Smythe/Shutterstock; 43 (LE), Todd Taulman/Shutterstock; 43 (RT), Tischenko Irina/Shutterstock; 44, Morgan Lane Photography/Shutterstock; 45 (LE), NoDerog/iStockphoto.com; 45 (RT), Tatiana Popova/Shutterstock; 46, M. Willis/Shutterstock; 47, Cardiae/Shutterstock; 48, Gianna Stadelmyer/Shutterstock; 50, Victorian Traditions/Shutterstock; 51 (LE), Svetlana Larina/Shutterstock; 51 (RT), Karen Roach/Shutterstock; 52, Thomas Mounsey/Shutterstock; 53 (LE), Diligent/Shutterstock; 53 (RT), Richard T. Nowitz; 54, Anyka/Shutterstock; 55 (LE), Dwight Smith/Shutterstock; 55 (RT), Matka Wariatka/Shutterstock; 56 (UP), Michael-John Wolfe/Shutterstock; 56 (LO), Chris Rainier/Getty Images; 56 (CTR), The Image Bank/Getty Images; 57 (UP LE), The Image Bank/Getty Images; 57 (LO RT), Kazuyoshi Nomachi/CORBIS; 57 (LO LE), Elio Ciol/CORBIS; 57 (CTR), Jodi Cobb; 57 (UP RT), Adrianna Williams/zefa/CORBIS; 58, Gary718/Shutterstock; 59, Pixel-Pets/Shutterstock; 60, Lisa F. Young/Shutterstock; 61 (LE), Ayazad/Shutterstock; 61 (RT), Perrush/Shutterstock; 62, Olga Lyubkina/Shutterstock; 63, Stephen Coburn/Shutterstock; 64 (LE), Luri/Shutterstock; 64 (RT), Salamanderman/Shutterstock; 65, Victorian Traditions/Shutterstock; 66, Timothy R. Nichols/Shutterstock; 67 (LE), Edyta Pawlowska/Shutterstock; 67 (RT), Getty Images; 68, Alan Freed/Shutterstock; 69, Michael Ledray/Shutterstock; 70, Ramona Heim/Shutterstock; 72, Denis Miraniuk/Shutterstock; 73 (LE), Ken Hurst/Shutterstock; 73 (RT), Sasa Petkovic/Shutterstock; 74, Roger Viollet Collection/Getty Images; 75 (LE), JuNe74/Shutterstock; 75 (RT), Bruce Shippee/Shutterstock; 76, Hulton Archive/Getty Images; 77, Image Source/Getty Images; 78 (LE), Digital Vision/Getty Images; 78 (RT), Carlos E. Santa Maria/Shutterstock; 79, Tatiana Morozova/Shutterstock; 80, Anyka/Shutterstock; 81 (LE), Tomislav Forgo/Shutterstock; 81 (RT), Joyride/iStockphoto.com; 82, Eyedear/Shutterstock; 83, Karina Maybely Orellana Rojas/Shutterstock; 84, Digital Vision/Getty Images; 85 (LE), Mario Bruno/Shutterstock; 85 (RT), Ana Vasileva/Shutterstock; 86, Heather Prosch-Jensen/Shutterstock; 87, Blue Lantern Studio/CORBIS; 88, Blue Lantern Studio/CORBIS; 89, Photodisc/Getty Images; 90 (LE), Yanik Chauvin/Getty Images; 90 (RT), Bettmann/CORBIS; 91, ene/Shutterstock; 92 (UP), Scott Rothstein/Shutterstock; 92 (LO), Adalberto Roque/AFP/Getty Images; 92 (CTR), HANA/Shutterstock; 93 (RT CTR), MaxPhoto/Shutterstock; 93 (UP RT), James L. Stanfield; 93 (LO LE), Bocos Benedict/Shutterstock; 93 (UP LE), Raymond Gehman/CORBIS; 93 (LO RT), Thierry Roge/Reuters/CORBIS; 93 (LE CTR), Werner Forman/CORBIS; 94, alexal/Shutterstock; 95 (LE), Kenneth Vincent Summers/Shutterstock; 95 (RT), Hulton Archive/Getty Images; 96, Glenda M. Powers/Shutterstock; 97, Mike Stobe/Getty Images; 98, Samuel Acosta/Shutterstock;

Shutterstock; 199 (UP), Willee Cole/Shutterstock; 199 (LO), Hulton Archive/Getty Images; 200, Catalin Plesa/Shutterstock; 201, Elnur/Shutterstock; 202 (LE), Anastasiya Igolkina/Shutterstock; 202 (RT), Landholt/Shutterstock; 203 (LE), Sean O. S. Barley/Shutterstock; 203 (RT), Travis Manley/Shutterstock; 204, Graca Victoria/Shutterstock; 205 (LE), Catalin Plesa/Shutterstock; 205 (RT), objectsforall/Shutterstock; 206 (UP), The Art Archive/CORBIS; 206 (CTR), Alinari Archives/CORBIS; 206 (LO), Plush Studios/Plush Studios/zefa/CORBIS; 207 (UP LE), Araldo de Luca/CORBIS; 207 (UP RT), Hulton Archive/Getty Images; 207 (LE CTR), Hulton Archive/Getty Images; 207 (RT CTR), Victorian Traditions/Shutterstock; 207 (LO RT), iofoto/Shutterstock; 207 (LO LE), H. Armstrong Roberts/Retrofile/Getty Images; 208 (LE), kozvic49/Shutterstock; 208 (RT), Osa/Shutterstock; 209, Lein de León Yong/Shutterstock; 210, Adrian Hughes/Shutterstock; 211, National Geographic; 212 (LE), sopovdenis/Shutterstock; 212 (RT), Sean O. S. Barley/Shutterstock; 213, Derek L. Miller/Shutterstock; 214, Bruce Rolff/Shutterstock; 215 (LE), Skocko/Shutterstock; 215 (RT), Pelham James Mitchinson/Shutterstock; 216, John Clines/Shutterstock; 217 (LE), Farrphresco/Shutterstock; 217 (RT), March Of Time/Time Life Pictures/Getty Images; 218, Marianne de Jong/Shutterstock; 220, STILLFX/Shutterstock; 221 (LE), Andrey Khrolenok/Shutterstock; 221 (RT), Scott Waldron/Shutterstock; 222 (LE), Donald Gargano/Shutterstock; 222 (RT), Morgan Lane Photography/Shutterstock; 223, Thomas M. Perkins/Shutterstock; 224, National Geographic; 225 (LE), Digitalife/Shutterstock; 225 (RT), Roger Viollet/Getty Images; 226 (LE), Vladimir Mucibabic/Shutterstock; 226 (RT), Doug Nelson/iStockphoto.com; 227, STILLFX/Shutterstock; 228, RAFA FABRYKIEWICZ/Shutterstock; 229, Cindy Haggerty/Shutterstock; 230 (LE), Galina Barskaya/Shutterstock; 230 (RT), Mike Flippo/Shutterstock; 231, Fantasista/Shutterstock; 232, Denis Pepin/Shutterstock; 233 (LE), Marcel Jancovic/Shutterstock; 233 (RT), Rod Ferris/Shutterstock; 234, Elnur/Shutterstock; 235, Tania A/Shutterstock; 236, Bettmann/CORBIS; 237 (LE), National Geographic; 237 (RT), Ami Parikh/Shutterstock; 238, J. Helgason/Shutterstock; 239 (LE), National Geographic; 239 (RT), Morgan Lane Photography/Shutterstock; 240 (LE), Dzarek/Shutterstock; 240 (RT), Hulton Archive/Getty Images; 241, Miguel Angel Salinas Salinas/Shutterstock; 242 (UP), FPG/Getty Images; 242 (CTR), Werner Forman/CORBIS; 242 (LO), Kolganov Igor/Shutterstock; 243 (UP LE), Luca/CORBIS; 243 (UP RT), Ted Thai//Time Life Pictures/Getty Images; 243 (LE CTR), Cary Sol Wolinsky; 243 (RT CTR), Derek Hayah/George H.H. Huey/Corbis; 243 (LO LE), Urbano Delvalle/Time Life Pictures/Getty Images; 243 (LO RT), Frédéric Neema/Sygma/CORBIS; 244, Bull's-Eye Arts/Shutterstock; 245 (LE), Paul Reid/Shutterstock; 245 (RT), Racheal Grazias/Shutterstock; 246, Steve Snowden/Shutterstock; 247, Racheal Grazias/Shutterstock; 248 (LE), Four Oaks/Shutterstock; 248 (RT), Sergei Didyk/Shutterstock; 250, Johanna Goodyear/Shutterstock; 252, Robert Davies/Shutterstock; 253 (LE), Laitr Keiows/Shutterstock; 253 (RT), Objectsforall/Shutterstock; 254, Regien Paassen/Shutterstock; 255 (LE), Luminis/Shutterstock; 255 (RT), Herbert Gehr/Time Life Pictures/Getty Images; 256, Shane White/Shutterstock; 257, Shutterstock; 258 (LE), Valery Potapova/Shutterstock; 258 (RT), Vasily Smirnov/Shutterstock; 259 (LE), Bettmann/CORBIS; 259 (RT), James Steidl/Shutterstock; 260 (UP), Mansell/Time & Life Pictures/Getty Images; 260 (LO), De Agostini Picture Library/Getty Images; 261 (UP LE), Courtesy Faber-Castell; 261 (LO RT), Reddogs/Shutterstock; 261 (UP), EML/Shutterstock; 261 (LO LE), Bettmann/CORBIS; 261 (UP RT), Marc Dietrich/Shutterstock; 262, Newphotoservice/Shutterstock; 263 (LE), jocicalek/Shutterstock; 263 (RT), Wally Stemberger/Shutterstock; 264, Hannamariah/Barbara Helgason/Shutterstock; 265, Mel Stoutsenberger/Shutterstock; 266 (LE), Romanchuck Dimitry/Shutterstock; 266 (RT), DreamTimeStudio/Shutterstock; 267, Roman Sigaev/Shutterstock; 268, Elemental Imaging/Shutterstock; 269 (LE), Rafael Ramirez Lee/Shutterstock; 269 (RT), Saveliev Alexey Alexsandrovich/Shutterstock; 270, J. Helgason/Shutterstock; 271 (LE), David Benton/Shutterstock; 271 (RT), Lars Christensen/Shutterstock; 272, RCPPHOTO/Shutterstock; 273, Kenneth William Caleno/Shutterstock; 274 (LE), Jocicalek/Shutterstock; 274 (RT), B. Hathaway/Shutterstock; 275, Germany Feng/Shutterstock; 276, Jaroslaw Grudzinski/Shutterstock; 277 (LE), Gerald LaFlamme/Shutterstock; 277 (RT), Popperfoto/Getty Images; 278 (LE), Fotocrisis/Shutterstock; 278 (RT), James Steidl/Shutterstock; 279, U. P. Images Photo/Shutterstock; 280, Tina Rencelj/Shutterstock; 281 (LE), Juris Sturainis/Shutterstock; 281 (RT), Claudio Bertoloni/Shutterstock; 282, Brasiliao-Media/Shutterstock; 283 (LE), Steve Vanhorn/iStockphoto.com; 283 (RT), Andy Piatt/Shutterstock; 284, TheBand/Shutterstock; 285, Jaimie Duplass/Shutterstock; 286, Bob Ainsworth/Shutterstock; 287 (LE), Alexei Daniline/Shutterstock; 287 (RT), Oddphoto/Shutterstock; 288, Fotocrisis/Shutterstock; 289, Jesse Kunerth/Shutterstock.

Index

C

Cabbage Patch Kids (dolls) 243
Cadolle, Hermionie 165
Cameras 266
Campers 135
Camping 135, 156
Candles 253
Canned goods 16–17
Canoes 272
Carbon paper 262
Card games 227–228
Carnival (Mardi Gras) 51
Carnival rides 245–247
Carrier, Willis Haviland 148
Cars 271
Carver, George Washington 21
Caskets 91–93
Castle, W. B. 212
Catherine de Medici, Queen
        (France) 165, 175
Cats 115–116
Cattle 112
Cease-fires 104
Cell phones 267
    see also Text messaging
Celsius, Anders 280
Central heating 148
Cereal 15
Ceremonies and customs 70–101
Charles, Prince of Wales 82
Chaturanga 224, 225
Checkers 226
Checking accounts 287
Cheeses 31
Chesebrough, Robert A. 198
Chess 225
Chewing gum 41
Child, Julia 140
Children 84–88, 101
    see also Toys and games
Chivalry 76
Chocolate 37–38
Chopines 175, 176
Chopsticks 44–45
Christening 86

Christianity
    customs 73
    food and drink 29, 43
    holidays 54, 62, 64–65
    hospitals 130–131
    symbols 106–108
Christmas 41, 64–66
Chuppah (wedding canopy)
        81–82
Churches 133
Churchill, Winston 106, 205
Cigars 85
Cinco de Mayo 55
Cinderella (fairy tale) 88
Circumcision 57
Circuses 246–247
Civil War, U.S. 56–57, 131,
        267, 268
Clapping 119
Claude, Georges
        261–262
Clement VI, Pope 74
Cleopatra 199, 203
Cloche hats 172
Clocks and clockmaking
        149–150, 152–153
    see also Time and timekeeping
Clogs (shoes) 174
Clothes dryers 186, 189
Clothes iron 187
Clothes washer 189
Clothespins 186–187
Clothing *see* Garments
        and accessories
Clovers, four-leaf 114–115
Cochrane, Josephine Garis 153
Coffee 25–26
Coffins 91–93
Coins 112–113, 286
Cold cuts (meats) 32–33
Cologne 209–210
Colt, Samuel 277
Columbarium 92
Combs 205
Communication 257–267
Communion wine 29
Compacts (cosmetics) 203

Computers 262–263
Concorde (SST) 272
Condiments 19–23
Condominiums 137
Confucius 44
Contact lenses 274
Containers (food and beverage)
        42–47
Conté, Nicolas-Jacques 257
Contract bridge (card game)
        228
Cookies 38
Corsets 165
Cosmetics 200–210
Cotton, Charles 228
Cotton gin 255–256
Cough drops 212–213
Country clubs 248
Courtesies 72–76
Cowboy boots 176–177
Cowboy hats 170
Cowries 112
Cows 112
Cramer, Stuart W. 148
Cravats 184
Crayons 238
Credit cards 113, 287
Crêpes Suzette 14–15
Crinolines 166
Cristofori, Bartolomeo 249
Crossed fingers 105–106
Crossing your heart gesture
        106–107
Crossword puzzles 245
Crowns 172
Curm, George 36
Currency 112–113, 286–287
Curtsy 72
Customs and ceremonies
        70–101

D

Darrow, Charles B. 224–225
Davis, Jacob 161

saying "Amen" 73
weddings 79, 80, 81–82
Judson, Whitcomb 179
Jump ropes 220

K

Kachina dolls 243
Keaton, Buster 268
Kellogg, William "Will" Keith 15
Kelvin, Lord 280
Ken (doll) 240
Kennedy Center, Washington, D.C. 249
Ketchup 23
Key, Francis Scott 97–98
Kiss, Max 211–212
Kitchens 139–140
    appliances 150–151, 153
Kites 222–223
Knerr, Richard 237
Knives 43–44, 256
Knocking on wood 115
Kohl 200
Kwanzaa 66–67

L

Labor Day 60
Ladders 116–117
Laënnec, René-Théophile-Hyacinthe 281
Last Supper 29, 54
Laundry 186–189
Lawns 154–155
Laxatives 211–212
Lee, Ezra 278–279
Lee, William 173
Lent 51
Lightbulbs 147
Lighting 146–147, 253, 261–262
Lincoln Logs 236
Lind, James 212

Lipstick 201
Liquor 30
Lister, Joseph 215, 283, 285
Little Italy, New York, New York 35
"Little Miss Muffet" 87
Living rooms 139
Loafers (shoes) 174
Locks 145
Log cabins 134–135
Logan, John A. 57
Loincloths 164
Louis XIV, King (France) 177, 184
LOVE sculpture 110
Low, Juliette Gordon 100
Lunch bags 45
Lunch boxes 45

M

Mad hatters 171
Magic Slate (toy) 242
Magie, Lizzie 224
Magna Doodle (drawing toy) 243
Mah-jongg 228
Makeup 200–210
Malaria 30
Male symbol 111–112
Manners 72–76
Marbles 220–221
Marconi, Guglielmo 265
Mardi Gras 51
Margarine 20–21
Marine chronometers 149–150
Markets 133
Marriage 66, 77–83
Mascara 200
Matches 252, 253
Matronymics 87
Matryoshka dolls 243
Mausolea 91, 93
Mayonnaise 23
McNamara, Frank 287
Medicine and health 190–217, 280–285
    beautification products 200–210

corsets 165
gin and tonic 30
hearing aids 273
hospitals 130–131
hygiene 192–199
innovations 280–285
mad hatters 171
medications 211–217, 283
phossy jaw 253
vision aids 274
Medicine droppers 284
Medieval chivalry 76
Medieval scribes 258
Memorial Day 56–57
Menander (Athenian playwright) 204
Menstruation 199
Merlin, Joseph 270
Merry-go-rounds 245–246
Mexico 55
Michtom, Morris 238
Microscopes 274–275
Microwave ovens 150
Midwives 285
Military service 99, 120, 279
    see also Weapons
Mineral baths 25
Mineral water 24, 27
Miniature golf 235
Mobile homes 135
Money 112–113, 286–287
Monopoly 224–225
Montagu, John, Fourth Earl of Sandwich 15–16
Moon 60
Morgan, Garrett 111
Morrison, Walter Frederick 237
Mortgage buttons 137
Morton, Joy 19
Mosques 133
Mother's Day 55–56
Mourning buttons 178
Mouthwashes 195
MP3 players 265
Mummies 92
Musical instruments 248–249
Mustard 23

W

X

Y

Z

An Uncommon History of Common Things

Bethanne Patrick and John Thompson

Published by the National Geographic Society

John M. Fahey, Jr., President and Chief Executive Officer

Gilbert M. Grosvenor, Chairman of the Board

Tim T. Kelly, President, Global Media Group

John Q. Griffin, President, Publishing

Nina D. Hoffman, Executive Vice President;
    President, Book Publishing Group

Prepared by the Book Division

Kevin Mulroy, Senior Vice President and Publisher

Leah Bendavid-Val, Director of Photography Publishing
    and Illustrations

Marianne R. Koszorus, Director of Design

Barbara Brownell Grogan, Executive Editor

Elizabeth Newhouse, Director of Travel Publishing

Carl Mehler, Director of Maps

Staff for This Book

Susan Straight, Editor

Susan Hitchcock, Consulting Editor

Patricia C. Click, Consultant

Cliff Owen, Illustrations Editor

Carol Norton, Art Director

Sanaa Akkach, Designer

Judy Klein and Anne Cherry, Copy Editors

Trudy Pearson and Carol Stroud, Researchers

Tiffin Thompson, Editorial Assistant

Al Morrow, Design Assistant

Jennifer A. Thornton, Managing Editor

R. Gary Colbert, Production Director

Manufacturing and Quality Management

Christopher A. Liedel, Chief Financial Officer

Phillip L. Schlosser, Vice President

Chris Brown, Technical Director

Nicole Elliott, Manager

Monika D. Lynde, Manager

Rachel Faulise, Manager

ISBN 978-1-4262-0420-3
ISBN 978-1-4262-0421-0 (deluxe)

Library of Congress Cataloging-in-Publication Data

Patrick, Bethanne Kelly.
  An uncommon history of common things / by Bethanne Patrick, John Thompson.
    p. cm.
  Includes bibliographical references and index.
  ISBN 978-1-4262-0420-3 (direct mail)
  1. United States--Civilization--Miscellanea. 2. United States--Civilization--Chronology. I. Thompson, John M. (John Milliken), 1959- II. Title.
  E169.1.P26 2008
  973--dc22

                                    2008040447

Printed in U.S.A.
09/WPCT-CML/1

WITHDRAWN

40.00   1/11/10